COLLINS GCSE SCIENCES
Chemistry

Jane Morris

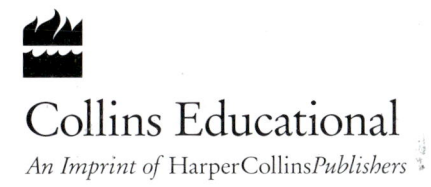

Collins Educational
An Imprint of HarperCollinsPublishers

Acknowledgements

Published by Collins Educational, an imprint of HarperCollins*Publishers* Ltd.
77–85 Fulham Palace Road, London W6 8JB.

© Jane Morris

First published 1997

ISBN 0 00 322386 8

Jane Morris asserts the moral right to be identified as the author of this work.

All rights reserved. No part of this publication may be reproduced, stored in a retrieval system or transmitted in any form or by any means, electronic, mechanical, photocopying, recording or otherwise, without the prior permission of the Publisher or a licence permitting restricted copying issued by the Copyright Licensing Agency Ltd, 90 Tottenham Court Road, London W1P 9HE.

British Library Cataloguing in Publication Data
A catalogue record for this book is available from the British Library.

Chapter 4 written by Lyn Nicholls

Edited by Jane Bryant

Design by Ken Vail Graphic Design, Cambridge

Cover design by Moondisks Ltd

Illustrations by Barking Dog Art and Ken Vail Graphic Design

Picture research by Dee Robinson

Index by Indexing Specialists

Production by Mandy Inness

Printed and bound by Scotprint, Musselborough, Scotland

Every effort has been made to contact the holders of copyright material, but if any have been inadvertantly overlooked, the publishers will be pleased to make the necessary arrangements at the first opportunity.

Cover photographs: (top) Tony Stone Images, (bottom) Science Photo Library

Title and contents page: Berthold/Rex Features

theme 1 header: Geray Sweeney/Impact Photos; theme 2 header: NASA; theme 3 and 4 header: Andrew Syred/Science Photo Library; theme 5 header: Tony Stone Images; theme 6 header: The Stock Market/Zefa

p2 Rex Features; p4 Alex Bartel/Science Photo Library; p6 J Allan Cash Ltd; p18 Geray Sweeney/Impact Photos; p19 Adam Woolfitt/Robert Harding Picture Library; p24 BOC Gases; p38 (middle left and centre) J Allan Cash Ltd.; p38 (middle right) Michael Mirecki/Impact Photos; p38 (bottom left) The British Petroleum Compacy plc; p38 (bottom right) Wildlife Matters; p39 Zefa; p40 ICI plc; p42 (both) BOC Gases; p43 (top left) Zefa; p43 (top centre) R Maisonneuve/Science Photo Library; p43 (top right) BOC Gases; p44 (top left) Wildlife Matters; p44 (middle left) Mike McQueen/Impact Photos; p44 (right) Charles D Winter/Science Photo Library; p45 (left) Nigel Davies/Impact Photos; p45 (top centre) PH Howard, E Simmons/LIAIS/Frank Spooner Pictures; p45 (right) Philippe Plailly/Science Photo Library; p48 (middle left) Imapct Photos; p48 (bottom left) Mark Edwards/Still Pictures;p52 NASA; p53NOAA/Science Photo Library; p54 Sander/Liaison/Frank Spooner Pictures; p61 Robert Harding Picture Library; p62 Robert Francis/Robert Harding Picture Library; p63 Explorer/F Gohier/Robert Harding Picture Library; p67 (left) Nik Wheeler/ Robert Harding Picture Library; p67 (right, all) GeoScience Features Picture Library; p68 (all) GeoScience Features Picture Library; p69 (all) GeoScience Features Picture Library; p71 (middle left) GeoScience Features Picture Library; p71 (bottom left) Tony Waltham/Nottingham University; p71 (bottom centre) Michael Holford/ Robert Harding Picture Library; p71 (right)Tony Waltham/ Robert Harding Picture Library; p76 Tony Waltham/Nottingham University; p78 (top) Homer Sykes/Impact Photos; p78 (bottom) Kodak; p79 Today/Rex Features; p80 Rex Features; p81 IBM; p88 Science Photo Library; p98 Andrew Syred/Science Photo Library; p105 The British Petroleum Company plc;.p106 Seiko UK; p108 Eric Schulzinger/Lockheed Advanced Development Company; p 145 Martin Bond/Science Photo Library; p146 Rex Features; p147 David Reed/Impact Photos; p148 Waterking JGB; p163 ICI plc; p164 Copper Development Association; p166 Zefa-Hummel; p167 The Aluminium Can Recycling Association; p168 Rex Features; p170 (top left) J Allan Cash Ltd.; p170 (top right) Mark Edwards/Still Pictures; p170 (bottom) J Allan Cash Ltd.; p172 Berthold/Rex Features; p173 (bottom left) Cunard; p173 (bottom right) Europa Manor Ltd.; p176 (bottom left) Photo Library International/Science Photo Library; p178 (middle right) J Allan Cash Ltd.; p176 (bottom right) Fex Features; p178 (top left) Ian West/Bubbles; p178 (top right) Bruce Stephens/Impact Photos; p179 Rex Features; p 180 (middle left) Fex Features; p180 (bottom left) Raleigh Industries ; p 180 (bottom middle) Zefa; p180 (bottom right) Garden Matters; p181)left) Zefa; p181 (right) The Aluminium Can Recycling Association; p189 (top left) Catherine Pouedras/Eurelios/Science Photo Library; p189 (middle) J Allan Cash Ltd.; p 193 NASA; p200 (middle left and middle) J Allan Cash Ltd.; pTony Stone Images; p201 (left) Wildlife Matters; p201 (right) J Allan Cash Ltd.; p206 Zefa; p209 Ben Radford/Allsport; p210 (middle) GeoScience Features Picture Library; p210 (bottom) The British Petroleum Company plc; p219 (top left) Zefa; p219 (top middle) J Allan Cash Ltd.; p228 Michael Holford; p229 (left and right) Zefa; p229 (middle)Tony Stone Images; p233 (middle)Didier Givois/Allsport; p233 (right) Tony Stone Images; p233 (bottom middle) Mike Powell/Allsport; p235 (left) Tony Stone Images; p235 (right) The Stock Market/Zefa.

Contents

What is matter?
1	Elements, compounds and mixtures	1
2	Solids, liquids and gases	18

Raw materials
3	The air	38
4	Rocks and minerals	57
5	The sea	75

More about atoms
6	Atomic structure	81
7	Periodic table	88
8	Chemical bonding	96

Measuring in chemistry
9	Moles and equations	113

Using chemistry in everyday life
10	Acids, bases and salts	131
11	Water and aqueous solutions	144
12	Electrolysis	156
13	Metals	166
14	Metals and redox reactions	183
15	Non-metals	191
16	Organic chemistry	209
17	Materials science	228

More chemical ideas
18	Energy	235
19	Rates of reaction	243
20	Reversible reactions	251
	Reference section	258
	Glossary	263
	Index	266

Elements, compounds and mixtures

Learning objectives

By the end of this chapter you should be able to:
- **define** an element and recognise common symbols
- **describe** physical changes
- **describe** how to separate mixtures based on relevant physical properties
- **understand** chemical change and recognise chemical properties
- **understand** what is meant by a molecule
- **write** balanced word and symbol equations, including state symbols

Chemists study the materials that make up the world, where those materials are found and how they can be made into useful substances.

1.1 Atoms and elements

Everything is made from atoms. An atom is the smallest particle that can be obtained by chemical means. Atoms are smaller than you can possibly imagine – all of them are less than 1 nm (1×10^{-9} or 0.000 000 001 m).

Figure 1 Atoms are measured in nanometres (symbol nm). One nanometre is 1×10^{-9} m (0.000 000 001 of a metre).

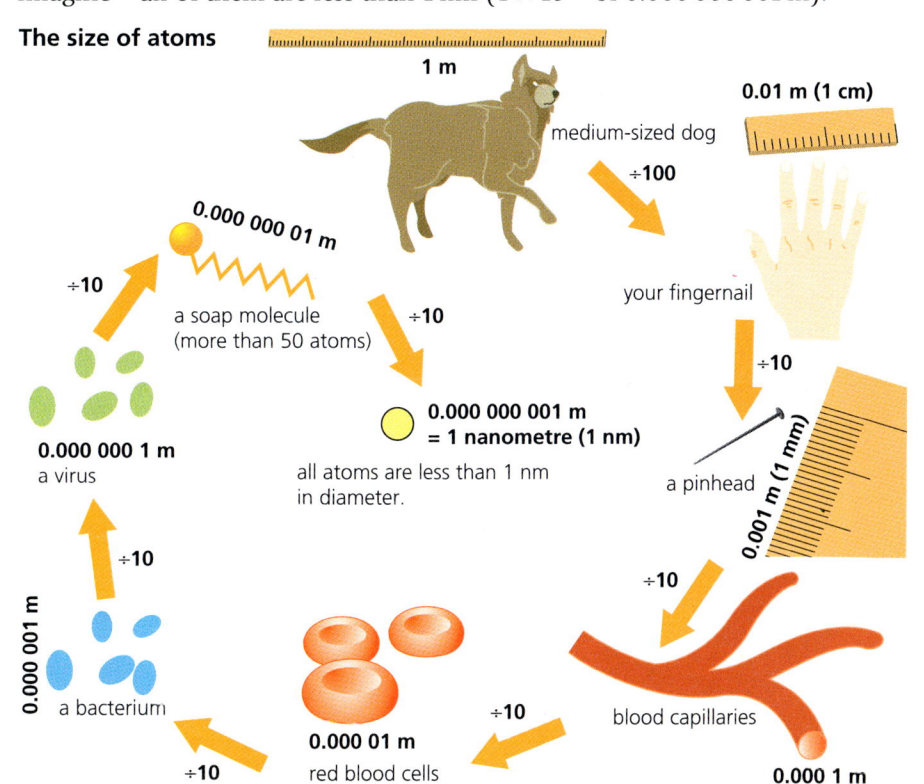

The size of atoms

- 1 m — medium-sized dog
- ÷100 → 0.01 m (1 cm) — your fingernail
- ÷10 → 0.001 m (1 mm) — a pinhead
- ÷10 → 0.000 1 m — blood capillaries
- ÷10 → 0.000 01 m — red blood cells
- ÷10 → 0.000 001 m — a bacterium
- ÷10 → 0.000 000 1 m — a virus
- ÷10 → 0.000 000 01 m — a soap molecule (more than 50 atoms)
- ÷10 → 0.000 000 001 m = 1 nanometre (1 nm) all atoms are less than 1 nm in diameter.

Table 1 The diameters of some atoms in nanometres

Atom	Diameter (nm)
Hydrogen	0.074
Carbon	0.15
Magnesium	0.32
Copper	0.26

What is matter?

A bottle of water contains a huge number of atoms. If all the atoms in a single bottle could be shared out among all the people alive in the world today, and if each person started counting the atoms at a rate of 100 per minute, it would take several hundred million years to count them all!

There are at least 109 different sorts of atom, which combine in many different ways to make different substances. A substance that is made up of only one type of atom is called an **element**. An element cannot be broken down into simpler substances by chemical means. You can see some examples in figure 2.

Note

Gold is an element, because in a nugget of pure gold you will only find atoms of gold – nothing else. Carbon is also an element, because it is made up only of carbon atoms.

Everyday objects made of elements

gold (Au) is a precious metal used in jewellery (often in combination with diamonds, which are another form of carbon)

carbon (C) is the black solid found in coal and charcoal

helium (He) is a low-density gas used to fill balloons

bromine (Br) is a dense red–brown liquid used in chemical laboratories

mercury (Hg) can be found in thermometers

nitrogen (N) is a colourless, odourless gas that is found in air

Figure 2 Many everyday objects are made from elements.

Look at figure 3. This is a list of many of the elements that are known. As well as its name, every element is given a symbol. The **chemical symbol** is a 'shorthand' way to represent that element. For most elements, the symbol is made up from of one or two letters from its name, but there are 11 elements whose symbols are very different from their names. This is usually because the symbol is taken from an old Latin or Greek name for the element. For example iron has the symbol 'Fe', because its Latin name is 'ferrum'.

1. List the other ten elements in figure 3 whose symbols are different from their names.
2. Write down the symbols for these elements:
   aluminium, boron, chlorine, copper, germanium, iodine, molybdenum, nitrogen, phosphorus, sodium, zinc.
3. What elements do these symbols represent?
   Ar, Br, Ca, F, Ga, H, In, La, Mg, Ni, O, Si, Ti, Zr

			H hydrogen														He helium
Li lithium	Be beryllium											B boron	C carbon	N nitrogen	O oxygen	F fluorine	Ne neon
Na sodium	Mg magnesium											Al aluminium	Si silicon	P phosphorus	S sulphur	Cl chlorine	Ar argon
K potassium	Ca calcium	Sc scandium	Ti titanium	V vanadium	Cr chromium	Mn manganese	Fe iron	Co cobalt	Ni nickel	Cu copper	Zn zinc	Ga gallium	Ge germanium	As arsenic	Se selenium	Br bromine	Kr krypton
Rb rubidium	Sr strontium	Y yttrium	Zr zirconium	Nb niobium	Mo molybdenum	Tc technetium	Ru ruthenium	Rh rhodium	Pd palladium	Ag silver	Cd cadmium	In indium	Sn tin	Sb antimony	Te tellurium	I iodine	Xe xenon
Cs caesium	Ba barium	La lanthanum	Hf hafnium	Ta tantalum	W tungsten	Re rhenium	Os osmium	Ir iridium	Pt platinum	Au gold	Hg mercury	Tl thallium	Pb lead	Bi bismuth	Po polonium	At astatine	Rn radon
Fr francium	Ra radium	Ac actinium															

Figure 3 This table shows some of the many elements known to scientists. Each one has its own symbol.

Summary of atoms and elements

- Atoms are the smallest particles obtained by chemical means.
- Elements are made from only one sort of atom. They cannot be broken down into simpler substances by chemical means.
- Every element has a symbol to represent it.

1.2 Physical change and mixtures

What is physical change?

If you take an ice cube out of the freezer and leave it in a warm room, it will melt. If you put the liquid water back into the freezer, it will turn back into ice. The water has undergone **physical change.** Physical change can be reversed quite simply by altering physical conditions such as temperature.

What is matter?

Figure 4 Physical changes.

sugar dissolves in water

ice melting in water and water evaporating to steam are both physical changes

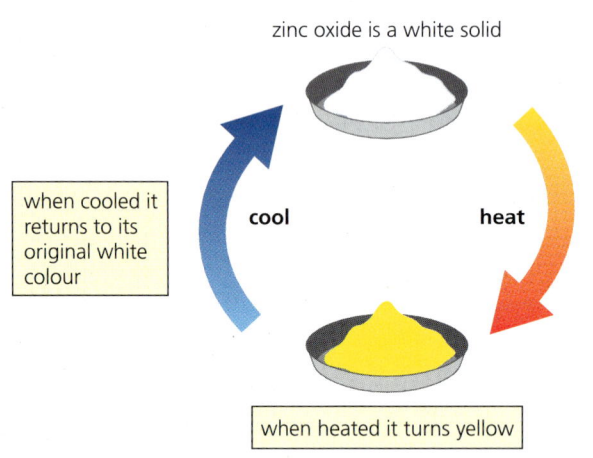

zinc oxide is a white solid

when cooled it returns to its original white colour

cool

heat

when heated it turns yellow

4 What other physical changes can you think of?

How can mixtures be separated?

Many materials are actually **mixtures** of substances. Mixtures can be separated by choosing a suitable physical property. Some of the physical properties that can be used to separate mixtures are:

- boiling point
- colour
- density
- hardness
- magnetism
- melting point
- solubility

For example, the mineral rock salt contains a mixture of particles of sandy grit and salt crystals. The rock salt can be separated from the grit using the property of solubility in water – salt dissolves in water but grit doesn't. The way this property can be used to separate the mixture is shown in figure 5.

An electromagnet can be used to separate iron and steel from other scrap metal.

Elements, compounds and mixtures

Separating out the components of rock salt

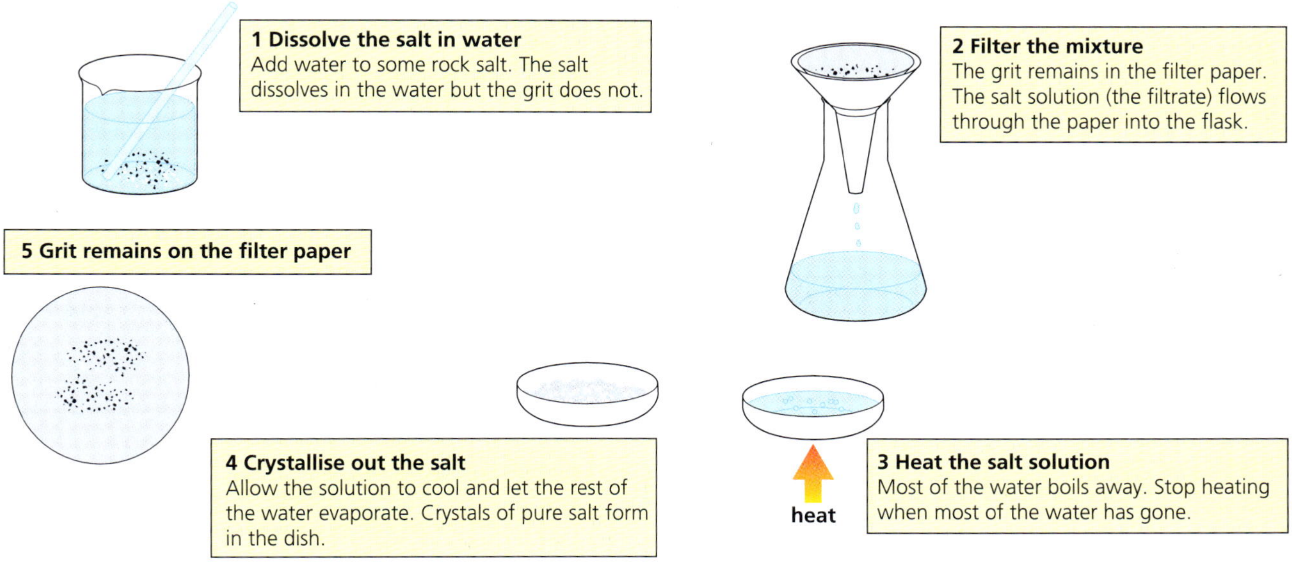

1 Dissolve the salt in water
Add water to some rock salt. The salt dissolves in the water but the grit does not.

2 Filter the mixture
The grit remains in the filter paper. The salt solution (the filtrate) flows through the paper into the flask.

5 Grit remains on the filter paper

4 Crystallise out the salt
Allow the solution to cool and let the rest of the water evaporate. Crystals of pure salt form in the dish.

3 Heat the salt solution
Most of the water boils away. Stop heating when most of the water has gone.

heat

Figure 5 Salt can be separated from grit using the physical property of solubility in water.

Making solutions

Here are some of the words used when dealing with solutions.

Word	Meaning
Solvent	The liquid used to dissolve substances
Solute	The substance that is dissolved in a solvent to make a solution. A solute can be a solid, a liquid or a gas
Saturated	A solution in which the amount of solute dissolved at a particular temperature is as high as possible
Dissolving	When a solute is taken up by a solvent in which it dissolves
Crystallising	When a hot saturated solution is cooled, or when the solution is left for the solvent to evaporate, crystals of the solute are formed from the solution
Filtrate	The liquid that is collected when a mixture is filtered

Mixture of iron filings and sulphur particles

The iron filings are attracted to the magnet and can be removed from the mixture.

magnet

The sulphur particles are not attracted to the magnet and stay in the dish

5 How would you separate out the components from a mixture of sawdust, sugar and iron filings?

6 Look at figure 6, which shows how to separate out a mixture of iron filings and sulphur. What physical property has been used?

7 How would you go about getting copper sulphate crystals from a solution of copper sulphate?

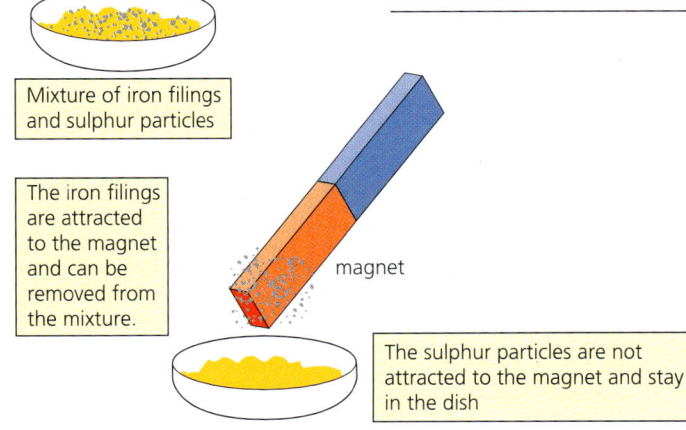

Figure 6 Separating a mixture of iron and sulphur.

What is matter?

What is distillation?

A mixture that everyone is familiar with is common salt dissolved in water – but how would you separate the salt from the water? Passing it through a filter paper won't work, because the salt particles are so much smaller than the gaps between the fibres of the paper, that the mixture passes straight through. If you boil the solution, or simply leave it to evaporate, you can remove the water, leaving the crystals of common salt in the dish.

By modifying this process to cool and condense the water coming off (distil the water), it can be collected separately from the salt crystals. This is known as simple distillation. A diagram of how simple distillation works is shown in figure 7.

8 What physical process causes water to collect on a bathroom window in cold weather?

9 Describe how you would obtain pure water from a sample of pond water.

Desalination is widely used to provide fresh water from sea water. So much fresh water is produced by this method that there is even enough for luxuries such as golf courses in some regions where it was not possible before.

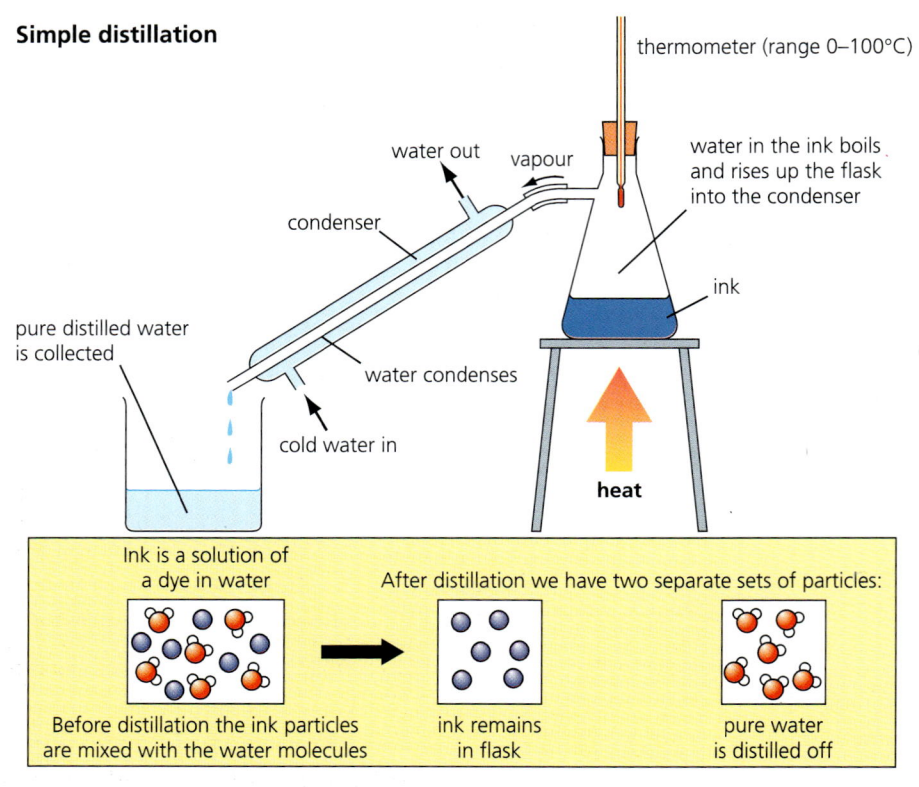

Simple distillation

Figure 7 Simple distillation can be used to separate pure water from a solution.

How can a mixture of liquids be separated?

A slightly different process is needed to separate a mixture of two or more liquids – this is **fractional distillation**. This method uses the physical property of boiling point – it depends on the liquids having different boiling points. Crude oil contains a mixture of liquids, each with a different boiling point. By slowly heating the mixture, each of the liquids will distil at a different temperature and can be collected separately, as you can see in figure 8. Liquids with similar boiling points that are distilled together are called **'fractions'**.

Elements, compounds and mixtures

Using a fractionating column

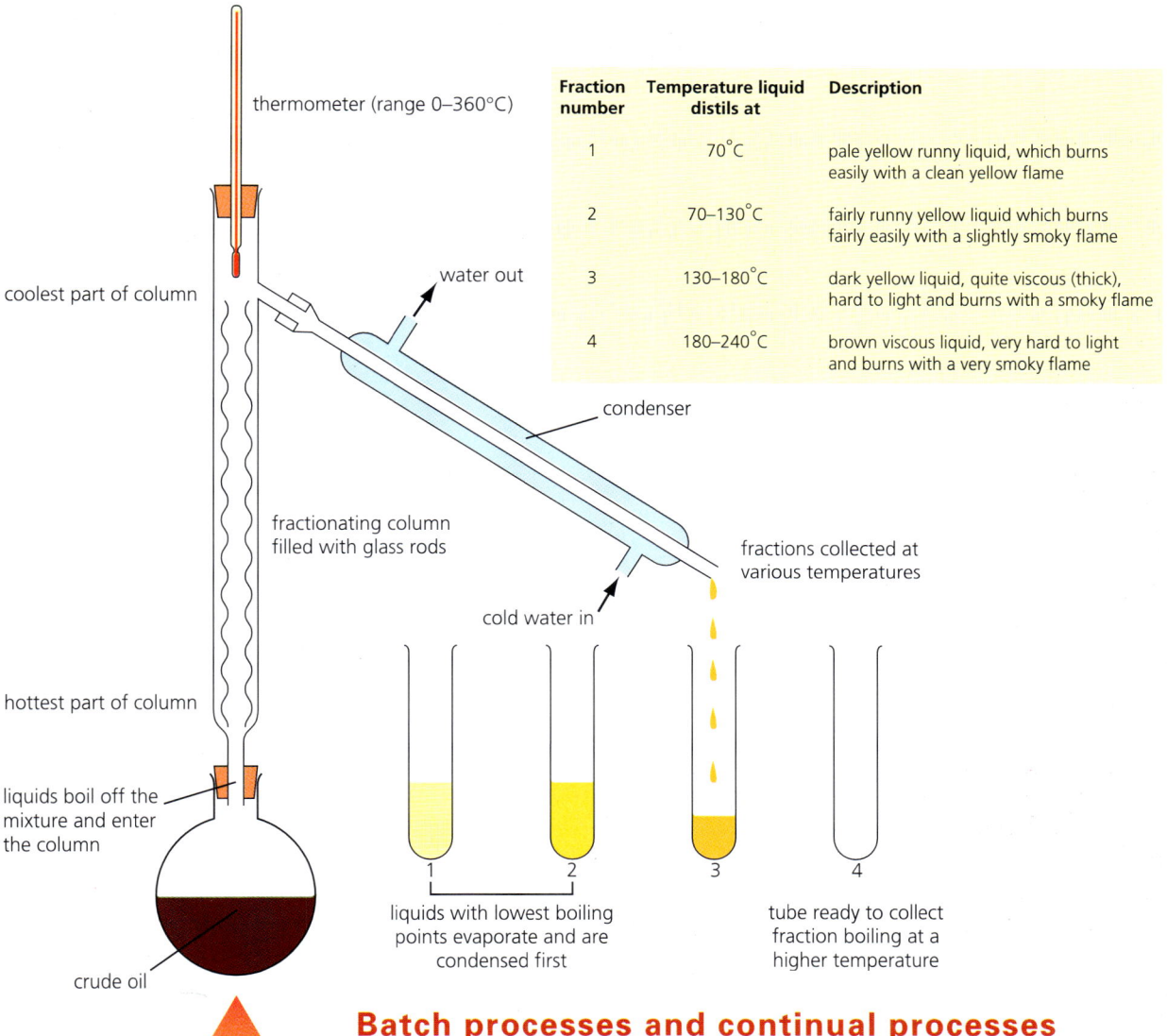

Fraction number	Temperature liquid distils at	Description
1	70°C	pale yellow runny liquid, which burns easily with a clean yellow flame
2	70–130°C	fairly runny yellow liquid which burns fairly easily with a slightly smoky flame
3	130–180°C	dark yellow liquid, quite viscous (thick), hard to light and burns with a smoky flame
4	180–240°C	brown viscous liquid, very hard to light and burns with a very smoky flame

Figure 8 Separating out the components of crude oil by fractional distillation.

Batch processes and continual processes

You can distil a single 'batch' of crude oil in your science laboratory by heating it in a flask, as shown in figure 8. As the temperature in the flask rises, the fractions with increasing boiling points are collected from the condenser. This is known as a **'batch process'**.

In an oil refinery, fractional distillation is done on a much larger scale for 24 hours a day. Oil is continually pumped into huge fractionating columns, and continually collected at a number of outlets in the column. This is much more economical for large-scale production, and is known as a **continuous process**. The machinery needed for this is very expensive, and the whole process is more profitable when it is running all the time, with people working in shifts. You will find more details about the oil industry and the chemicals involved in Chapter 16, *Organic chemistry*.

What is matter?

How can you separate liquids that don't mix completely?

Some liquids, such as alcohol, will dissolve completely in water in any proportions. Liquids that do this are said to be **miscible** with each other. The components of crude oil are also miscible with each other.

However, some liquids do not dissolve in each other – they are **immiscible**. For example, oil and water will not mix – they will always form two separate layers because the oil floats on the water. Immiscible liquids can be separated from each other using this physical property. To separate immiscible liquids you would use a separating funnel like the one in figure 9.

Separating immiscible liquids

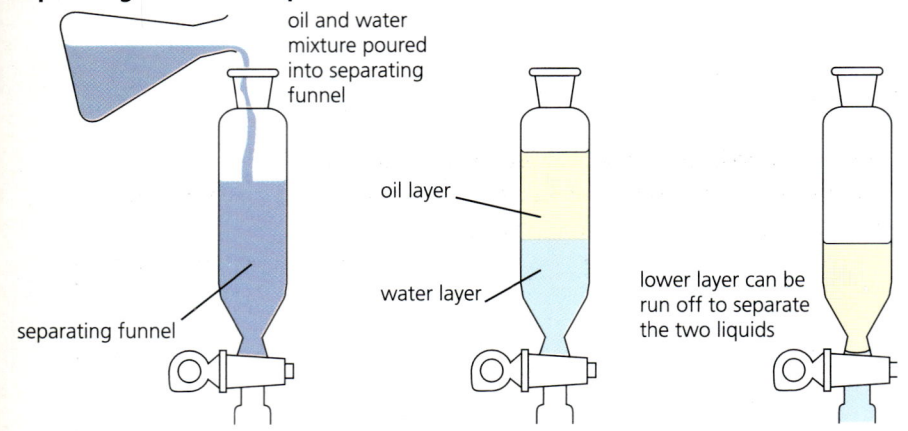

- oil and water mixture poured into separating funnel
- oil layer
- water layer
- lower layer can be run off to separate the two liquids
- separating funnel

Figure 9 Oil and water can be separated by running off each layer in turn.

What is chromatography?

Note

Chemists often want to find out the substances present in various mixtures. For example a forensic scientist might want to analyse the samples found at the scene of a crime to identify a culprit. A food scientist may need to know if food samples contain unacceptable levels of pesticides or whether food colourings are present. An analytical chemist may be asked to find out whether samples of river water contain various pollutants. All of these people might use chromatography to find the answers they need.

Chromatography is another way of separating out the different components of a mixture. A solution containing several different solutes can be separated by **paper chromatography**. This process is explained in figure 10.

Many different solvents or mixtures of solvents can be used in chromatography, and chemists often need to experiment before they find out exactly which solvent mixture works best for a particular mixture to be separated.

Chromatography can also be used to identify the substances in a mixture by putting an unknown mixture onto the paper together with a number of known pure substances that could be present in the mixture. By comparing the separated spots on the chromatogram, the exact contents of the mixture can be identified. An example of this is shown in figure 11.

Figure 10 Paper chromatography.

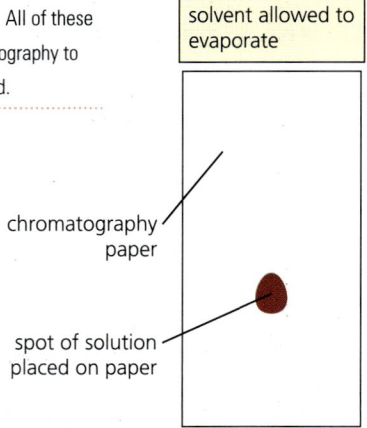

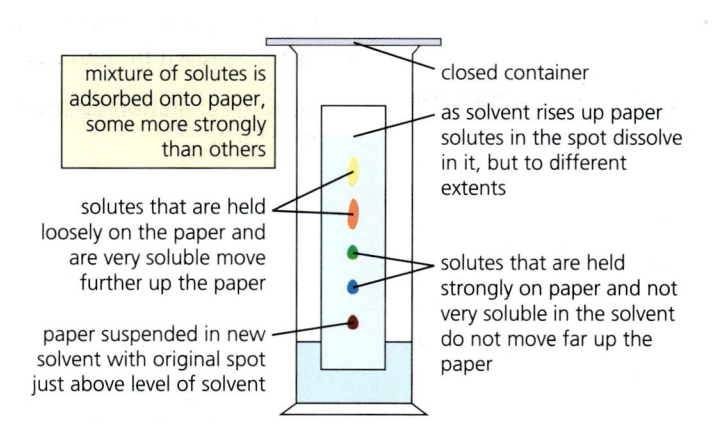

- solvent allowed to evaporate
- chromatography paper
- spot of solution placed on paper
- mixture of solutes is adsorbed onto paper, some more strongly than others
- solutes that are held loosely on the paper and are very soluble move further up the paper
- paper suspended in new solvent with original spot just above level of solvent
- closed container
- as solvent rises up paper solutes in the spot dissolve in it, but to different extents
- solutes that are held strongly on paper and not very soluble in the solvent do not move far up the paper

Elements, compounds and mixtures

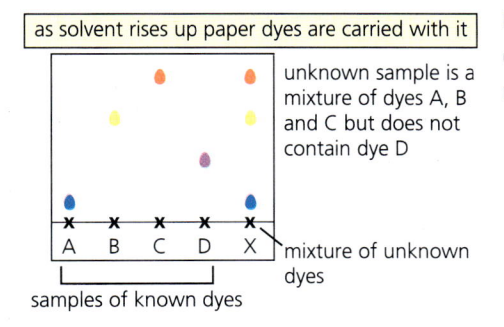

Figure 11 By comparing the spots on a chromatogram with 'standard' spots an unknown mixture can be identified.

as solvent rises up paper dyes are carried with it

unknown sample is a mixture of dyes A, B and C but does not contain dye D

A B C D X — mixture of unknown dyes

samples of known dyes

10 What physical property is used to separate substances in chromatography?
11 A food scientist is investigating the colourings used in a particular variety of sweets. She has extracted the dyes and has prepared chromatogram A below.

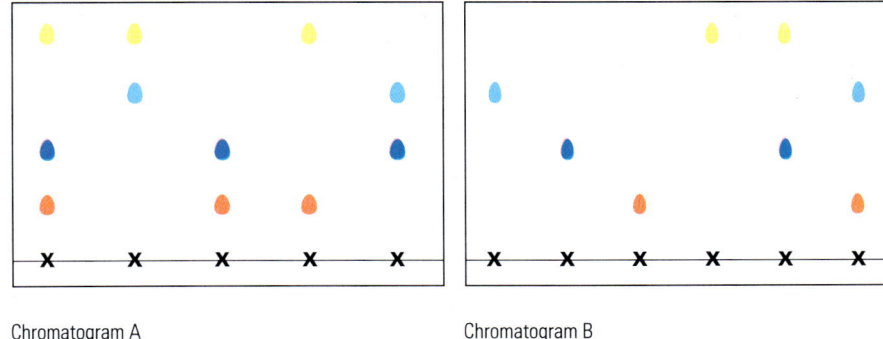

Chromatogram A

Chromatogram B

To help her identify the dyes extracted from the food she has also made a chromatogram of some standard food dyes she thinks might have been used (Chromatogram B).
How many different dyes has the manufacturer used?

What use is sublimation?

When some solids are warmed, they change straight to a gas without first melting to a liquid. The process of changing straight from a solid to a gas is called **sublimation**. When this vapour touches a cool surface it condenses back into a solid. For example, iodine sublimes when gently warmed. This physical property can be used to separate a mixture of iodine and common salt, as shown in figure 12.

Figure 12 Separating common salt and iodine.

Using sublimation to separate substances

← cold water from tap
→ water out
iodine crystals solidify on cold surface
iodine sublimes and rises up beaker, but salt does not
salt crystals remain in beaker

mixture of common salt and iodine crystals

gentle warming

12 How would you go about separating out the components of a mixture of salt, iron filings and iodine?

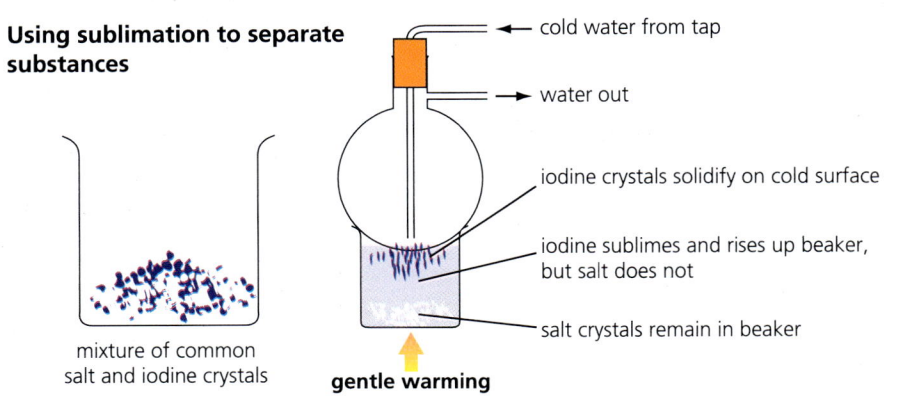

9

Summary of physical change and mixtures

- Physical change is a process brought about by changing physical conditions – such as temperature.
- Mixtures of substances can be separated using the differences in their physical properties.
- Simple distillation is used to separate a liquid and a solid dissolved in it.
- A mixture of liquids with different boiling points can be separated by fractional distillation.
- Liquids that are immiscible will not dissolve in each other – a separating funnel can be used to recover each liquid separately.
- Paper chromatography can be used to separate and identify a mixture of dissolved substances by noting how far up the paper they are carried by the solvent.
- When a substance changes from a solid to a gas, without going through a liquid phase in between, it has sublimed.

1.3 Chemical change and compounds

In a **chemical reaction** the materials that react together undergo **chemical change** to form new ones. This type of change is very different from physical change when substances stay the same but just appear in a different form (water is still water whether it is ice or vapour).

The **chemical properties** of a substance describe the ways it reacts chemically. For instance:

- whether it burns
- how it reacts with oxygen
- its reaction with water
- its reaction with chlorine

You can separate a mixture of substances using differences in their physical properties. An example of this is the mixture of iron and sulphur shown in figure 6. However, if you heat a mixture of iron and sulphur a chemical reaction will take place between the iron and the sulphur, and a new substance (called iron sulphide) will be formed. The way this happens is shown in figure 13.

Chemical change

mixture of iron filings (a grey metallic material) and sulphur (a yellow powder) in equal quantities

chemical reaction

iron sulphide formed – a grey solid that is a compound of iron and sulphur

heat

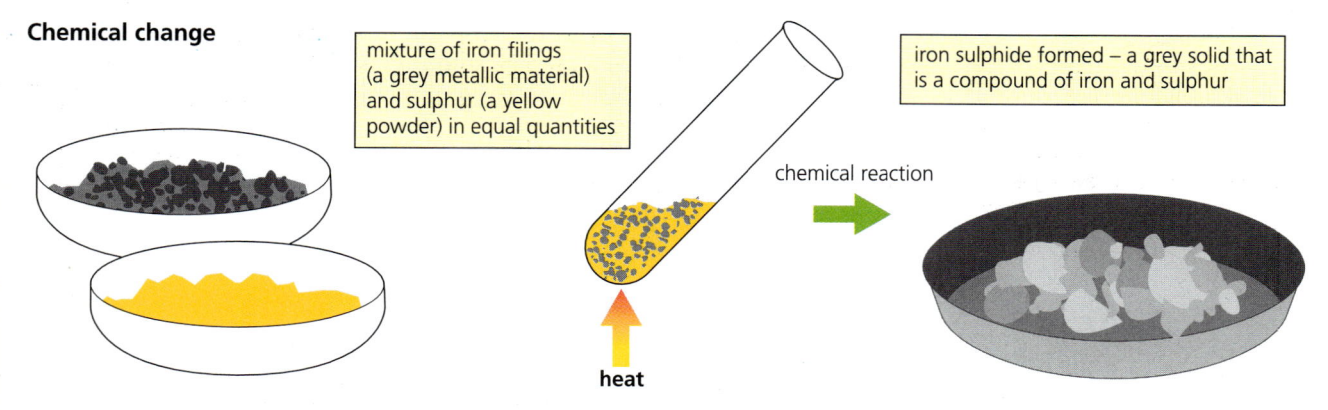

Figure 13 When a mixture of iron and sulphur is heated chemical change occurs and a new substance is formed.

Elements, compounds and mixtures

Iron sulphide is a **compound** of the elements iron and sulphur. A compound contains two or more elements chemically joined together. It can only be broken down into its elements again by using further chemical reactions.

13 Here is a list of solids that are changed by heating. For each one state how it changes and whether the change is physical or chemical.
   a Ice
   b Iodine
   c Salt
   d Sugar

14 For each of the following processes state what happens. Which ones involve chemical change?
   a Boiling water
   b Burning methane
   c Evaporating petrol
   d Melting sodium chloride

When chemical reactions like this happen, it is often possible to see changes taking place. Some of these are illustrated in figure 14.

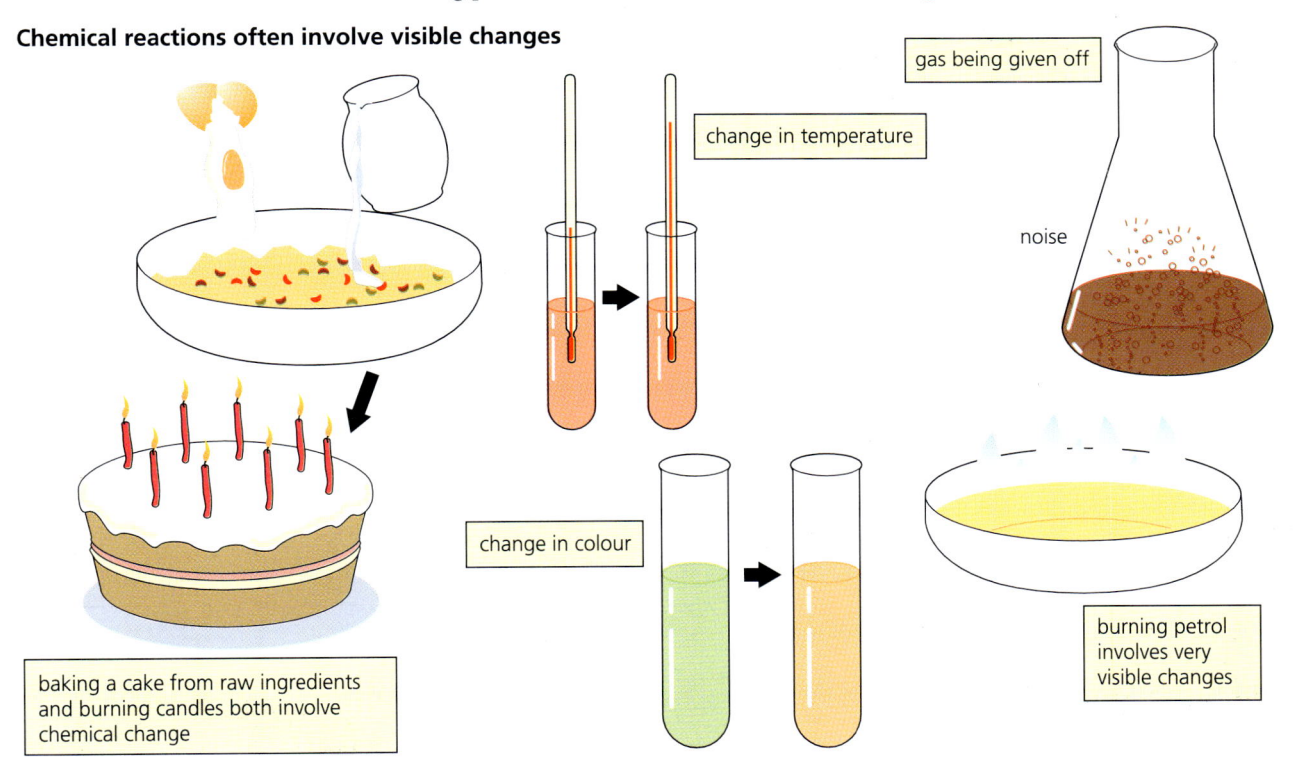

Chemical reactions often involve visible changes

gas being given off

change in temperature

noise

change in colour

baking a cake from raw ingredients and burning candles both involve chemical change

burning petrol involves very visible changes

Figure 14 Seeing chemical changes happen.

What are chemical formulae and how are they used?

When we want to write down what is present in a substance or what is happening in a chemical reaction we do not always have to write out long

11

What is matter?

The chemical formula for water

the H and the O show that water contains the elements hydrogen and oxygen

H_2O

the number in the formula shows that water contains two hydrogen atoms and one oxygen atom

H_2O

Figure 15 The chemical formula shows two main things – which elements are present and how much of each element is present.

descriptions in words. We use the chemical symbols (look back at figure 3) as 'chemical shorthand' to show which elements are present in a substance. The compound formed in a chemical reaction can be represented in chemical shorthand using a **chemical formula**. For example, the chemical formula for water is H_2O. The chemical formula gives useful information about a compound.

The plural of formula is **formulae** – the formulae of some common compounds are shown in table 2.

water molecules are made up of hydrogen and oxygen atoms

ammonia molecules are made up of hydrogen and nitrogen atoms

Table 2 Chemical formulae of some common compounds

Name	Formula	Each compound contains
ammonia	NH_3	one nitrogen atom for every three hydrogen atoms
carbon dioxide	CO_2	one carbon atom for evey two oxygen atoms
iron oxide	Fe_2O_3	two iron atoms for every three oxygen atoms
sodium chloride	$NaCl$	one sodium for every one chlorine
sulphuric acid	H_2SO_4	two hydrogen atoms for every one sulphur atom for every four oxygen atoms

15 Here is a list of the formulae of various chemical compounds:
$CaCO_3$, KNO_3, CH_4, $C_6H_{12}O_6$, HCl, NH_4NO_3, $AlCl_3$, C_2H_6O, NO_2, $CuSO_4 \cdot 5H_2O$
  a How many different elements does each formula represent?
  b How many atoms does each formula contain?

What are molecules?

Two or more atoms often join together chemically into groups called **molecules**. The smallest molecules contain only two atoms – these are called **diatomic** molecules. Some of the large molecules found in plastics or living things can contain hundreds of thousands of atoms. Molecules can come in many shapes and sizes.

molecules come in all sorts of sizes – from very small and simple ...

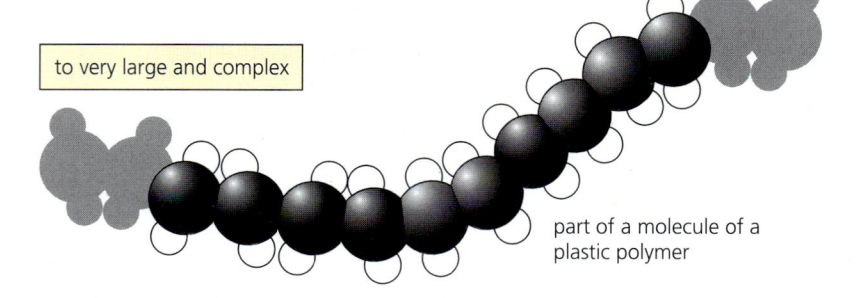

a hydrogen molecule

to very large and complex

part of a molecule of a plastic polymer

Figure 16 Molecules come in many shapes and sizes.

Elements, compounds and mixtures

Table 3 *Molecules can be elements or compounds*

Elements	Compounds
hydrogen H_2	Carbon dioxide CO_2
nitrogen N_2	Water H_2O
oxygen O_2	hydrogen chloride HCl

How do we write down what happens in chemical reactions?

A **chemical equation** shows what is happening in a chemical reaction. Chemical equations can be written as **word equations**, which show the names of the chemicals involved, or as **symbol equations**, which show the symbols or formulae of the chemicals involved.

Here is the equation for the reaction between the two elements iron and sulphur, written as both a word equation and a symbol equation.

| Word equation: | iron | + | sulphur | → | iron sulphide |
| Symbol equation: | Fe | + | S | → | FeS |

Here is another chemical equation, involving the two compounds copper oxide and sulphuric acid:

| Word equation: | copper oxide | + | sulphuric acid | → | copper sulphate | + | water |
| Symbol equation: | CuO | + | H_2SO_4 | → | $CuSO_4$ | + | H_2O |

When carbon burns in a coal fire it reacts with oxygen in the air to form carbon dioxide:

| Word equation: | carbon | + | oxygen | → | carbon dioxide |
| Symbol equation: | C | + | O_2 | → | CO_2 |

This means that: one atom of carbon reacts with one molecule of oxygen to form one molecule of carbon dioxide.

16 Which way of writing chemical reactions do you think is more useful, word equations or symbol equations? Why?

Here is the symbol equation for what happens when hydrogen burns in oxygen:

$$2H_2 + O_2 \rightarrow 2H_2O$$

The numbers before the H_2 and H_2O show the number of molecules of hydrogen and water that are involved in this reaction – this symbol equation means that:

| two molecules | react | one molecule | to give | two molecules |
| of hydrogen | with | of oxygen | | of water |

The symbol equation for a reaction is a 'shorthand' way of writing down what is happening, more quickly than writing it all out in words. Symbol equations provide information more concisely than word equations.

What do state symbols show?

Another useful piece of chemical shorthand, which is included in many equations, is the **state symbol**. This shows whether a substance in a reaction is a solid (symbol s), a liquid (l), a gas (g) or is dissolved in water (aqueous solution, symbol aq). The state symbols are written after the symbol or formula.

Here are some of the equations we have already used, rewritten to include the state symbols.

Burning carbon in oxygen:

Symbol equation:	$C(s)$	+	$O_2(g)$	→	$CO_2(g)$
Means that:	solid copper	reacts with	oxygen gas	to give	carbon dioxide gas

Reacting copper oxide with sulphuric acid:

Symbol equation:	$CuO(s)$	+	$H_2SO_4(aq)$	→	$CuSO_4(aq)$ + $H_2O(l)$
Means that:	solid copper oxide	reacts with	sulphuric acid dissolved in water (it is a dilute acid)	to give	copper sulphate dissolved in water and liquid water.

17 Look back at the reaction for burning hydrogen in oxygen on page 13 and rewrite it to include the state symbols.

Water is used to dissolve many substances, and so the (aq) state symbol appears often. Sometimes water is itself involved in a chemical reaction (as in the reaction between copper oxide and sulphuric acid above). When water appears as part of an equation like this, it is written as $H_2O(l)$, *never* as $H_2O(aq)$.

18 Why do you think you should not write $H_2O(aq)$ in an equation?

How do you know which way a reaction is proceeding?

The arrow in the equation tells which way the reaction is going. The substances present at the start of the reaction are called the **reactants**. They are always shown on the left-hand side of the equation (to the left of the arrow).

The **products** of the reaction are the new substances that are formed. They are always shown on the right-hand side of the equation (to the right of the arrow).

For example:

$$CuO(s) + H_2SO_4(aq) \rightarrow CuSO_4(aq) + H_2O(l)$$

reactants – the substances reacting together at the start

products – the new substances formed

Elements, compounds and mixtures

Why should chemical equations be balanced?

When chemical reactions are written down they should be 'balanced'. In a **balanced equation** the number of atoms of each element on both sides of the equation are the same. But why is it important that an equation is balanced?

The **Law of Conservation of Mass** answers this question. Antoine Lavoisier was a French chemist who discovered this law, which states that:

"matter cannot be created or destroyed in a chemical reaction – the mass of the products must equal the mass of reactants"

To make sure that this law is followed, there must always be the same number of atoms present at the end of the reaction as there were at the start – the equation must be balanced.

To balance an equation you must count up the number of atoms of each element involved and ensure that they are the same on both sides of the equation. This could mean that the number in front of some formulae will have to change. For example, if water is involved in an equation the number of molecules may have to be changed from one (H_2O) to two ($2H_2O$) or even three ($3H_2O$).

Note

You should *never* attempt to balance an equation by simply altering a formula – the formula for a chemical *never* changes. For example, the formula for water is *always* H_2O and you should never change it to H_3O or HO_2 simply to try to balance an equation.

WORKED EXAMPLES

1 Methane burns in oxygen to give carbon dioxide and water. Write a balanced equation for this reaction.

First, write down the formulae for each of the reactants and products:

	reactants		products
	methane + oxygen	→	carbon dioxide + water
Unbalanced equation:	$CH_4 + O_2$	→	$CO_2 + H_2O$
Count the atoms to see if it is balanced:	1 carbon atom		1 carbon atom
	4 hydrogen atoms		2 hydrogen atoms
	2 oxygen atoms		3 oxygen atoms
Balance the number of hydrogen atoms, by changing the H_2O on the right to $\mathbf{2}H_2O$:	$CH_4 + O_2$	→	$CO_2 + \mathbf{2}H_2O$
			there are now 4 hydrogen atoms here
Now balance the number of oxygen atoms, by changing the O_2 on the left to $\mathbf{2}O_2$:	$CH_4 + \mathbf{2}O_2$	→	$CO_2 + 2H_2O$
	there are now 4 oxygen atoms here		
Balanced equation:	$CH_4 + 2O_2$	→	$CO_2 + 2H_2O$
	1 carbon atom		1 carbon atom
	4 hydrogen atoms		4 hydrogen atoms
	4 oxygen atoms		4 oxygen atoms

number of atoms in reactants = number of atoms in products

What is matter?

2 A solid oxide of iron with the formula Fe_2O_3 reacts with hydrogen gas to form solid iron metal and steam vapour. Write a balanced equation for this reaction, including state symbols.

Unbalanced equation:	$Fe_2O_3 + H_2$	→	$Fe + H_2O$
Count the atoms to see if it is balanced:	2 iron atoms		1 iron atom
	3 oxygen atoms		1 oxygen atom
	2 hydrogen atoms		2 hydrogen atoms

Balance the number of iron atoms,
by changing the Fe on the right to **2**Fe: $Fe_2O_3 + H_2$ → **2**Fe + H_2O
↑
there are now 2 iron atoms here

Balance the number of oxygen atoms: $Fe_2O_3 + H_2$ → 2Fe + **3**H_2O
↑
there are now 3 oxygen atoms here

Balance the number of hydrogen atoms: $Fe_2O_3 +$ **3**H_2 → 2Fe + 3H_2O
↑
there are now 6 hydrogen atoms

Balanced equation:	$Fe_2O_3 + 3H_2$	→	$2Fe + 3H_2O$
	2 iron atoms		2 iron atoms
	3 oxygen atoms		3 oxygen atoms
	6 hydrogen atoms		6 hydrogen atoms

number of atoms in reactants = number of atoms in products

Use the information given to decide the state symbols:

$Fe_2O_3(s) + 3H_2(g)$ → $2Fe(s) + 3H_2O(l)$

19 Balance these symbol equations:
- **a** $Al + Cl_2 \rightarrow AlCl_3$
- **b** $C + CO_2 \rightarrow CO$
- **c** $CuO + HCl \rightarrow CuCl_2 + H_2O$
- **d** $C_2H_6 + O_2 \rightarrow CO_2 + H_2O$
- **e** $Al + HCl \rightarrow AlCl_3 + H_2$
- **f** $C_2H_4 + O_2 \rightarrow CO_2 + H_2O$
- **g** $H_2S + O_2 \rightarrow H_2O + SO_2$
- **h** $H_2 + Cl_2 \rightarrow HCl$
- **i** $Na_2CO_3 + HCl \rightarrow NaCl + H_2O + CO_2$
- **j** $SO_2 + O_2 \rightarrow SO_3$

Summary of chemical change and compounds

- A compound contains two or more elements chemically joined together.
- The chemical formula of a compound shows which elements are present and in what proportions.
- When a chemical reaction happens, one or more new elements or compounds are always formed.
- A molecule contains two or more atoms chemically joined together. Molecules may be elements or compounds.
- A chemical equation shows the formulae of the reactants and products in a chemical reaction.
- Balancing an equation involves showing the correct proportion of each chemical involved in the reaction.
- State symbols show the state of a substance in an equation – a solid (s), a liquid (l), a gas (g) or dissolved in water (aq).

Examination style questions

1 The diagram below shows the apparatus that could be used to separate pure water from sea water.

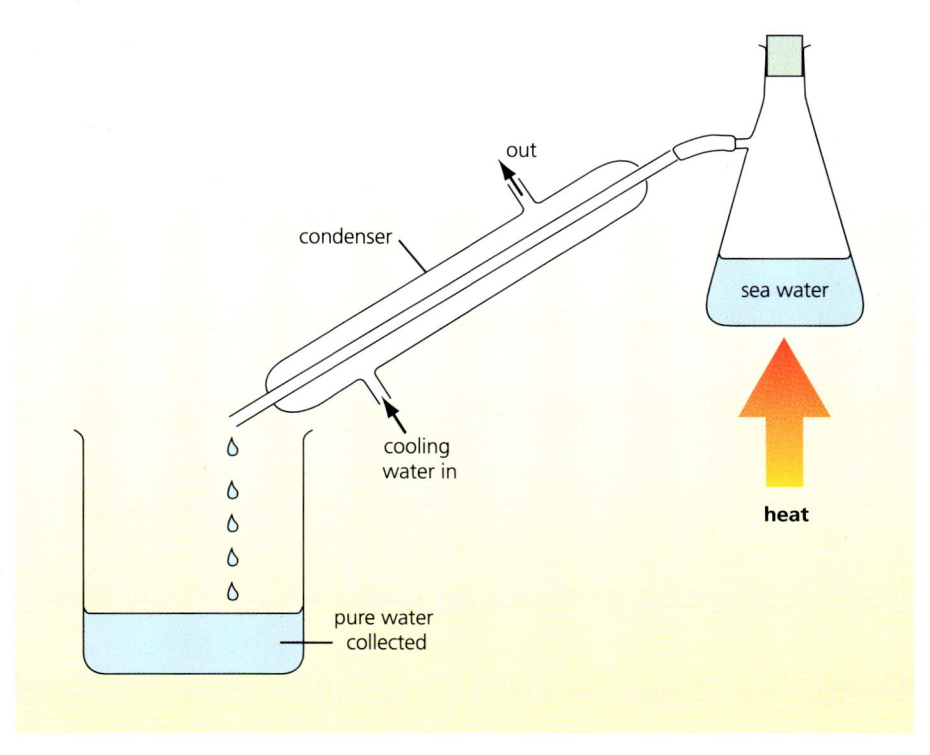

a What process is being carried out here?
b Give one of the physical properties of sea water that makes it different from pure water
c A thermometer is helpful in this process
i Where is the most useful place to put the thermometer?
ii Where is the best place for the thermometer bulb?
iii Thermometers are available to measure the following temperature ranges:
0–50°C, -10–110°C, 0–360°C. Which would be the most useful for this experiment?
d Why is cold water passed through the condenser?
e It is possible for desert countries with little fresh water to distil sea water in this way, but the process is very expensive. Why?

2 Balance the following chemical equations.
a $CO + O_2 \rightarrow CO_2$
b $Fe + O_2 \rightarrow Fe_2O_3$
c $Na + H_2O \rightarrow NaOH + H_2$
d $Al + I_2 \rightarrow AlI_3$
e $C_3H_8 + O_2 \rightarrow CO_2 + H_2O$
f $C_4H_8 + O_2 \rightarrow CO_2 + H_2O$
g $Ag_2CO_3 \rightarrow Ag + CO_2 + O_2$
h $KNO_3 \rightarrow KNO_2 + O_2$
i $NaHCO_3 \rightarrow Na_2CO_3 + CO_2 + H_2O$
j $CuSO_4 + KI \rightarrow CuI + K_2SO_4 + I_2$

Solids, liquids and gases 2

Learning objectives

By the end of this chapter you should be able to:

- **describe** the physical properties of solids, liquids and gases
- **explain** the properties of materials using the Kinetic Theory
- **explain** the energy changes involved in changes of state
- **calculate** the density of a substance from its mass and volume
- **calculate** the effects of changes in pressure, temperature and volume on a gas using the gas laws
- **predict** the state of a material at room temperature from its melting and boiling points
- **relate** the uses of solids, liquids and gases to their particular properties

2.1 States of matter

How do solids, liquids and gases differ?

Figure 1 A substance can change from one state to another depending on the physical conditions.

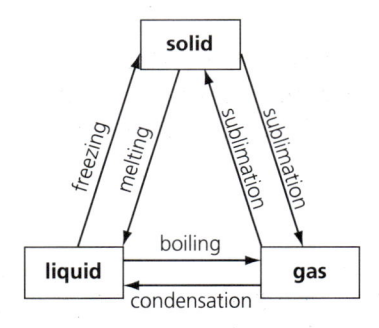

Almost all substances can be classified as **solids**, **liquids** or **gases** or as various mixtures of these three. These are described as the three **states of matter**, and they each have different properties, depending on how strongly the particles are held together.

- Solids have a fixed volume and shape.
- Liquids have a fixed volume but no definite shape. They take up the shape of the container in which they are held.
- Gases have no fixed volume or shape. They spread out to fill whatever container or space they are in.

Substances don't always exist in the same state – depending on the physical conditions they change from one state to another.

Some substances can exist in all three states in the natural world – a good example of this is water.

Water covers nearly four-fifths of the Earth's surface. Here all three states of matter exist together – solid water (the ice) is floating in liquid water (the ocean) and the surrounding air contains water vapour (the clouds).

Matter can, in fact, exist in states other than the three described here – for example plasma. Your teacher should be able to tell you more about this.

Solids, liquids and gases

Why do solids, liquids and gases behave differently?

The ways that solids, liquids and gases behave can be explained if we think of all matter as being made up of very small particles that are in constant motion. This idea has been summarised in the **Kinetic Theory of Matter**.

Particles in a liquid can move around. When they are heated the particles move around even more.

When particles are heated they vibrate faster. Vibrating particles bump into neighbouring particles and make them vibrate more too.

Particles in a solid are packed closely together. The particles vibrate from side to side only.

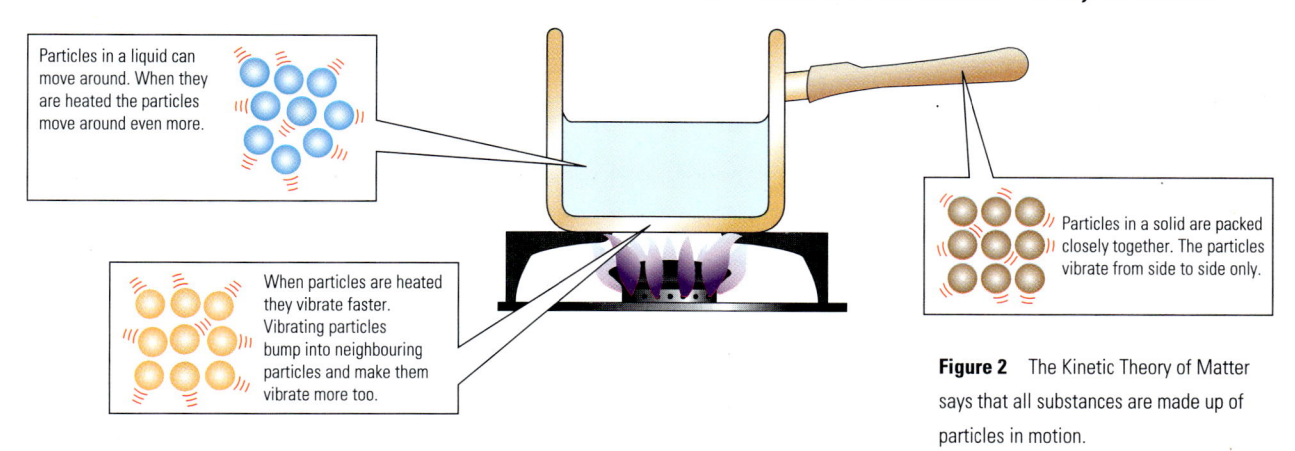

Figure 2 The Kinetic Theory of Matter says that all substances are made up of particles in motion.

Summary of States of matter

- Most substances exist in three states – solid, liquid or gas.
- Substances can change from one state to another.
- The properties of each state of matter can be explained by the Kinetic Theory of Matter.

2.2 Properties of solids

Solids have many interesting properties. If you are sitting on a chair as you read this book you are relying on some of the properties of solids – the chair doesn't flow all over the floor as a liquid would or escape out of the window like a gas!

Why is the shape of solids fixed?

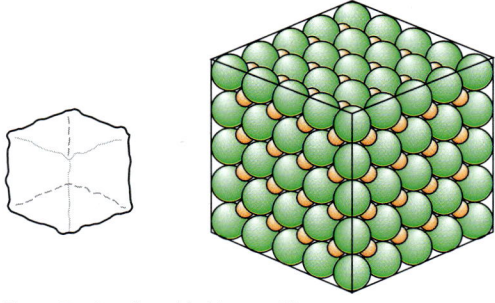

If you have ever seen or grown crystals of copper sulphate or sodium chloride you will know that each substance has its own **crystal shape**. This is because the particles are always arranged in a particular way. Sodium chloride crystals, for example, are always cube-shaped.

Although the crystals of a substance are always the same shape they can, of course, be of different sizes. A **giant structure** contains the same arrangement repeated over and over again. As the crystal gets larger the giant structure is repeated – but the arrangement is the same whatever the size.

Figure 3 A sodium chloride crystal is cube-shaped because of the way the ions are arranged.

What is matter?

Figure 4 As a crystal gets larger the arrangement of particles is repeated over and over. This is called a giant structure.

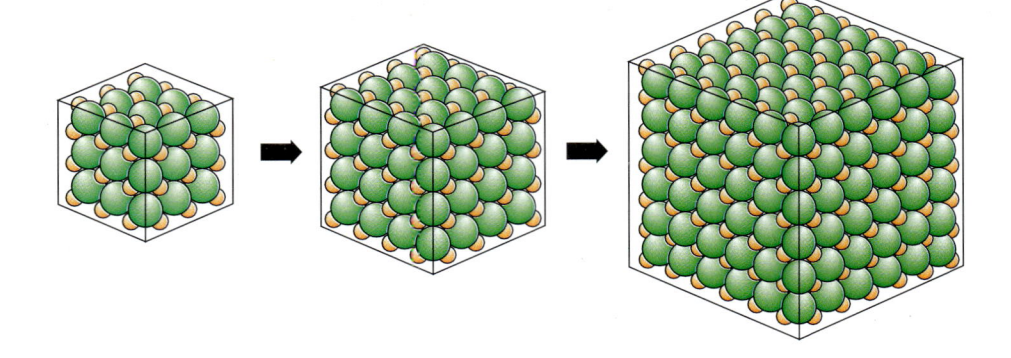

How are solids affected by pressure?

The particles in a solid are held together tightly by the bonds between them, and don't move around. Because the particles stay in one place, the volume is always the same. This also means that solids can't be compressed (they are **incompressible**).

What happens when solids are heated or cooled?

The particles in a solid vibrate slightly rather than move around. When a solid is heated the particles vibrate more and the substance expands. If a substance is cooled down the particles vibrate less and it contracts.

Figure 5 Heating and cooling solids.

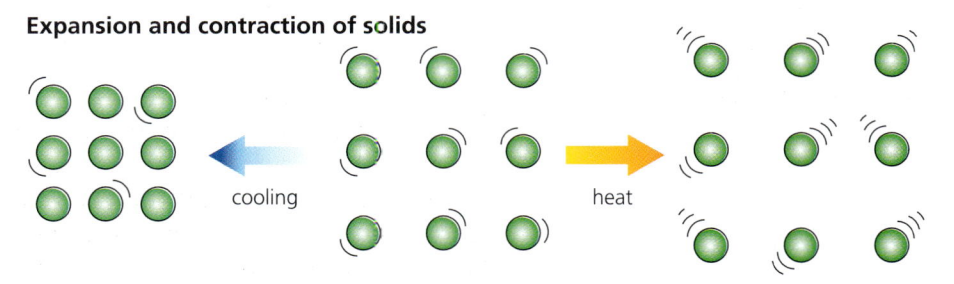

Expansion and contraction of solids

cooling ← → heat

The property of expansion on heating can be used to make something a perfect fit. As the barrel hoops cool the wood of barrel is pulled tightly together. In a similar way the property of contraction on cooling can be used to make a perfect fit. One material can be cooled so that it fits into a slot on another, as the cooled material warms it expands to fit the slot.

Summary of properties of solids

- Solids have a fixed shape.
- Solids have fixed volume.
- Solids cannot be compressed.
- Solids expand when heated and contract when cooled.

2.3 Properties of liquids

How do particles in a liquid behave?

The particles in a liquid behave differently from the particles in a solid. They are further apart, and so the bonds between them are not as strong as in a solid. Bonds between particles in a liquid are also constantly being broken and formed. This makes the liquid flow more easily than a solid and a liquid will take up the shape of whatever container it is in.

Figure 6 Melting solids

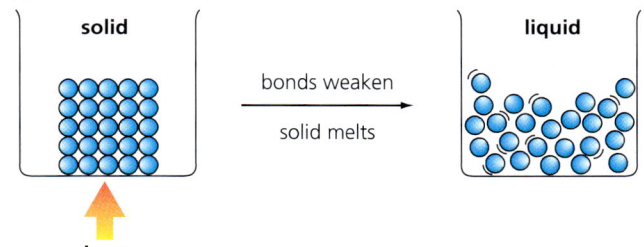

Movement of molecules in a beaker of water

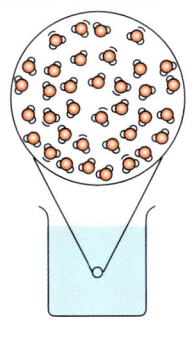

Figure 7

In 1827 a botanist called Robert Brown was studying pollen grains in water under his microscope. He noticed that the pollen grains were moving around in a random way. He discovered that the pollen grains were being moved by the much smaller water molecules bumping into them. Although the water molecules were too small to be seen, their motion could be followed by the way the pollen grains moved around. This form of motion was named **Brownian motion**, after the man who discovered it. By studying Brownian motion we can discover more about the ways particles in a liquid behave.

Can liquids be compressed?

Although the molecules in a liquid are moving around more than they do in a solid, they are held together fairly strongly, so the volume of a given mass of a liquid at a constant temperature doesn't change.

The particles are also packed quite closely together and can't be pushed together much – so liquids are not easily compressed.

What is matter?

What is diffusion?

If a crystal of potassium permanganate is placed into a beaker of water the water molecules will bump into its particles and dissolve some of them. These particles will slowly be moved around the beaker, and this can be seen by the colour slowly spreading throughout the beaker. The process of spreading out of particles like this is called **diffusion**.

Figure 8 If a few crystals of potassium permanganate are put into a beaker of water the colour will slowly spread throughout the beaker as the potassium permanganate diffuses through the water.

Diffusion in liquids

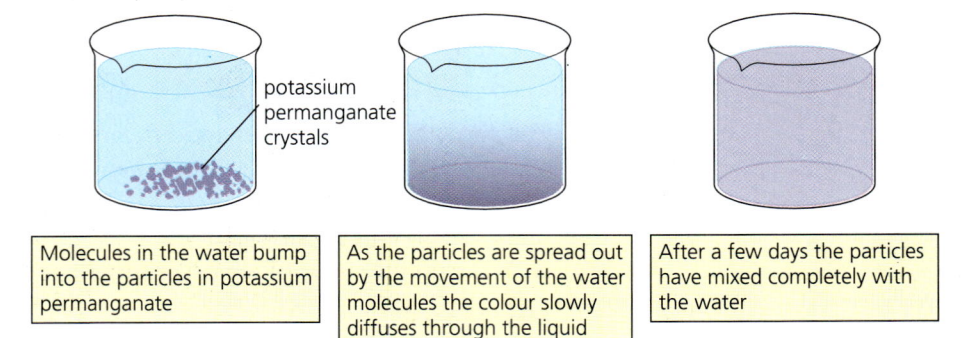

| Molecules in the water bump into the particles in potassium permanganate | As the particles are spread out by the movement of the water molecules the colour slowly diffuses through the liquid | After a few days the particles have mixed completely with the water |

Diffusion occurs more rapidly if the liquid is hot – for example a spoonful of sugar will dissolve more quickly in a cup of hot tea than in a cold one. This is because the particles of a hot liquid have more energy than in a cold one. They therefore move around more quickly, spreading particles more rapidly throughout the liquid.

Summary of properties of liquids

- A liquid has no fixed shape – it will take up the shape of its container.
- A liquid does have a fixed volume – it cannot easily be compressed.
- Particles spread throughout a liquid by diffusion.

2.4 Properties of gases

Gases have some properties that are very similar to the properties of liquids, but also have their own unique properties – for example they do not have a fixed shape or volume, and will spread out to fill whatever container they are in.

How do particles of a gas move about?

The particles in liquids and gases both move randomly. However, the particles in a gas have much more energy and so move more quickly. The movement of gas particles can be studied by looking at the Brownian motion of smoke particles in a smoke cell, as shown in figure 9.

Solids, liquids and gases

Figure 9 A smoke cell.

- microscope
- Smoke particles are seen under the microscope as bright, randomly moving specks
- light source
- Cell containing smoke particles in air. The individual molecules in the air are too small to see, but their effects on the smoke particles are visible
- smoke particles
- Molecules in the air move randomly and collide with smoke particles, moving them around
- The path taken by an individual gas molecule is quite random. Gas molecules move very quickly, only changing direction when they collide with each other or with other particles such as the walls of the container

Does diffusion occur in gases?

Again, like liquids, gases will diffuse in all directions – and again, because the energy of the gas particles is higher the particles move around more quickly. Diffusion in a gas is much more rapid than in liquids.

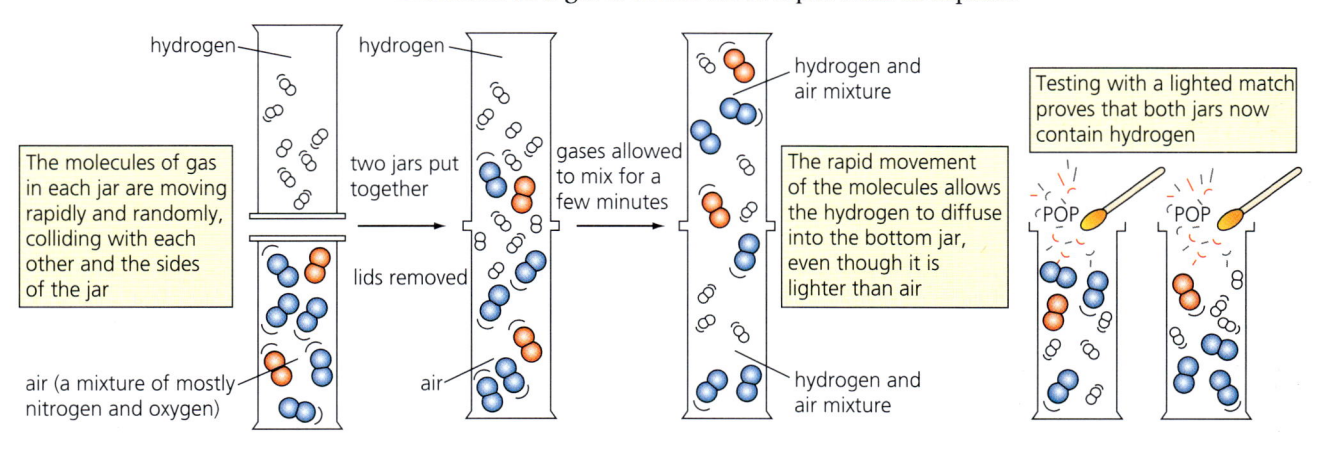

- hydrogen
- The molecules of gas in each jar are moving rapidly and randomly, colliding with each other and the sides of the jar
- air (a mixture of mostly nitrogen and oxygen)
- two jars put together
- lids removed
- gases allowed to mix for a few minutes
- hydrogen and air mixture
- The rapid movement of the molecules allows the hydrogen to diffuse into the bottom jar, even though it is lighter than air
- hydrogen and air mixture
- Testing with a lighted match proves that both jars now contain hydrogen
- POP   POP

Figure 10 Diffusion of the molecules in hydrogen and air.

- white ring where gases A+B meet
- cotton wool soaked in solution A
- cotton wool soaked in solution B

The **rate of diffusion** of a gas depends on its mass – molecules with a higher mass move more slowly than ones with a lower mass, as the experiment in figure 11 shows.

Figure 11 Ammonia and hydrogen chloride diffuse down a tube and react to form ammonium chloride. Because the ammonia molecules have a smaller mass than the hydrogen chloride molecules, they will move down the tube quicker and the reaction will not take place at the centre of the tube.

23

What is matter?

1 Four experiments were set up to investigate diffusion in gases. The experimental set-ups are shown in figure 12.

Figure 12 Experiments to study diffusion in gases.

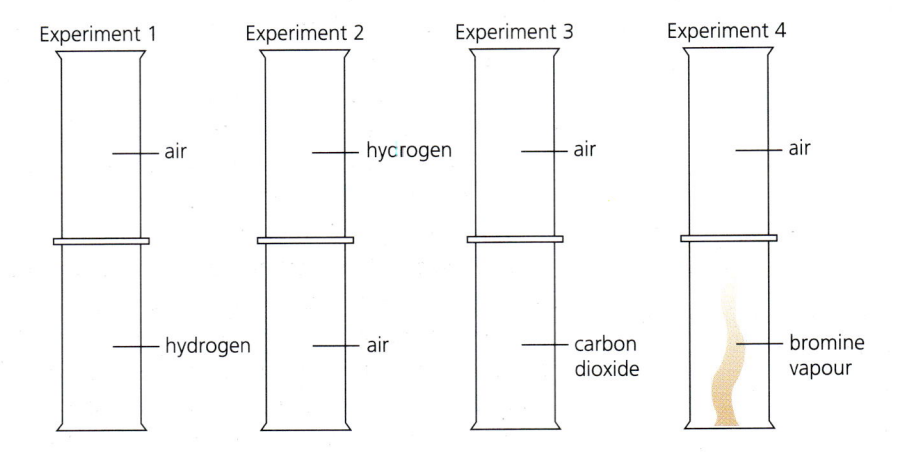

Experiment 1: air (top) / hydrogen (bottom)
Experiment 2: hydrogen (top) / air (bottom)
Experiment 3: air (top) / carbon dioxide (bottom)
Experiment 4: air (top) / bromine vapour (bottom)

At the start of each experiment, the dividing plate is removed and the gas jars left connected for about 20 minutes.

a In experiments 1 and 2 after 20 minutes the top jars were tested with a lighted match. What would you expect to happen in each one?

b In experiment 3, after 20 minutes each jar was tested by shaking with limewater. What would you expect to see?

c What would you expect to see in the apparatus in experiment 4 after 20 minutes?

2 When a bottle of perfume is opened on one side of a room the smell can be detected at the other side within a few minutes, even if the doors and windows are closed. How can this happen?

What happens when pressure is put upon a gas?

Unlike solids and liquids, gases can be compressed. This is because the particles in a gas are widely spaced and there is room for them to be squeezed into a smaller volume.

This property of gases is very useful – for example large volumes of gases can be compressed into cylinders for easy transportation.

Compressing a gas

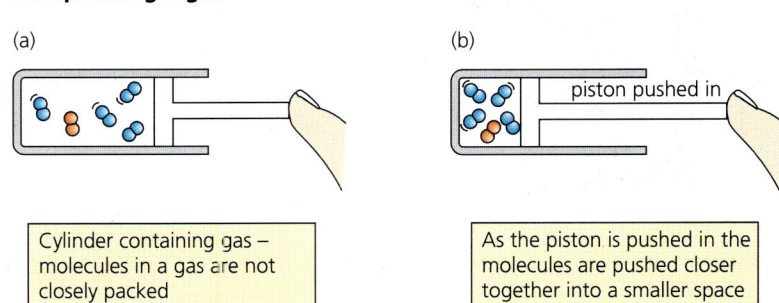

(a) Cylinder containing gas – molecules in a gas are not closely packed

(b) As the piston is pushed in the molecules are pushed closer together into a smaller space

Gases are transported compressed into cylinders.

Figure 13 A gas can be squeezed into a much smaller volume.

24

Gas pressure

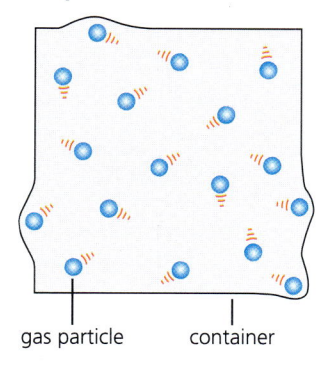

Figure 14 Gas pressure is caused by millions of tiny particles colliding with the walls of the container.

The particles of a gas are constantly moving rapidly. They move in straight paths and at steady speeds and only change direction when they collide with something – other particles or the walls of the container they are in (you can see the effects of this in the smoke cell described above). These collisions cause **gas pressure**.

As we have already discovered, the speed of motion of particles in a gas depends on their mass and the temperature – large particles move more slowly than smaller ones, hot particles move more quickly than cold ones. It follows that the same mass or volume of a gas will exert more pressure when it is hot than when it is cold.

The air around us pushes down and in upon us all the time, but we don't feel the pressure because our bodies exert an equal outward pressure. Normal atmospheric pressure is about 100 kPa (about 100 kN/m^2). We don't feel the collisions of the millions of particles of air crashing into us because the molecules are very much smaller than we are. In space there is no air, and so no air pressure. Astronauts in space need to wear special pressurised sealed suits. Without a pressure suit an astronaut would explode!

Gases will respond to changes in pressure, temperature and volume in ways that can be predicted. These responses have been summed up in several **gas laws**.

How are gas pressure and volume linked?

To investigate the relationship between the pressure of a gas and its volume you could gradually compress a sample of gas, recording the pressure and the volume at regular intervals. You must keep the temperature of the gas and the number of particles of gas constant during the experiment.

Boyle's law

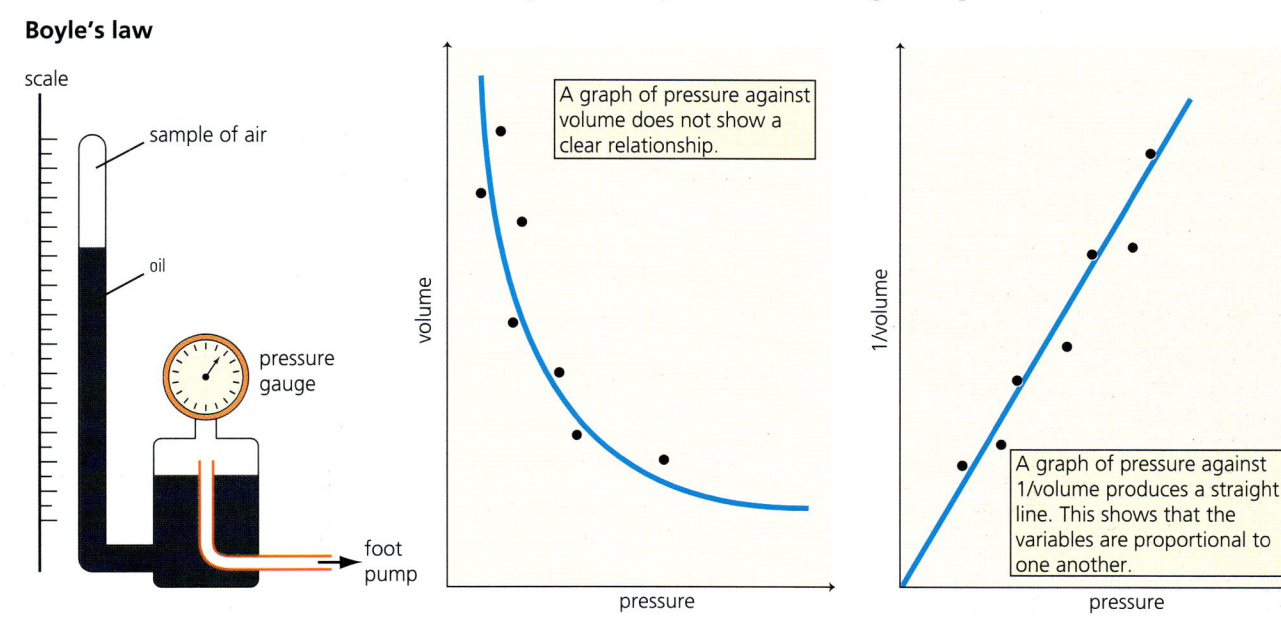

A graph of pressure against volume does not show a clear relationship.

A graph of pressure against 1/volume produces a straight line. This shows that the variables are proportional to one another.

Figure 15 You could use this apparatus to explore the link between pressure and volume of a gas.

What is matter?

Why Boyle's law works

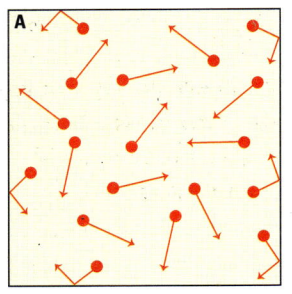

Each container holds the same number of gas particles, but in B, whose volume is twice that of A, the pressure is half that in A.

Figure 16

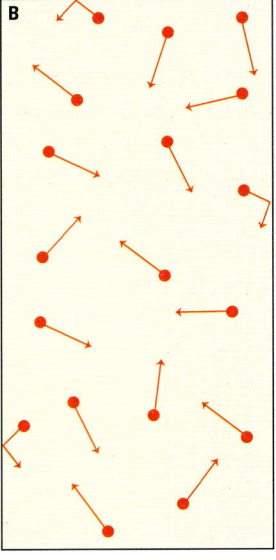

The particles in B have further to travel between collisions than in A. Because collisions with the sides of the container are less frequent, the pressure in B is lower.

As you can see from figure 15, provided the temperature is kept constant, the pressure of a fixed mass of a gas is inversely proportional to its volume:

| pressure | ∝ | 1/volume |
| P | ∝ | 1/V |

This is **Boyle's law**. It is named after Robert Boyle, who discovered in 1662 the link between pressure and volume in gases.
Expressing this another way:

| pressure × volume | = | a constant. |

3 A sample of pure oxygen gas had a volume of 50 cm³ at room temperature and pressure. How would the volume change if:
 a the pressure was doubled
 b the pressure was halved
while the temperature was kept constant?

What is the link between gas volume and temperature?

In 1787 Jacques Charles discovered that the volume of a fixed mass is directly proportional to its absolute temperature – if a fixed mass of a gas is heated at a constant pressure its volume increases and as it is cooled its volume decreases.

Charles' law

- open end
- acid droplet
- narrow glass tube
- sample of air
- scale
- closed end

Because the bore of the tube is a constant diameter, the length of the air sample is proportional to the volume.

The tube is warmed, and as the air sample expands, it pushes the droplet along.

If you extrapolate the graph you can estimate the temperature when the air bubble has zero length.

length of air bubble

absolute zero

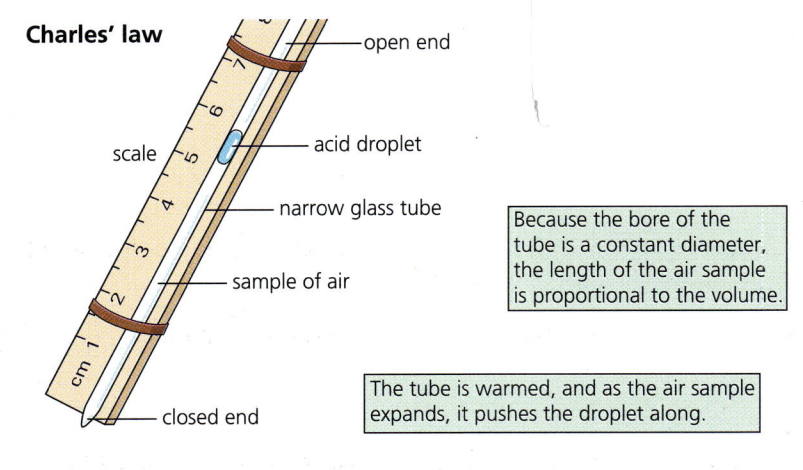

Figure 17 As a gas is cooled at constant pressure its volume decreases until it becomes a liquid.

This has become known as **Charles' law**:

| volume | ∝ | temperature |
| V | = | constant × T |

26

Absolute zero and the Kelvin scale of temperature

When gases are cooled to very low temperatures they will eventually condense to a liquid (at point X on the graph in figure 18). If we continue the line back from X it will always cross the temperature axis at −273 °C, no matter which gas is being studied. This temperature is known as **absolute zero**.

Absolute zero

By extrapolating the graph we can estimate the temperature when the volume is zero – this is **absolute zero**

Figure 18 Absolute zero is the temperature at which the volume of a gas is zero.

Kelvin scale / Celsius scale

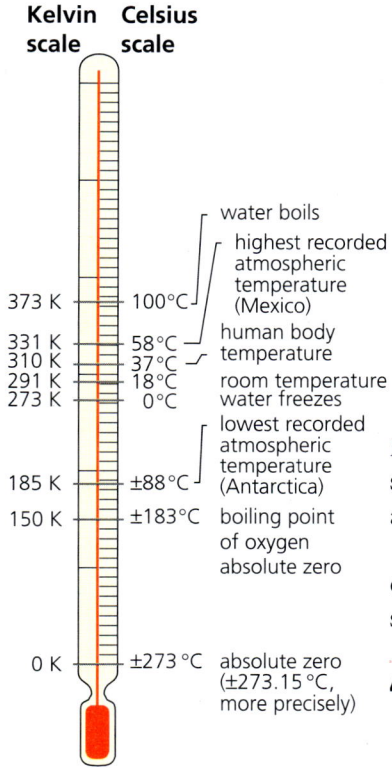

- 373 K — 100 °C — water boils
- highest recorded atmospheric temperature (Mexico)
- 331 K — 58 °C
- 310 K — 37 °C — human body temperature
- 291 K — 18 °C — room temperature
- 273 K — 0 °C — water freezes
- 185 K — ±88 °C — lowest recorded atmospheric temperature (Antarctica)
- 150 K — ±183 °C — boiling point of oxygen
- absolute zero
- 0 K — ±273 °C — absolute zero (±273.15 °C, more precisely)

Figure 19 Absolute zero is the starting point for the Kelvin scale of temperature measurement.

No temperatures have ever been measured below absolute zero, and although scientists have been able to cool substances down to a temperature approaching absolute zero, no one has ever actually reached it.

The **Kelvin scale** of temperature measurement starts at absolute zero. It is often used in scientific calculations and equations rather than the Celsius scale of measurement.

4 What would the following temperatures be in Kelvins?
  a 0 °C
  b 100 °C
  c 25 °C
  d 50 °C
  e −150 °C
  f −190 °C

The formal definition of Charles' law uses the absolute temperature measured in **Kelvins**. This law can be put another way:

$$\text{volume} = \text{constant} \times \text{absolute temperature}$$

Can the gas laws be combined?

We can combine Boyle's and Charles' laws into a single equation for a fixed mass of a gas:

$$\frac{\text{pressure} \times \text{volume}}{\text{absolute temperature}} = \text{constant}$$

or

$$\frac{PV}{T} = \text{constant}$$

This is known as the **gas equation**.

We can use the gas equation to make useful predictions about how a gas will behave under certain conditions of pressure, temperature and volume. For example, it can be used to compare a gas under two sets of conditions:

$$\frac{\text{initial pressure} \times \text{initial volume}}{\text{initial temperature}} = \frac{\text{final pressure} \times \text{final volume}}{\text{final temperature}}$$

$$\frac{P_1 V_1}{T_1} = \frac{P_2 V_2}{T_2}$$

WORKED EXAMPLE

A volume of 200 cm³ of ammonia gas at 500°C and 220 kPa is cooled to 0°C and the pressure reduced to 101 kPa. What will be the final volume of the gas?

Use the equation:

$$\frac{P_1 V_1}{T_1} = \frac{P_2 V_2}{T_2}$$

We put the first set of conditions here at the left-hand side and the final set of conditions on the right. But first we must change the temperatures given to Kelvins, because they have been given in degrees Celsius and the gas equation uses absolute temperature.

$$500°C = (500 + 273)K$$
$$= 773K$$
$$0°C = (0 + 273)K$$
$$= 273K$$

Now put the values into the gas equation:

$$\frac{220 \times 200}{773} = \frac{101 \times V_2}{273}$$

By rearranging the equation we can calculate V_2:

$$V_2 = \frac{273 \times 220 \times 200}{773 \times 101}$$
$$= 154 \text{ cm}^3$$

---

5 A sealed container of oxygen has a volume of 500 cm², and is maintained at a pressure of 100 kPa. Calculate the new pressure if the container is cooled from 25°C to 0°C.

6 Use your knowledge of the gas equation to find out the following:

a 50 cm³ of oxygen at 2 atmospheres pressure and 50°C is cooled to 0°C at the same pressure. What volume will it now occupy?

b 150 cm³ of chlorine gas is heated from 20°C to 100°C at atmospheric pressure. What new volume will the gas occupy?

c 200 cm³ of nitrogen gas at 100 kPa and 25°C is heated to 150°C and the pressure increased to 250 kPa. What final volume will the gas occupy?

Solids, liquids and gases

Summary of properties of gases

- Gases have no fixed shape or volume – they spread out to fill the space available.
- The rate of diffusion in gases is related to the temperature and the size of the particles.
- Gases can be compressed easily.
- Gases exert pressure.
- The pressure of a gas is inversely proportional to its volume.
- The volume of a gas is directly proportional to its absolute temperature.
- The gas equation can be used to predict the properties of a gas under a certain set of conditions.

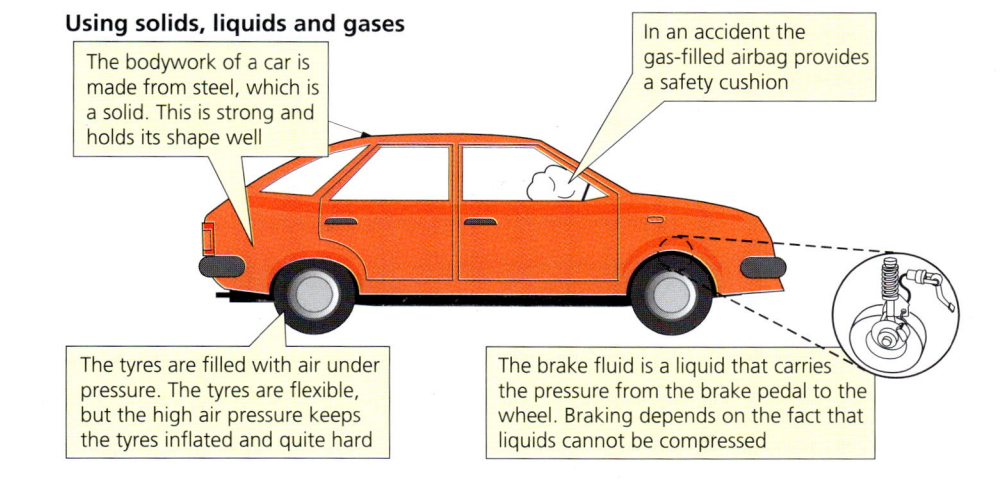

Figure 20 Using solids, liquids and gases

The bodywork of a car is made from steel, which is a solid. This is strong and holds its shape well

In an accident the gas-filled airbag provides a safety cushion

The tyres are filled with air under pressure. The tyres are flexible, but the high air pressure keeps the tyres inflated and quite hard

The brake fluid is a liquid that carries the pressure from the brake pedal to the wheel. Braking depends on the fact that liquids cannot be compressed

7 Which properties are being put to use in:
   a a chair made of wood?
   b the steel in a car body?
   d the water in a fish tank?
   e the air in a bicycle tyre?

Density

The density of a substance is the mass of a particular volume. Every substance has its own particular density – some examples are given in figure 21.

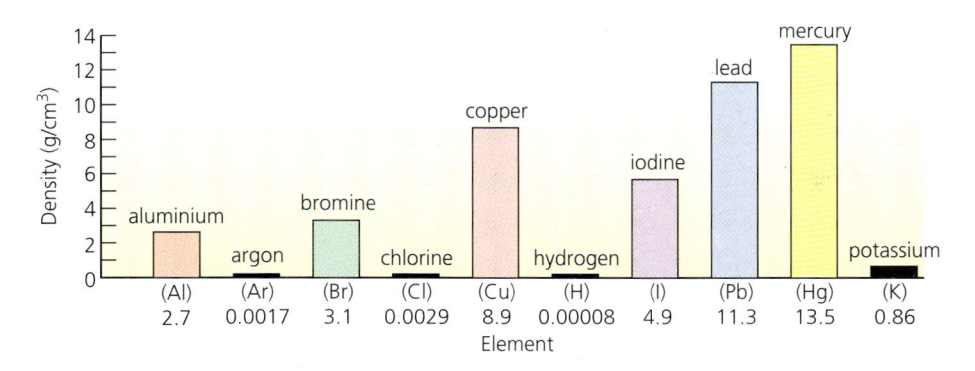

Figure 21 Densities of some common elements at 20°C.

Element	(Al)	(Ar)	(Br)	(Cl)	(Cu)	(H)	(I)	(Pb)	(Hg)	(K)
Density (g/cm³)	2.7	0.0017	3.1	0.0029	8.9	0.00008	4.9	11.3	13.5	0.86

All substances expand and contract with changes in temperature so lists of densities you will find in reference books always give the densities at a particular temperature. This means that the values can be compared with each other.

29

What is matter?

The densities of chemicals are quoted in different ways depending on where you look the information up – you will find them quoted as:

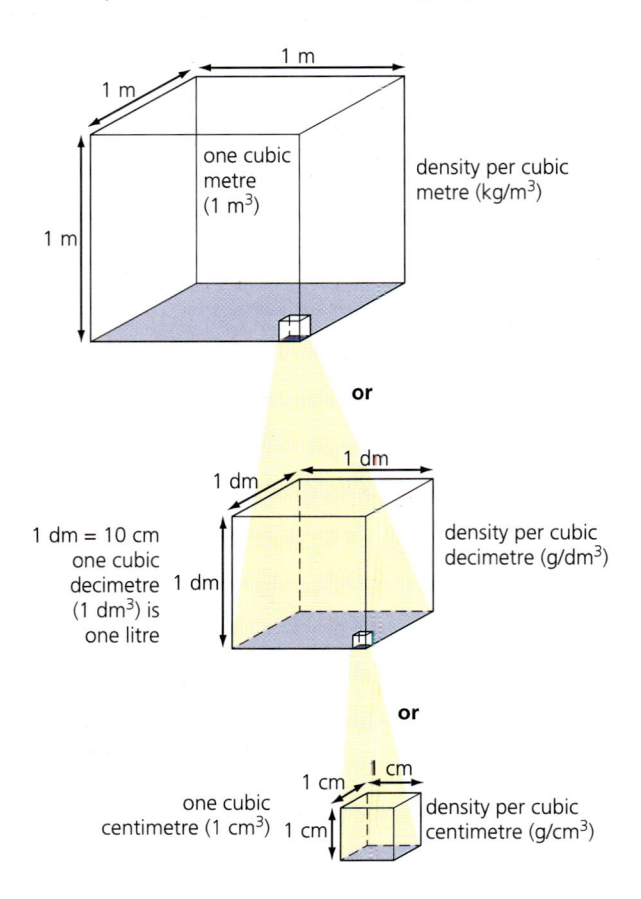

- one cubic metre (1 m³) — density per cubic metre (kg/m³)

or

- 1 dm = 10 cm, one cubic decimetre (1 dm³) is one litre — density per cubic decimetre (g/dm³)

or

- one cubic centimetre (1 cm³) — density per cubic centimetre (g/cm³)

You must be very careful to make sure you are comparing like with like!

How are density, mass and volume related?

Density is related to mass and volume by the following equation:

$$\text{density} = \frac{\text{mass}}{\text{volume}}$$

This equation can be rearranged in two ways:

$$\text{mass} = \text{density} \times \text{volume}$$

and

$$\text{volume} = \frac{\text{mass}}{\text{density}}$$

These equations can be used to find out the properties of substances under different conditions.

Solids, liquids and gases

WORKED EXAMPLES

1 A 10 cm³ block of iron has a mass of 79 g. What is its density?

Using the equation:

$$\text{density} = \frac{\text{mass}}{\text{volume}}$$

$$= \frac{79}{10}$$

$$= 7.9 \text{ g/cm}^3$$

2 Sodium has a density of 0.97 g/cm³. What volume would 10.0 g of sodium occupy?

Using the equation:

$$\text{volume} = \frac{\text{mass}}{\text{density}}$$

$$= \frac{10.0}{0.97}$$

$$= 10.3 \text{ cm}^3$$

Note

When calculating from scientific data think carefully about the accuracy of the numbers you are using. Always quote your answer to the same degree of accuracy as the question. For example, in Worked example 2 your calculator might have given the answer 10.309 278 35 but the numbers in the question were quoted only to three significant figures. In this case the answer should be corrected to 10.3, which is also to three significant figures.

8 The density of water is 1.00 g/cm³. Which of the following substances will sink in water?

	A	B	C	D	E
Density (g/cm³)	0.50	1.74	0.97	0.00133	10.50

9 A 20 cm³ solid block of sulphur has a mass of 42 g. Calculate the density of sulphur.

10 A block of copper measures 20 cm × 4.0 cm × 2.0 cm. Use the value for the density of copper in figure 21 to work out the mass of the block.

2.5 Changes of state

When a solid melts to a liquid it changes from the solid state to the liquid state. Similarly, when a liquid boils or evaporates it has changed from the liquid state to the gaseous state.

How do substances change state?

The everyday changes of state can be explained by the ideas in the Kinetic Theory of Matter, discussed earlier.

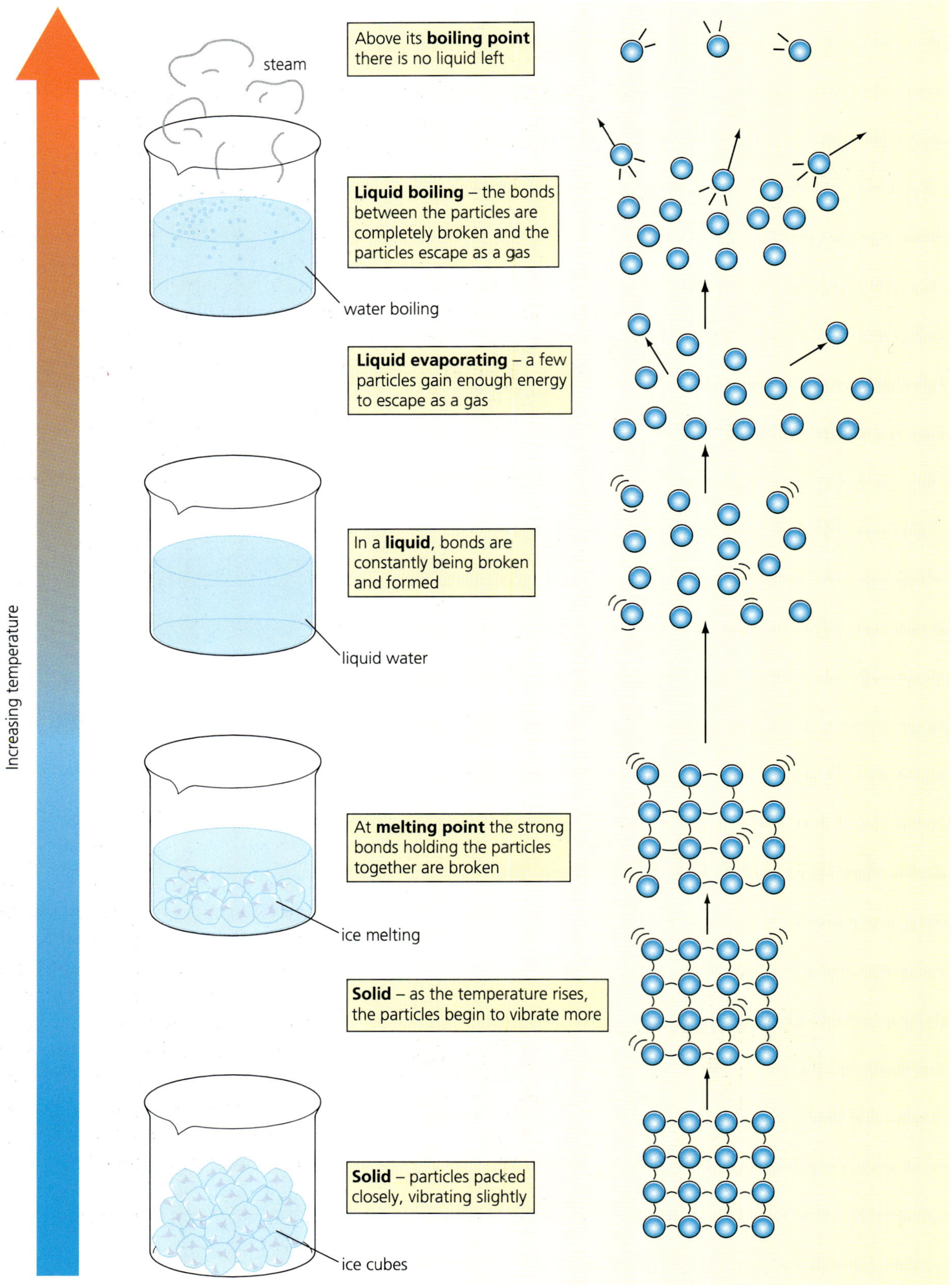

What is matter?

Increasing temperature →

steam

Above its boiling point there is no liquid left

Liquid boiling – the bonds between the particles are completely broken and the particles escape as a gas

water boiling

Liquid evaporating – a few particles gain enough energy to escape as a gas

In a liquid, bonds are constantly being broken and formed

liquid water

At melting point the strong bonds holding the particles together are broken

ice melting

Solid – as the temperature rises, the particles begin to vibrate more

Solid – particles packed closely, vibrating slightly

ice cubes

Figure 22 State changes can be explained by the Kinetic Theory of Matter.

What happens when a substance is heated?

Only at absolute zero are the particles in a substance completely stationary. Above absolute zero, the particles start to vibrate. Eventually they will reach a point where their energy is so great that the bonds holding them together break apart and the substance melts. While the bonds are breaking, although energy is being applied to the particles, it is all being used to break the bonds and the temperature of the melting solid does not increase. This temperature is known as a substance's **melting point**. Once all the solid has melted the temperature of the new liquid will start to rise again.

As more heat is supplied, the particles in the liquid move around faster and faster until some of them gain enough energy to escape from the surface of the water, even though the liquid has not yet reached boiling point. This is called **evaporation**. The warmer the liquid becomes, the more particles will have enough energy to escape and the faster evaporation becomes. Finally the particles have enough energy to break completely the bonds between them and they are free to become a gas – the liquid boils. At atmospheric pressure, the temperature at which a liquid boils is called its **boiling point.**

Figure 23 At its boiling point the particles in a liquid have enough energy to escape as a gas.

Once all the liquid has become gas, no bonds are left to be broken and the temperature will start to rise again.

Not all substances boil at the same temperature because the energy needed to break the bonds between particles is different for different substances. Liquids that need more energy to boil are said to have higher boiling points. For example, water boils at 100°C but cooking oil boils at temperatures at over 200°C.

11 Why would boiling cooking oil cause more serious burns than boiling water?

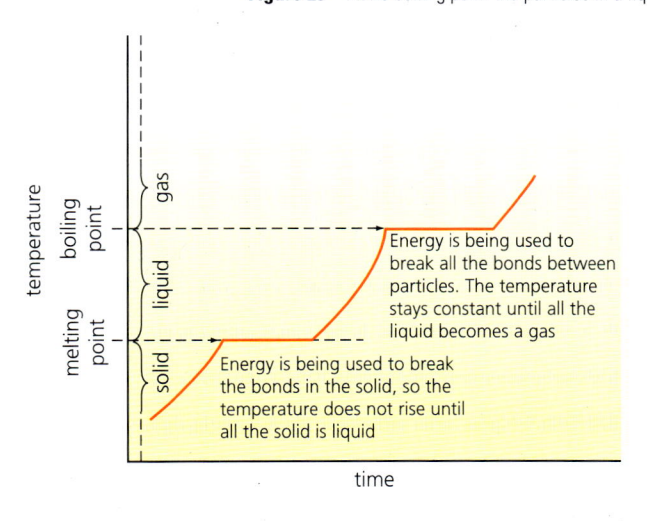

Figure 24 Temperature changes during heating.

What is matter?

What processes occur during condensing and freezing?

If a gas is cooled it will condense and become a liquid again. The temperature at which a gas condenses is called its **condensation point** and it is the same as the boiling point of the liquid. The temperature will stay constant at this stage because the bonds between the particles are reforming. Once all the gas has condensed to liquid the temperature will begin to drop again as the particles move more slowly and move closer together.

As cooling continues, the particles lose energy so that eventually permanent bonds are formed between particles. When this happens the liquid solidifies, or freezes, and becomes a solid again. The temperature this happens at is called the **freezing point** – it is the same as the melting point.

How can we measure state changes?

A good way of measuring the melting (or freezing) point of a solid is to cool a liquid slowly and measure the temperature at regular intervals. The apparatus that can be used for this is shown in figure 25.

The temperature will stay constant for a while as the liquid freezes. By plotting a graph of temperature against time you will be able to find the melting point.

You can measure the boiling point of a liquid in much the same way – by slowly heating a liquid and measuring the temperature just above the surface at regular intervals (see figure 27).

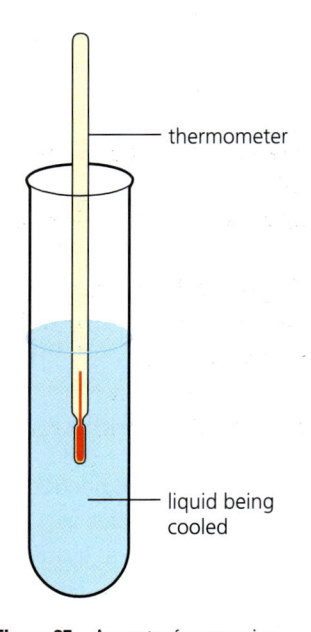

Figure 25 Apparatus for measuring the freezing point of a liquid.

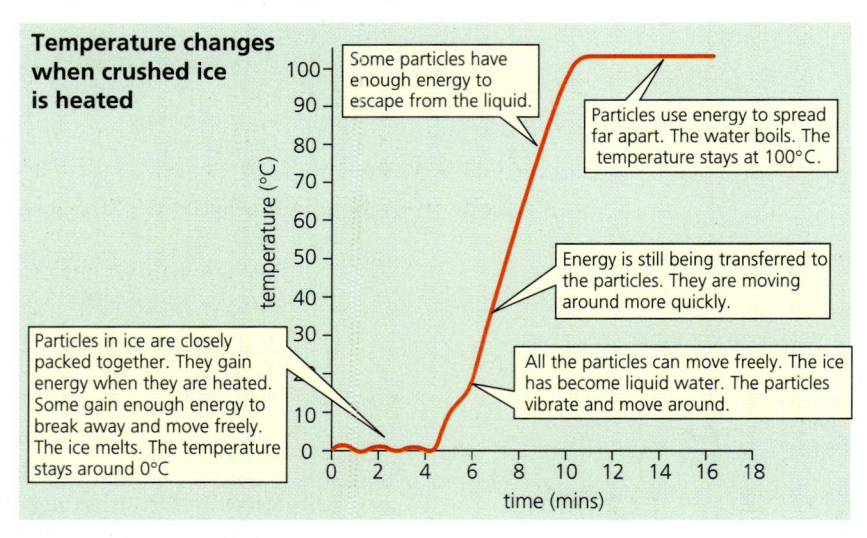

Figure 26 What happens when ice is heated.

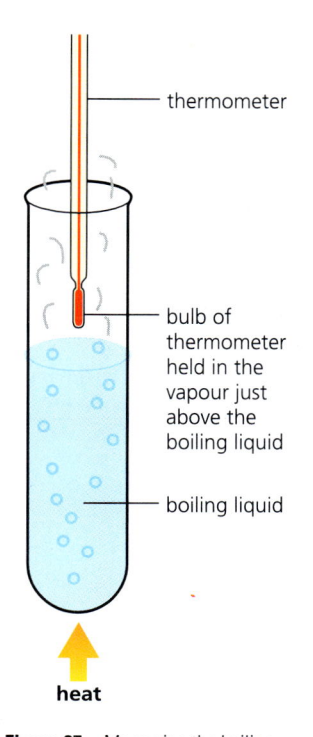

Solids, liquids and gases

12 Why should the thermometer bulb be placed just above the surface of the liquid, not in it?

13 The graph shows the temperature of a sample of pure gold as it was heated. Which parts of the graph correspond to:
  a gold as a solid
  b gold as a liquid
  c gold as a gas
  d gold melting
  e gold boiling?

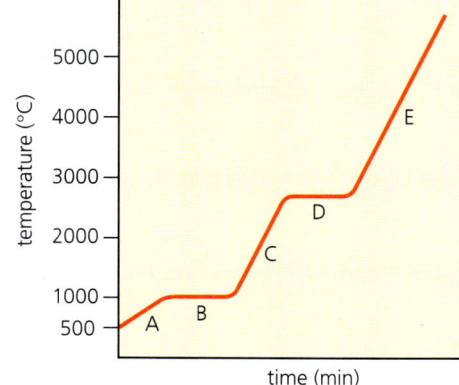

14 Some substances, like iodine, change straight from a solid to a gas (they sublime, as described in the last chapter). How would you go about measuring the temperature at which a solid sublimes (its sublimation point) at constant pressure?

Figure 27 Measuring the boiling point of a liquid.

How do impurities affect state changes?

The melting and boiling points of a pure substance are clear and sharp, but what happens if there are impurities in the substance?

Look at the curves in figure 28. One is of a pure substance, the other is that of the same substance with some impurities in it.

As you can see, the impurities have lowered the melting point. If you tried this experiment for yourself, you would also find that instead of having a sharp melting temperature the impure substance will melt over a range of temperatures. Impurities have a similar effect on boiling – they raise the boiling point.

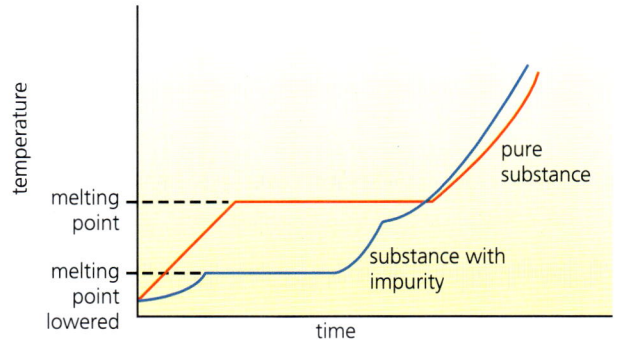

Figure 28 When an impurity is added to a liquid its melting point changes.

15 Why do you think that putting salt on your front step in winter is useful?

16 Salt raises the boiling point of water. Do you think vegetables cooked in salt water will cook more quickly or more slowly than in pure water? Why?

35

What is matter?

Solid, liquid or gas?

If you know the melting and boiling points of a substance you should be able to work out whether it is likely to be a solid, a liquid or a gas at any particular temperature.

Solid, liquid or gas?

e.g. water melts at 0°C
Water is a liquid between 0°C and 100°C
e.g. water boils at 100°C

Melting point — A substance is a solid below its melting point

Room temperature 20°C

A substance is a liquid between its melting and boiling points

Boiling point — A substance is a gas above its boiling point

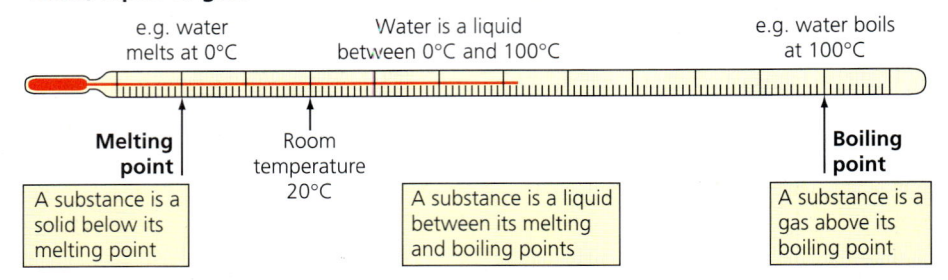

Figure 29 Determining the state of a substance.

17 Nearly all substances exist as one of the three main states of matter. Look at the figure below.

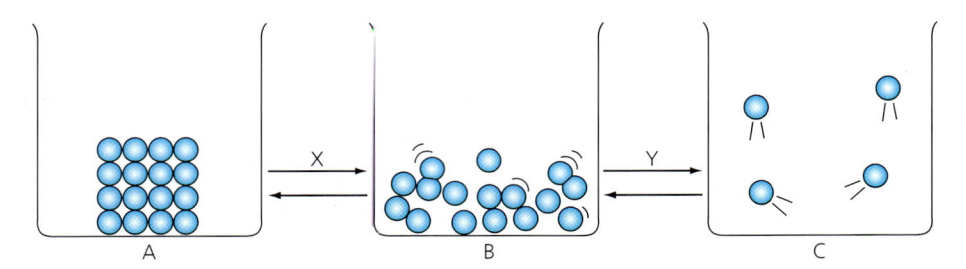

A → X → B → Y → C

a Which physical states are represented by A, B and C?
b Name the changes X and Y

18 Phosphorus has a melting point of 44°C and boils at 281°C. What state is it in at room temperature (20°C)?

19 The table below shows the melting and boiling point of some substances

Element	Melting point (°C)	Boiling point (°C)
A	1050	3200
B	−189	−186
C	−7	59
D	−101	−35
E	1063	2970
F	−39	357
G	3410	5930

a i which substances are solids at 20°C?
  ii which are liquids at 20°C?
  iii which are solids at 20°C?
b which substance has:
  i the highest boiling point?
  ii the lowest melting point?
c which substance is liquid over the greatest range of temperature?

Summary of changes of state

- Changes of state can be explained by the Kinetic Theory of Matter.
- When a substance is heated the energy supplied is used to break bonds between particles.
- When a substance is cooled bonds reform and energy is released.
- The melting point of a substance is the temperature at atmospheric pressure at which a solid becomes a liquid.
- The boiling point of a substance is the temperature at atmospheric pressure at which a liquid becomes a gas.
- Impurities in a substance raise its boiling point and lower its melting point.

Examination style questions

1. A pressurised container of helium gas had a mass of 20.790 kg. The cylinder was used to fill 200 balloons, each of which contained an average of 3 litres of the gas. The final mass of the cylinder was found to be 20.742 kg.

   a What was the total volume of helium gas used?

   b What was the loss in mass of the cylinder

   i in kilograms?

   ii in grams?

   c Use your answers to **a** and **b** to find the mass of 1 litre of helium.

2. Study the following table of data:

Substance	Melting point (°C)	Boiling point (°C)
A	0	100
B	190	510
C	−112	−82
D	−117	79
E	−85	−35

   a Which of these substances has the highest melting point?

   b Which substance has the lowest boiling point?

   c Which substances are liquid at room temperature (20°C)?

   d Which substance is a liquid over the greatest temperature range?

   e Which substance could be used to measure temperatures between −80°C and −30°C? Why?

3. Ethanoic acid is the substance that gives vinegar its characteristic flavour. Pure ethanoic acid melts at 17°C and boils at 118°C. A sample of pure ethanoic acid is heated from 0°C to 150°C over a period of 15 minutes.

   a Draw a graph to show how the temperature of the acid changes over the period.

   b Explain the shape of the graph you have drawn

   c In vinegar, ethanoic acid is usually diluted with water. What will be the effect of adding a little water to ethanoic acid on

   i the melting point

   ii the boiling point?

37

the air 3

USING HIRS 2 AND MSU DATA

Degrees Kelvin

NASA

Learning objectives

By the end of this chapter you should be able to:

- **explain** what is meant by natural materials and raw materials
- **explain** the finite nature of most resources
- **recall** the composition of the atmosphere
- **describe** how gases are extracted from air by fractional distillation
- **describe** the properties of the main gases in the atmosphere
- **describe** the main causes of air pollution
- **list** some of the problems caused by air pollution
- **describe** ways of controlling air pollution

3.1 Raw materials

Humans have made use of the materials in the world around them for many thousands of years. Some materials we use directly, by shaping them or using them to make useful objects – these are called **natural materials**. Examples of natural materials are wood and stone. Other substances seem to be not very useful in themselves – until they have been processed into useful materials or chemicals. These are known as **raw materials** and include crude oil, plant extracts and even the air we breathe.

Natural materials include wood, stone and wool.

Raw materials include North Sea oil and coppiced wood such as willow.

38

Although many thousands of substances are used as raw materials, they are in **finite supply**. Eventually their supply will run out. For example, the metal tungsten is used to make light bulb filaments because it has a very high melting point and glows white hot while still remaining solid. There is only a limited supply of tungsten compounds in the Earth's crust. Although some new supplies are being discovered and some metal is recycled, the metal is being used up. As supplies decrease the price of tungsten will rise so high that it will be too expensive for most purposes and we will have to find alternatives.

This is true for many other raw materials, and the only long-term answer to their use is either to extend recycling or to seek alternative materials that are more plentiful.

Summary of raw materials

- Natural materials can be used directly to make useful objects.
- Raw materials are used to manufacture useful chemicals and other substances.
- Raw materials are in finite supply, and will eventually be used up.

3.2 The air

The air around us is something we all take for granted. We cannot see it, it usually has no smell, and we only feel it on a windy day. Yet without this vital mixture of gases, life on Earth as we know it would be impossible.

The Earth's atmosphere is vital for all living things.

What makes up the air?

Air is a mixture of many gases – the main components of air are shown in figure 1.

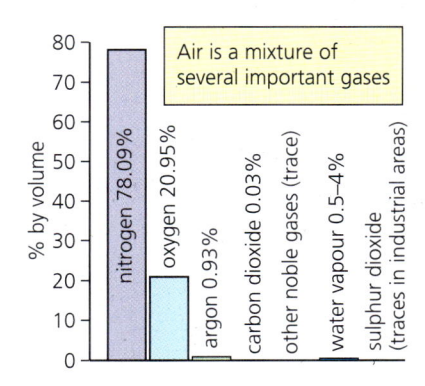

Figure 1 The composition of the atmosphere.

Air is a mixture of several important gases

% by volume
- nitrogen 78.09%
- oxygen 20.95%
- argon 0.93%
- carbon dioxide 0.03%
- other noble gases (trace)
- water vapour 0.5–4%
- sulphur dioxide (traces in industrial areas)

Raw materials

Figure 2 Determining the proportion of the air that is oxygen.

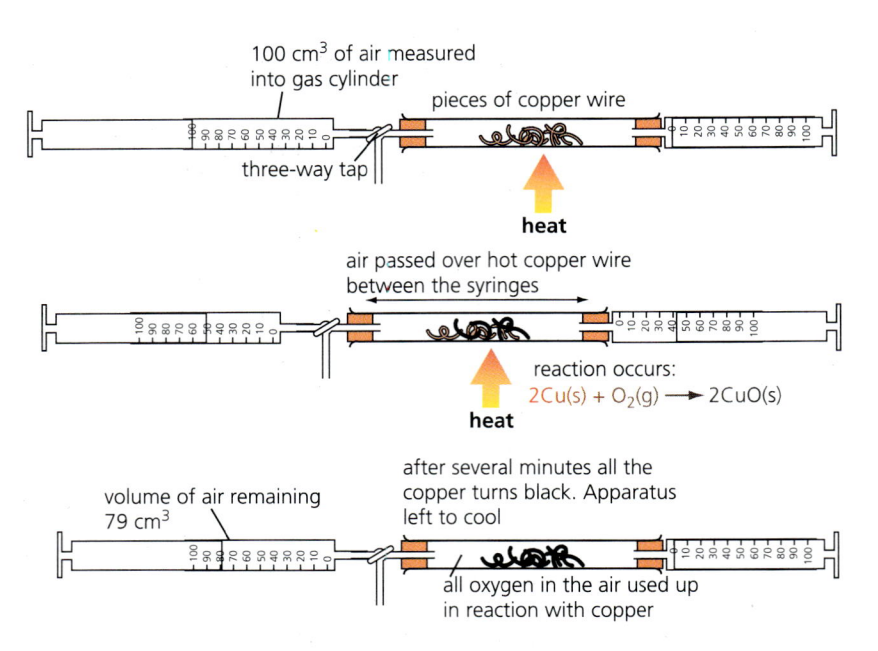

100 cm³ of air measured into gas cylinder
pieces of copper wire
three-way tap
heat

air passed over hot copper wire between the syringes
reaction occurs:
$2Cu(s) + O_2(g) \rightarrow 2CuO(s)$
heat

volume of air remaining 79 cm³
after several minutes all the copper turns black. Apparatus left to cool
all oxygen in the air used up in reaction with copper

How can the components of air be separated?

Figure 3
Fractional distillation of liquid air

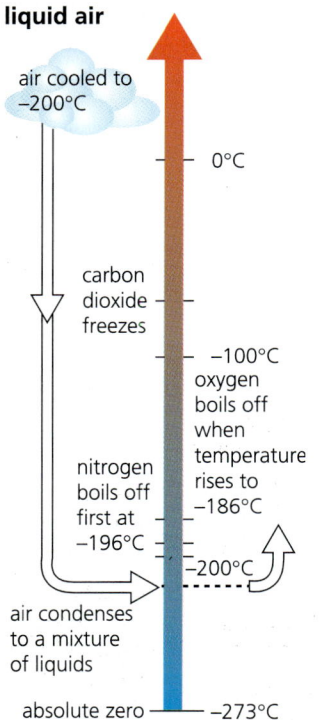

air cooled to −200°C
0°C
carbon dioxide freezes
−100°C
oxygen boils off when temperature rises to −186°C
nitrogen boils off first at −196°C
−200°C
air condenses to a mixture of liquids
absolute zero —— −273°C

Air is a mixture of gases. If it is cooled to about −200°C it will condense to form a very cold mixture of liquids. This liquid air can then be separated into its various components by fractional distillation (see Chapter 1, *Elements, compounds and mixtures*). If the temperature of the liquid air is allowed to rise, each gas will distil off at its own boiling point and can be collected separately.

This plant is used for the fractional distillation of air.

Summary of the air

- Air is a mixture of gases, mainly nitrogen (78%) and oxygen (21%).
- Liquid air can be separated into its components by fractional distillation.

1 Table 1 shows the boiling points of some of the gases found in air.

Table 1

Gas	Boiling point (°C)
argon	−182
helium	−269
hydrogen	−252
krypton	−152
neon	−246
nitrogen	−196
oxygen	−183
radon	−62
sulphur dioxide	−10
xenon	−108

Rearrange the gases into the order in which they would boil off during fractional distillation.

2 Which one of the following statements most closely describes air?
    a a compound
    b an element
    c a mixture of compounds
    d a mixture of elements
    e a mixture of compounds and elements

3.3 Gases in the air

Each gas in the air has its own unique properties.

Why is nitrogen so unreactive?

The most important thing about nitrogen is that it does not react easily with other substances. This is one of the main reasons why there is so much of it in the air.

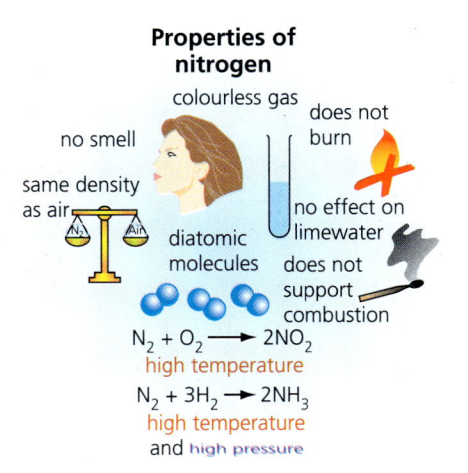

Properties of nitrogen
- colourless gas
- no smell
- same density as air
- diatomic molecules
- does not burn
- no effect on limewater
- does not support combustion

$N_2 + O_2 \longrightarrow 2NO_2$
high temperature

$N_2 + 3H_2 \longrightarrow 2NH_3$
high temperature and **high pressure**

Figure 4 The properties of nitrogen.

Raw materials

Nitrogen is so unreactive because the bond holding the two nitrogen atoms together in a molecule is very strong. Before nitrogen can react with other elements it must be given enough energy to break this bond.

Nitrogen is used to cool foods rapidly so that decomposition is slowed. Other foods are stored in packaging filled with nitrogen for the same reason.

Why is oxygen so important?

Oxygen is essential for life. Most living things need oxygen for respiration. Even plants and animals living in water use oxygen, which is dissolved in the water.

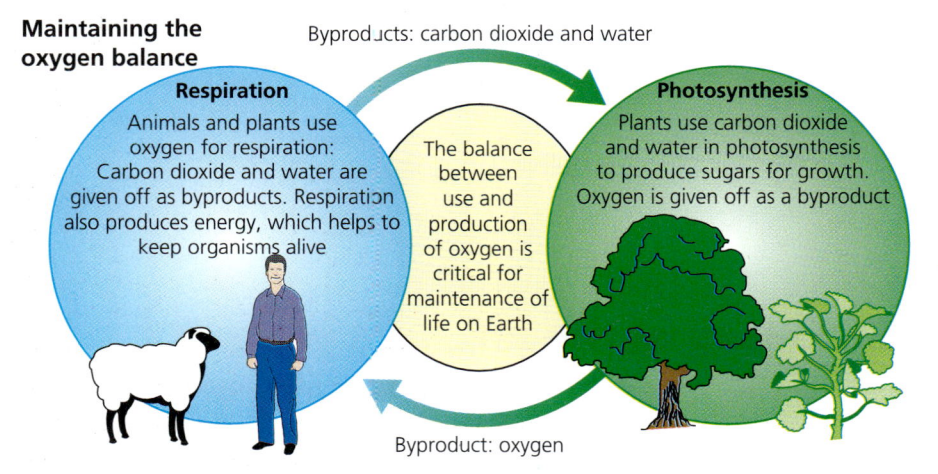

Maintaining the oxygen balance

Byproducts: carbon dioxide and water

Respiration
Animals and plants use oxygen for respiration: Carbon dioxide and water are given off as byproducts. Respiration also produces energy, which helps to keep organisms alive

The balance between use and production of oxygen is critical for maintenance of life on Earth

Photosynthesis
Plants use carbon dioxide and water in photosynthesis to produce sugars for growth. Oxygen is given off as a byproduct

Byproduct: oxygen

Figure 5 The proportion of oxygen in the atmosphere is a result of the balance between respiration and photosynthesis.

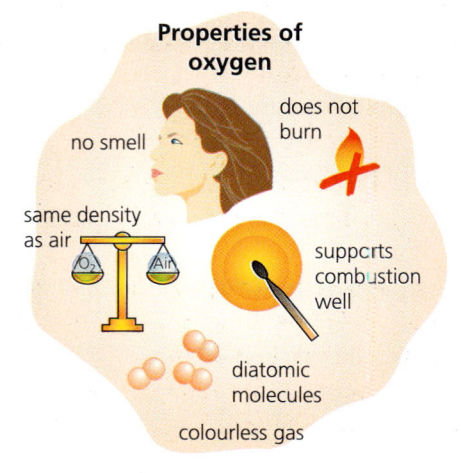

Figure 6 The properties of oxygen.

Properties of oxygen
- no smell
- does not burn
- same density as air
- supports combustion well
- diatomic molecules
- colourless gas

The rocks and minerals in the Earth's crust also contain many compounds of oxygen. Half of the Earth's crust is made up of compounds of oxygen and various other elements. For example, sand is mostly silicon dioxide (SiO_2) and clay is a compound containing oxygen, aluminium, hydrogen and silicon. The water that covers four-fifths of the Earth's surface contains 89% by mass of oxygen chemically joined to hydrogen.

The air

We use oxygen for many processes including steel production, cutting metals and respiration.

How does oxygen react with other elements?

Oxygen reacts readily with other elements to form compounds called **oxides**. In the reaction the other element is said to have been **oxidised** and the reaction that has occurred is called an **oxidation** reaction.

Figure 7 **Making oxides in the lab**

Making oxygen: add a sprinkling of manganese dioxide powder to 10cm³ of hydrogen peroxide solution

Use the following elements to see what will form: magnesium ribbon, zinc granules, copper turnings, iron wool, carbon granules, powdered sulphur (do this in a fume cupboard)

Oxygen collects in the boiling tube

bubbles of oxygen gas

water

Heat your element with a bunsen burner. As soon as it starts to burn put it in the boiling tube of oxygen. The oxide will form in the tube

hydrogen peroxide solution

Some oxidation reactions happen very quickly, giving off a great deal of heat and light – and a flame is seen. This type of reaction is called **combustion**, or burning. The energy transferred in combustion is enough to turn the substance that burns into a gas, which then reacts with oxygen.

For example, carbon is the main element present in coal, which burns in air or oxygen to form a gas:

$$C(s) + O_2(g) \rightarrow CO_2(g)$$

Combustion reactions release a large amount of energy largely as heat. These reactions happen rapidly and often involve the formation of large volumes of gas.

Other oxidation reactions give off less energy than combustion. Because of this the reaction happens without a flame being seen. For example the reactive metal sodium is kept under a layer of oil to protect it. In contact with air, sodium reacts to form sodium oxide. This oxidation reaction slowly gives off heat energy but does not involve a flame:

$$4Na(s) + O_2(g) \rightarrow 2Na_2O(s)$$

Raw materials

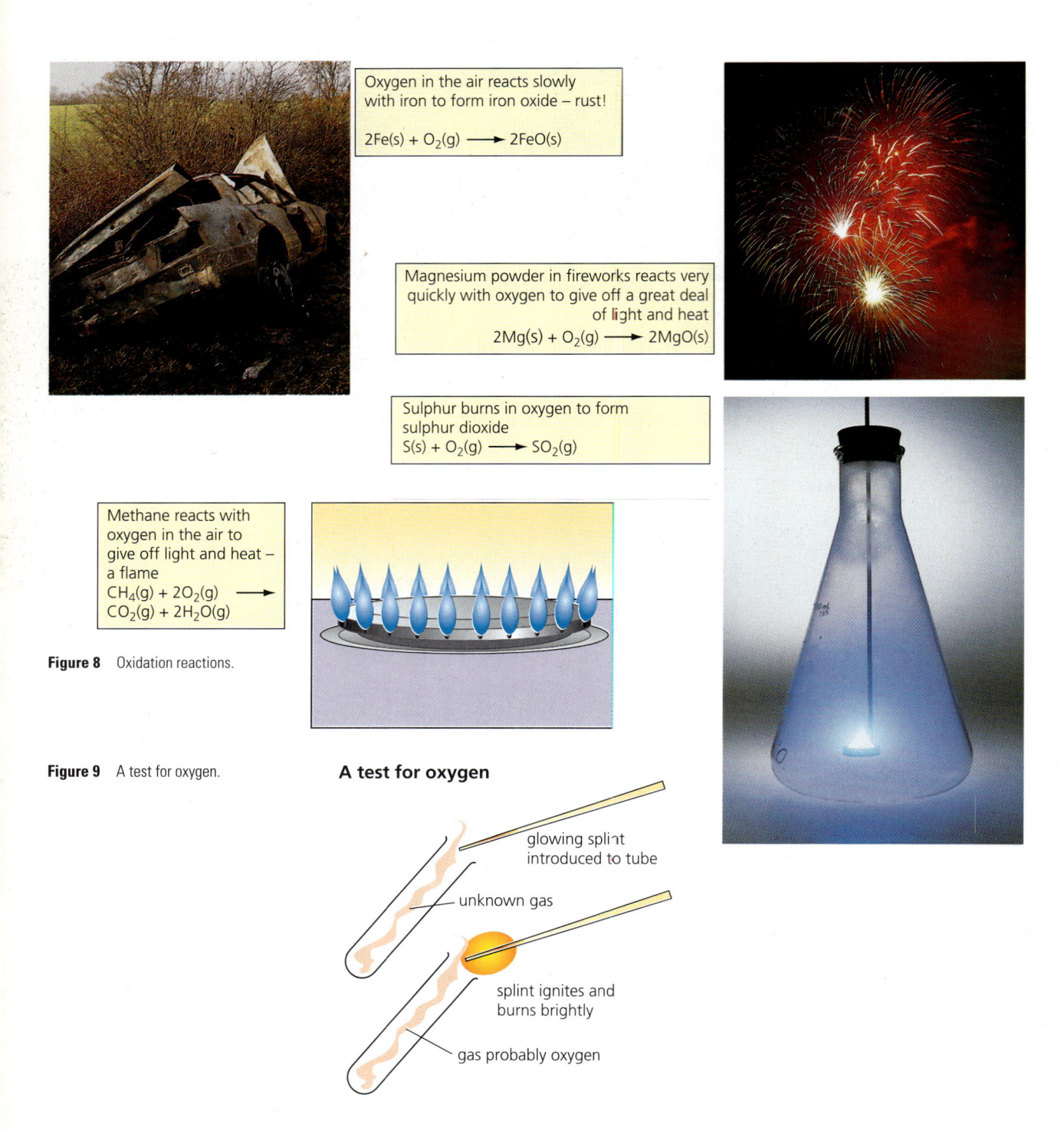

Oxygen in the air reacts slowly with iron to form iron oxide – rust!

$2Fe(s) + O_2(g) \longrightarrow 2FeO(s)$

Magnesium powder in fireworks reacts very quickly with oxygen to give off a great deal of light and heat

$2Mg(s) + O_2(g) \longrightarrow 2MgO(s)$

Sulphur burns in oxygen to form sulphur dioxide

$S(s) + O_2(g) \longrightarrow SO_2(g)$

Methane reacts with oxygen in the air to give off light and heat – a flame

$CH_4(g) + 2O_2(g) \longrightarrow CO_2(g) + 2H_2O(g)$

Figure 8 Oxidation reactions.

Figure 9 A test for oxygen.

A test for oxygen

- glowing splint introduced to tube
- unknown gas
- splint ignites and burns brightly
- gas probably oxygen

What are the noble gases?

The so-called 'noble' gases are helium, neon, argon, krypton, xenon and radon. They are all very unreactive. All the noble gases are made up of isolated single atoms – they are so unreactive that they don't even form molecules. This unreactivity might make you think that the noble gases would be of very little use – but in fact they are useful *because* they don't react.

The air

Noble gases are useful because they are so unreactive.

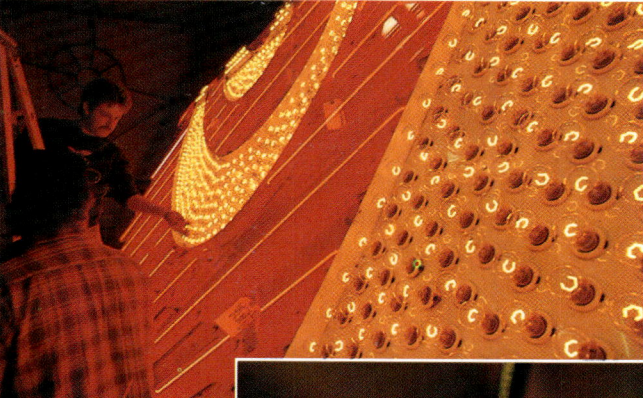

Neon and argon are used in street lights.

Helium is used to blow up childrens balloons.

Xenon is used in the excimer lasers used in surgery.

Summary of gases in the air

- Nitrogen is a gas composed of diatomic molecules.
- Nitrogen is unreactive because the bond between the atoms in a nitrogen molecule is very strong.
- Oxygen is a very reactive gas made from diatomic O_2 molecules.
- Oxygen combines with many elements in oxidation reactions to form oxides.
- When oxidation produces a lot of light and heat energy a flame is produced – this is combustion.
- Oxygen is needed by living things for respiration and is given out by plants in photosynthesis.
- Noble gases are very unreactive.
- Noble gases all consist of single atoms.

3 Nitrogen gas can be made to react with oxygen, but only at very high temperatures. Why is so much energy needed?

4 What changes are likely to happen in the Earth's atmosphere if the human and animal populations increase, while at the same time areas with many green plants are cut down? Why is this a cause for concern?

5 Devise a table to illustrate two physical properties and one chemical property of the following gases: nitrogen, oxygen, helium and argon.

6 Describe one everyday process that involves oxidation and one that involves combustion. Write balanced symbol equations for these reactions.

Raw materials

3.4 Pollution of the air

Ever since people learnt to control fire the smoke from their fires has poisoned and contaminated (polluted) the air. Small amounts of pollutants (the substances that cause pollution) are usually washed away by the rain or broken down by bacteria to harmless products, but large amounts damage the environment.

The industrial revolution changed the natural balance of the environment as the new industries started to burn fuel on a very large scale. In this century, car ownership has increased greatly and all over the world vehicles are producing exhaust gases that have a considerable effect on the environment. Factories still pour waste products into the air and the water, with many effects on all that breathe air and use water.

How do waste gases in the air cause harm?

Sulphur dioxide and some nitrogen oxides are dangerous acid gases. Sulphur dioxide comes from the oxidation of sulphur in the fossil fuels we burn. Nitrogen oxides are produced by reactions between nitrogen and oxygen in the air at high temperatures – for example in car engines. The nitrogen oxides are given off as a mixture of acid gases when fossil fuels are burned.

Sulphur dioxide and the nitrogen oxides can drift down to the ground near where they are produced, and can seriously affect animals and plants they touch.

Effect of sulphur dioxide on animals and plants

Animals
- Increase in deaths due to heart or blood vessel diseases
- Increase in normal death rate
- Significant health effects
- Bronchitis patients become more ill
- Health effects suspected
- More difficult to breathe

Plants
- Growth slowed and many leaves damaged in pine trees
- Plants damaged
- 81% of pine trees do not produce cones
- Obvious damage to leaves of trees and shrubs
- Damage to plants unknown

Length of time exposed to sulphur dioxide: 3 sec, 30 sec, 5 min, 1 hr, 8 hrs, 1 day, 4 days, 1 mth, 1 yr, 10 yrs

Concentration of sulphur dioxide/ppm: 0.01, 0.1, 1, 10

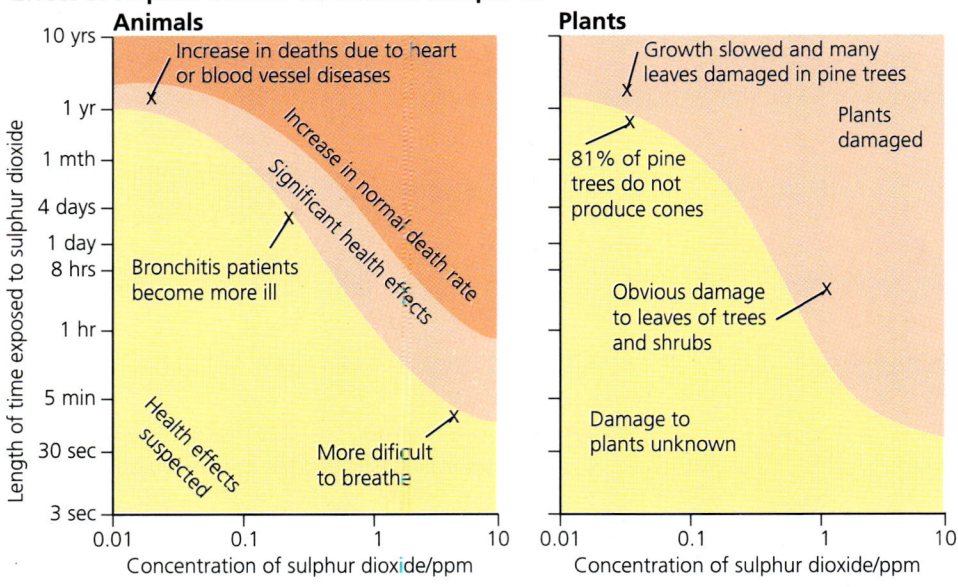

Figure 10

To get over this problem, tall chimneys are used to push the gases high up into the atmosphere away from the ground. Unfortunately, they then react with rain in the air and fall back to Earth as acid rain.

The air

Figure 11 Acid gases and the formation of acid rain.

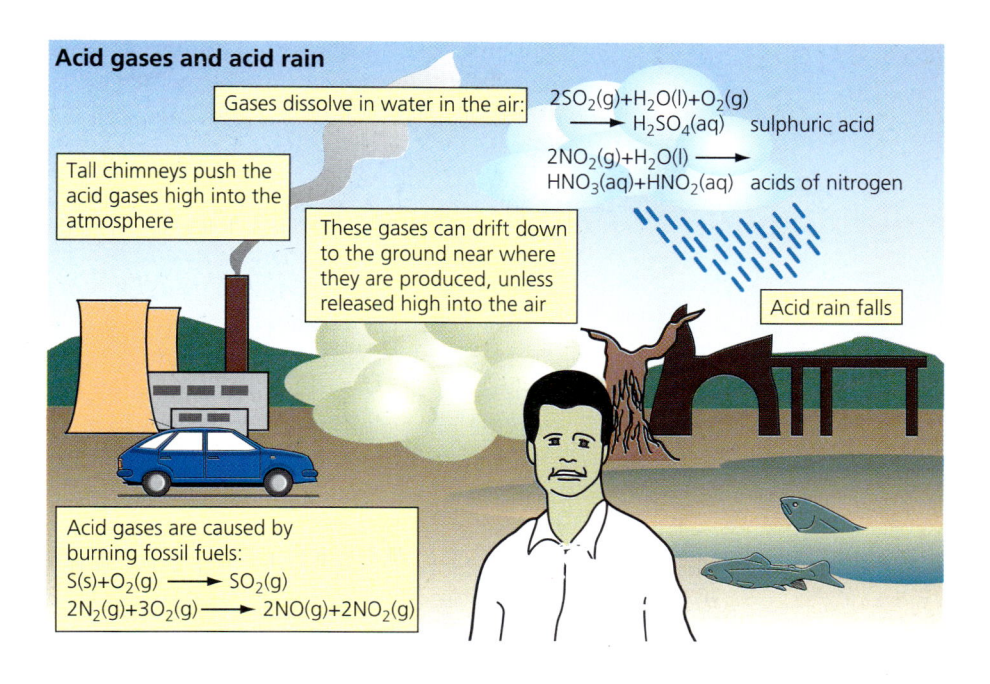

Acid gases and acid rain

Gases dissolve in water in the air:
$$2SO_2(g) + H_2O(l) + O_2(g) \longrightarrow H_2SO_4(aq) \quad \text{sulphuric acid}$$
$$2NO_2(g) + H_2O(l) \longrightarrow HNO_3(aq) + HNO_2(aq) \quad \text{acids of nitrogen}$$

Tall chimneys push the acid gases high into the atmosphere

These gases can drift down to the ground near where they are produced, unless released high into the air

Acid rain falls

Acid gases are caused by burning fossil fuels:
$$S(s) + O_2(g) \longrightarrow SO_2(g)$$
$$2N_2(g) + 3O_2(g) \longrightarrow 2NO(g) + 2NO_2(g)$$

What damage does acid rain do?

When oxides of non-metals dissolve in water they produce acidic solutions. Clean, unpolluted rainwater is naturally slightly acidic (about pH 6) because carbon dioxide from the air dissolves in it to make dilute carbonic acid. Small amounts of sulphur dioxide and oxides of nitrogen also dissolve in rainwater to make dilute acids. This natural low level of acidity is quite harmless and forms a useful part of the cycle of erosion and deposition of rocks and minerals (see Chapter 4, *Rocks and minerals*).

Acid rain only started to be a problem in the last few hundred years – when industry developed. Since the industrial revolution millions of tonnes of acid gases have been released into the atmosphere from power stations, factories and motor vehicles.

As car ownership has increased over recent years, so the amount of nitric acid in the rain has increased.

Figure 12

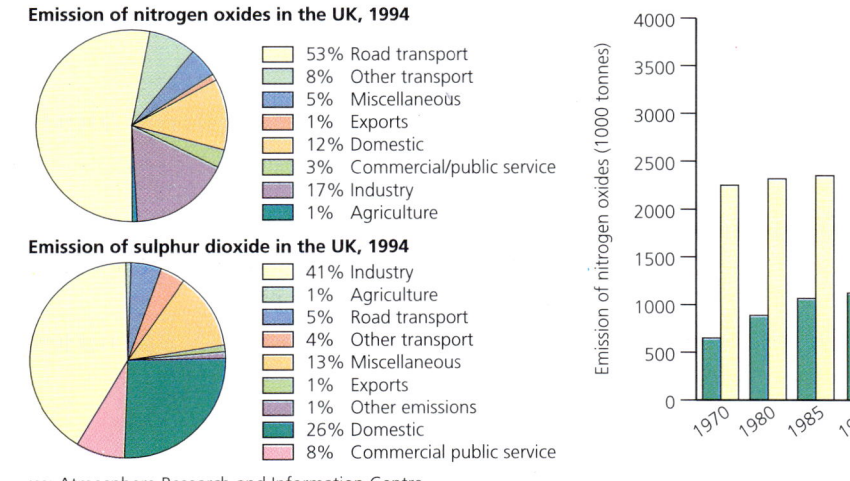

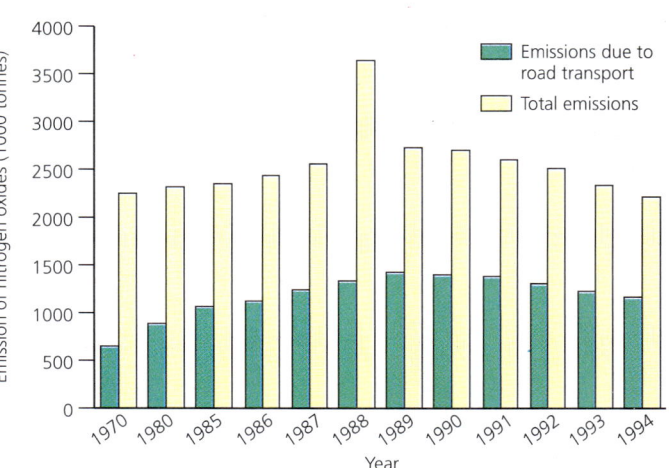

Emission of nitrogen oxides in the UK, 1994

- 53% Road transport
- 8% Other transport
- 5% Miscellaneous
- 1% Exports
- 12% Domestic
- 3% Commercial/public service
- 17% Industry
- 1% Agriculture

Emission of sulphur dioxide in the UK, 1994

- 41% Industry
- 1% Agriculture
- 5% Road transport
- 4% Other transport
- 13% Miscellaneous
- 1% Exports
- 1% Other emissions
- 26% Domestic
- 8% Commercial public service

Source: Atmosphere Research and Information Centre

Raw materials

Acid rain can damage both buildings and living things. Many buildings are made from limestone or marble, which are both forms of calcium carbonate. This reacts with the acid in rainwater, and dissolves away:

$$CaCO_3(s) + 2HNO_3(aq) \rightarrow Ca(NO_3)_2(aq) + H_2O(l) + CO_2(g)$$
calcium carbonate + nitric acid → calcium nitrate + water + carbon dioxide

Acid rain can also damage trees and other plants. It can damage leaves and it reacts with many vital nutrients in the soil so that these are washed away and are no longer available to the tree.

Acid rain also dissolves aluminium compounds in the soil and washes them into rivers and streams. Aluminium in the water supply may be harmful – and aluminium is thought to be involved in the development of Alzheimer's disease. Similarly a change in pH can affect the whole ecology of freshwater rivers and lakes and eventually kill off many species of plants and fish.

Acid rain has dissolved much of the limestone used in many of Europe's oldest buildings.

Solubility of aluminium at different ph levels

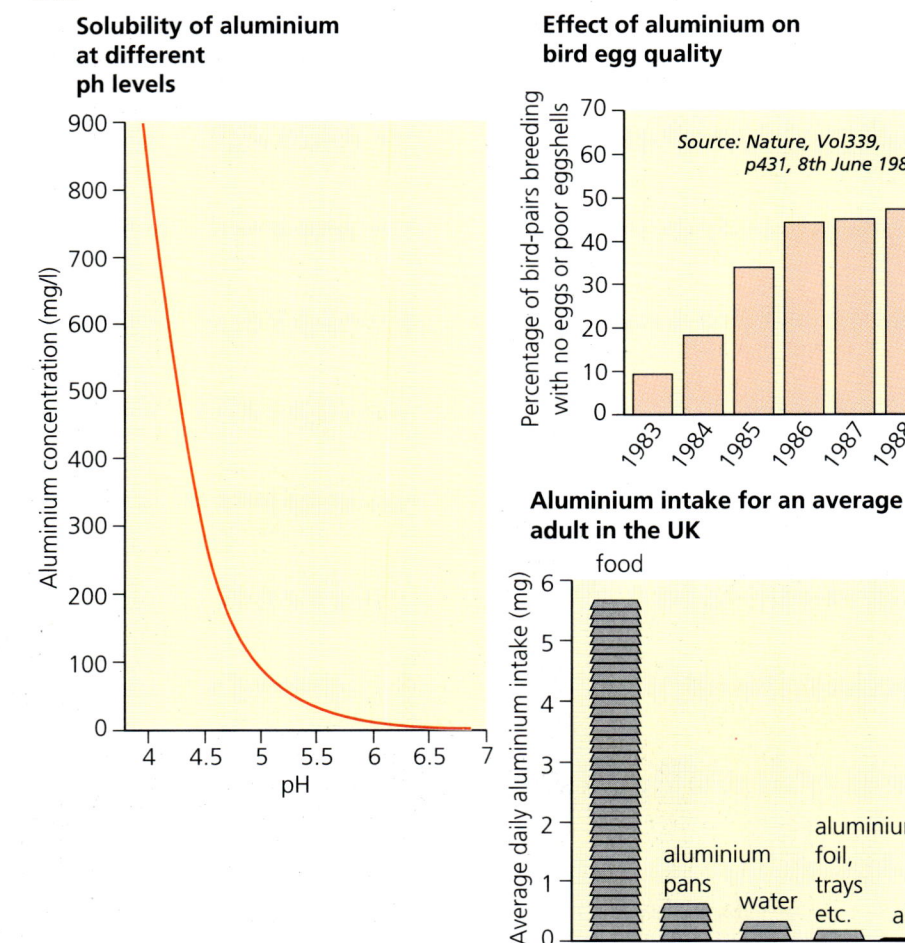

Effect of aluminium on bird egg quality

Source: Nature, Vol339, p431, 8th June 1989

Aluminium intake for an average adult in the UK

Figure 13

Lime being dumped from a helicopter into a dying lake in Sweden. The lime neutralises the acid which is killing the lake.

The air

How can acid rain be prevented?

The only effective way to deal with acid rain is to reduce the production of acid gases that get into the atmosphere in the first place. Very little can be done to combat its effects once it falls.

All new cars are fitted with catalytic converters which remove the oxides of nitrogen from the exhaust gases and turn them back into harmless gases. The problem of the sulphur dioxide emitted by power stations is less easy to solve. It is very expensive to remove sulphur from coal or oil before it is burned. Some types of coal contain very little sulphur, but these are very expensive. It is possible to remove the sulphur dioxide from waste gases before they are released to the atmosphere. This is done in a 'flue gas desulphurisation' (FGD) plant.

A 'greener' boiler

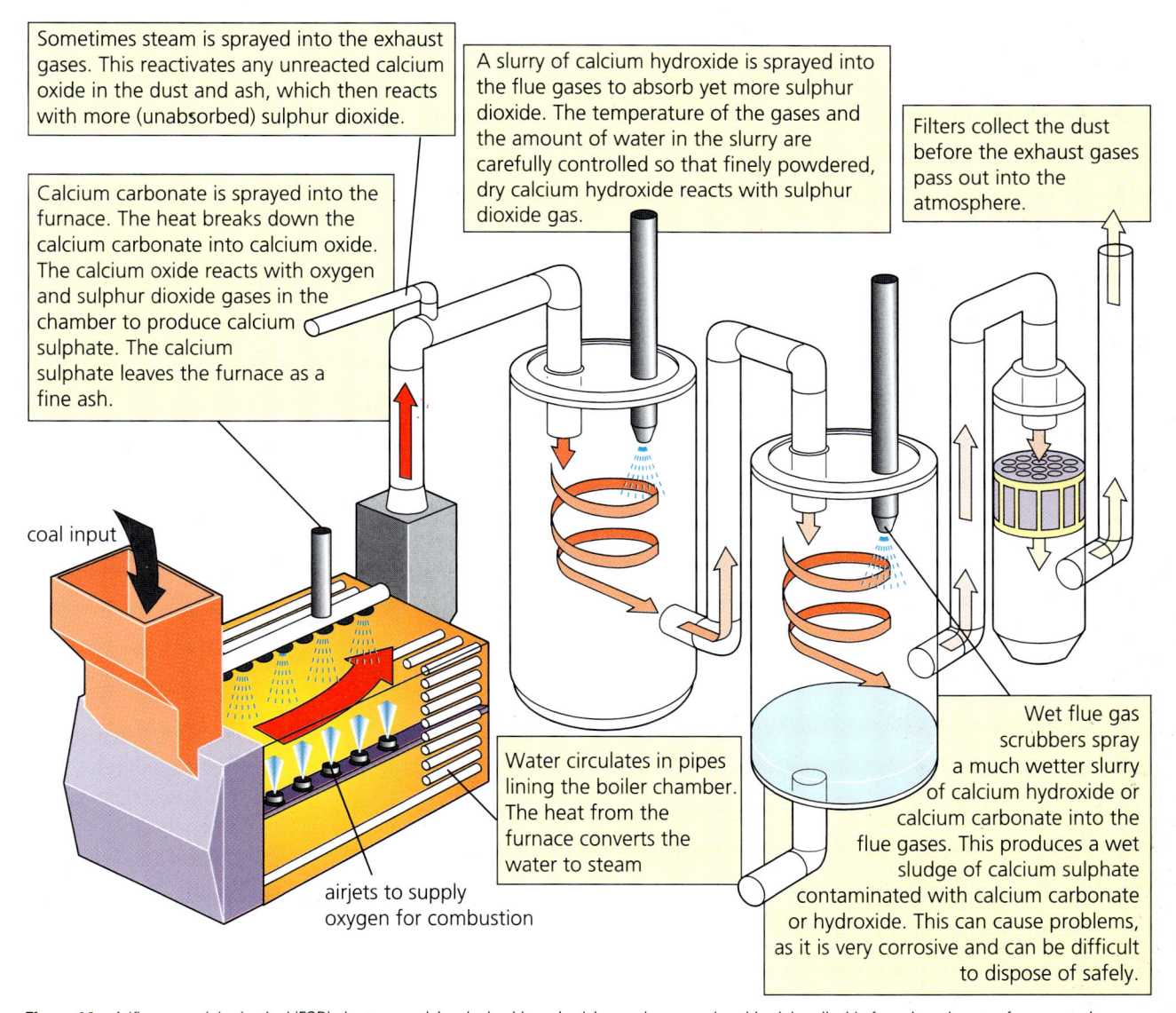

Sometimes steam is sprayed into the exhaust gases. This reactivates any unreacted calcium oxide in the dust and ash, which then reacts with more (unabsorbed) sulphur dioxide.

A slurry of calcium hydroxide is sprayed into the flue gases to absorb yet more sulphur dioxide. The temperature of the gases and the amount of water in the slurry are carefully controlled so that finely powdered, dry calcium hydroxide reacts with sulphur dioxide gas.

Filters collect the dust before the exhaust gases pass out into the atmosphere.

Calcium carbonate is sprayed into the furnace. The heat breaks down the calcium carbonate into calcium oxide. The calcium oxide reacts with oxygen and sulphur dioxide gases in the chamber to produce calcium sulphate. The calcium sulphate leaves the furnace as a fine ash.

coal input

Water circulates in pipes lining the boiler chamber. The heat from the furnace converts the water to steam

airjets to supply oxygen for combustion

Wet flue gas scrubbers spray a much wetter slurry of calcium hydroxide or calcium carbonate into the flue gases. This produces a wet sludge of calcium sulphate contaminated with calcium carbonate or hydroxide. This can cause problems, as it is very corrosive and can be difficult to dispose of safely.

Figure 14 A 'flue gas sulphurisation' (FGD) plant uses calcium hydroxide and calcium carbonate to 'scrub' sulphur dioxide from the exhausts of power stations. The process produces calcium sulphate (gypsum), which can be used in the construction industry.

Raw materials

These plants are expensive to run and increase the cost of the electricity produced. Unless power stations are compelled by law to limit the amount of sulphur dioxide they produce, the economic pressures on their business will lead to continued pollution.

Why is the greenhouse effect so worrying?

As long ago as the end of the last century a Swedish chemist called Arrhenius became worried that the amount of carbon dioxide released into the atmosphere by burning coal would warm up the Earth's surface and cause changes in the climate. Much research has gone on into this effect recently, and there has been a lot of debate involving both scientists and politicians.

Some gases in the Earth's atmosphere have an effect that is like that of a garden greenhouse. Energy that is radiated from the surface of the Earth is absorbed and trapped by these gases – causing the greenhouse effect.

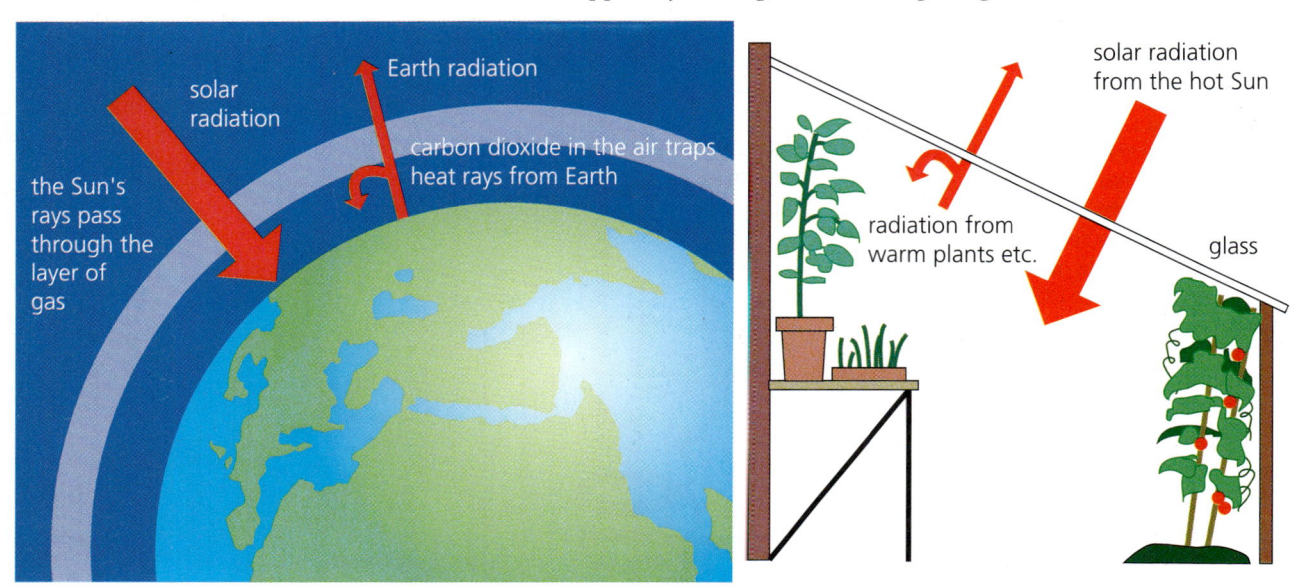

Figure 15 The greenhouse effect.

The main gases causing the greenhouse effect are carbon dioxide and methane. These are known as **greenhouse gases.**

As with some other pollution issues, the greenhouse effect is a natural process whose balance is being upset by human activity. The Earth's natural greenhouse effect keeps the temperature on the surface of the planet relatively even. The moon has no atmosphere and therefore no greenhouse effect to protect it, and its temperature fluctuates widely. During the day, the temperature on the moon rises to 102 °C and at night it falls to −150 °C.

Since the industrial revolution, the amount of carbon dioxide in the Earth's atmosphere has risen considerably. It is estimated that over 20 000 000 000 tonnes of carbon dioxide are released to the air each year from burning fossil fuels.

Table 2 *Greenhouse gases*

	Carbon dioxide (CO$_2$)	Methane (CH$_4$)	Chlorofluorocarbons (CFCs)	Nitrous oxide (N$_2$O)	Ozone (O$_3$) close to the Earth's surface
annual increase (%)	0.5	1	6	—	—
time taken to break down (years)	7	10	15 000	170	2–3 weeks
how strongly it traps energy (compared with carbon dioxide)	1	30	10–20 000	150	2000
total contribution to greenhouse effect (%)	50	18	14	6	10
source	burning fossil fuels	formed in intestines of cows and sheep; also in breakdown of organic chemicals by bacteria without enough oxygen, e.g. in rice fields	coolants in fridges and air conditioners; also used in foam and aerosol sprays	bacteria in the soil and breakdown of nitrate fertilisers; burning fossil fuels and wood	around 75% of ozone is made when sunlight affects car exhaust fumes

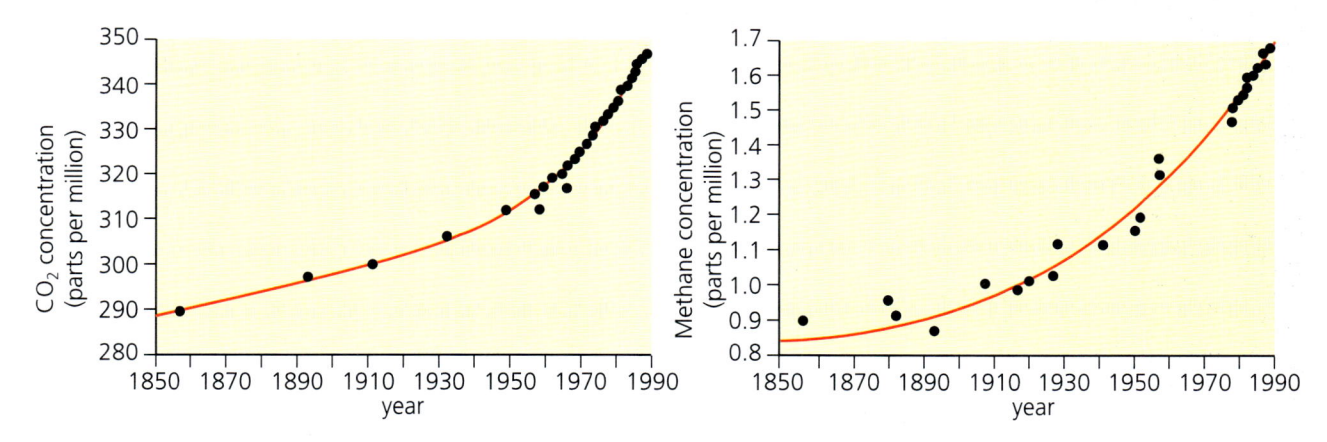

Figure 16 Levels of carbon dioxide in the Earth's atmosphere have risen since the industrial revolution.

It is difficult to make direct connections between the level of greenhouse gases and climate change because so many complex variables are involved. But many people are becoming very concerned that the greenhouse effect will have unpredictable consequences on the world's climate. Even fairly small increases in temperature (this is called 'global warming') can change weather patterns – causing drought in some areas and flooding and violent storms in others. The polar ice caps contain huge amounts of frozen water, and if these continue to melt, then sea levels will rise and low-lying countries may be flooded.

Raw materials

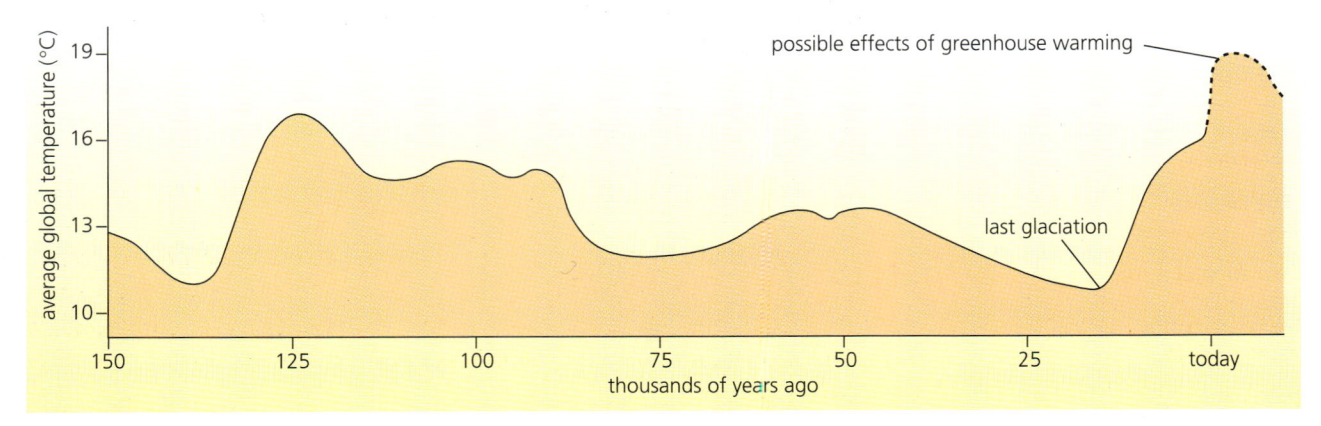

Figure 17 Global warming.

This satellite map shows the average surface temperature of the world, with the coolest areas in mauve and the hottest in black. Will the greenhouse effect permanently change these patterns?

How can the greenhouse effect be reduced?

The way to reduce the greenhouse effect is to cut down considerably on the amount of greenhouse gases released into the air. Governments must agree on national and international levels to make such changes. However, these decisions are difficult for politicians to make because they mean that pollution must be stopped before it happens – which can be expensive.

How does ozone depletion affect life on Earth?

The sun's radiation gives the warmth and light that makes life on Earth possible. The sun also emits ultra-violet radiation, which can damage living things. Nearly all of this harmful radiation is absorbed by the ozone layer. Ozone is a gas made from triatomic molecules of oxygen – its formula is O_3. Ozone is in short supply in the upper atmosphere, but at ground level it is produced as a pollutant, particularly from complex chemical reactions in vehicle exhausts. It is also a greenhouse gas.

Ozone is formed in the upper atmosphere by the effects of ultra-violet radiation on oxygen in a two-step reaction:

$$O_2 \xrightarrow{\text{ultra-violet light}} O\cdot + O\cdot$$
free oxygen atoms (free radicals)

$$O\cdot + O_2 + M \rightarrow O_3 + M$$
ozone (M = an inert particle)

The air

Ozone is destroyed by a combination of two reactions, which are also initiated by ultra-violet light:

$$O_3 \xrightarrow{\text{ultra-violet light}} O_2 + O\cdot$$
$$O\cdot + O_3 \xrightarrow{\text{ultra-violet light}} 2O_2$$

The formation and breakdown of ozone would be kept in natural balance if there were no other radicals in the atmosphere. But chemicals such as the chlorofluorocarbons (CFCs) that are used in fridges, freezers, air conditioners, as aerosol propellants and as solvents break down to radicals in the upper atmosphere:

$$CF_2Cl_2 \xrightarrow{\text{ultra-violet light}} \underset{\substack{\text{chlorine}\\\text{free}\\\text{radical}}}{Cl\cdot} + \underset{\substack{\text{CFC}\\\text{free}\\\text{radical}}}{CF_2Cl\cdot}$$

These free radicals destroy ozone. During this process they are recycled:

$$Cl\cdot + O_3 \rightarrow ClO\cdot + O_2$$
$$ClO\cdot + O\cdot \rightarrow Cl\cdot + O_2$$
net effect: $O\cdot + O_3 \rightarrow 2O_2$

So, only a few atoms of a CFC can destroy a great many ozone molecules.

Satellites which have examined the ozone layer in the atmosphere have revealed that it is getting thinner over Antarctica – a 'hole' is forming. A similar, but smaller, hole is appearing over the Arctic.

The only way of dealing effectively with this problem is for everyone to stop producing and using CFCs. Some countries have started to do this but the problem could continue for at least another generation.

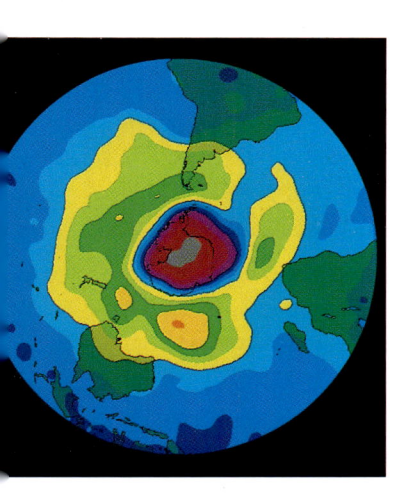

A 'hole' in the ozone layer the size of the United States of America appears over Antarctica each spring. This allows harmful ultra-violet rays from the sun to reach the Earth's surface.

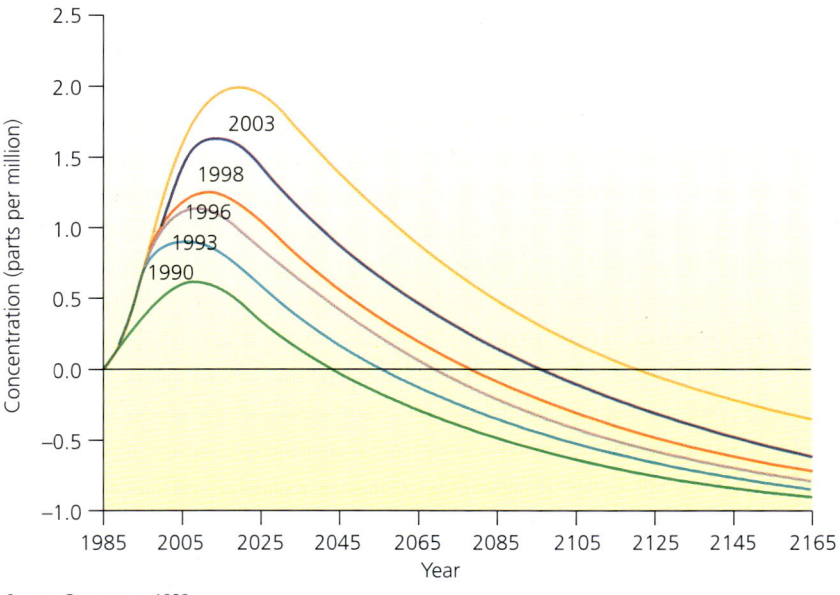

Figure 18 If all countries had achieved 100% reduction in Montreal Protocol CFCs by 1990, it would still take until 2050 for chlorine in the stratosphere to return to 1985 levels. If this reduction was delayed until 1998, chlorine would not return to 1985 levels until 2100.

Source: Greenpeace, 1988

Raw materials

CASE STUDY: THE MOTOR CAR

Many aspects of the way we live today cause problems with pollution and there is no one easy solution. Use of motor vehicles is one such example. Many people aspire to own a car, since it allows personal freedom of movement. This in turn has led to many problems.

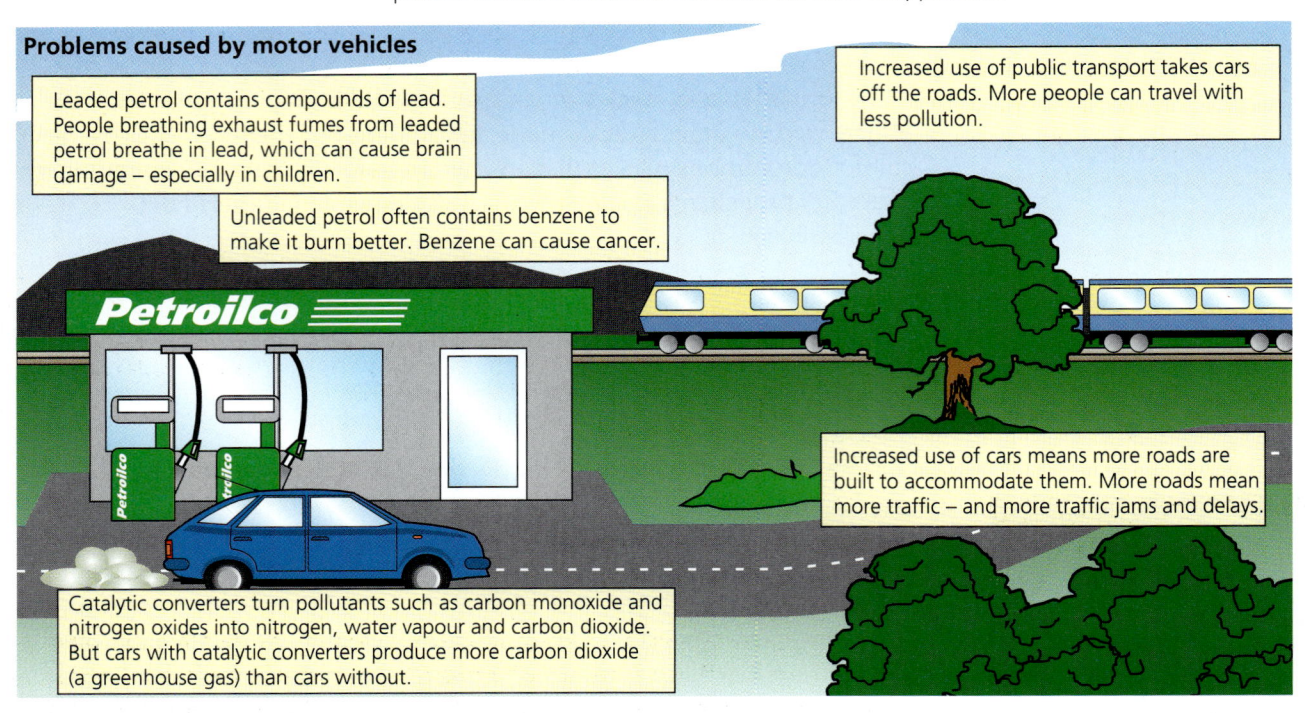

Problems caused by motor vehicles

Leaded petrol contains compounds of lead. People breathing exhaust fumes from leaded petrol breathe in lead, which can cause brain damage – especially in children.

Unleaded petrol often contains benzene to make it burn better. Benzene can cause cancer.

Increased use of public transport takes cars off the roads. More people can travel with less pollution.

Increased use of cars means more roads are built to accommodate them. More roads mean more traffic – and more traffic jams and delays.

Catalytic converters turn pollutants such as carbon monoxide and nitrogen oxides into nitrogen, water vapour and carbon dioxide. But cars with catalytic converters produce more carbon dioxide (a greenhouse gas) than cars without.

Exhaust gases build up in urban areas where the car is used most – the worst pollutants from cars are carbon monoxide, unburned hydrocarbons and nitrogen oxides. During prolonged dry sunny spells, these gases can react to form a 'photochemical smog' which can make breathing problems worse and trigger asthma attacks.

The Los Angeles skyline is often hazy because of a photochemical smog. There are more cars in this area than anywhere else on Earth. The coastal weather conditions combine with the exhaust gases to form a blanket of smog over the city.

In many cities the air quality is monitored and the people informed when the air is heavily polluted so that those who are likely to be badly affected can stay indoors.

There are no easy solutions to this problem. One answer is to provide better public transport, so that more people travel in fewer vehicles. Another has been to fit all new cars with catalytic converters. Once these warm up to operating temperature, they convert about 90% of the worst exhaust pollutants into nitrogen, water and carbon dioxide. Unfortunately, catalytic converters reduce engine efficiency, cause more fuel to be burned, and so release more carbon dioxide – which fuels the greenhouse effect. The unleaded petrol that is needed by cars with catalytic converters also contains benzene, which can cause cancer.

Summary of pollution of the air

- Non-metal oxides in the air dissolve in rainwater to form acid rain.
- Acid rain damages both buildings and living organisms.
- Acid rain can be prevented by stopping the release of acid gases into the air.
- The greenhouse effect may have long-term effects on the Earth's climate.
- Greenhouse gases include carbon dioxide and methane.
- The ozone layer high in the Earth's atmosphere prevents harmful ultra-violet radiation from reaching the surface.
- Chlorofluorocarbons are destroying the ozone layer.

Examination style questions

1. The following list shows some of the gases that might be present in a sample of polluted air:
   ammonia
   carbon dioxide
   carbon monoxide
   nitrogen
   nitrogen dioxide
   oxygen
   sulphur dioxide
   Which of these gases might cause rain to become acidic? Give the name of the acid formed in each case.

2. Make out a table that summarises the main facts about air pollution as follows: list the names of substances that pollute the air, where they come from, what sort of pollution is produced and how this might be controlled. Head the four columns as follows:

Name	Source	Effect	Control

3. A sample of 60 cm³ of air was pushed several times over a sample of the hot solid A, shown in the diagram below:

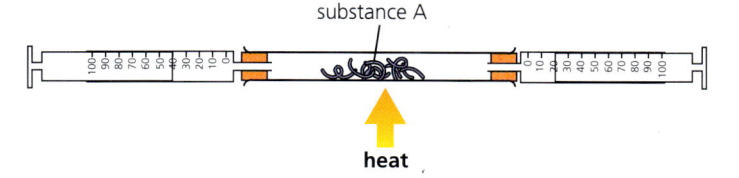

When there was no further change in volume, the apparatus was allowed to cool to room temperature. The final volume of gas remaining was found to be 47.4 cm³.

   a Why was the apparatus allowed to cool to room temperature before the final reading was taken?
   b What is the name of substance A?
   c Write a balanced chemical equation for the reaction taking place in the apparatus
   d What is the name of the main gas left over at the end of the experiment?
   e Calculate the percentage of oxygen present in the sample of air in this experiment
   f Name two noble gases also found in air

Raw materials

4 The following table shows information about the three main gases present in air:

Gas	Percentage in the air	Boiling point (K)	Cost (pence per litre)
argon	1	87	350
nitrogen	79	77	70
oxygen	21	90	70

a If a fractional distillation plant took in 100 000 litres of air, how many litres of each of these three gases would be collected?
b Calculate the cost of producing this amount of each gas.
c Give one use of each gas.
d Many of the uses of nitrogen depend on the fact that it does not easily react with other substances. Why is nitrogen so unreactive?
e One use of nitrogen is to flush out the inside of oil tankers, which become filled with petrol fumes. Why is nitrogen used for this purpose instead of air?

5 Carbon dioxide is formed in many natural and industrial processes. It is a gas that is vital for life as well as a source of pollution.
a Name one natural process and one activity of humans that involve carbon dioxide being released into the atmosphere.
b What is the name of the process by which green plants remove carbon dioxide from the atmosphere?
c Give two ways in which excess carbon dioxide can be a pollutant in the air.

Rocks and minerals 4

Learning objectives

By the end of this chapter you should be able to:
- **describe** the structure of the Earth
- **explain** how the Earth's magnetic field varies with time
- **describe** a theory about the origin of the Earth
- **explain** how tectonic plates account for earthquakes, volcanoes, mountains and rift valleys
- **classify** rocks as sedimentary, igneous or metamorphic
- **give evidence** for the age of rocks
- **describe** the rock cycle
- **explain** physical and chemical weathering, transportation and erosion
- **define** a rock, a mineral and an ore

4.1 The structure of the Earth

Which parts of the Earth contain rocks?

The Earth is composed of several different layers.
- The **inner core** is at the centre of the Earth. Its temperature is over 4300°C.
- The **outer core** has the same temperature as the inner core, but because it is under less pressure it is probably liquid.

Scientists think that the inner and outer cores are kept at this temperature by large amounts of heat energy released by the decay of radioactive elements. This is similar to what happens inside a nuclear reactor. The heat lost outwards to the surface of the Earth is replaced by more heat generated in the core.

- The **mantle** consists of cooler, more solid rock which moves very slowly.
- The **crust** is the thin outer layer of solid rock. It is thinnest under the oceans and thicker under the continents. Most (about 90%) of the Earth's crust is made from compounds of oxygen, silicon, aluminium, iron, calcium, sodium, potassium and magnesium.

The crust is made of **rocks**.

Gutenburg discontinuity This is the junction between the mantle and the core

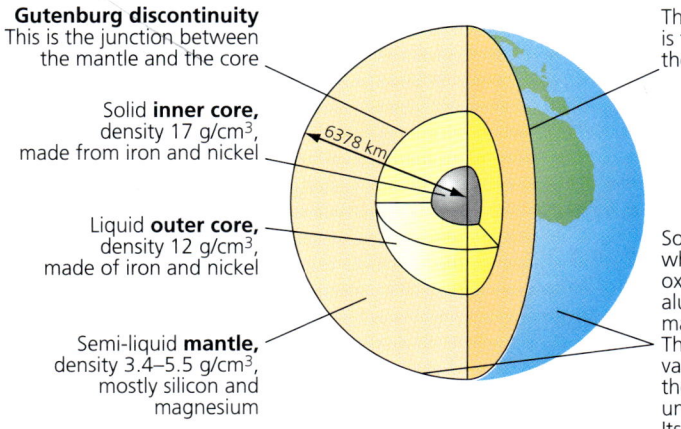

Solid **inner core**, density 17 g/cm^3, made from iron and nickel

6378 km

Liquid **outer core**, density 12 g/cm^3, made of iron and nickel

Semi-liquid **mantle**, density 3.4–5.5 g/cm^3, mostly silicon and magnesium

The **Moho discontinuity** is the junction between the crust and the mantle

Solid **crust,** made of rocks which are compounds of oxygen, silicon, calcium, aluminium, sodium, magnesium and potassium. The thickness of the crust varies from 5–10 km under the oceans to 30–90 km under the continents. Its density is between 2 and 3 g/cm^3

Figure 1 The structure of the Earth.

Raw materials

Why does the Earth have a magnetic field?

The Earth behaves like a giant magnet. This is because movement of rock on the crust sets up convection currents in the mantle and liquid outer core, which generate electric currents. These electric currents produce the Earth's internal electromagnet. The inner Earth is far too hot for a permanent magnet to form. At present, the magnetic north tilts 4° west from the geographical north.

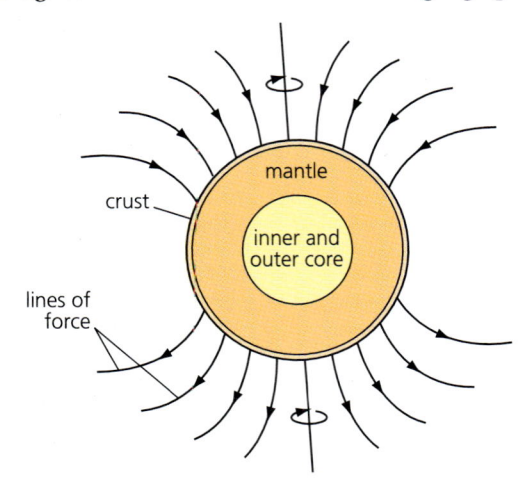

Figure 2 The Earth behaves like a simple bar magnet.

Is magnetic north always the same?

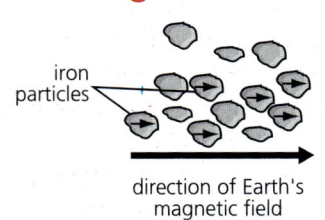

Figure 3 Magnetised particles of iron align themselves with the Earth's magnetic field.

Particles of iron in a magnetic field line up with the direction of the magnetic field as they become magnetised.

Some rocks in the Earth's crust, such as basalt and sandstone, contain large amounts of iron. Scientists have studied the direction of the iron particles in older rocks and have discovered that the Earth's magnetic field has varied in the past. In fact, the whole magnetic field has reversed itself 171 times during the past 76 million years. When this happens the magnetic north pole becomes the south pole and vice versa.

Small variations in the position of magnetic north occur constantly. In 1580 in London, the compass needle pointed 11° to the east but in 1660 it pointed due north and by 1820 it was 24° to the west. It is now only 4° to the west. These changes are thought to be due to changes in the direction of the **convection currents** in the core.

Does the structure of the Earth help us understand its origin?

One theory of the Earth's origin is that it started as a giant ball of molten rock. As it cooled, rafts of solid rock formed on the outside. These eventually joined up and formed the Earth's **tectonic plates**. Volcanoes frequently erupted all over the new surface, giving out ammonia, carbon dioxide, methane and steam. These gases eventually reacted to form the Earth's atmosphere. **Radioactive decay** studies tell us that the Earth is roughly 4500 million years old. If we think of this on the scale of a 24 hour clock, humans arrived at only one minute to midnight!

Rocks and minerals

1 Does the model shown in figure 4 explain why the core is made from nickel and iron?
2 What do you think might have happened to the smoothness of the surface as the Earth cooled?
3 Do you think the Earth will continue to cool? Explain your reasons.

Figure 4   **A theory of the origin of the Earth**

The Earth started as a giant ball of molten rock

As heat radiated away into space the Earth cooled and a crust formed

Volcanoes erupted over the Earth's surface, producing ammonia, carbon dioxide, methane and steam – the first atmosphere

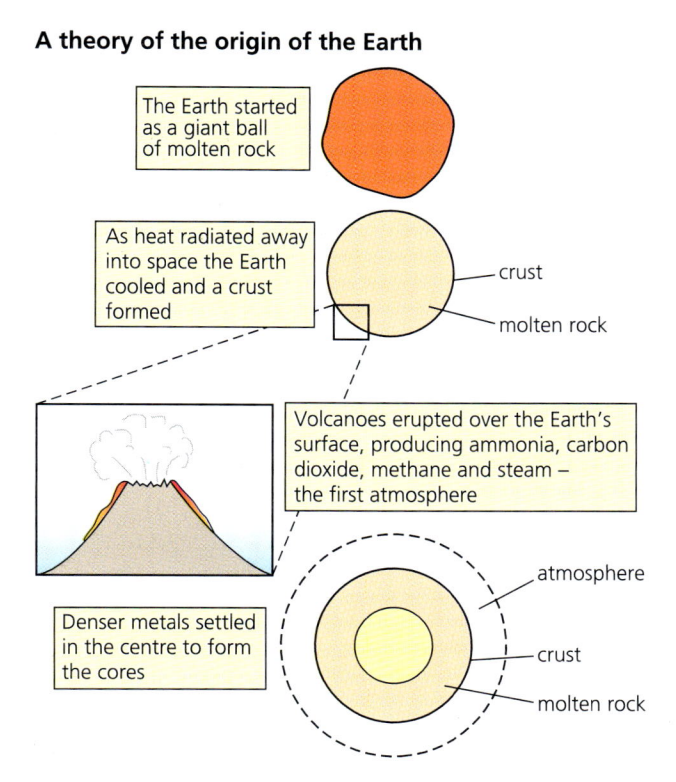

Denser metals settled in the centre to form the cores

What is radioactive decay?

Half-lives

Some atoms form **isotopes** which are radioactive and decay. This usually means that they give off particles and become different elements. The time taken for half the atoms in a sample to decay is called its **half-life**. Each radioactive element has its own half-life. You will find more about isotopes in Chapter 6, *Atomic structure* and half-lives in Chapter 20, *Radioactivity*.

The radioactivity that remains in a rock sample can be used to calculate the age of the rock. The best elements for dating rocks are **potassium**, which has an isotope with a half-life of 1300 million years, and **rubidium**, which has an isotope with a half-life of 47 000 million years. So far, the oldest rocks known come from Greenland and are 4000 million years old. Rocks over 4200 million years old were collected from the Moon by the Apollo crews. Meteorites are up to 4600 million years old, which is probably the age of the planets.

Figure 5 The rate of decay of an isotope decreases over time.

4 Look at figure 5. How old is a sample containing half the original number of radioactive atoms?

Raw materials

Table 1 *Radioactive isotopes of elements decay to form other elements*

Radioactive element	Half life (in millions of years)	Decays into
^{238}U	4500	^{206}Pb
^{40}K	1300	^{40}Ar
^{87}Rb	47 000	^{87}Sr

Summary of the structure of the Earth

- The Earth consists of an inner and outer core, the mantle and the crust.
- The Earth has a magnetic field.
- The Earth's magnetic north is not constant.
- Radioactive isotopes can be used to date rocks.

4.2 Plate tectonics

Has the map of the world always been the same?

The outer layer of the Earth, the crust, is not one continuous shell of rock but is made from several very large slabs of rock which float on the slowly moving mantle. The plates move because of the huge convection currents in the mantle. These slabs of rock are called **tectonic plates**. They can move as much as 5 cm a year.

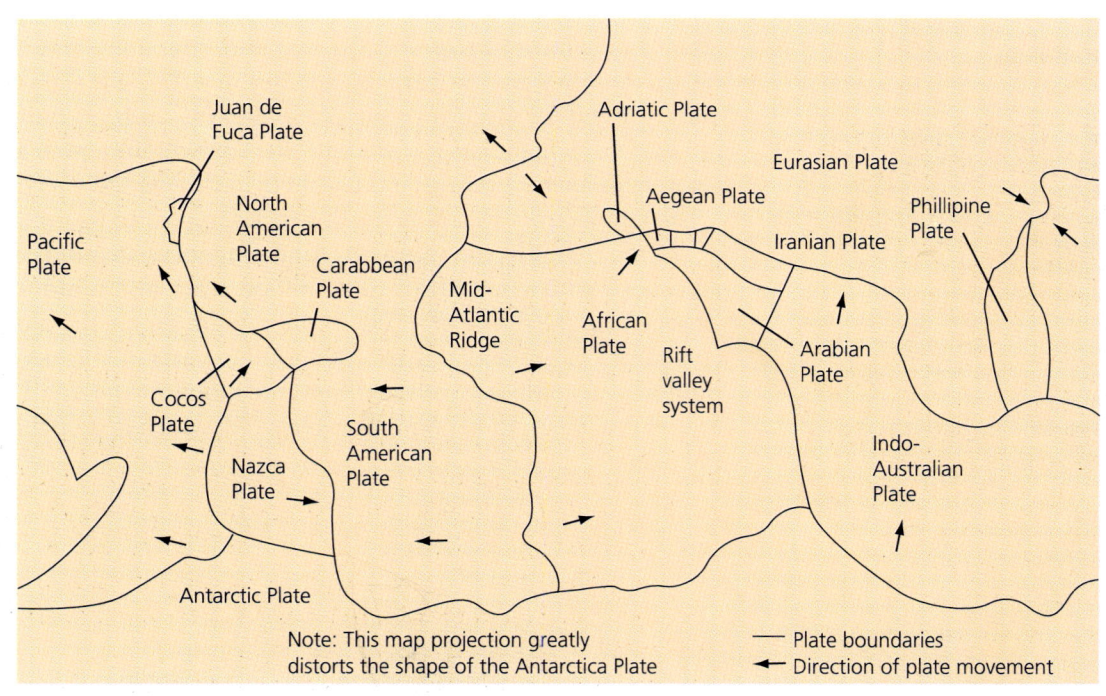

Figure 6 The Earth's tectonic plates.

5 Draw a diagram to explain how convection currents could arise in the mantle.

60

Rocks and minerals

Over millions of years, whole continents have moved thousands of miles. The UK was once thought to have been near the equator (this was when our coal reserves formed from tropical rain forests). South America and Africa were once thought to have been joined together. Measurements from space satellites have confirmed that the Atlantic ocean is getting wider by 5 cm a year. Figure 7 shows how evidence from rock types supports this theory.

Figure 7 The rock types found in Africa and South America are very similar. This suggests that the two continents were once joined together.

Rock types in Africa and South America

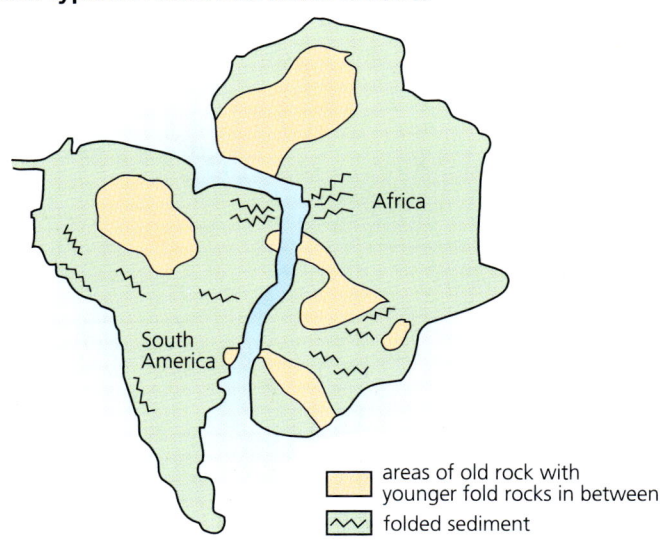

- areas of old rock with younger fold rocks in between
- folded sediment

How does movement of tectonic plates affect the landscape?

The Nazca plate sinks beneath the South American plate as the two plates come together. The South American plate has been lifted up to form the Andes mountain range.

The Earth's crust that lies under the oceans is called the **oceanic crust.** The crust under the continents is called **continental crust.**

Oceanic crust is heavier than continental crust. If an oceanic plate and a continental plate are moving together, then the heavier oceanic crust will sink under the lighter continental plate. The continental crust is lifted up and can form high **mountain ranges**.

This is called a **destructive margin**, because crustal rocks are dragged into the mantle and are melted again. You can see the ways movement of tectonic plates affects the landscape in figure 8.

Energy is needed to melt the crustal rock and the magma cools, becomes more dense and sinks towards the core. Hotter magma from below rises to the Earth's crust to take its place. This sets up the convection currents, which provide the energy to drag the tectonic plates across the surface of the mantle.

At the place where two tectonic plates are moving apart, a **constructive margin** forms. Liquid rock from the mantle rises to fill the spaces left by the plate movement and **volcanoes** form.

Sometimes two plates simply slide past each other. This is called a **conservative** margin. **Earthquakes** occur at conservative margins, but volcanoes or mountains don't.

If two plates that are both under continental crust collide, **fold mountains** are formed. The Alps, the Himalayas and the Pyrenees formed this way.

Raw materials

Figure 8

Movement at a destructive margin

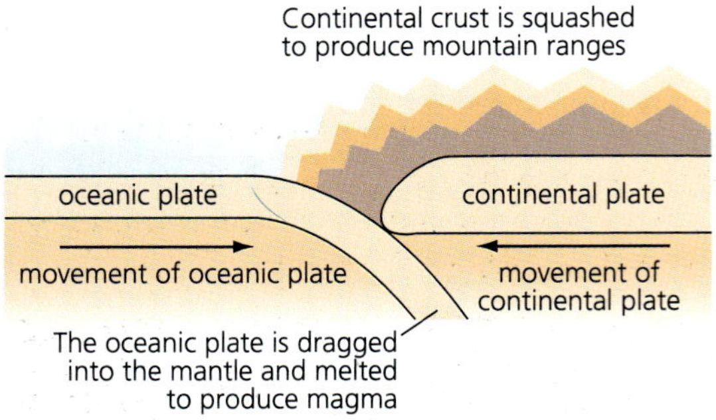

Continental crust is squashed to produce mountain ranges

oceanic plate — continental plate
movement of oceanic plate → ← movement of continental plate

The oceanic plate is dragged into the mantle and melted to produce magma

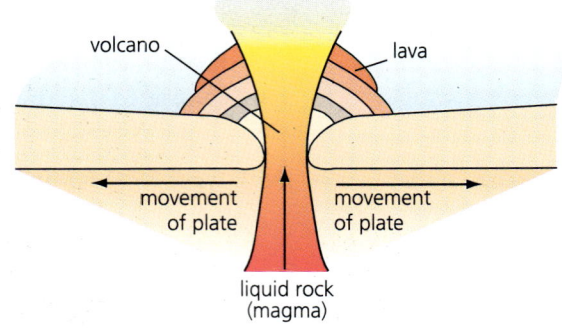

Movement under continental crust

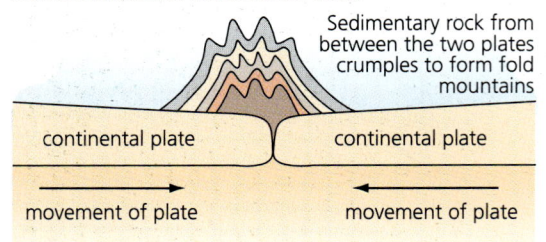

Sedimentary rock from between the two plates crumples to form fold mountains

continental plate — continental plate
movement of plate → ← movement of plate

Movement at a constructive margin

volcano — lava
← movement of plate | movement of plate →
liquid rock (magma)

Formation of a rift valley

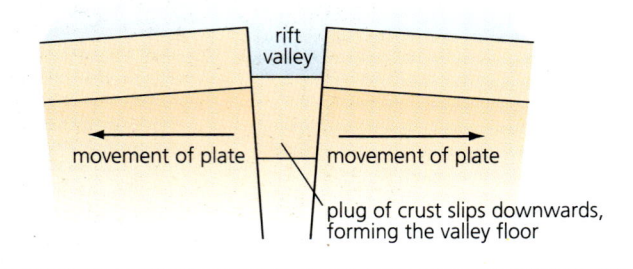

rift valley
← movement of plate | movement of plate →
plug of crust slips downwards, forming the valley floor

Volcanoes and rift valleys form at constructive margins.

6 Which tectonic plates move to form the Himalaya mountains?
7 Which plates form the constructive margin at the Mid-Atlantic ridge?
8 Why do you think the margin of tectonic plates moving apart is called a constructive margin?

In the seas around Japan are chains of volcanic islands which have been formed from constructive margins. The mid-Atlantic ridge is a chain of mountains running through the Atlantic ocean. Iceland is one of these mountains which rises above the surface of the ocean. The Mid-Atlantic ridge (figure 6) is another example of what happens when tectonic plates move apart.

Rift valleys may also form when plates move apart. When a rift valley forms a central plug of crust slips downwards to form the valley floor.

What other evidence is there for the tectonic plate theory?

9 The tectonic plate theory was developed in the 1960s. Why is it still considered a theory and not scientific fact?

When scientists first studied the alignment of iron particles in rocks to determine past positions of magnetic north, they found that the results from different continents were wildly different from each other. Their results only made sense when they allowed for the movement of the continents – that is, when they took the tectonic plate theory into account.

Summary of plate tectonics

- The Earth's crust is made up of tectonic plates.
- The tectonic plates are constantly moving.
- Volcanoes, earthquakes, mountains and rift valleys can occur at tectonic plate boundaries.

Rocks and minerals

4.3 Earthquakes and volcanoes
Why do earthquakes occur?

Earthquakes do not just occur randomly. The epicentre of an earthquake is nearly always found near faults or the boundaries of tectonic plates. Earthquakes happen when plates are moving in opposite directions. If stresses build up and then are suddenly released, an earthquake occurs.

Los Angeles is on the boundaries of the North American plate and the Pacific plate. This is a conservative margin. It is called the San Andreas fault.

10 Look back at figure 6 and use it to predict the areas of the world where earthquakes are most likely to occur.

What can we learn from earthquakes?

Earthquakes send out waves which travel in rock in different ways, depending on:
- the density of the rock
- the state of the rock (whether it is solid or liquid)
- the angle at which the waves hit the rock.

If we can measure the ways the waves are moving we can deduce information about the type and structure of rock they are moving through.

Seismographs are machines that detect vibrations in the Earth such as the waves caused by an earthquake. By taking readings all round the world, we can find out how earthquake waves spread out and detect any activity which could indicate that another earthquake is likely.

11 What is the change in state between:
  a the mantle and the outer core
  b the outer and inner core?

Raw materials

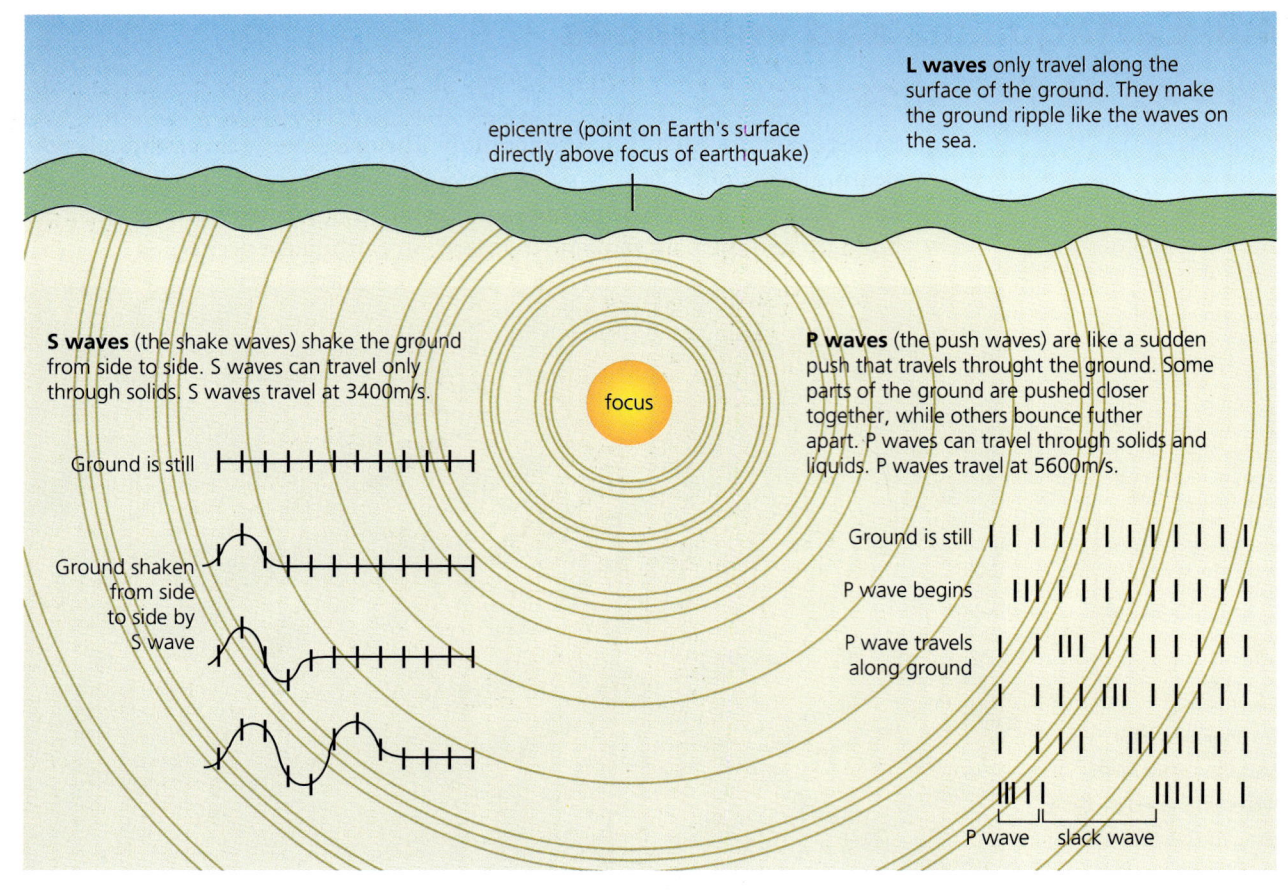

L waves only travel along the surface of the ground. They make the ground ripple like the waves on the sea.

epicentre (point on Earth's surface directly above focus of earthquake)

S waves (the shake waves) shake the ground from side to side. S waves can travel only through solids. S waves travel at 3400m/s.

Ground is still

Ground shaken from side to side by S wave

focus

P waves (the push waves) are like a sudden push that travels throught the ground. Some parts of the ground are pushed closer together, while others bounce futher apart. P waves can travel through solids and liquids. P waves travel at 5600m/s.

Ground is still

P wave begins

P wave travels along ground

P wave   slack wave

Figure 9 The waves that travel outwards from the centre of an earthquake are very similar to sound waves. There are three types of wave.

Figure 10 The velocity of earthquake waves.

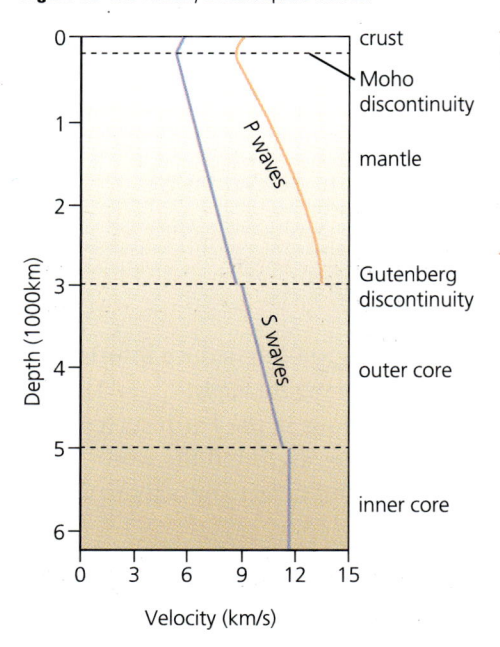

crust
Moho discontinuity
mantle
Gutenberg discontinuity
outer core
inner core

Depth (1000km)
Velocity (km/s)

12 Look at the graph in figure 10.
   a What happens to the P waves at the Gutenburg discontinuity?
   b What happens to the S waves at the discontinuity?
   c What does this suggest?

What causes volcanoes?

Rocks pushed down into the Earth are slowly heated and eventually melt. Molten rock is called **magma**. Because magma is less dense than solid rock, it will rise, forcing its way up through any crack or hole in the Earth's crust. This forms a **volcano** on the surface. Magma on the surface is called **lava**. Volcanoes can cause devastation over large areas of land and produce toxic sulphur dioxide and hydrogen sulphide gases.

Cross-section of a volcano

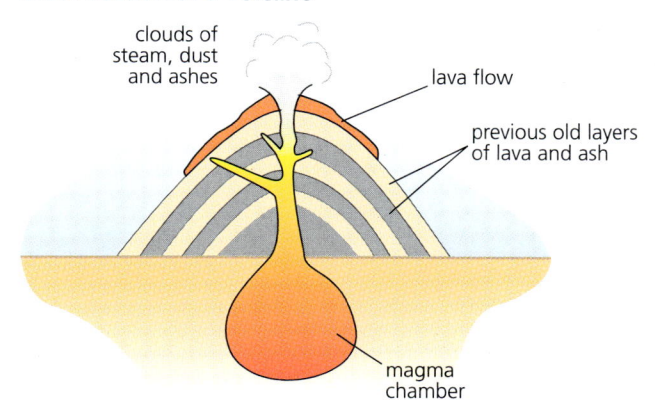

Figure 11

Summary of earthquakes and volcanoes

- Earthquakes occur when tectonic plates are moving in opposite directions.
- By measuring the ways earthquake waves move we can find out about the rock they are moving through.
- Volcanoes are formed when molten rock forces its way through weaknesses in the Earth's crust.

4.4 The Earth's crust

How do we classify rocks?

Rocks are difficult to classify according to the chemicals they are made from because many of them look the same. Rocks are usually classified, according to how they were formed, into three main types:
- sedimentary rocks
- igneous rocks
- metamorphic rocks

Sedimentary rock

Sedimentary rocks are formed by layers of sediment (small particles) which are deposited on top of each other over thousands of years.

Raw materials

The layers gradually build up and press down on the layers of older sediment beneath them, squeezing out the water. The sediments become cemented together by salts crystallising out of the water. Millions of years later, the sediments form new rocks. The process is called **consolidation**.

Sedimentary rocks often contain **fossils** of plants and animals that were living when the sediment was laid down. These provide us with clues as to the age of the rock. (Some of the clues fossils leave behind are shown in figure 12.)

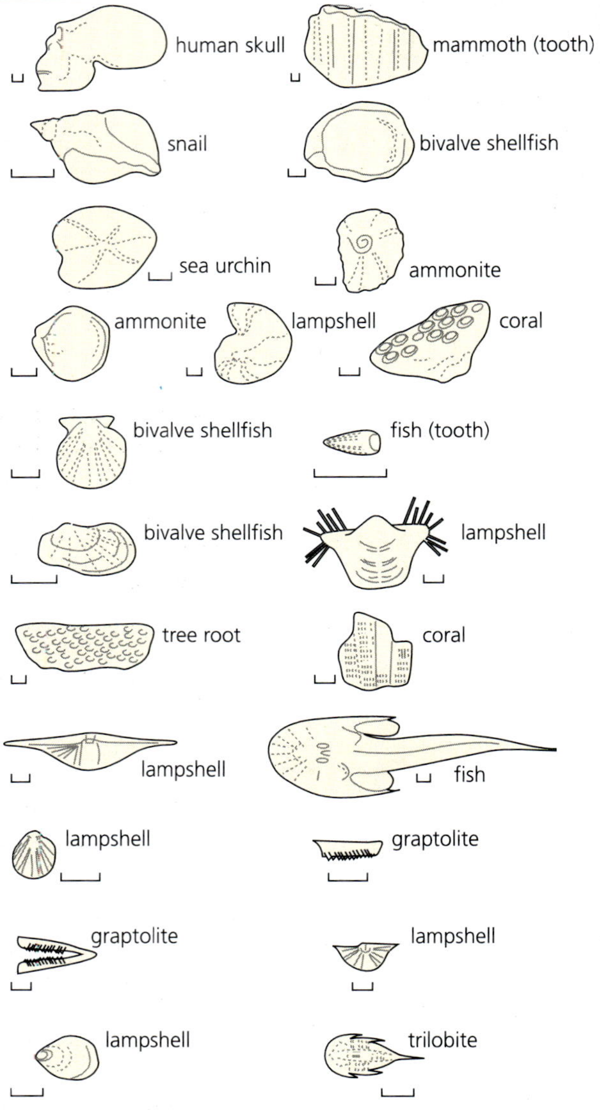

Time period	Millions of years ago	Some typical British fossils
Quaternary	0 – 2	human skull, mammoth (tooth)
Tertiary	up to 65	snail, bivalve shellfish
Cretaceous	up to 136	sea urchin, ammonite
Jurassic	up to 190	ammonite, lampshell, coral
Triassic	up to 225	bivalve shellfish, fish (tooth)
Permian	up to 280	bivalve shellfish, lampshell
Carboniferous	up to 355	tree root, coral
Devonian	up to 395	lampshell, fish
Silurian	up to 440	lampshell, graptolite
Ordovician	up to 500	graptolite, lampshell
Cambrian	up to 570	lampshell, trilobite
Precambrian	over 570	Few fossils are found in Precambrian rocks

Figure 12 The fossils present in a sample of sedimentary rock are indicators of its age.

Rocks and minerals

The layers in sedimentary rock are called **beds** and the joins between them are called **bedding planes**. Sedimentary rocks cover 75% of the continents.

Table 2 Sedimentary rocks can be formed from clay, sand and pebbles

Particles	Sedimentary rock formed	
clay	mudstone	
sand	sandstone	
pebbles	conglomerate	

The layers of sedimentary rock in the sides of the Grand Canyon have been exposed by erosion. The oldest sedimentary rocks are at the bottom of the canyon.

Igneous rock

Igneous rocks are rocks that have been molten and form when the lava from a volcano solidifies. Igneous rock is hard and contains many small crystals. There are two main types of igneous rock:
- Magma solidifying on the surface of the Earth forms **extrusive igneous rock**.
- Some igneous rocks are formed when lava pushes its way towards the Earth's surface, but does not reach it. These are called **intrusive igneous rocks.**

Figure 13 Magma intrusions solidify to form intrusive igneous rock.

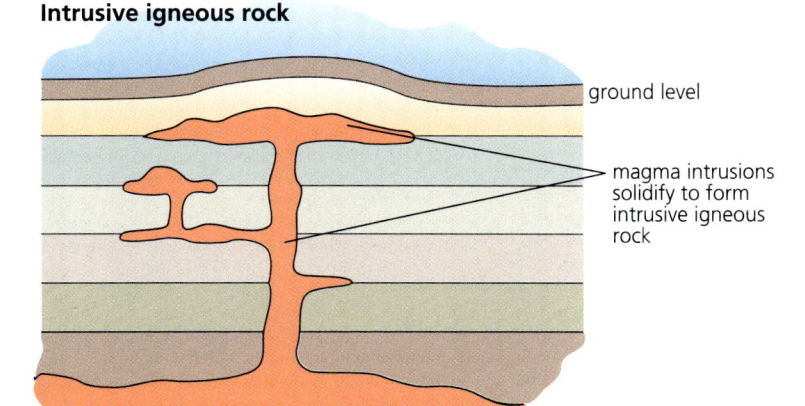

Intrusive igneous rock

Intrusive igneous rocks usually cool slowly. This results in the formation of larger crystals, such as can be seen in the photograph of Cornish granite overleaf. Slow cooling allows the particles time to align themselves in a regular crystal pattern. Extrusive igneous rocks usually cool quickly and the crystals formed are very small, such as those in basalt. Basalt is solid lava.

Raw materials

13 Which of the intrusive igneous rocks in these photographs would you expect to have the smallest crystals? Why?

The crystal size in igneous rocks depends on the rate of cooling. Cornish granite formed as an intrusive igneous rock. Former surface layers of rock have since been eroded away, leaving the granite exposed.

Formation of metamorphic rock

Skeleton particles

loose grains

Limestone

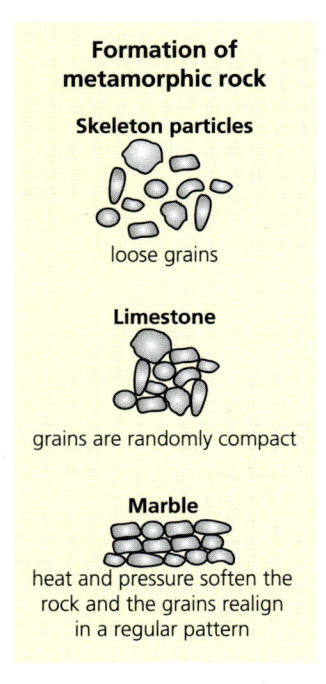

grains are randomly compact

Marble

heat and pressure soften the rock and the grains realign in a regular pattern

Figure 14 Microscopic changes occur as sedimentary or igneous rocks are changed into metamorphic rocks.

Metamorphic rock

Metamorphic rocks are formed by the action of heat and pressure on other rock types. Limestone, chalk and marble are all forms of calcium carbonate, $CaCO_3$. Limestone and chalk are sedimentary rocks – chalk formed from crushed algae and limestone formed from the crushed skeletons of tiny shellfish. After many years the layers built up until they were hundreds of metres thick. If limestone is pushed deep into the Earth the heat and pressure change it into **marble**. Marble is a metamorphic rock. You can see the microscopic changes that take place in figure 14.

Metamorphic rocks are often found around a volcano where the magma heats the surrounding rock.

Different amounts of heat and pressure produce different degrees of metamorphism.

At low temperatures and high pressure, mudstone and shale forms slate.

Slate is used as a roofing material.

Rocks and minerals

At higher temperatures and high pressure, mudstones and shales form schist.

At even higher temperatures, gneiss is formed.

Can rocks change from one form to another?

Over millions of years, sedimentary, igneous and metamorphic rocks are recycled. This cycle is called the **rock cycle**.

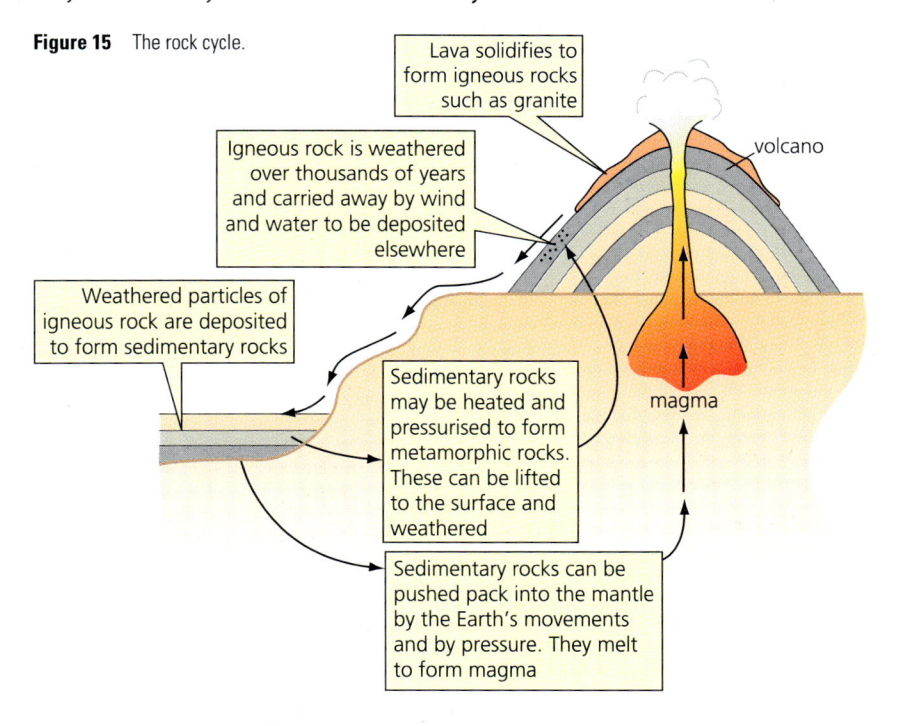

Figure 15 The rock cycle.

- Lava solidifies to form igneous rocks such as granite
- Igneous rock is weathered over thousands of years and carried away by wind and water to be deposited elsewhere
- Weathered particles of igneous rock are deposited to form sedimentary rocks
- Sedimentary rocks may be heated and pressurised to form metamorphic rocks. These can be lifted to the surface and weathered
- Sedimentary rocks can be pushed pack into the mantle by the Earth's movements and by pressure. They melt to form magma

volcano, magma

14 What energy sources are needed to operate the rock cycle?

Raw materials

Summary of the Earth's crust

- Rocks are classified as sedimentary, igneous or metamorphic, depending on the way they form.
- The fossils present in sedimentary rock give clues as to its age.
- The age of igneous rock can be deduced from the size of the crystals present.
- Metamorphic rocks are formed by the action of heat and pressure on other types of rock.
- Rocks are recycled over millions of years in the rock cycle.

4.5 Weathering of rocks

How is soil made from rocks?

Weathering is the process that breaks up rocks into small particles, such as those found in soil. This process takes thousands of years. If the rock particles are then transported elsewhere, they can cause **erosion** of the landscape. Rocks are weathered in two ways:
- **physical weathering** or
- **chemical weathering**.

What is physical weathering?

Weathering can be caused by changes in temperature or by the effects of water.

Weathering by temperature

Rocks expand in the heat and contract when it is cold. When changes in temperature are extreme, like those you would find in a desert, rocks expand during the day and contract during the cooler night. Because most rocks are made from minerals that expand at different rates the rock eventually cracks.

Weathering by water

Water can collect in cracks in rocks. If the temperature falls below 0°C, the water freezes. When water freezes, it expands and the force produced can make the rock crack. When the temperature rises the water melts again and can flow further into a crack, to freeze again when it gets cold. The effect of this on rocks is called the **freeze-thaw effect**.

Rocks and minerals

Figure 16 Rocks can be broken down by weathering in many different ways.

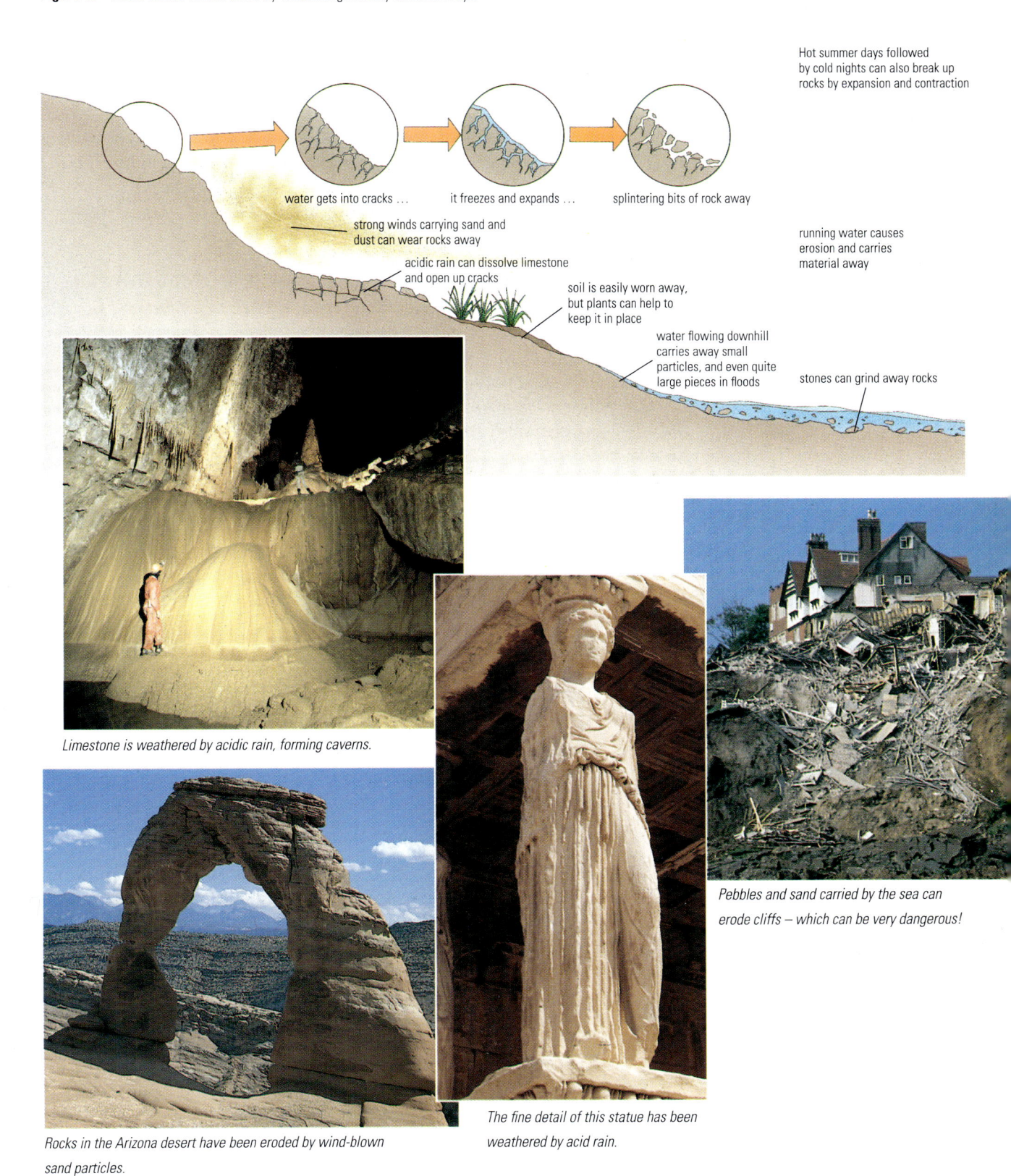

Hot summer days followed by cold nights can also break up rocks by expansion and contraction

water gets into cracks … it freezes and expands … splintering bits of rock away

strong winds carrying sand and dust can wear rocks away

acidic rain can dissolve limestone and open up cracks

soil is easily worn away, but plants can help to keep it in place

running water causes erosion and carries material away

water flowing downhill carries away small particles, and even quite large pieces in floods

stones can grind away rocks

Limestone is weathered by acidic rain, forming caverns.

Pebbles and sand carried by the sea can erode cliffs – which can be very dangerous!

Rocks in the Arizona desert have been eroded by wind-blown sand particles.

The fine detail of this statue has been weathered by acid rain.

71

What is chemical weathering?

Rainwater is naturally weakly acidic. The acid in rainwater reacts with rocks made from calcium carbonate, such as limestone, to form soluble compounds of calcium. These dissolve in the ground water and the limestone is eroded away. Caves and caverns in limestone areas are made in this way.

This type of weathering also affects marble statues and buildings. In recent years, the process has been accelerated by acid rain caused by acid gases in the air (see Chapter 3, *The air*, for more about acid rain and its effects).

How do weathered rock particles shape the landscape?

The fragments of rock produced by weathering are often **transported** a long way from their original rock. They can be transported by gravity, wind or moving water (river, sea or ice). These particles act like sandpaper and wear away other rocks, causing **erosion** of the landscape.

Particles of eroded rock eventually settle and form sediments. Rivers may deposit sediments in channels and flood plains. As rivers slow down near the sea, the deposited sediments form deltas. The layers of sediment eventually form sedimentary rocks.

How is soil classified?

Soils are usually classified according to the diameter of the particles present:
- **sandy** soils have rock particles between 2.0 mm and 0.02 mm
- **silt** soils have rock particles between 0.02 mm and 0.002 mm
- **clay** soils have rock particles between 0.002 mm and 0.0002 mm.

A good soil contains a 1:2 mixture of clay to sand – it is called a **loam**.

Table 3 Characteristics of soils

Soil type	Water content	Air content	Mineral content	Workability
sandy	drains quickly, so generally low	good air supply	minerals washed out	easy
loam	correct water content	sufficient air supply	sufficient mineral content	workable
clay	can become waterlogged	poor air supply	good mineral content	sticky and heavy

Summary of weathering of rocks

- Physical weathering can be caused by changes in temperature and the freeze-thaw effect of water.
- Chemical weathering is caused by the acid content of rainwater.
- Transportation of weathered rock particles by gravity, wind and water is called erosion.
- Eroded particles eventually settle to form sediments and soil.
- Soils are classified according to particle size as sandy, loam or clay.

4.6 Rocks and minerals
How are useful materials obtained from rocks?

The Earth's crust consists of **rocks**. Rocks are usually mixtures of **minerals**. A mineral is any solid element or compound found in the ground. Minerals which contain metals are called **ores**.

15 Which of these are rocks, which are minerals and which are ores? Explain your choices.
- **a** iron(II) oxide
- **b** calcium carbonate
- **c** silicon dioxide
- **d** shale
- **e** granite
- **f** limestone
- **g** copper carbonate
- **h** aluminium oxide

Figure 17 The main elements in the Earth's crust. These combine in many ways to make up minerals, ores and rocks. Most of the rocks on Earth are made up of silicates.

Elements in the Earth's crust

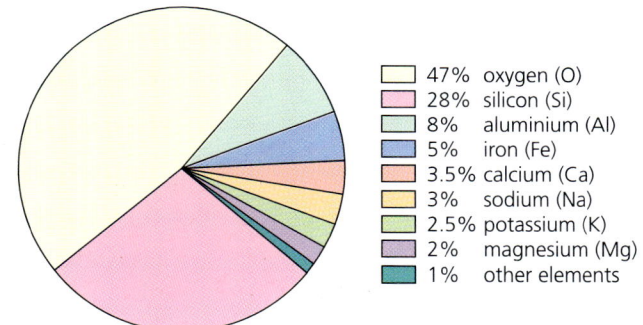

- 47% oxygen (O)
- 28% silicon (Si)
- 8% aluminium (Al)
- 5% iron (Fe)
- 3.5% calcium (Ca)
- 3% sodium (Na)
- 2.5% potassium (K)
- 2% magnesium (Mg)
- 1% other elements

Aluminium is a hard silvery coloured metal, with a low density. It is the third most common element in the Earth's crust. It is found in the ore bauxite. Aluminium compounds, such as bauxite, are very stable; they can only be extracted by **electrolysis**. (See Chapter 12, *Electrolysis*.)

Iron is the second most common metal in the Earth's crust and is the most widely used of all metals. Over 400 million tonnes of iron are produced each year throughout the world. Iron is extracted from its ores haematite and magnetite in a blast furnace.

Calcium carbonate, as chalk, limestone and marble, is the second most common mineral in the Earth's crust. Uses of calcium carbonate include:
- neutralising acid soil
- manufacturing iron and steel
- manufacturing cement and concrete
- manufacturing lime.

Raw materials

Limestone is quarried from the Earth's crust. Unfortunately, the purest limestone deposits are usually found in areas of great natural beauty. It is calculated that if quarrying in the Peak District continues at its present rate, about one-quarter of the district will be removed within the lifetimes of today's children.

16 List the pros and cons of quarrying limestone in an area of outstanding natural beauty. Consider the views of the local residents, the local economy, the environmentalists, the quarrying company and the public demand for limestone products.

Summary of rocks and minerals

- Rocks are mixtures of minerals.
- Most of the rocks in the Earth's crust are made of silicates.
- Minerals that contain metals are called ores.
- Useful materials are extracted from ores, but the process of extraction from the ground can damage the environment.

The sea 5

Learning objectives

By the end of this chapter you should be able to:
- **list** the main components of sea water
- **describe** the electrolysis of brine, and what the products of this process are used for
- **explain** how magnesium is extracted from sea water and describe some of its uses
- **understand** how bromine is extracted from sea water and list some of its uses
- **describe** how sea water can be polluted and suggest ways of dealing with marine pollution

As rain falls through the air, acid gases in the air dissolve in it and it becomes acidic (look back at Chapter 3, *The air*, for more about how this happens). This acid rainwater flows over rocks, soils and organic matter and dissolves small amounts of substances. By the time the water reaches the oceans it has many solids dissolved in it. These can be extracted and are useful raw materials for manufacturing processes.

5.1 The chemicals in sea water

The sea is salty, and most of the salt in it is the chemical we put on our food (sodium chloride). This salt is the basic raw material for a whole industry.

Although sea water is referred to as 'salt water' (or 'brine') it actually contains many different substances – sea water even contains tonnes of dissolved gold!

Unfortunately, valuable metals like gold are present in very low concentrations, and no-one has discovered an economic way to extract them from the sea. However, sea water also contains a number of compounds of metals and non-metals and some of these can be separated out and extracted further for use.

Figure 1 Sea water contains many dissolved solids which are washed into the oceans by rivers.

The ions present in sea water

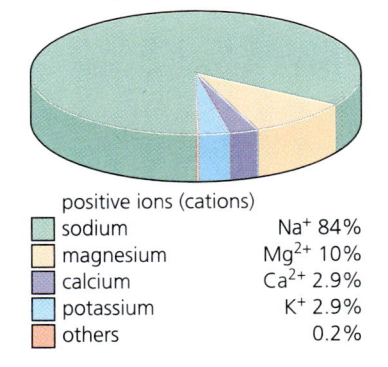

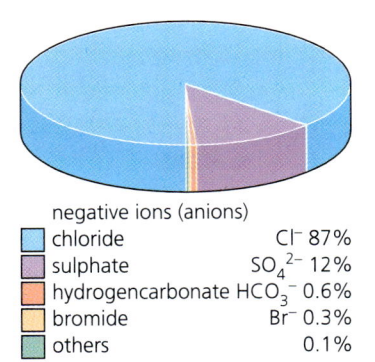

positive ions (cations)
- sodium Na^+ 84%
- magnesium Mg^{2+} 10%
- calcium Ca^{2+} 2.9%
- potassium K^+ 2.9%
- others   0.2%

negative ions (anions)
- chloride Cl^- 87%
- sulphate SO_4^{2-} 12%
- hydrogencarbonate HCO_3^- 0.6%
- bromide Br^- 0.3%
- others   0.1%

75

Raw materials

> 1 Name three compounds that are found dissolved in sea water. Briefly describe the process by which these dissolved compounds may have come to be present in the oceans.
> 2 Which is the most abundant compound in brine?

How is salt extracted from the sea?

Most of the table salt we use comes from salt mines. Underground deposits of salt were formed millions of years ago as ancient seas evaporated, leaving the solid salt behind. In countries where the sun shines a lot salt can be obtained easily from sea water. The water is left to evaporate in shallow lagoons. The solution of salt becomes more and more concentrated until the salts crystallise out and can be collected. If you use 'sea salt' on your food it will have been prepared this way.

Most of our salt is mined from large mines like this one in Cheshire. In many other countries salt is extracted from seawater instead.

What happens during electrolysis of brine?

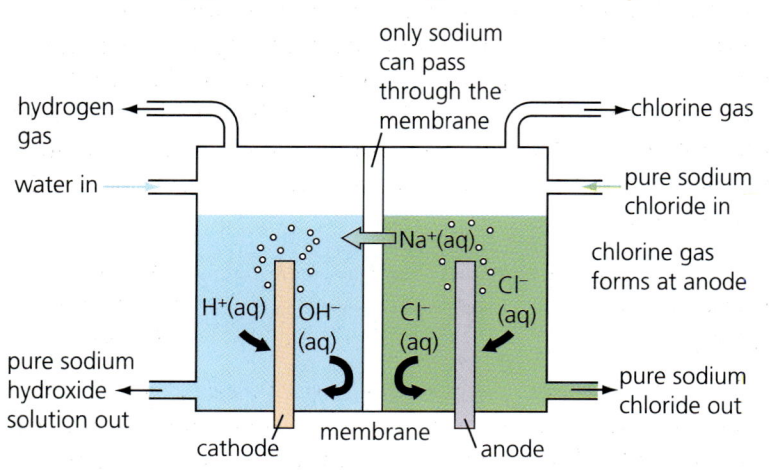

Brine is mostly a solution of sodium chloride in water, containing positive sodium ions and negative chloride ions. If an electric current is passed through the solution useful chemicals are produced. This process is called **electrolysis**, and you will find out more about it in Chapter 12, *Electrolysis*.

Brine is electrolysed in a membrane cell. You can see what happens in a membrane cell in figure 2.

Figure 2 A membrane cell during the electrolysis of brine.

The net result in these cells is:

Sodium chloride + water → sodium hydroxide + chlorine + hydrogen
2NaCl(aq) + 2H$_2$O(l) → 2NaOH(aq) + Cl$_2$(g) + H$_2$(g)

Each of these three products is collected separately and used in industry, as shown in figure 3.

Figure 3 What we can make with salt.

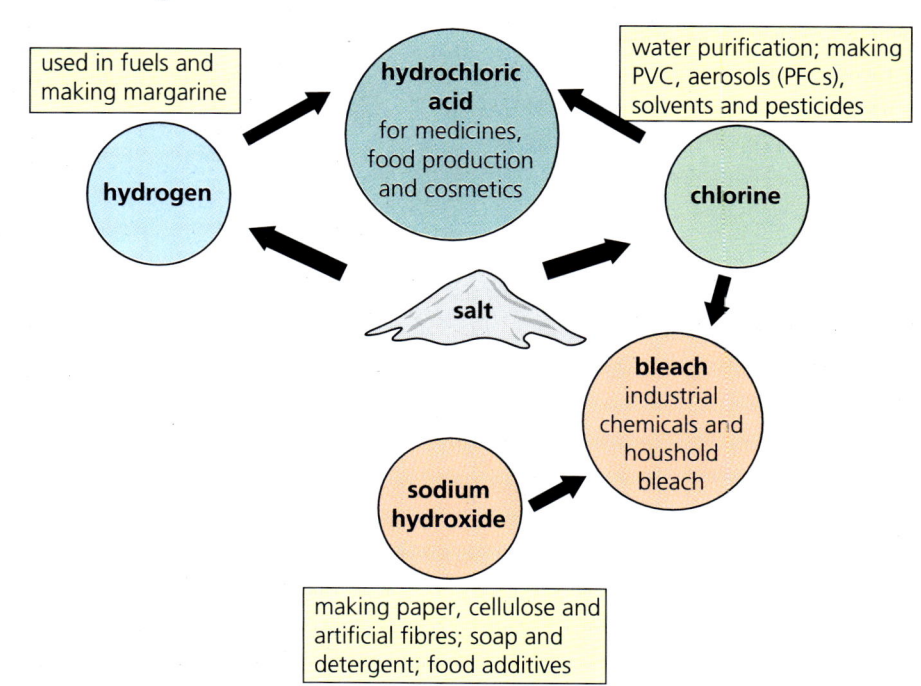

- hydrogen — used in fuels and making margarine
- hydrochloric acid — for medicines, food production and cosmetics
- chlorine — water purification; making PVC, aerosols (PFCs), solvents and pesticides
- bleach — industrial chemicals and houshold bleach
- sodium hydroxide — making paper, cellulose and artificial fibres; soap and detergent; food additives

3 Suggest some everyday uses for the chemicals produced by the electrolysis of brine.

How is magnesium extracted from sea water?

Each cubic mile of sea water contains more than five million tonnes of magnesium, which is present as salts such as magnesium chloride (MgCl$_2$), magnesium sulphate (MgSO$_4$) or magnesium bromide (MgBr$_2$). Such salts can be extracted by evaporating off the water and crystallising out the salts. Solid magnesium chloride extracted from sea water in this way is heated until it melts and an electric current is then passed through the liquid. Magnesium metal is formed at the negatively charged cathode, and this is drawn off and allowed to cool into a block.

	electrolysis	cathode		anode
magnesium chloride	→	magnesium metal	+	chlorine gas
MgCl$_2$(l)	→	Mg(l)	+	Cl$_2$(g)

The magnesium formed is used to make low-density strong alloys (for example with aluminium or zinc) used in the construction of aircraft and cars, in fireworks and in sacrificial protection of other metals against corrosion.

Raw materials

4 Magnesium metal has a low density, and is useful for making lightweight alloys, when blended with other metals.

a Describe briefly how magnesium is extracted from naturally occurring raw materials.

b Magnesium burns readily in air with a brilliant white flame. Write a chemical equation for this combustion reaction, and suggest a use to which this reaction could be put.

c Magnesium forms useful alloys with metals such as aluminium and zinc. What is an alloy? Suggest why magnesium might be useful to alloy with these metals.

Burning magnesium. Magnesium burns with a brilliant light, and this property is used in distress flares.

How is bromine extracted from the sea?

Another useful substance that is extracted from sea water is the element bromine. Although sea water contains only a small amount of compounds of bromine, mostly as magnesium bromide ($MgBr_2$), it is still economically worthwhile to extract it.

To extract the bromine, chlorine gas is bubbled through sea water. It reacts with the dissolved magnesium bromide to give off bromine vapour:

$$Cl_2(g) + MgBr_2(aq) \rightarrow Br_2(g) + MgCl_2(aq)$$

This is known as a **displacement reaction** – the bromide ions in the salt have been displaced by chlorine. The bromine vapour is then further processed to concentrate and purify it to liquid bromine.

Bromine itself has few uses because it is very dangerous, but compounds of bromine are used in the manufacture of leaded petrol, in medicine and in photography.

5 a What is a displacement reaction?

b Name a compound of bromine found in sea water, and write a balanced equation for the reaction of chlorine with this compound.

c Suggest some uses for bromine or its compounds.

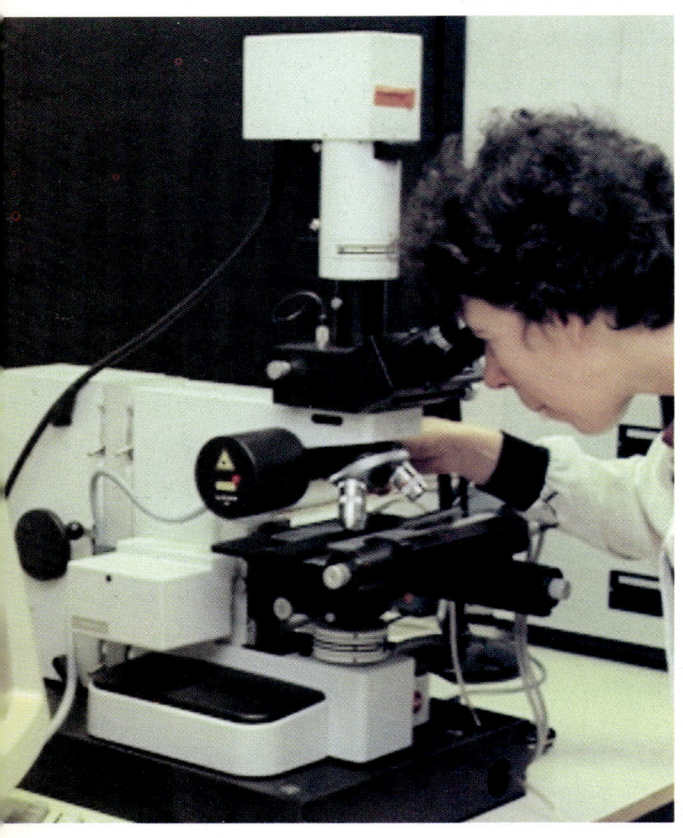

Developing photographs. One important compound of bromine is silver bromide. This compound is an important part of photographic film.

Summary of chemicals in water

- Sea water contains many dissolved salts.
- Electrolysis of brine produces chlorine, hydrogen and sodium hydroxide solution.
- Magnesium is extracted from magnesium chloride in sea water by evaporation, crystallisation and electrolysis.
- Magnesium is used in distress flares, low-density alloys and corrosion prevention.
- Bromine is obtained from sea water by a displacement reaction with chlorine.
- Compounds of bromine are used in medicine, photography and the manufacture of leaded petrol.

5.2 Pollution at sea

Oceans cover four-fifths of the Earth's surface. They are essential to regulate life on Earth. But the oceans and the organisms that live there are under attack. For many years, humans have treated the oceans like a huge dumping ground. Sewage sludge, chemicals, many kinds of rubbish and even radioactive waste have all been dumped at sea, in the belief that this was the end of the problem. In places where very polluted rivers have flowed into the sea many waste materials have built up round the coast. This has put the whole marine environment in danger, and has affected many plants and animals.

Who is responsible for oil slicks?

Almost a quarter of the ships in the world carry one type of cargo – crude oil. Sometimes accidents occur and the oil leaks into the sea. Small accidental oil spills may cause local problems, but the oil is eventually broken down by natural processes. Large spills can be disastrous for the whole marine environment.

Oil is also lost when the ships' tanks are washed out and in a process called ballasting (empty oil tanks are filled with sea water to stop the ship floating too high in the water; this oily water must then be flushed out before more oil can be taken on board). Cleaning and ballasting are particularly harmful because they are usually done when the ship is in or near a port and unless great care is taken they can pollute the nearby coastline. A more major problem is caused by tanker crews illegally washing out their tanks at sea, rather than paying to have it safely done in port.

When crude oil is spilled into the sea many seabirds become coated in oil and will die unless they can be caught and carefully cleaned.

Raw materials

How can oil spills be cleaned up?

Various methods are used to clear up oil spills, but none of them are fully effective. Chemicals (such as detergents) are sprayed onto the oil to make it disperse but these are usually poisonous and can cause almost as much damage to wildlife as the oil.

Cleaning up oil spillages.

As with other pollution problems, it is much better to prevent the pollution in the first place than to try to deal with it once it has happened.

6 Suggest two problems caused by spillages of crude oil at sea.
7 How can spillages of crude oil onto sea water be dealt with?
8 Suggest two other ways in which the seas have been polluted by human activity.
9 Discuss briefly some of the ways in which pollution at sea might be prevented.

As people become more aware of the problems of pollution, they are putting pressure on their governments to reduce and eventually stop dumping waste at sea.

Summary of pollution at sea

- Crude oil is spilled into the sea accidentally and also by illegal washing out of oil tanks.
- Oil spillages are a major problem to marine wildlife.

Atomic structure

6

Learning objectives

By the end of this chapter you should be able to:
- **draw** the structure of simple atoms
- **explain** the terms atomic number and mass number
- **describe** isotopes
- **explain** relative atomic mass
- **describe** simple electronic configurations

Atoms are the smallest particles that can be obtained by chemical means. They are too small to see directly – about 100 million laid side to side would measure 1 cm. Atoms are measured in nanometres – one nanometre is 1×10^{-9} m, or 0.000 000 001 m.

lithium 0.123	beryllium 0.089	boron 0.080	carbon 0.077	nitrogen 0.075	oxygen 0.073	fluorine 0.071	neon 0.160
sodium 0.157	magnesium 0.136	aluminium 0.125	silicon 0.118	phosphorus 0.110	sulphur 0.102	chlorine 0.099	argon 0.190

Figure 1 Atomic radii (in nanometres) and relative sizes of some atoms.

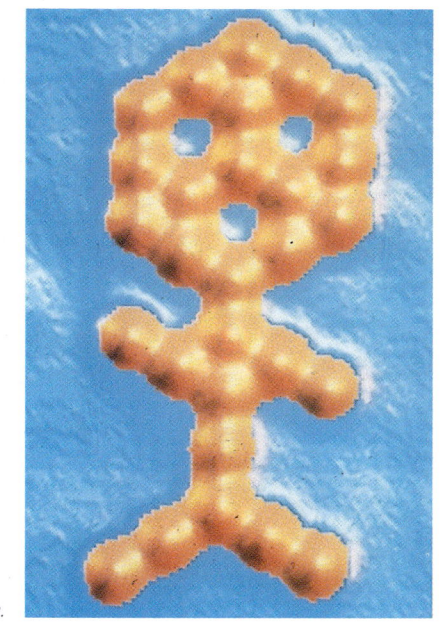

A company logo picked out in the atoms of a surface.

6.1 Inside the atom

What are atoms made of?

Scientists have been able to break atoms down into their constituent sub-atomic particles. Atoms consist of a nucleus, which is made of protons and neutrons (together these are called nucleons). Protons have a positive charge but neutrons have no charge. This gives the nucleus an overall positive charge. Electrons orbit the nucleus in areas called shells. Electrons are negatively charged. An atom contains equal numbers of protons and electrons so their charges cancel each other out. The attraction of the positive nucleus holds the electrons in the atom.

More about atoms

Figure 2 The structure of an atom.

It is difficult to draw the electronic structure of atoms in three dimensions, so throughout the book they will be shown more simply, like this

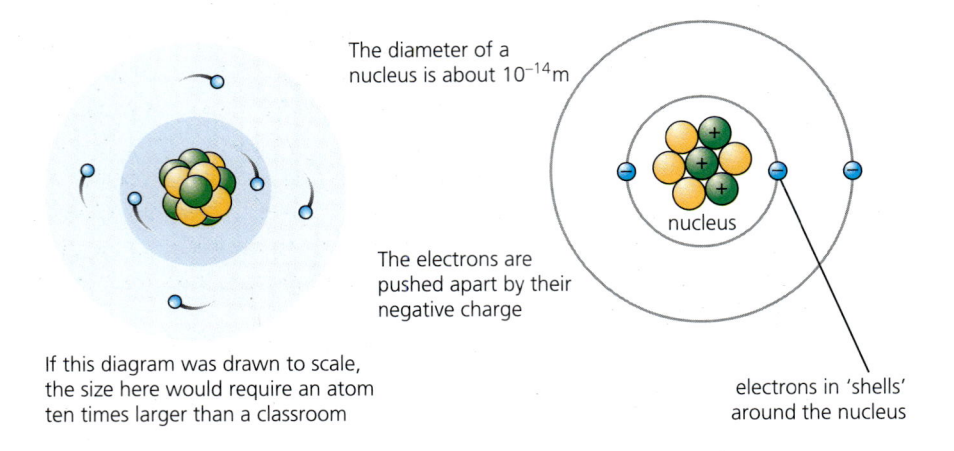

The diameter of a nucleus is about 10^{-14} m

The electrons are pushed apart by their negative charge

If this diagram was drawn to scale, the size here would require an atom ten times larger than a classroom

nucleus

electrons in 'shells' around the nucleus

These sub-atomic particles are extremely small, but they do have mass – although it is very small. For example, the mass of a proton is about 1.67×10^{-27} kg. A neutron has almost the same mass as a proton, but electrons are so light we consider their mass negligible. Nearly all the mass of an atom is therefore concentrated in the nucleus.

The mass of sub-atomic particles is usually quoted in relative units, with protons and neutrons being given relative masses of 1.

Table 1 Mass and charge of sub-atomic particles

Particle	Relative charge	Relative mass (units)
proton	+1	1
neutron	0	1
electron	−1	negligible

The masses of atoms and their particles are measured in atomic mass units. 1 unit = 1.661×10^{-27} kg.

1 Where in the atom do you find most of its mass?

2 a Which particles are found in the nucleus?
   b Why do you think electrons are often referred to as having negligible mass?
   c Explain why atoms have no overall charge.

Atomic structure

What makes chemicals different?

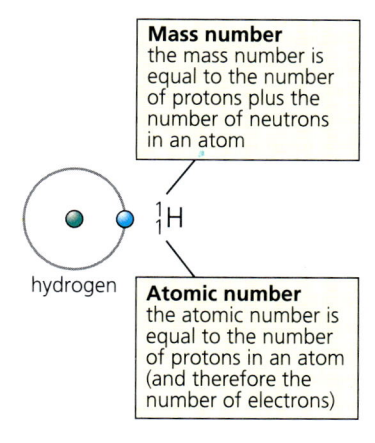

Mass number
the mass number is equal to the number of protons plus the number of neutrons in an atom

^1_1H

hydrogen

Atomic number
the atomic number is equal to the number of protons in an atom (and therefore the number of electrons)

^4_2He

helium

^7_3Li

lithium

Figure 3 Atomic number and mass number.

We now know of 109 different sorts of atom, each one having its own unique arrangement of protons, neutrons and electrons.

The number of protons in an atom is called the **atomic number**. Each element has a different atomic number. The atoms of different elements also have different numbers of electrons arranged around the nucleus. Electron arrangement affects how the atoms combine together and how elements behave in chemical reactions. The number of neutrons in a nucleus can vary and there is no easy way to predict exactly how many neutrons will be present.

Each atom is also given a **mass number**, which is equal to the sum of the number of protons and neutrons in the atom. The relative mass of various atoms can be compared using their mass numbers.

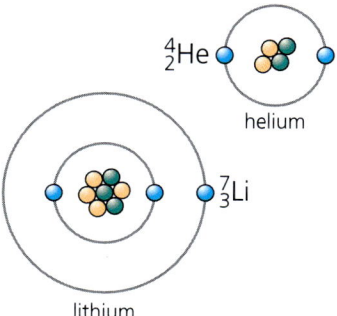

3 Copy out and complete the following table.

Element	Symbol	Atomic number	Mass number	Number of protons	Number of neutrons
carbon	$^{12}_6C$	?	?	6	?
chlorine	$^{35}_{17}Cl$	?	?	?	18
nitrogen	$^{14}_7N$	?	14	?	?
uranium	$^{238}_{92}U$	92	?	?	?

Summary of inside the atom

- An atom is the smallest particle that can be obtained by chemical means.
- Atoms are composed of a central nucleus, containing protons and neutrons. The nucleus is surrounded by electrons.
- Protons have a positive charge, electrons have a negative charge and neutrons are electrically neutral.
- An atom contains the same number of protons as electrons, so overall its electrical charge is zero.
- The atomic number is the number of protons in an atom.
- The mass number of an atom is the total number of protons and neutrons.

More about atoms

6.2 Comparing atoms
Are all the atoms in an element identical?

Some elements contain atoms with differing masses. This is because they contain different numbers of neutrons, although all the atoms of a particular element contain the same number of protons. Atoms of the same element which have the same number of protons but different numbers of neutrons are called **isotopes**. They behave in the same way in chemical reactions but they have a different mass.

Figure 4 Isotopes of carbon.

	Number of protons	Number of neutrons	Number of electrons	Written
carbon–12	6	6	6	$^{12}_{6}C$
carbon–13	6	7	6	$^{13}_{6}C$
carbon–14	6	8	6	$^{14}_{6}C$

Symbols are used to represent all the information about various isotopes in a short-hand way – as you can see in figure 5.

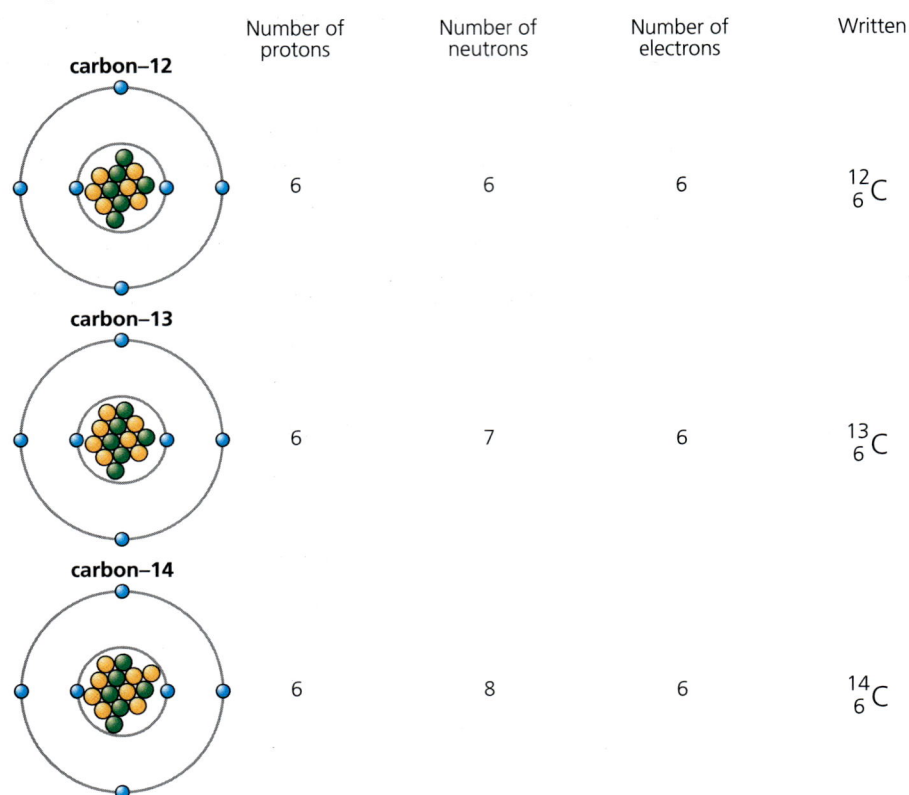

Figure 5 Chlorine has two isotopes – chlorine-35 and chlorine-37.

chlorine-35 $\quad$ chlorine-37

$^{35}_{17}Cl \qquad ^{37}_{17}Cl$

mass number = number of protons + neutrons

atomic number = number of protons

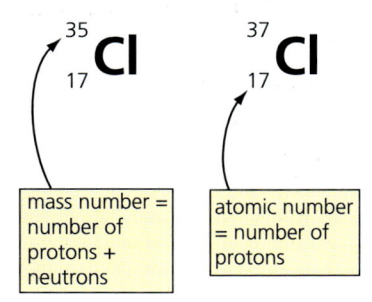

4 Copy and complete the table below for the isotopes of hydrogen.

Isotope	Atomic number	Mass number	Number of neutrons
hydrogen	1	1	?
deuterium	?	2	1
tritium	1	?	2

5 Suggest a reason why water which contains a lot of deuterium atoms is often called 'heavy water'.

6 The element chlorine consists of two isotopes: chlorine-35 and chlorine-37. How many protons and neutrons are there in the nucleus of each of these isotopes?

Atomic structure

What is relative atomic mass?

The actual mass of atoms is very small indeed – for example a single atom of oxygen has a mass of

0.000 000 000 000 000 000 000 015 057 049 g!

It would therefore be impractical to use the actual mass of atoms in chemical calculations – the average calculator would simply run out of digits! To make calculations simpler, all atoms are compared with the mass of an atom of carbon-12 and given a **relative atomic mass**. This is the average mass of an atom of that element compared with one-twelfth the mass of an atom of carbon-12. The relative atomic mass is given the symbol A_r. Note that, since these values are relative numbers, they do not have any units.

A full table of relative atomic mass values appears at the back of this book, but to explain the concept further the values for the first ten elements are given in table 2.

Table 2 Relative atomic mass values for the first ten elements in the periodic table

Atomic number	Name	Symbol	Relative atomic mass (A_r)
1	hydrogen	H	1.0
2	helium	He	4.0
3	lithium	Li	6.9
4	beryllium	Be	9.0
5	boron	B	10.8
6	carbon	C	12.0
7	nitrogen	N	14.0
8	oxygen	O	16.0
9	fluorine	F	19.0
10	neon	Ne	20.2

How is relative atomic mass calculated?

You will see from table 2 that many of the values for relative atomic mass are not whole numbers. This is because many elements consist of a mixture of isotopes.

For example, chlorine has a relative atomic mass of 35.5 because it exists as a mixture of 75% – chlorine-35 and 25% chlorine-37. This can be calculated as follows:

$$\text{relative mass of each isotope} \quad \underset{26.25}{\underbrace{\left(\frac{75 \times 35}{100}\right)}_{\text{chlorine-35}}} \quad + \quad \underset{9.25}{\underbrace{\left(\frac{25 \times 37}{100}\right)}_{\text{chlorine-37}}}$$

relative atomic mass = 35.5

More about atoms

7 Find out:
  a The relative atomic mass of mercury.
  b An atom which has twice the mass of calcium.
  c An atom which has twice the mass of oxygen.
8 How can you tell from an atom's relative atomic mass whether it has isotopes?

How are electrons arranged in an atom?

As the number of protons increases the number of negatively charged electrons also increases. The electrons orbit the nucleus in a series of cloud-like 'shells'. Each shell is larger and can hold more electrons than the one inside it. Electrons will fill up one shell before going into the next one.

Shell 1	can hold up to	2 electrons
Shell 2	can hold up to	8 electrons
Shell 3	can hold up to	18 electrons, although it becomes quite stable once it contains 8 electons

The arrangement of electrons in a particular atom is known as its electronic configuration. The electronic configurations for some elements are shown in figure 6.

Figure 6

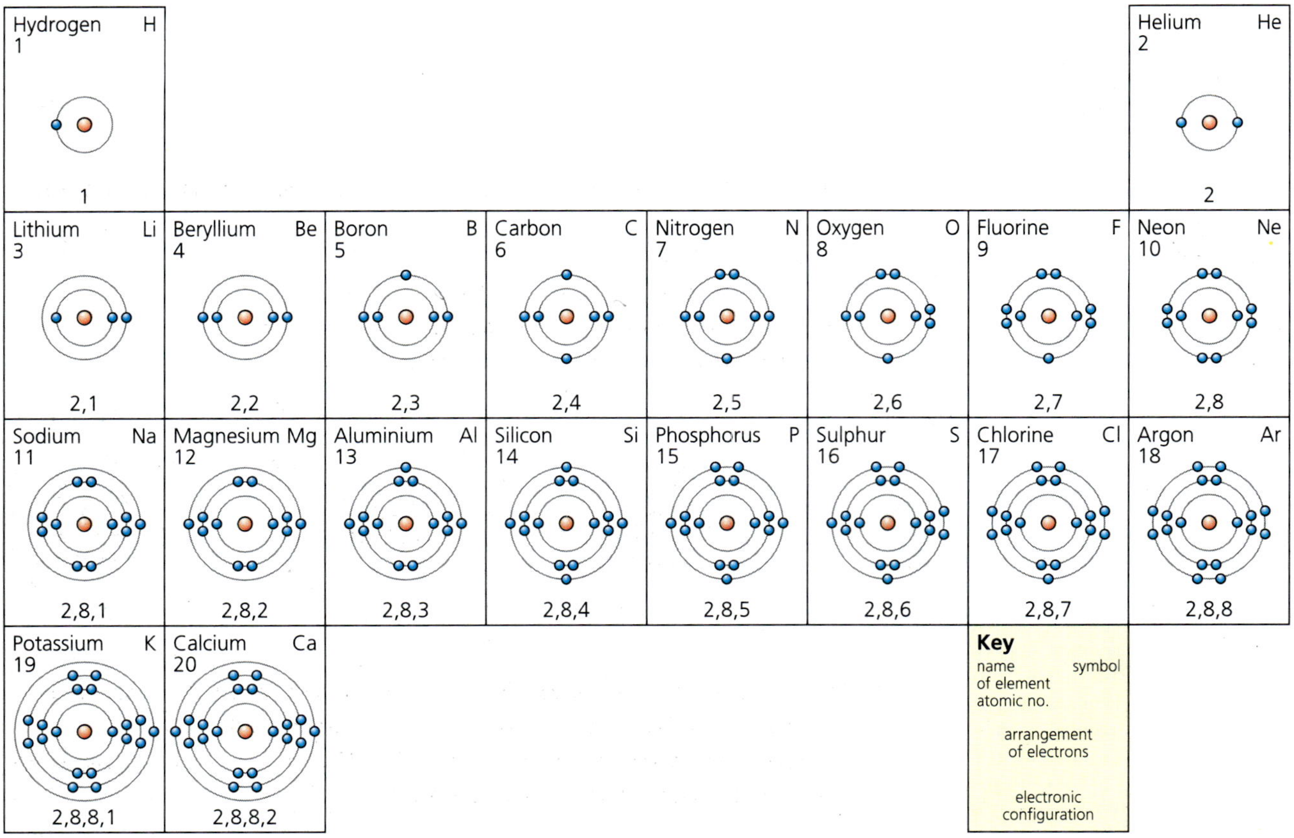

Hydrogen H 1 — 1							Helium He 2 — 2
Lithium Li 3 — 2,1	Beryllium Be 4 — 2,2	Boron B 5 — 2,3	Carbon C 6 — 2,4	Nitrogen N 7 — 2,5	Oxygen O 8 — 2,6	Fluorine F 9 — 2,7	Neon Ne 10 — 2,8
Sodium Na 11 — 2,8,1	Magnesium Mg 12 — 2,8,2	Aluminium Al 13 — 2,8,3	Silicon Si 14 — 2,8,4	Phosphorus P 15 — 2,8,5	Sulphur S 16 — 2,8,6	Chlorine Cl 17 — 2,8,7	Argon Ar 18 — 2,8,8
Potassium K 19 — 2,8,8,1	Calcium Ca 20 — 2,8,8,2						

Key
name — symbol
of element
atomic no.
arrangement of electrons
electronic configuration

Atomic structure

9 The electronic configurations of various elements are given in the table below. For each one, draw a diagram to show the arrangement of electrons in shells around the central nucleus.

Element	Symbol	Electronic configuration
helium	He	2
carbon	C	2, 4
neon	Ne	2, 8
potassium	K	2, 8, 8, 1

10 Give the symbols for the elements with the following electronic configurations:
   a 2, 1   **b** 2, 7   **c** 2, 8, 1   **d** 2, 8, 8   **e** 2, 8, 8, 1

Summary of comparing atoms

- All atoms of a particular element have the same number of protons.
- Isotopes are atoms of the same element that have a different number of neutrons. They have the same atomic number but different mass numbers.
- The carbon-12 scale is used to compare the mass of all atoms with carbon-12. It is a relative scale and so has no units.
- The relative atomic mass (A_r) is the average mass of an atom compared with one-twelfth the mass of one atom of carbon-12.
- Electrons are arranged around the nucleus of an atom in a series of shells.
- The electronic configuration of an atom shows the number of electrons present in each shell.

Examination style questions

1 Look at figure 7 and answer the following questions, making use of the information in the tables throughout this chapter:
   a What element does atom A represent?
   b What is the electronic configuration of atom B?
   c How many electrons should be shown in atom C?
   d How many protons should be present in the nucleus of atom D?

Figure 7

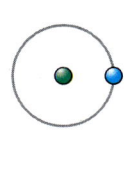

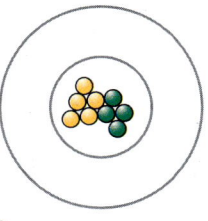

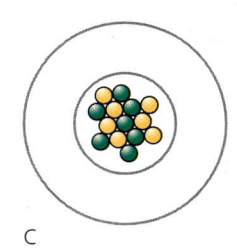

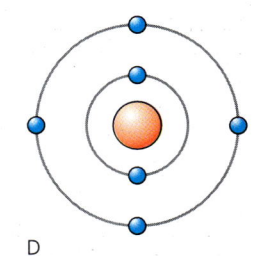

A   B   C   D

2 The element bromine (atomic number 35) consists of two isotopes, bromine-79 and bromine-81.
   a List the numbers of each sub-atomic particle in each of these two isotopes.
   b Bromine consists of approximately 50% bromine-79 and 50% bromine-81. Use this information to calculate the average relative atomic mass of bromine.

87

The periodic table

7

Learning objectives
By the end of this chapter you should be able to:
- **outline** the history of the modern periodic table
- **recall** how elements are arranged in the periodic table
- **define** groups and periods
- **describe** the positions of metals and non-metals in the periodic table
- **connect** the electronic configuration of an atom to its position in the periodic table

7.1 Introducing the periodic table

People have known about and studied the properties of elements that are found naturally in the Earth's crust (such as gold or copper) for thousands of years. As they learned to extract more elements from their compounds further elements were discovered. By the middle of the nineteenth century over 60 elements were known. Scientists began to look for a logical way to classify them.

How was the periodic table developed?

In 1864, a British chemist called John **Newlands** tried to arrange the elements in order of their relative atomic masses. When he did this, he discovered that elements with similar properties 'periodically' occurred – this gave rise to the name 'periodic table'. However, several elements did not fit into Newlands' arrangement of elements, and his ideas were not widely accepted.

A few years later, in 1869, a Russian chemist called Dmitri **Mendeleev** looked again at the way elements could be arranged.

Mendeleev arranged the known elements in order of atomic mass, with the atoms with the lowest mass first, and put them into groups with similar physical and chemical properties. He insisted that his table should be arranged to show repeating patterns or **'periodicity'**, which meant that gaps had to be left for, as yet, undiscovered elements.

Mendeleev used his ideas to predict the existence of an element which had not yet been discovered. He suggested that this element would appear in the table between silicon and tin and called it 'eka-silicon', which means 'below silicon'. He described the appearance of eka-silicon, its relative atomic mass and some of its physical and chemical properties. Roughly 15 years later, the element germanium was discovered, and was found to have almost exactly the properties that Mendeleev had predicted.

Dmitri Mendeleev was born in Siberia in 1834. He was a brilliant chemist and teacher. Mendeleev's arrangement of elements formed the basis of the modern periodic table.

The periodic table

Row	Group I --- R_2O	Group II --- RO	Group III --- R_2O_3	Group IV RH_4 RO_2	Group V RH_3 R_2O_5	Group VI RH_2 RO_3	Group VII RH R_2O_7	Group VIII --- RO_4
1	H = 1							
2	Li = 7	Be = 9.4	B = 11	C = 12	N = 14	O = 16	F = 19	
3	Na = 23	Mg = 24	Al = 27.3	Si = 28	P = 31	S = 32	Cl = 35.5	
4	K = 39	Ca = 40	-- = 44	Ti = 48	V = 51	Cr = 52	Mn = 55	Fe = 56, Co = 59, Ni = 59, Cu' = 63
5	(Cu = 63)	Zn = 65	-- = 68	-- = 72	As = 75	Se = 78	Br = 80	
6	Rb = 85	Sr = 87	?Yt = 88	Zr = 90	Nb = 94	Mo = 96	-- = 100	Ru = 104, Rh = 104, Pd = 106, Ag = 108
7	(Ag = 108)	Cd = 112	In = 113	Sn = 118	Sb = 122	Te = 125	I = 127	
8	Cs = 133	Ba = 137	?Di = 138	?Ce = 140	--	--	--	----

Figure 1 Part of Mendeleev's original periodic table of 1871.

The periodic table that is used today is based on the ideas of Mendeleev. In the modern periodic table, the elements are arranged in order of atomic number rather than atomic mass.

Figure 2 Mendeleev's ideas about periodicity.

1. The elements, if arranged according to their atomic weights, exhibit an evident periodicity of properties.
2. Elements which are similar as regards their chemical properties have atomic weights which are either of nearly the same value (e.g. platinum, iridium, osmium) or which increase regularly (e.g. potassium, rubidium, caesium).
3. The arrangement of the elements, or of groups of elements in order of their atomic weights corresponds to their so-called valencies as well as, to some extent, to their distictive chemical properties – as is apparent among other series in that of lithium, beryllium, boron, carbon, nitrogen, oxygen and fluorine.
4. We must expect the discovery of many yet unknown elements, for example, elements analoguous to aluminium and silicon, whose atomic weight would be between 65 and 75.

Source: Dmitri Mendeleev

How are elements arranged in the periodic table?

Basic information about each element (its name, symbol, atomic number and relative atomic mass) is recorded in a small box, as shown in the example in figure 3.

Illustrating an element

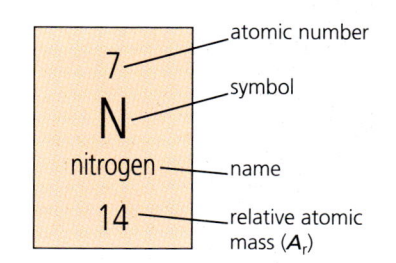

7 — atomic number
N — symbol
nitrogen — name
14 — relative atomic mass (A_r)

Figure 3 In the periodic table, basic information about each element is recorded in small boxes like this one.

More about atoms

1. Give the name and symbol of:
   a. a metal that is solid
   b. a metal that is liquid
   c. a non-metal that is solid
   d. a non-metal that is liquid
   e. a non-metal that is a gas at room temperature and pressure.
2. When elements are arranged in order of their atomic numbers, there are several places in the periodic table where the relative atomic mass does not show a similar regular increase. Can you find two places where the relative atomic mass decreases while the atomic number goes up? Can you suggest a reason for this decrease?

If all this information for each of the 109 known elements was arranged in a long line, from lowest atomic number to highest, it would become unmanageable. We know that elements with similar properties appear at intervals, or 'periodically', and by cutting up this imaginary line, elements with similar properties can be grouped together. This gives us the basic shape of the periodic table we use today.

Classifying elements

1 H hydrogen 1							2 He helium 4
3 Li lithium 7	4 Be beryllium 9	5 B boron 11	6 C carbon 12	7 N nitrogen 14	8 O oxygen 16	9 F fluorine 19	10 Ne neon 20
11 Na sodium 23	12 Mg magnesium 24	13 Al aluminium 27	14 Si silicon 28	15 P phosphorus 31	16 S sulphur 32	17 Cl chlorine 35.5	18 Ar argon 40
19 K potassium 39							

Figure 4 If the elements are arranged in a long line, and the line cut up into groups of elements with similar properties, we obtain the basic shape of the modern periodic table.

3. Give the names and symbols of the elements in Period 3.
4. Give the names and symbols of the elements in group VII.

Periods

The horizontal rows of elements in the table are known as **periods**. There are seven periods in all.

Groups

The vertical columns in the periodic table are divided into eight **groups**. The elements in each group have similar properties. In the simplest versions of the periodic table, the central block of metals – the transition metals – is not divided into groups. Transition metals have many similar properties and they are usually studied as a block.

The periodic table

Figure 5 The periodic table.

Periodic table of the elements

Groups	I	II												III	IV	V	VI	VII	0
Periods																			
1	1 H hydrogen 1																		2 He helium 4
2	3 Li lithium 7	4 Be beryllium 9												5 B boron 11	6 C carbon 12	7 N nitrogen 14	8 O oxygen 16	9 F fluorine 19	10 Ne neon 20
3	11 Na sodium 23	12 Mg magnesium 24												13 Al aluminium 27	14 Si silicon 28	15 P phosphorus 31	16 S sulphur 32	17 Cl chlorine 35.5	18 Ar argon 40
4	19 K potassium 39	20 Ca calcium 40	21 Sc scandium 45	22 Ti titanium 48	23 V vanadium 51	24 Cr chromium 52	25 Mn manganese 55	26 Fe iron 56	27 Co cobalt 59	28 Ni nickel 59	29 Cu copper 64	30 Zn zinc 65		31 Ga gallium 70	32 Ge germanium 73	33 As arsenic 75	34 Se selenium 79	35 Br bromine 80	36 Kr krypton 84
5	37 Rb rubidium 85.5	38 Sr strontium 88	39 Y yttrium 89	40 Zr zirconium 91	41 Nb niobium 93	42 Mo molybdenum 96	43 Tc technetium 98	44 Ru ruthenium 101	45 Rh rhodium 103	46 Pd palladium 106	47 Ag silver 108	48 Cd cadmium 112		49 In indium 115	50 Sn tin 119	51 Sb antimony 122	52 Te tellurium 128	53 I iodine 127	54 Xe xenon 131
6	55 Cs caesium 133	56 Ba barium 137	57 La lanthanum 139	72 Hf hafnium 178.5	73 Ta tantalum 181	74 W tungsten 184	75 Re rhenium 186	76 Os osmium 190	77 Ir iridium 192	78 Pt platinum 195	79 Au gold 197	80 Hg mercury 201		81 Tl thallium 204	82 Pb lead 207	83 Bi bismuth 209	84 Po polonium 210	85 At astatine 210	86 Rn radon 222
7	87 Fr francium 223	88 Ra radium 226	89 Ac actinium 227	104 Db dubnium 261	105 Jl joliotium 262	106 Rf rutherfordium	107 Bh bohrium	108 Hn hahnium	109 Mt meitnerium										

58 Ce cerium 140	59 Pr praseodymium 141	60 Nd neodymium 144	61 Pm promethium 147	62 Sm samarium 150	63 Eu europium 152	64 Gd gadolinium 157	65 Tb terbium 159	66 Dy dysprosium 162.5	67 Ho holmium 165	68 Er erbium 167	69 Tm thulium 169	70 Yb ytterbium 173	71 Lu lutetium 175
90 Th thorium 232	91 Pa protactinium 231	92 U uranium 238	93 Np neptunium 237	94 Pu plutonium 242	95 Am americium 243	96 Cm curium 247	97 Bk berkelium 247	98 Cf californium 251	99 Es einsteinium 254	100 Fm fermium 253	101 Md mendelevium 256	102 No nobelium 254	103 Lr lawrencium 257

Key:
- atomic no.
- symbol
- name
- relative atomic mass

metal / non-metal

The lines of elements going across are called **periods**
There are seven periods in the table

The columns of elements going down are called **groups**
Elements in the same group usually have similar properties

Summary of introducing the periodic table

- Elements in the periodic table are arranged in ascending atomic number order.
- The periodic table is so-called because 'periodically' elements occur with similar properties.
- The modern form of the periodic table was suggested by Dmitri Mendeleev.
- A group is a vertical column of elements with similar properties.
- A period is a horizontal row of elements.

7.2 The periodic table and atomic structure

Elements are arranged in the periodic table in **atomic number** order. An element's position in the table is related to the arrangement of sub-atomic particles in its atoms.

The arrangement of electrons in an atom determines its chemical properties. When elements or compounds react the arrangement of electrons around each atom is always altered in some way.

Why are the noble gases so unreactive?

The elements in Group 0 (the **'noble'** gases) are all colourless unreactive gases made of isolated single atoms. All the noble gases have eight electrons in their outer shell (look back at Chapter 6, *Atomic structure*, if you need reminding about electron shells).

Table 1 Electronic configuration of Group 0 elements

Name	Symbol	Electronic configuration
helium	He	2
neon	Ne	2, 8
argon	Ar	2, 8, 8
krypton	Kr	2, 8, 18, 8
xenon	Xe	2, 8, 18, 18, 8

There is a special stability associated with this arrangement of electron shells, which makes atoms with this arrangement very unreactive.

5 Write out the electronic configuration of the element argon. Use this electronic configuration to explain why argon is useful in light bulbs.

The periodic table

How are the properties of the Group I elements related to their electronic configuration?

The elements in Group I are called the **alkali metals**. All elements in Group I have only one electron in their outer shell. This electron is easily lost in chemical reactions, which means that the elements in Group I are very reactive.

Table 2 Electronic configuration of Group I elements

Name	Symbol	Electronic configuration
lithium	Li	2, 1
sodium	Na	2, 8, 1
potassium	K	2, 8, 8, 1
rubidium	Rb	2, 8, 18, 1
caesium	Cs	2, 8, 18, 18, 1

6 Group I elements include the metals lithium, sodium and potassium.
  a What feature in their electronic configuration do these elements have in common?
  b How do these electron arrangements explain the fact that these elements become much more reactive going down the group?

Going down the group, the atoms get larger as successive shells of electrons are added and the negatively charged electrons are further away from the positively charged protons in the nucleus. This means that they are held to the atom less strongly and can escape more easily.

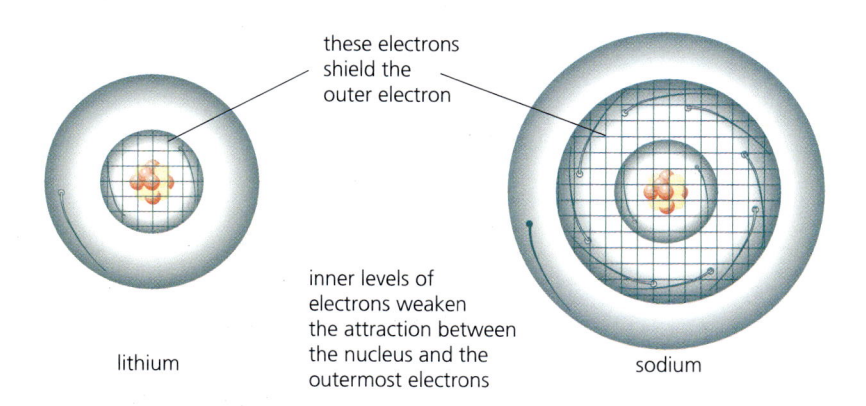

Figure 6 Outer electron shells are shielded from the nucleus by the inner shells.

For this reason the metals become increasingly more reactive further down the group. When these metals react they lose the single electron in their outer shell and form positively charged ions.

More about atoms

How does the configuration of Group VII elements affect their properties?

The non-metallic elements in Group VII are known as the **halogens**. All the elements in Group VII have seven electrons in their outer shell.

Table 3 *Electronic configuration of Group VII elements*

Name	Symbol	Electronic configuration
fluorine	F	2, 7
chlorine	Cl	2, 8, 7
bromine	Br	2, 8, 18, 7
iodine	I	2, 8, 18, 18, 7

This means that each of these elements is one electron short of a stable full-shell arrangement. When these elements are involved in chemical reactions, they gain an electron from other atoms to acquire a stable full-shell arrangement.

The negatively charged electrons are attracted to the atom by the positively charged nucleus. The smaller the atom the closer the electrons are to the nucleus and the more strongly electrons are attracted to the nucleus. Fluorine is the smallest, and therefore the most reactive, element in Group VII. As we go down the group, more electron shells are added, the atoms get larger and electrons are not attracted as readily. This means that the elements get less reactive going down the group.

How is electronic structure related to periods?

As we go across a period, each successive element gains one proton, one electron and a variable number of neutrons. You can see how this works in figure 7.

Group I	Group II	Group III	Group IV	Group V	Group VI	Group VII	Group 0
Sodium	Magnesium	Aluminium	Silicon	Phosphorus	Sulphur	Chlorine	Argon
2,8,1	2,8,2	2,8,3	2,8,4	2,8,5	2,8,6	2,8,7	2,8,8

The number of electrons in the outer shell is the same as the number of the group

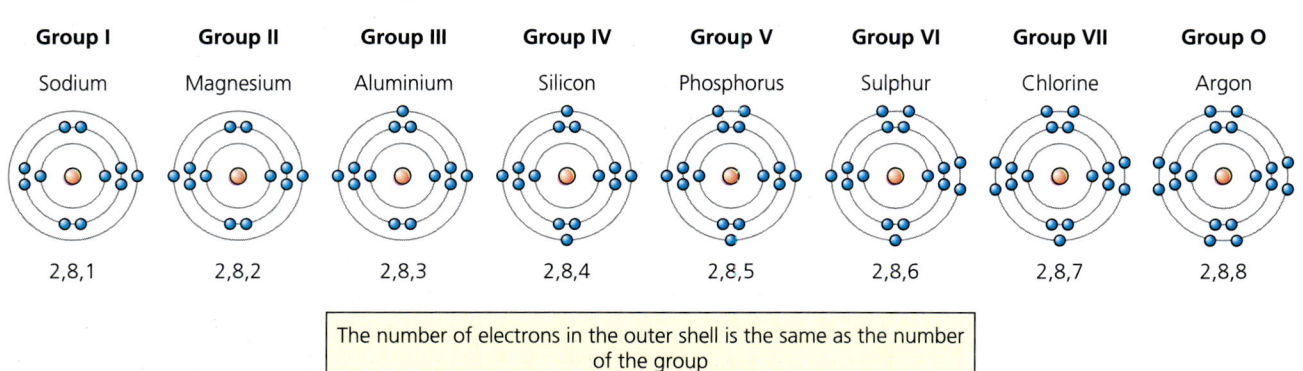

Figure 7 Going across a period, each element gains an electron. This figure shows the electronic configurations for the elements in period 3.

Summary of the periodic table and atomic structure

- All chemical reactions involve a change in the arrangement of electrons around atoms.
- Elements in the same group have the same number of electrons in their outer shell.
- The noble gases (Group 0 elements) all have eight electrons in their outer shell, which makes them especially stable.
- The number of electrons in the outer shell of an atom is the same as the number of the group in which it is found.

Examination style questions

1 Use your knowledge of the periodic table to answer the following questions.
   a Find an element that is in the same period as potassium.
   b Which element has the electron arrangement 2, 8, 4?
   c Name the least reactive element in Group I.
   d Which is the most reactive element in Group VII?
   e Name the element that has a relative atomic mass of 20.
   f Which element has no neutrons?

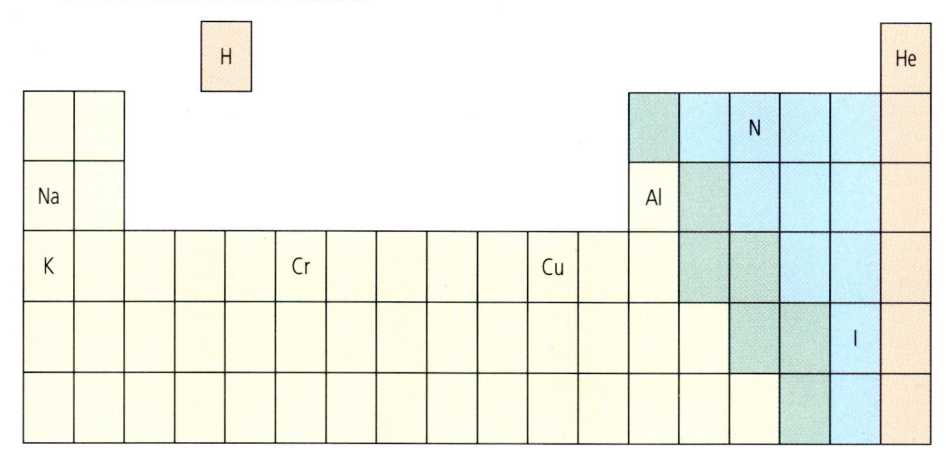

2 Study the periodic table outline given above.
Using only the elements shown in the grid:
   a Write the name and symbol of
   i a metal
   ii a non-metal.
   b Write the name and symbol of two elements in the same group.
   c Write the name and symbol of two metals in the same period.
   d Write the name and symbol of a gas that is not known to form any compounds.
   e Give the name and formulae of two compounds formed by the elements shown on this grid.

Chemical bonding

8

Learning objectives

By the end of this chapter you should be able to:

- **explain** why noble gases exist as isolated single atoms and form few compounds
- **understand** how ionic compounds are formed
- **define** ions and radicals
- **describe** the bonding in sodium chloride
- **relate** the physical properties of ionic compounds to their structure
- **derive** the formulae of ionic compounds from the charges on ions
- **explain** how covalent bonds are formed
- **describe** covalent bonding in simple molecules
- **show** how the forces within molecules are different from the forces between molecules
- **describe** giant structures
- **describe** bonding in metals

Scientists have discovered a total of 109 elements, but relatively few of these occur naturally on Earth. Most elements react with each other to form compounds. Atoms can join together in several different ways. By understanding how the atoms in a substance bond we can understand its properties.

8.1 The noble gases

The noble gases (Group 0 of the periodic table) are unusual because they exist as isolated single atoms. They are very unreactive and form few compounds – only very reactive elements like fluorine can 'force' some noble gases to react and form compounds.

The unreactivity of noble gases can be explained by looking at their electronic configuration.

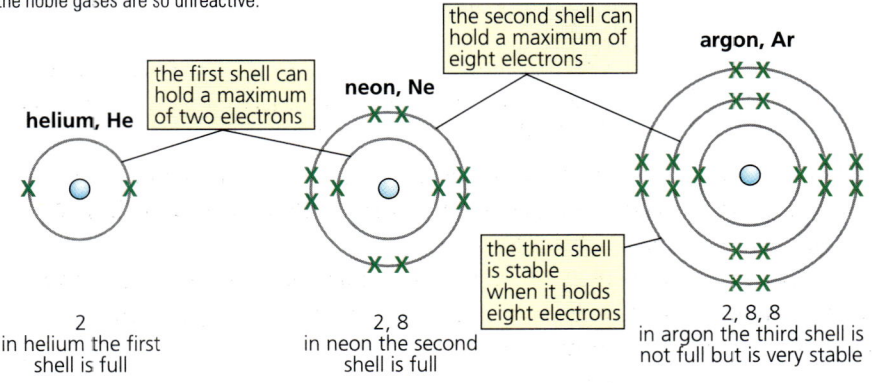

Figure 1 The outer shell of electrons in the noble gases is particularly stable, and joining with other atoms would mean losing this stability. This is why the noble gases are so unreactive.

helium, He — the first shell can hold a maximum of two electrons
2
in helium the first shell is full

neon, Ne — the second shell can hold a maximum of eight electrons
2, 8
in neon the second shell is full

argon, Ar — the third shell is stable when it holds eight electrons
2, 8, 8
in argon the third shell is not full but is very stable

Other elements have partially filled outer electron shells. When atoms join together, they nearly always do so in order to gain a full or stable outer shell of electrons. This usually happens in one of two ways – by transferring electrons from one atom to another or by sharing electrons between atoms.

Chemical bonding

Summary of the noble gases

- The outer electron shell of the noble gases is very stable, making these elements rather unreactive.
- Atoms join together to gain a full or stable outer shell of electrons.

8.2 Ionic bonding

Metallic elements can combine with non-metallic elements by transferring electrons between them – this is called ionic bonding.

How are ionic bonds formed?

By losing an electron a metallic atom gains a stable outer electron shell – and gains a positive charge. The non-metallic atom gains the electron – this helps to make its outer shell more stable and gives it a negative charge in the process. An example of what happens in ionic bonding is shown in figure 2.

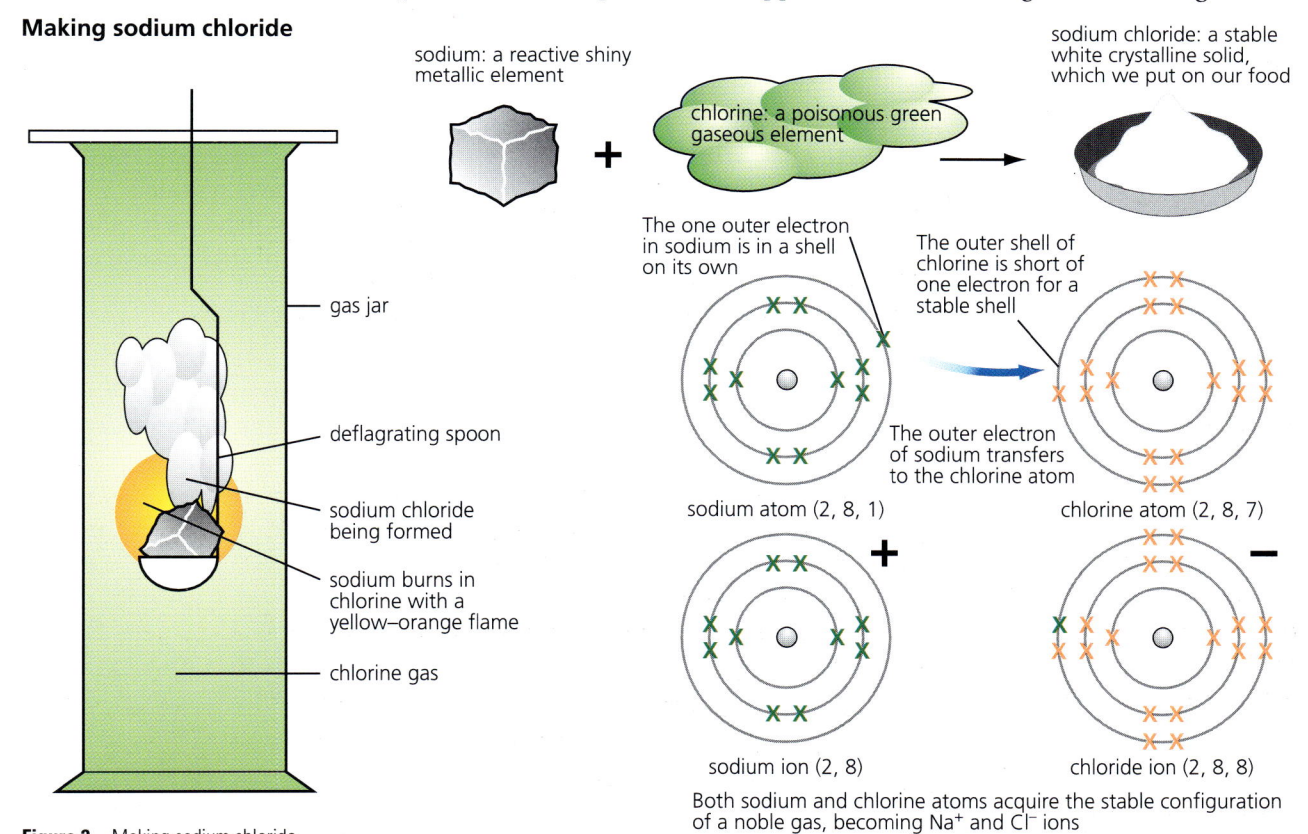

Making sodium chloride

Figure 2 Making sodium chloride.

To signify that a non-metallic atom like chlorine has become an ion the ending of its name is changed. A chlor*ine* atom becomes a chlor*ide* ion, a brom*ine* atom becomes a brom*ide* ion.

The sodium and chloride ions attract each other very strongly because the opposite charges attract. This electrostatic attraction is quite powerful and holds the ions together strongly in a solid structure.

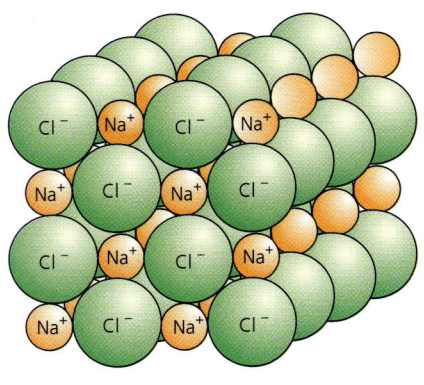

More about atoms

Figure 3 The structure and properties of sodium chloride.

PROPERTIES	EXPLANATION
hard, shiny crystals	ions are packed closely together in a regular arrangement
high melting point	strong electrostatic forces hold the ions together
solid does not conduct electricity	ions and electrons held firmly in place and cannot move to carry current
soluble in water (although this is not true of all ionic compounds – in some the ions are held so strongly together they won't dissolve)	water molecules attract the ions and take them into solution
liquid or aqueous solution conducts electricity	ions are free to move around and carry current

At room temperature and pressure, ions don't exist independently – they are always joined together as solid ionic compounds. For example, you would never find a container of sodium ions – they would always be combined with negative ions such as chloride.

The regular arrangement of ions in an ionic compound is repeated throughout the whole structure. Such an arrangement of particles is called a giant structure. All ionic compounds are made from giant structures of ions.

Which elements form ions?

When ions are formed, atoms lose or gain electrons so as to get a full outer shell of electrons. This is the very stable arrangement found in noble gases.

Figure 4 **Some atoms in period 2**

lithium, Li
atomic number 3

2, 1

Lithium easily loses one electron to form an ion:

$Li \longrightarrow Li^+ + e^-$

All metals lose electrons and form positive ions

carbon, C
atomic number 6

2, 4

Carbon would need to lose or gain four electrons before it would have a stable outer shell and form a stable ion. This needs so much energy it does not usually happen

Some non-metals with partly filled electron shells do not form ions

fluorine, F
atomic number 9

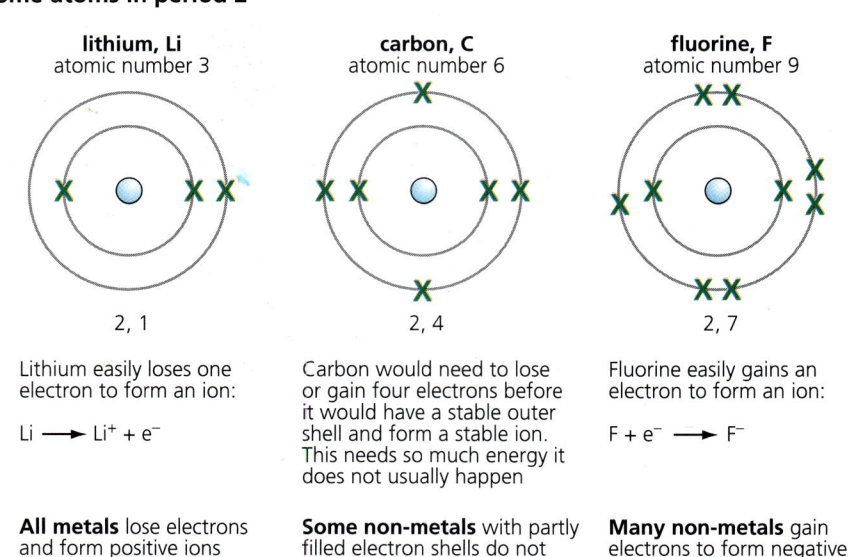

2, 7

Fluorine easily gains an electron to form an ion:

$F + e^- \longrightarrow F^-$

Many non-metals gain electrons to form negative ions

Chemical bonding

How do ions with more than one charge arise?

Some elements, especially the transition metals, can form ions with differing charges depending on the conditions. For example an iron atom can form 2+ or 3+ ions by losing two or three electrons.

Table 1 *Ions with more than one charge*

Name	Symbol	Example
iron (II)	Fe^{2+}	iron (II) chloride ($FeCl_2$)
iron (III)	Fe^{3+}	iron (III) oxide (Fe_2O_3)
copper (I)	Cu^+	copper (I) iodide (CuI)
copper (II)	Cu^{2+}	copper (II) sulphate ($CuSO_4$)

What are radicals?

Small groups of atoms can also gain electrical charge and become ions. Ions formed like this are called radicals.

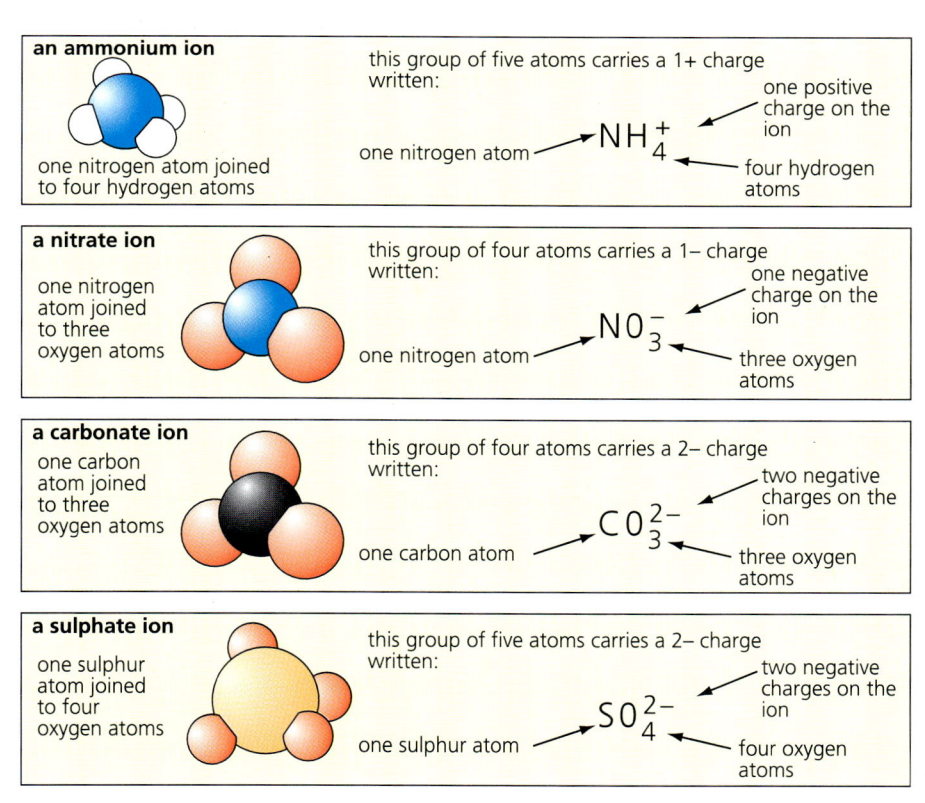

an ammonium ion
one nitrogen atom joined to four hydrogen atoms
this group of five atoms carries a 1+ charge written:
NH_4^+
one nitrogen atom — one positive charge on the ion — four hydrogen atoms

a nitrate ion
one nitrogen atom joined to three oxygen atoms
this group of four atoms carries a 1− charge written:
NO_3^-
one nitrogen atom — one negative charge on the ion — three oxygen atoms

a carbonate ion
one carbon atom joined to three oxygen atoms
this group of four atoms carries a 2− charge written:
CO_3^{2-}
one carbon atom — two negative charges on the ion — three oxygen atoms

a sulphate ion
one sulphur atom joined to four oxygen atoms
this group of five atoms carries a 2− charge written:
SO_4^{2-}
one sulphur atom — two negative charges on the ion — four oxygen atoms

Figure 5 Some common radicals.

More about atoms

Table 2 *The charges on some common ions*

Positively charged ions (mostly metals)

1+	2+	3+
lithium, Li^+	magnesium, Mg^{2+}	aluminium, Al^{3+}
sodium, Na^+	calcium, Ca^{2+}	chromium, Cr^{3+}
potassium, K^+	barium, Ba^{2+}	iron (III), Fe^{3+}
silver, Ag^+	zinc, Zn^{2+}	few 3+ ions exist as they are hard to form
copper (I), Cu^+	lead, Pb^{2+}	
mercury (I), Hg^+	copper (II), Cu^{2+}	
hydrogen, H^+	iron (II), Fe^{2+}	
ammonium, NH_4^+	mercury (II), Hg^{2+}	

(a few 4+ ions exist, but they are very hard to form)

Negatively charged ions (non-metals and most radicals)

1−	2−	3−
fluoride, F^-	oxide, O^{2-}	nitride N^{3-}
chloride, Cl^-	sulphide, S^{2-}	phosphate PO_4^{3-}
bromide, Br^-	carbonate, CO_3^{2-}	few 3− ions exist as they are hard to form
iodide, I^-	sulphate, SO_4^{2-}	
hydroxide, OH^-	chromate, CrO_4^{2-}	
nitrate, NO_3^-	dichromate, $Cr_2O_7^{2-}$	
hydrogencarbonate, HCO_3^-		

How is the formula of an ionic compound worked out?

When writing the formula of an ionic compound it is important to make sure that the electrical charges are in balance. The total positive charge present must be balanced by an equal negative charge.

For example, when sodium chloride forms:

one sodium ion	combines with	one chlorine ion	to form	sodium chloride
Na^+	+	Cl^-	→	NaCl
1 positive charge	+	1 negative charge	→	no overall charge

In calcium chloride, calcium has two positive charges and needs two chloride ions to balance it:

one calcium ion	combines with	two chloride ions	to form	calcium chloride
Ca^{2+}	+	$Cl^- Cl^-$	→	$CaCl_2$
2 positive charges	+	2×1 negative charge	→	no overall charge

Note that when the formula of an ionic compound is written down, the positive ion is usually written first and the negative ion second.

Chemical bonding

Write the two ions involved side by side:

magnesium ion   bromide ion
    Mg^{2+} Br^{1-}

Take the number of the charge diagonally opposite like this:

$Mg^{2+} \searrow Br^{1-} \rightarrow Mg_1Br_2$ or $MgBr_2$

Other examples:
aluminium oxide:
$Al^{3+} \searrow O^{2-} \rightarrow Al_2O_3$

copper (II) nitrate:
$Cu^{2+} \searrow NO_3^{1-} \rightarrow Cu(NO_3)_2$

calcium oxide:
$Ca^{2+} \searrow O^{2-} \rightarrow Ca_2O_2$
– this is then written CaO

Figure 6 A short cut to finding the formula of an ionic compound.

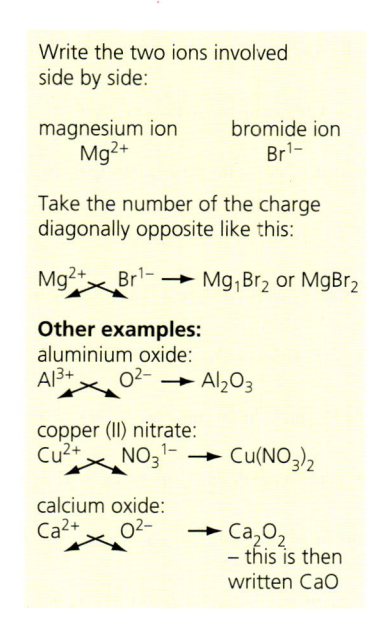

More care is needed when writing the formula of a compound that contains a radical. For example, in sodium nitrate

one sodium ion	combines with	one nitrate ion	to form	sodium nitrate
Na^+	+	NO_3^-	→	$NaNO_3$
1 positive charge	+	1 negative charge	→	no overall charge

When calcium nitrate is formed, the calcium ion needs two nitrate ions to balance the electrical charge. To show this in the formula, the nitrate ion is shown in brackets:

one calcium ion	combines with	two nitrate ions	to form	calcium nitrate
Ca^{2+}	+	$NO_3^- NO_3^-$	→	$Ca(NO_3)_2$
1 positive charge	+	2×1 negative charge	→	no overall charge

the number outside the brackets shows how many nitrate ions are present

Summary of ionic bonding

- An ion is an atom or group of atoms with an electrical charge.
- Metals usually form positive ions, non-metals negative ions.
- Ionic compounds are formed by electron transfer.
- Ionic compounds have distinct physical properties which can be explained by their structure.
- In the formula of an ionic compound the positive charges must balance the negative charges.

1. Write down the names of the ionic compounds that are represented by the following formulae:
   - **a** ZnO
   - **b** $CaCl_2$
   - **c** Al_2O_3
   - **d** K_2SO_4
   - **e** $FeBr_3$
   - **f** NH_4I
   - **g** $MgCO_3$
   - **h** NH_4NO_3
   - **i** $Cu(NO_3)_2$
   - **j** Fe_2O_3

2. Work out the formulae of the following ionic compounds:
   - **a** potassium iodide
   - **b** calcium carbonate
   - **c** ammonium chloride
   - **d** sodium nitrate
   - **e** iron (II) fluoride
   - **f** chromium oxide
   - **g** silver oxide
   - **h** zinc sulphate
   - **i** barium chromate
   - **j** iron (III) phosphate.

More about atoms

3 Work out the formulae of the following ionic compounds:
   a ammonium sulphate
   b ammonium dichromate
   c iron (III) nitrate
   d copper (I) sulphate
   e aluminium nitrate
   f calcium hydroxide
   g magnesium hydrogencarbonate
   h potassium chromate
   i chromium nitrate
   j lead nitrate.

4 The table below gives some information about five substances, two of which are known to be ionic compounds.

Substance	Melting point (°C)	Boiling point (°C)	Conductivity solid	Conductivity liquid	Conductivity aqueous solution
A	0	100	no	no	no
B	801	1467	no	yes	yes
C	−77	−33	no	no	yes
D	407	862	no	yes	insoluble
E	1083	2595	yes	yes	insoluble

Which two letters represent these ionic compounds? Give reasons for your answers.

5 Study the following table:

Substance	Number of protons	Number of neutrons	Number of electrons
A	9	10	10
B	12	12	12
C	19	20	18
D	6	8	6

   a Which is a positive ion?
   b Which is a negative ion?
   c Which is a metal atom?
   d Which letter represents an isotope of $^{12}_{6}C$?

8.3 Covalent bonding

Another important way atoms join together is by forming covalent bonds. A covalent bond is formed when non-metal atoms share electrons.

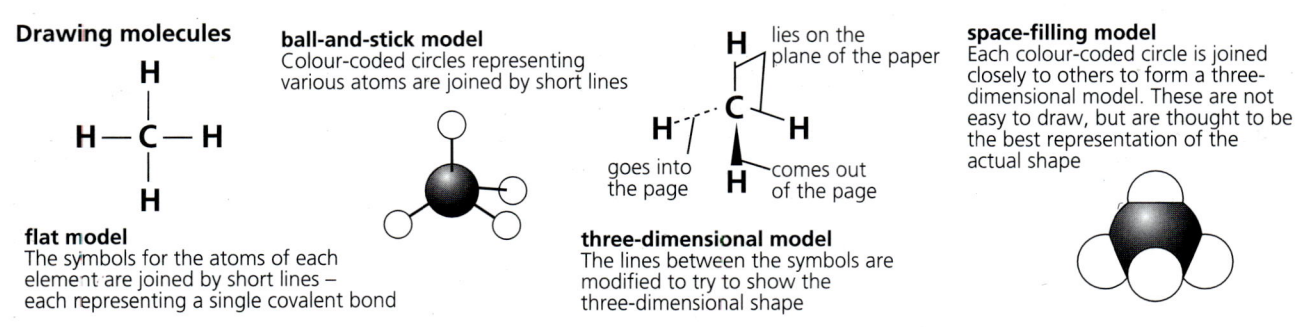

Drawing molecules

flat model
The symbols for the atoms of each element are joined by short lines – each representing a single covalent bond

ball-and-stick model
Colour-coded circles representing various atoms are joined by short lines

three-dimensional model
The lines between the symbols are modified to try to show the three-dimensional shape

H lies on the plane of the paper
goes into the page
comes out of the page

space-filling model
Each colour-coded circle is joined closely to others to form a three-dimensional model. These are not easy to draw, but are thought to be the best representation of the actual shape

Figure 7 Models of molecules. The same molecule can be drawn in several different ways.

Chemical bonding

Covalent bonds are found in both elements and compounds. A compound where the atoms are joined by covalent bonds is methane. Methane consists of small molecules where a single carbon atom is joined to four hydrogen atoms with covalent bonds.

hydrogen

each hydrogen atom has one electron occupying the outer electron shell

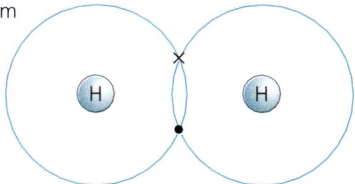

the two electrons are shared between the two atoms, giving the molecule the electronic configuration of helium, a noble gas

The bonding can be shown in a dot–and–cross diagram, in which dots and crosses represent electrons:

H×.H

Dot–and–cross diagrams don't imply that there are two different kinds of electrons. All electrons are identical. They just make it easier to show where the different electrons come from.

chlorine

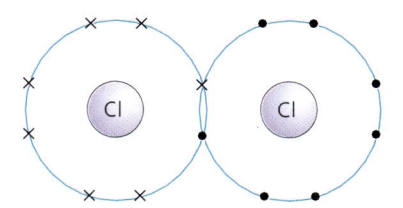

two electrons in the outer shells are shared, giving each atom the configuration of neon, a noble gas (only the electrons in the highest energy level are shown)

Figure 8 Covalent bonding in non-metals.

A single covalent bond is made by sharing one pair of electrons but it is possible for two atoms to share two or even three electron pairs. This leads to multiple covalent bonds.

Single covalent bonds in molecules

methane

Only the electrons in the outer shell are shown

The four 'bonded pairs' of electrons in methane repel each other. This results in the four hydrogens being evenly spread around the central carbon in a tetrahedral shape

water

Figure 9 Covalent bonding in compounds.

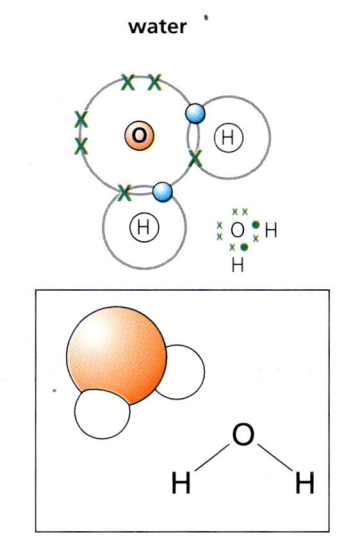

103

More about atoms

Double and triple covalent bonds

carbon dioxide

Four electrons are shared in each covalent bond; two from carbon and two from each oxygen atom. This arrangement is called a double bond

$$O=C=O$$

nitrogen

Six electrons are shared in each bond – three from each atom. This arrangement is called a triple bond. The triple bond in nitrogen is extremely strong

$$N\equiv N$$

Figure 10

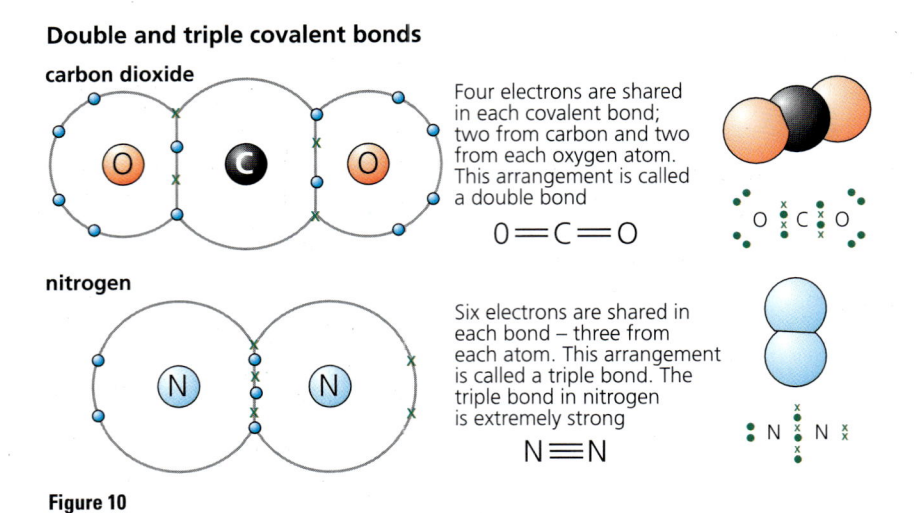

How strong are the covalent bonds between small molecules?

The covalent bonds that hold atoms together within a molecule (the *intra*molecular bonds) are quite strong. When water is boiled in a kettle, the bonds within the molecule stay in place. These strong intramolecular forces stop water decomposing into hydrogen and oxygen when it is boiled. However the *inter*molecular forces (the forces between molecules) are relatively weak and so water can be boiled at a fairly low temperature. Elements and compounds that are made from small molecules all have relatively weak intermolecular forces, which means that they all have fairly low melting and boiling points.

Table 3 *Some small molecules. Elements and compounds made from small molecules are usually gases, or solids and liquids with low melting and boiling points. This is because the intermolecular forces are relatively weak and easily broken*

	Formula	Melting point (°C)	Boiling point (°C)	State at 20°C
Elements:				
hydrogen	H_2	−259	−252	gas
oxygen	O_2	−218	−183	gas
bromine	Br_2	−7	59	liquid
iodine	I_2	114	184	solid
Compounds:				
ammonia	NH_3	−77	−33	gas
hydrogen chloride	HCl	−115	−85	gas
ethanol	C_2H_6O	−117	79	liquid
water	H_2O	0	100	liquid

Chemical bonding

Forces between molecules

hydrogen

Forces between hydrogen molecules are very weak. Hydrogen needs to be cooled down to −252°C before it will condense to form a liquid

melting point −259°C
boiling point −252°C

water

Forces between water molecules are still fairly weak but are stronger than those between hydrogen molecules. This means that water has a higher boiling point than hydrogen

melting point 0°C
boiling point 100°C

iodine

melting point 114°C
boiling point 184°C

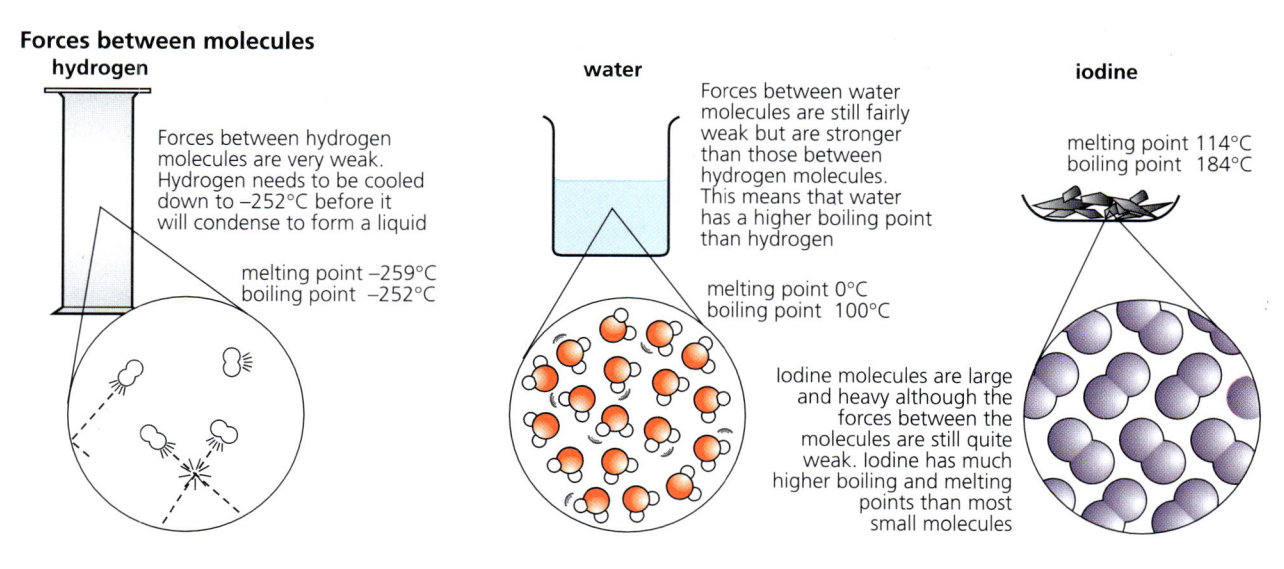

Iodine molecules are large and heavy although the forces between the molecules are still quite weak. Iodine has much higher boiling and melting points than most small molecules

Figure 11 The state of a substance at room temperature depends on the strength of the forces holding the molecules together.

How large can molecules be?

Molecules occur in many different sizes, from as small as two atoms to hundreds or even thousands of atoms. The atoms in large molecules are also joined together by covalent bonds. Such large molecules are nearly always compounds, and because of their size and high relative molar mass, they are always solids at room temperature. Many large molecules are found in plant and animal tissue. For example the cells of all living things contain molecules of DNA, which carry important genetic information (figure 12). Large molecules can also be synthesised for various uses. One example is poly(ethene), which can be used to make plastic bags.

Figure 12 The atoms in large molecules are held together by covalent bonds. Poly(ethene) melts when gently heated and can be rolled into flexible sheets. On its own it is transparent but other substances can be added to it to colour it and make it opaque. One disadvantage is that it is not biodegradable, so careless disposal can cause litter problems.

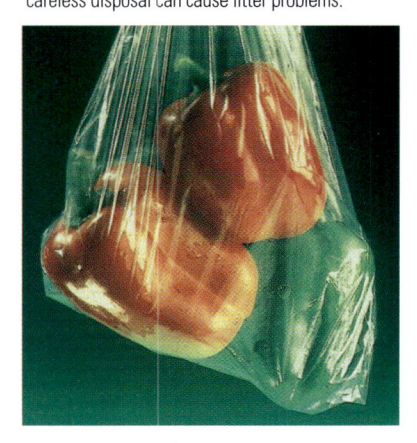

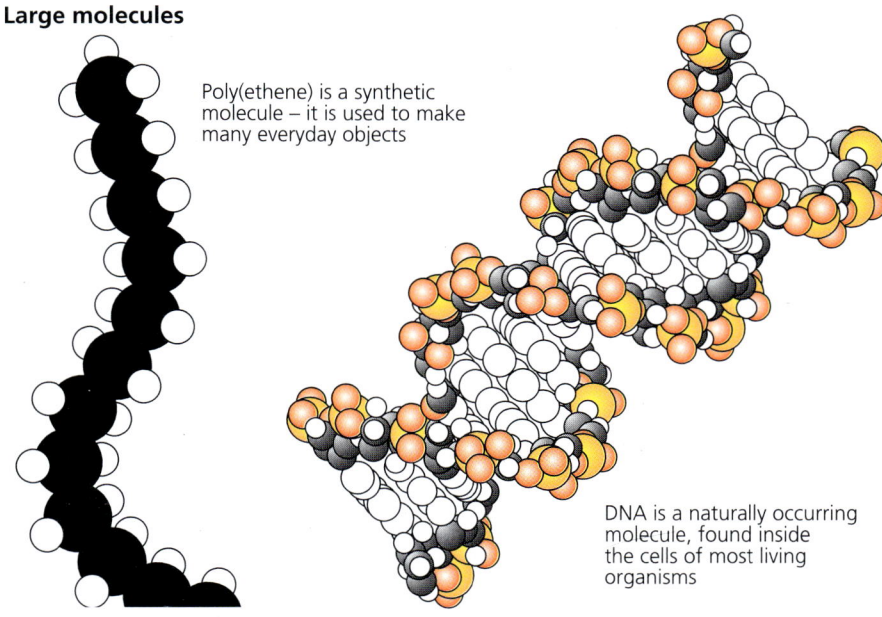

Large molecules

Poly(ethene) is a synthetic molecule – it is used to make many everyday objects

DNA is a naturally occurring molecule, found inside the cells of most living organisms

105

More about atoms

What are giant atomic structures?

When atoms of a non-metallic substance are joined together throughout the whole of the substance by covalent bonds, they can form a giant structure of atoms. Giant atomic structures contain a regular arrangement of atoms that is repeated throughout the structure.

The element carbon can form giant atomic structures, with the atoms bonding to each other in different ways – as diamond, graphite and as buckminster fullerene, for example (figure 13). In all of these structures, carbon atoms are joined throughout the structure by strong covalent bonds. Giant atomic structures can also occur in compounds – for example in silicon dioxide, SiO_2, which is found in sand.

Figure 13

Giant atomic structures

diamond

Every carbon atom bonds to four other carbon atoms

graphite

Flat sheets of carbon atoms are bonded into hexagons

buckminster fullerene

Newly discovered giant structure of carbon containing 60 carbon atoms arranged in hexagons and pentagons

silicon dioxide

Silicon dioxide is a three-dimensional structure of silicon and oxygen atoms joined by covalent bonds

Quartz is a mineral composed of silicon dioxide that vibrates when a small electrical current is passed through it. These vibrations are very fast and consistent, so quartz crystals are used in the construction of accurate clocks and watches.

Chemical bonding

The atoms in a giant structure are very hard to pull apart because the covalent bonds are so strong. This means that these substances have high melting points (for example, graphite melts at 3730°C). Giant atomic structures joined by covalent bonds do not conduct electricity. The reason for this is that outer electrons are 'localised' by forming covalent bonds and none are available to carry a current. The main exception to this is graphite, where some electrons are available to carry the current.

Some atoms in period 3

sodium, Na	silicon, Si	chlorine, Cl
atomic number 11	atomic number 14	atomic number 19
2, 8, 1	2, 8, 4	2, 8, 7
Sodium can easily lose one electron to form a positive ion	Silicon would need to gain or lose four electrons to form an ion. This needs so much energy it does not happen	Chlorine can either gain an electron to form a negative ion or it can share electrons to form a covalent bond
All sodium compounds are ionic – an example is sodium chloride, Na$^+$Cl$^-$	Silicon always forms covalent bonds. An example is silane, SiH$_4$:	Chlorine can form ionic or covalent bonds – examples are potassium chloride (K$^+$Cl$^-$), an ionic compound, and chlorine (Cl$_2$) and hydrogen chloride (HCl), molecules containing covalent bonds
All metals can form positively charged ions. Only a few metals can share electrons to form covalent bonds	Non-metals with partly filled electron shells usually form covalent bonds	Non-metal atoms with nearly full electron shells form either negative ions or covalent bonds

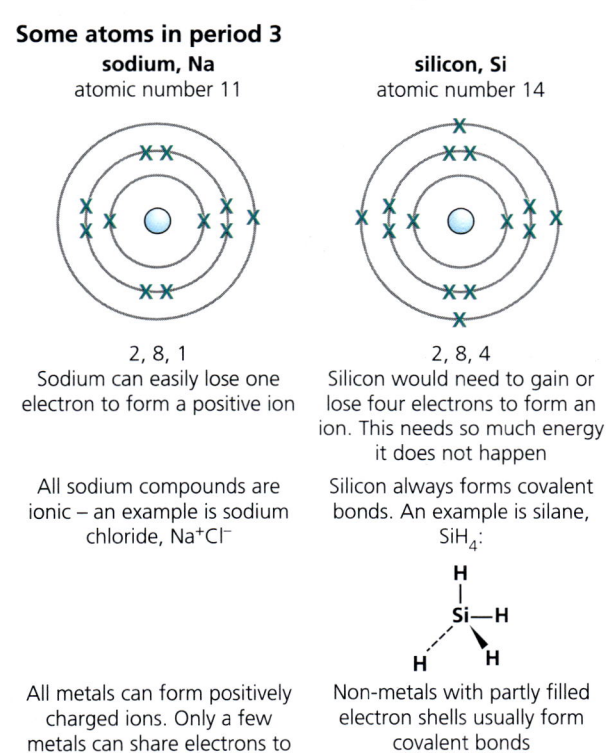

Figure 14

Summary of covalent bonding

- Covalent bonds are formed by atoms sharing electrons.
- Some atoms are able to share two or three pairs of electrons, forming double or triple covalent bonds.
- As molecules get larger the melting and boiling points rise.
- Compounds made of large molecules have high melting and boiling points because the intermolecular forces are relatively strong.
- Some non-metal atoms can join with covalent bonds to form giant structures of atoms.

107

More about atoms

8.4 Bonding in metals

The atoms in metals are joined with metallic bonds – the atoms in a solid metal are also arranged in a giant structure. Metallic bonds are quite strong, which means that metal atoms can be hard to pull apart. This leads to most metals having high boiling and melting points. All metals (except mercury) are solid at room temperature.

Many parts of aircraft are constructed of aluminium or some of its alloys. This is because it is strong but light. The atoms in aluminium are held together by strong metallic bonds and form a giant structure of atoms.

In metallic bonds the outer electrons are free to move from atom to atom. Outer electrons overlap on adjacent atoms, and this overlapping extends throughout the metal. This means that the electrons form a 'sea' of negative charge surrounding the positive metal ions (cations). Such electrons are free to move through the metal. They no longer belong to one particular atomic nucleus and are said to be 'delocalised'.

If a potential difference is applied across a metal, the delocalised electrons will move towards the positive terminal. Since an electric current consists of a flow of electrons, all metals can conduct electricity, even when liquid.

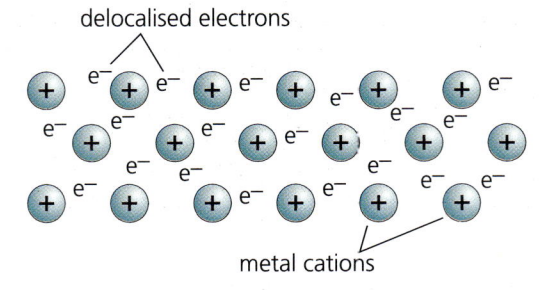

All metals conduct electricity, even when they are liquid.

Summary of bonding in metals

- Metallic bonds are strong, so most metals are solid at room temperature.
- The electrons in a metal are 'delocalised', so metals conduct electricity, even when they are liquid.

8.5 Bonding and properties

The ways that atoms in a substance are joined together determine its properties. If we look at the periodic table we can see overall patterns in the properties of compounds formed by elements in groups and periods.

For example, elements in the same group form compounds with similar formulae because they have similar arrangements of electrons.

Table 4 *Elements in the same group have similar electron arrangements and therefore form similar compounds*

Group I elements and compounds

Element	Symbol	Electronic configuration	Ion	Chloride	Oxide	Nitrate
lithium	Li	2, 1	Li^+	LiCl	Li_2O	$LiNO_3$
sodium	Na	2, 8, 1	Na^+	NaCl	Na_2O	$NaNO_3$
potassium	K	2, 8, 8, 1	K^+	KCl	K_2O	KNO_3
rubidium	Rb	2, 8, 18, 8, 1	Rb^+	RbCl	Rb_2O	$RbNO_3$
caesium	Cs	2, 8, 18, 18, 8, 1	Cs^+	CsCl	Cs_2O	$CsNO_3$

Group IV elements and compounds

Element	Symbol	Electronic configuration	Hydride	Oxide
carbon	C	2, 4	CH_4	CO_2
silicon	Si	2, 8, 4	SiH_4	SiO_2
germanium	Ge	2, 8, 18, 4	GeH_4	GeO_2
tin	Sn	2, 8, 18, 18, 4	SnH_4	SnO_2
lead	Pb	2, 8, 18, 32, 18, 4	PbH_4	PbO_2

6 The figure below illustrates various arrangements of atoms:

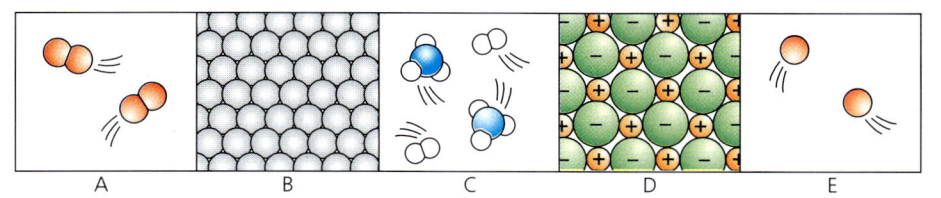

A   B   C   D   E

Which of these diagrams represents:

   a a mixture of gases?
   b a solid metal?
   c sodium chloride?
   d a noble gas?
   e oxygen gas?

More about atoms

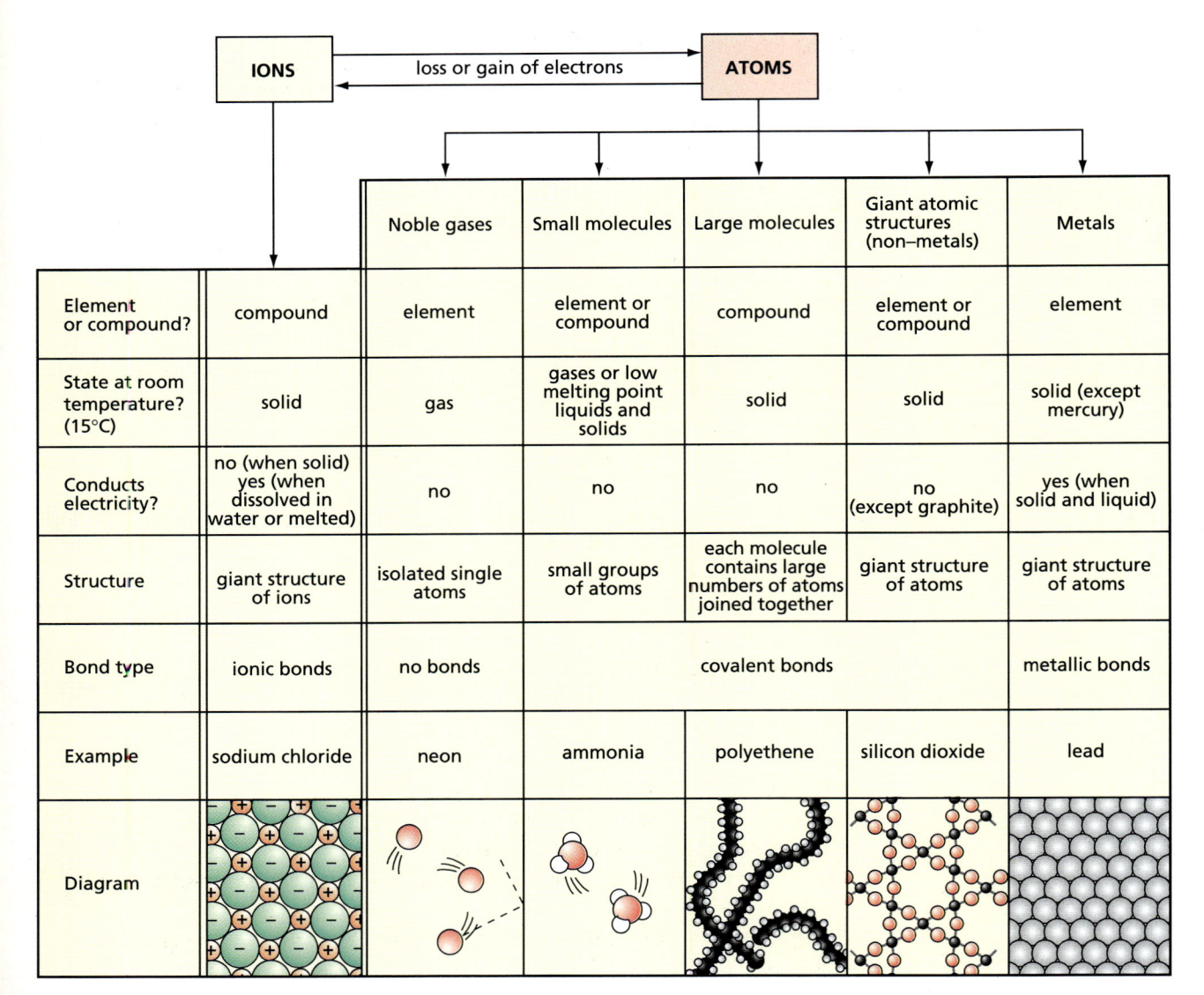

		Noble gases	Small molecules	Large molecules	Giant atomic structures (non–metals)	Metals
Element or compound?	compound	element	element or compound	compound	element or compound	element
State at room temperature? (15°C)	solid	gas	gases or low melting point liquids and solids	solid	solid	solid (except mercury)
Conducts electricity?	no (when solid) yes (when dissolved in water or melted)	no	no	no	no (except graphite)	yes (when solid and liquid)
Structure	giant structure of ions	isolated single atoms	small groups of atoms	each molecule contains large numbers of atoms joined together	giant structure of atoms	giant structure of atoms
Bond type	ionic bonds	no bonds	covalent bonds	covalent bonds	covalent bonds	metallic bonds
Example	sodium chloride	neon	ammonia	polyethene	silicon dioxide	lead

IONS ← loss or gain of electrons → ATOMS

Figure 15 Bonding and properties.

7 Draw two labelled diagrams to illustrate the arrangement of electrons in a nitrogen atom and in a hydrogen atom.
Ammonia (NH$_3$) is a small molecule joined by covalent bonds. Use the two diagrams you have drawn to draw the arrangement of electrons in a molecule of ammonia.

8 Write out the electronic configurations of:
   a a magnesium atom
   b a magnesium ion, Mg^{2+}
   c a phosphorus atom
   d a fluoride ion
   e a neon atom
   f a sodium ion

9 Draw out a table with the following headings:

Metal	Symbol	Melting point (°C)	Boiling point (°C)	State at room temperature (15°C)

Complete the table for:
a aluminium
b copper
c mercury
d zinc.

10 Why do most metals have quite high melting and boiling points?

Examination style questions

1 Use the information in table 2 to write the formulae of the following compounds:
   a potassium sulphate
   b silver nitrate
   c zinc oxide
   d calcium fluoride
   e ammonium nitrate
   f copper (II) chloride.

2 Name the compounds that have the following formulae:
   a $ZnSO_4$
   b $CuBr_2$
   c Fe_2S_3
   d $NaNO_3$

3 Sodium burns in chlorine to form sodium chloride.
   a Name the type of bonding present in sodium chloride.
   b Write out the electronic configuration of sodium and chlorine, and use these to explain how this bond is formed.
   c State two physical properties of sodium chloride, and explain how the type of bonding present gives rise to these properties.

4 The diagrams on the left show the electron shells present in water and hydrogen fluoride.
   a Copy out and complete these diagrams to show the electrons present.
   b Name the type of bonding present in these compounds.
   c State one physical property of water, and explain how the type of bonding present gives rise to this property.

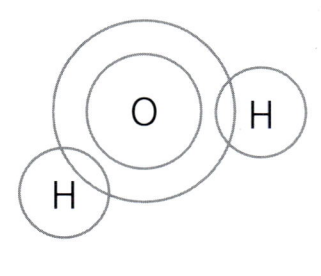

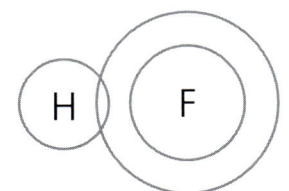

More about atoms

5 The table that follows contains information about the physical properties of various substances.

Substance	Melting point (°C)	Boiling point (°C)	Electrical conductivity Solid	Liquid	Aqueous solution
A	1537	2927	good	good	insoluble
B	−7	59	poor	poor	good
C	−117	79	poor	poor	poor
D	0	100	poor	poor	poor
E	−115	−85	poor	poor	good
F	801	1467	poor	good	good
G	−182	−161	poor	poor	insoluble
H	650	1107	good	good	insoluble
I	1407	2357	poor	poor	insoluble

The questions that follow can be answered by the substances in the table – used once, more than once or not at all.

At room temperature and pressure, which of these substances:

a could be water
b is a gas that does not react with water
c is a liquid made from small molecules
d is a metal
e is a gas made from small molecules that reacts with water to produce a solution containing ions.
f is a water-soluble ionic compound
g is a solid with a giant covalent structure of atoms?

6 The following table shows the atomic structure of various particles.

Substance	Number of protons	Number of neutrons	Number of electrons
A	6	6	6
B	11	12	10
C	6	8	6
D	9	10	10
E	19	20	19

a Which is a metal atom?
b Give the letter which represents a positive ion.
c Which letter represents a negative ion?
d List the two isotopes of the same element.

112

Moles and equations 9

Learning objectives

By the end of this chapter you should be able to:

- **calculate** the number of moles of a substance from its mass, using Avogadro's number
- **calculate** relative molar mass
- **explain** the difference between empirical and molecular formulae
- **deduce** the formulae of compounds from the masses reacting
- **apply** Avogadro's law to calculate the number of moles of a gas from its volume
- **explain** what is meant by the molarity of a solution
- **calculate** the number of moles present in an aqueous solution
- **write** balanced symbol equations

9.1 Measuring substances

When chemists manufacture a substance they need to be able to calculate the amounts of reactants and products. A substance can be measured in a number of ways – by finding its mass or its volume for example. A chemist may also measure the amount of a substance in **moles**. This chapter explains what the mole is, why it is so useful in chemistry and how it can be applied.

Why do chemists use the mole?

Chemists need to know how many particles of one substance react with another before they can write the formula or the equation for the reaction. The formula shows how many of each sort of atom are present in a substance – for example the formula for water, H_2O, tells us that two hydrogen atoms combine with one oxygen atom in each molecule of water. An equation indicates how many particles of one substance react with another. The equation

$$2H_2(g) + O_2(g) \rightarrow 2H_2O(l)$$

means that

| two molecules of hydrogen | combine with | one molecule of oxygen | to make | two molecules of water |

How do chemists find out how many particles of oxygen and hydrogen react together to make water? Knowing the mass is not enough because, as we discovered in Chapter 6, *Atomic structure*, different atoms have different masses. Someone might do an experiment and find out that:

113

Measuring in chemistry

| 4 g hydrogen | + | 32 g oxygen | → | 36 g water |

but on its own this information is not very useful because oxygen atoms are 16 times as heavy as hydrogen atoms, and this needs to be taken into account when working out how many particles are reacting.

Chemists use the **mole** to help them find out how many particles are present in a substance.

What is the mole?

A mole contains 6.023×10^{23} particles. One mole of atoms of any element contains 6.023×10^{23} atoms. People also refer to a mole of molecules, a mole of ions or a mole of electrons – in each case they mean 6.023×10^{23} particles. This number is called **Avogadro's number**, or the Avogadro constant, after the nineteenth century Italian chemist Amadeo Avogadro.

As atoms all have different masses, a mole of atoms of one element will have a different mass from a mole of atoms of another. For example, the following all contain 6.023×10^{23} atoms:

| 12 g | 24 g | 32 g | 56 g | 64 g |
| Carbon | Magnesium | Sulphur | Iron | Copper |

All of these are the relative atomic masses of the elements in grams. So, a mole of atoms of an element will have a mass equal to its relative atomic mass, in grams. For example, one mole of carbon-12 atoms has a mass of 12 g, and two moles of carbon-12 atoms a mass of 24 g.

Table 1 Moles and structure

Substance	Symbol or formula	Structure	One mole is called...
carbon	C	giant structure of atoms	one mole of carbon atoms
chlorine	Cl_2	diatomic molecules	one mole of chlorine molecules
magnesium	Mg	giant structure of atoms	one mole of magnesium atoms
sodium chloride	NaCl	giant structure of ions	one mole of sodium chloride
water	H_2O	molecules	one mole of water molecules

How is the mole used in calculations?

The mass of one mole of an element is easy to work out – it is simply its relative atomic mass (A_r) in grams. The relationship between mass, relative atomic mass and number of moles can be expressed by this equation:

$$\text{number of moles} = \frac{\text{mass (in grams)}}{A_r}$$

This equation can be rearranged to give the mass of a substance:

$$\text{mass} = \text{number of moles} \times A_r$$

or its relative atomic mass:

$$A_r = \frac{\text{mass}}{\text{number of moles}}$$

WORKED EXAMPLES

1 What is the mass of 0.0025 mole of iron atoms? (A_r of iron is 56)

Choose an equation that will give the mass:

mass = moles × A_r

= 0.0025 × 56

= 0.14 g

2 How many moles are there in 16 g copper? (A_r of copper is 64)

The question asks the moles of copper, so choose an equation that will give moles:

moles = $\frac{\text{mass}}{A_r}$

= $\frac{16}{64}$

= 0.25 moles

---

1 Use relative atomic mass values to work out how many moles there are in:
  a 8 g helium atoms
  b 12 g magnesium atoms
  c 4 g carbon atoms
  d 4.5 g aluminium atoms.
2 Calculate the mass of:
  a 0.1 moles of iron atoms
  b 5 moles of neon atoms
  c 0.02 moles of chromium atoms
  d 0.05 moles of bromine atoms.

What is relative molar mass?

It is also possible to use the mole to find out how many particles of a compound are present. The mass of one mole of a compound is called its **relative molar mass** and is given the symbol M_r. The relative molar mass is calculated by adding up the relative atomic mass values of the elements present.

Measuring in chemistry

WORKED EXAMPLES

1 Find the mass of one mole of copper (II) oxide, CuO.

write down the formula:	Cu		O
this means	one copper	and	one oxygen
write the A_r values:	64	+	16
add these up:		80	

The mass of one mole of copper (II) oxide is 80 g

2 Find the mass of one mole of calcium nitrate, $Ca(NO_3)_2$.

write down the formula:	Ca	(N	$O_3)_2$	
this means	one calcium	two nitrogens	six oxygens	
write the A_r values:	40	+ (2×14)	+ (6×16)	
add these up:		164		

The mass of one mole of calcium nitrate is 164 g

3 Find the mass of one mole of the following compounds:
  a methane, CH_4
  b water, H_2O
  c propane, C_3H_8
  d calcium hydroxide, $Ca(OH)_2$
  e copper (II) nitrate, $Cu(NO_3)_2$

4 Work out many moles there are in:
  a 25 g calcium carbonate, $CaCO_3$
  b 6.6 g carbon dioxide, CO_2
  c 3.1 g copper (II) carbonate, $CuCO_3$
  d 5.28 g ammonium sulphate, $(NH_4)_2SO_4$

Can the mole be applied to molecules?

Substances that have molecular structures can also be measured in moles. A mole of molecules always contains 6.023×10^{23} molecules, and its mass can be calculated from the relative molar mass of the substance.

Cl_2
$35.5 + 35.5$
$71g = M_r$

one mole of chlorine molecules contains 6.023×10^{23} molecules

H_2O
$1+1+16$
$M_r = 18g$

one mole of water molecules contains 6.023×10^{23} molecules

$C_{12}H_{22}O_{11}$
$(12 \times 12) + (22 \times 1) + (11 \times 16)$
$M_r = 342g$

one mole of sugar molecules contains 6.023×10^{23} molecules

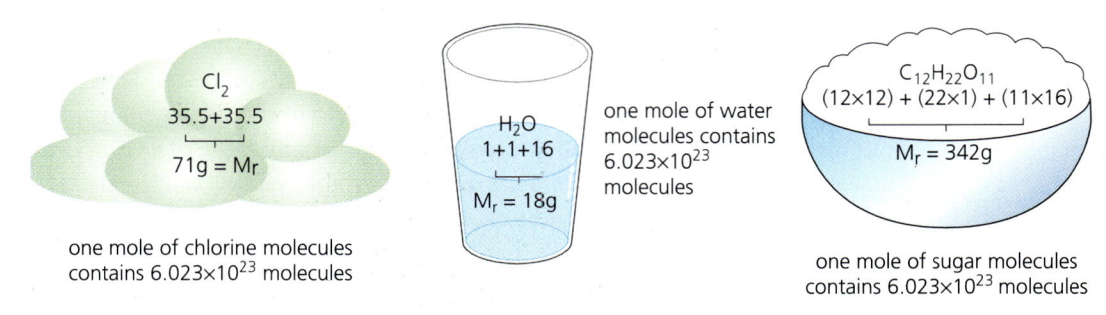

Figure 1

Moles and equations

Atoms	Elements only — all metals, some non-metals, noble gases	Aluminium	one mole of aluminium **atoms** (mass 27.0g)	a mole of **atoms** contains 6.023×10^{23} atoms
		Carbon	one mole of carbon **atoms** (mass 12.0g)	
		Helium airship	one mole of helium **atoms** (mass 4.0g)	
Molecules	Elements	Oxygen	one mole of oxygen **molecules** (mass 32.0g)	one mole of **molecules** contains 6.023×10^{23} molecules
		Bromine	one mole of bromine **molecules** (mass 159.8g)	
		Iodine	one mole of iodine **molecules** (mass 253.8g)	
	or Compounds	Ammonia	one mole of ammonia **molecules** (mass 17.0g)	
		Water	one mole of water **molecules** (mass 18.0g)	
Ions	Compounds only	Sodium chloride	one mole of sodium chloride 1 mole of sodium chloride contains: 6.023×10^{23} sodium **ions** and 6.023×10^{23} chloride **ions**	

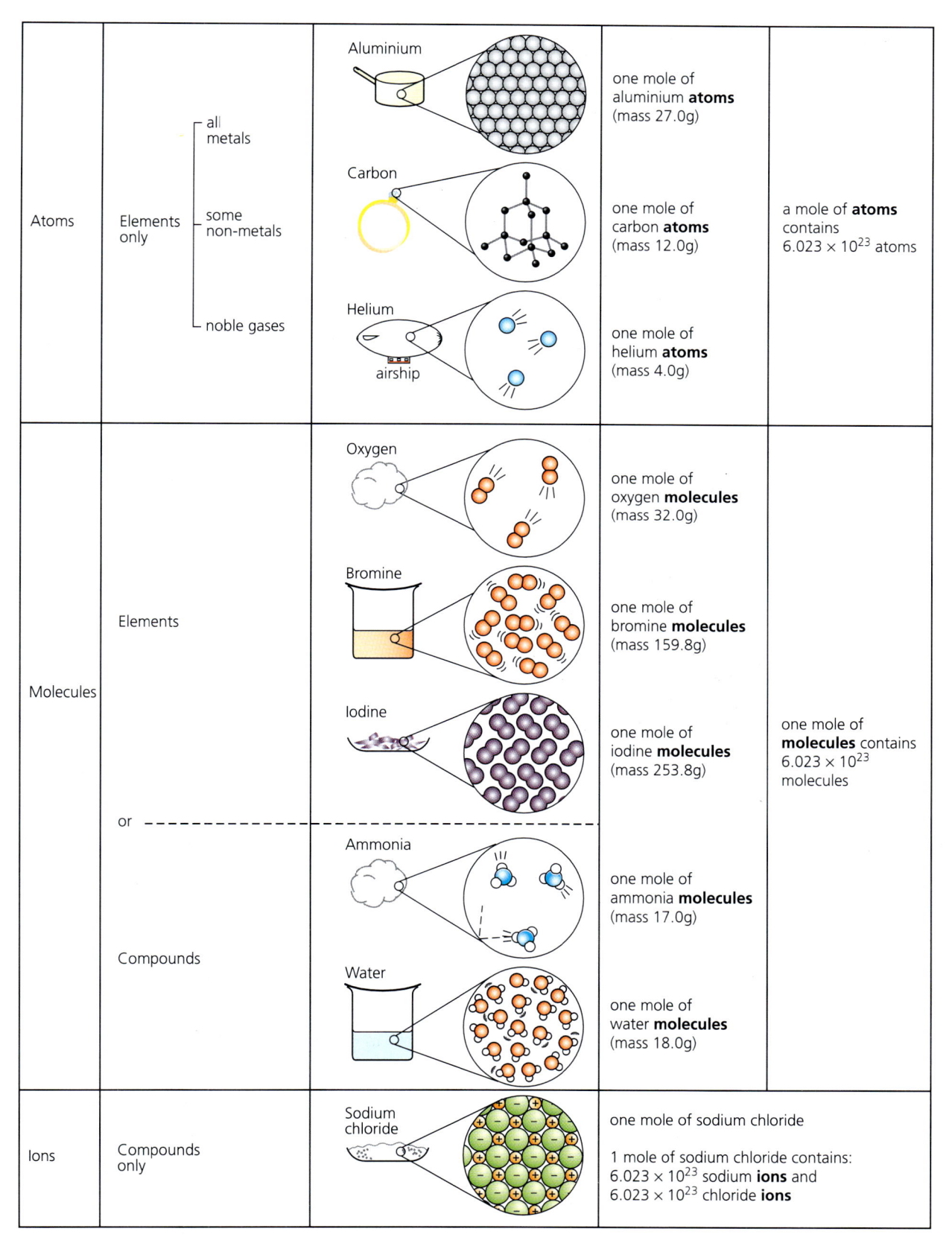

Figure 2 It is important to know the structure of an element or compound. This helps us to describe correctly and understand one mole of a substance.

117

Measuring in chemistry

Chemists working in the laboratory need to measure out many different amounts of compounds. Varying amounts of compounds can be measured in moles in a similar way to previous calculations by using the formula

$$\text{number of moles} = \frac{\text{mass}}{M_r}$$

This can be rearranged to give:

$$\text{mass} = \text{number of moles} \times M_r$$

WORKED EXAMPLES

1 How many moles are there in 27 g of water, formula H_2O?

These calculations involve two steps. The first step is to calculate the M_r. The second is to use this value to find the number of moles.

find the M_r of water: H_2 $\quad$ O
$\qquad\qquad\qquad\quad$ (1 + 1) + 16
$\qquad\qquad\qquad\qquad\quad$ 18

find moles of water: $\text{moles} = \dfrac{\text{mass}}{M_r}$

$\qquad\qquad\qquad\qquad = \dfrac{27}{18}$

$\qquad\qquad\qquad\qquad = 1.5 \text{ moles}$

2 What is the mass of 0.025 moles of calcium carbonate, formula $CaCO_3$?

find the M_r: Ca   C O_3
$\qquad\qquad\quad$ 40   12   (3 × 16)
$\qquad\qquad\qquad\quad$ 100

find mass: $\text{mass} = \text{moles} \times M_r$

$\qquad\qquad\qquad = 0.025 \times 100$

$\qquad\qquad\qquad = 2.5 \text{ g}$

5 Calculate the mass of:
   a 0.02 moles of water, H_2O
   b 0.004 moles of calcium carbonate, $CaCO_3$
   c 2.5 moles of sulphuric acid, H_2SO_4
   d 0.35 moles of methane, CH_4

Summary of measuring substances

- Chemists measure the amount of a substance in moles.
- One mole of atoms of an element contains its relative atomic mass in grams.
- The number of particles in a mole is called Avogadro's number, which is 6.023×10^{23}.
- The relative molar mass, M_r, is used to find the mass of one mole of a compound.

9.2 Finding chemical formulae

When chemists are investigating a compound, one of the first things they want to know is its chemical formula. One way of doing this is to find the mass of each element in the compound and then use the mole to find the chemical formula. An example of how this is done is shown in figure 3.

Making magnesium oxide

Find the mass of a crucible and lid.

Break up enough magnesium to half fill the crucible. Find the new mass of the crucible and lid, then work out the mass of magnesium.

Heat the crucible gently with a Bunsen burner. Lift the lid slightly every now and then.

After heating for 5 minutes, switch the Bunsen burner off. Leave the crucible to cool down for 5 minutes.

Find the mass of the crucible, lid and its contents (magnesium oxide). Work out the mass of magnesium oxide inside the crucible. By subtraction, now work out the mass of oxygen that has reacted.

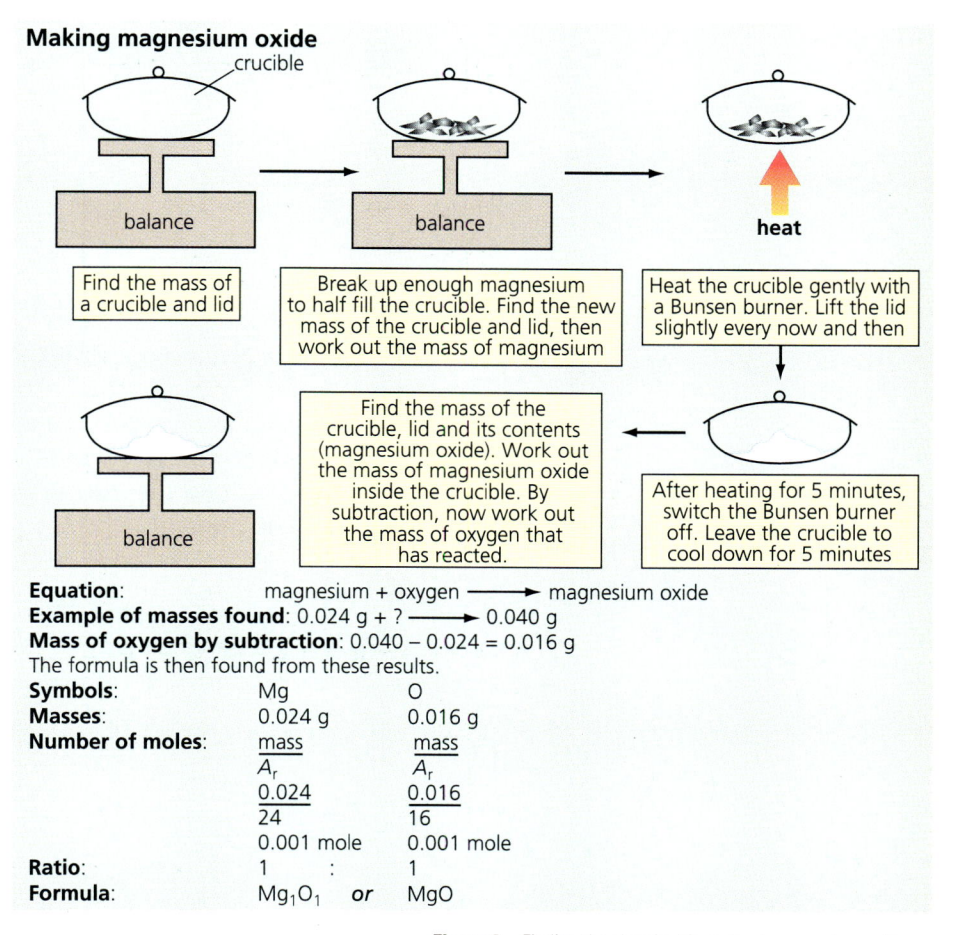

Equation: magnesium + oxygen ⟶ magnesium oxide
Example of masses found: 0.024 g + ? ⟶ 0.040 g
Mass of oxygen by subtraction: 0.040 − 0.024 = 0.016 g
The formula is then found from these results.

Symbols:	Mg	O
Masses:	0.024 g	0.016 g
Number of moles:	$\dfrac{mass}{A_r}$	$\dfrac{mass}{A_r}$
	$\dfrac{0.024}{24}$	$\dfrac{0.016}{16}$
	0.001 mole	0.001 mole
Ratio:	1 :	1
Formula:	Mg_1O_1 or	MgO

Figure 3 Finding the chemical formula of magnesium oxide.

WORKED EXAMPLES

1 Find the formula of the oxide of carbon formed when 0.3 g carbon reacts with 0.8 g oxygen (C = 12, O = 16)

symbols:	C		O
masses:	0.3 g		0.8 g
moles:	$\dfrac{0.3}{12}$		$\dfrac{0.8}{16}$
	0.025		0.05
ratio:	1	:	2
formula:		CO_2	

2 A compound was found to contain 52.2% carbon, 13.0% hydrogen and 34.8% oxygen by mass. Find its simplest formula (C = 12, H = 1, O = 16).

When a question gives a percentage by mass, assume that 100 g of the compound is present, and use the individual percentage figures to calculate the number of moles.

symbols:	C	H	O
masses:	52.2 g	13.0 g	34.8 g
number of moles:	$\dfrac{52.2}{12}$	$\dfrac{13.0}{1}$	$\dfrac{34.8}{16}$
	4.35	13.0	2.18
ratio:	2 :	6 :	1
formula:		C_2H_6O	

What is the difference between empirical and molecular formulae?

The **empirical formula** of a compound is the simplest ratio of elements in that compound.

The actual number of moles of each element in one mole of a compound is known as the **molecular formula**. To find the molecular formula of a compound, you need to know the mass of one mole as well as the amount of each individual element present.

WORKED EXAMPLE

A sugar with a molar mass of 180 was found to contain 40.0% carbon, 6.67% hydrogen and 53.33% oxygen by mass. Find its empirical formula and its molecular formula (C = 12, H = 1, O = 16).

symbols:	C	H	O
mass:	40.0 g	6.67 g	53.33 g
moles:	$\dfrac{40.0}{12}$	$\dfrac{6.67}{1}$	$\dfrac{53.33}{16}$
	3.33	6.67	3.33
ratio:	1 :	2 :	1

empirical formula (simplest ratio): CH_2O

find mass of empirical formula: $\underbrace{12 + 2 + 16}_{30}$

compare with M_r: 180

M_r is six times the mass of the empirical formula

molecular formula is therefore six times the empirical formula: $C_6H_{12}O_6$

6 Use relative atomic mass values to find the simplest formulae of the following compounds:
   a the oxide that is formed when 2.24 g of iron reacts with 0.96 g of oxygen
   b the oxide formed when 1.24 g of phosphorus reacts with excess oxygen to give 2.84 g of oxide
   c the fluoride produced when 0.20 g of calcium reacts with fluorine to give 0.39 g of product
   d the hydrocarbon formed when 9.0 g of carbon react with 2.0 g of hydrogen.
7 Calculate the empirical formula and the molecular formula for:
   a a hydrocarbon with an M_r of 78 containing 92.31% carbon and 7.69% hydrogen by mass
   b 11.0 g of a hydrocarbon with an M_r of 44, which is found to contain 9.0 g of carbon.
   c an oxide of phosphorus with an M_r of 284, which contains 43.66% phosphorus and 56.34% oxygen by mass
   d a sulphur-based acid with an M_r of 82 containing 2.44% hydrogen, 39.02% sulphur and 58.54% oxygen by mass.

Summary of finding chemical formulae

- The formula of a compound can be found from reacting masses of elements.
- The empirical formula of a compound shows the simplest ratio of elements present.
- The molecular formula of a compound shows the actual number of moles of each element present in one mole of that compound.

9.3 The mole in gases and solutions
How can the number of moles of a gas be calculated?

In many chemical reactions gases react or are given off. If the number of moles of a gas can be found then formulae and equations for reactions involving gases can be written.

It is possible to find the mass of a gas, and turn this into moles using the equations described earlier in the chapter. For a dense gas like carbon dioxide, this can be quite accurate, but for gases of a low density like hydrogen the measurements might not be very accurate.

The most useful way to measure the amount of a gas is to find its volume at a particular temperature. At 273 K and one atmosphere of pressure one mole of any gas occupies 22.4 dm³ (or 22 400 cm³). These conditions are known as **standard temperature and pressure** (often shortened to 'STP'). At room temperature and pressure (this is usually taken to be 293 K and one atmosphere pressure) one mole of any gas will occupy 24 dm³.

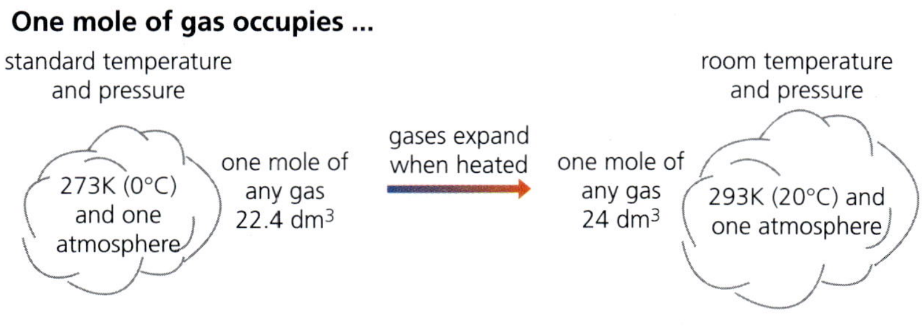

One mole of gas occupies ...

standard temperature and pressure
273K (0°C) and one atmosphere — one mole of any gas 22.4 dm³

gases expand when heated →

room temperature and pressure
one mole of any gas 24 dm³ — 293K (20°C) and one atmosphere

Figure 4 One mole of a gas.

Measuring in chemistry

One mole of any gas will always contain Avogadro's number (6.023×10^{23}) of atoms or molecules. Equal volumes of all gases at the same temperature and pressure will always contain equal numbers of molecules. This is known as **Avogadro's law**.

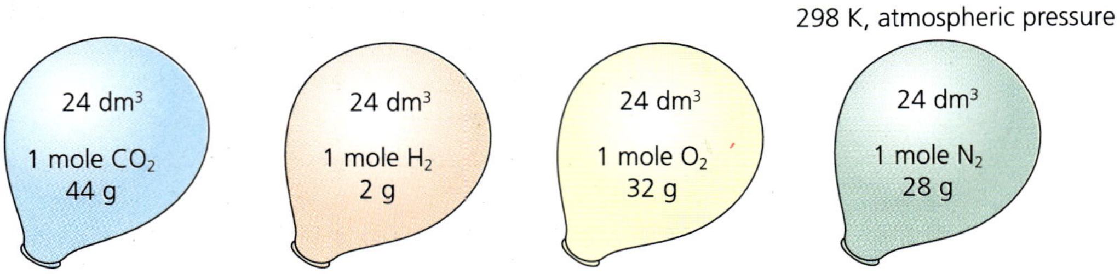

298 K, atmospheric pressure

- 24 dm³ — 1 mole CO_2 — 44 g
- 24 dm³ — 1 mole H_2 — 2 g
- 24 dm³ — 1 mole O_2 — 32 g
- 24 dm³ — 1 mole N_2 — 28 g

Figure 5 Molar volumes of gases.

$$\text{The number of moles of a gas} = \frac{\text{volume of gas}}{\text{volume of 1 mole}}$$

Chemists will work this out in one of two ways:
at STP:

$$\text{moles of a gas} = \frac{\text{volume of gas (cm}^3\text{)}}{22\,400}$$

or at room temperature and pressure:

$$\text{moles of a gas} = \frac{\text{volume of gas (cm}^3\text{)}}{24\,000}$$

These equations can be rearranged as follows:

$$\text{volume} = \text{moles} \times 22\,400 \quad \text{(at STP)}$$

or

$$\text{volume} = \text{moles} \times 24\,000$$
(at room temperature and pressure)

WORKED EXAMPLES

1 How many moles are present in 336 cm³ of nitrogen gas, when measured at STP?

$$\begin{aligned}
\text{number of moles} &= \frac{\text{volume}}{22\,400} \\
&= \frac{336}{22\,400} \\
&= 0.015 \text{ moles}
\end{aligned}$$

2 What volume is occupied by 0.02 moles of carbon dioxide gas at room temperature and pressure?

$$\begin{aligned}
\text{volume} &= \text{moles} \times 24\,000 \\
&= 0.02 \times 24\,000 \\
&= 480 \text{ cm}^3
\end{aligned}$$

Moles and equations

8 How many moles are present at STP in:
   a 224 cm^3 hydrogen
   b 560 cm^3 methane
   c 5 600 cm^3 ammonia
   d 336 cm^3 carbon dioxide
   e 44.8 dm^3 oxygen.

9 How many moles do the following gases contain at room temperature and pressure?
   a 120 cm^3 propane
   b 240 cm^3 chlorine
   c 6 000 cm^3 neon
   d 12 dm^3 neon
   e 96 dm^3 helium.

10 Find the volume of the following gases at STP:
   a 0.1 moles argon
   b 0.25 moles carbon dioxide
   c 2 moles krypton
   d 0.04 moles sulphur dioxide
   e 0.002 moles butane.

11 What volume would each of the gases in question 10 occupy at room temperature and pressure?

How are moles measured in solutions?

Many chemicals are used in the laboratory as aqueous solutions – that is, dissolved in water. Chemists usually measure how concentrated a solution is by finding out how many moles of a substance are dissolved in each litre of solvent.

The number of moles of substance contained in each litre of a solution is called its **molarity**. If one mole of any substance is dissolved in water and then made up to a volume of one litre it produces a 'one **molar** solution'. By dissolving different amounts of solid in water and making the volume up to one litre solutions of different molarities can be prepared.

Figure 6

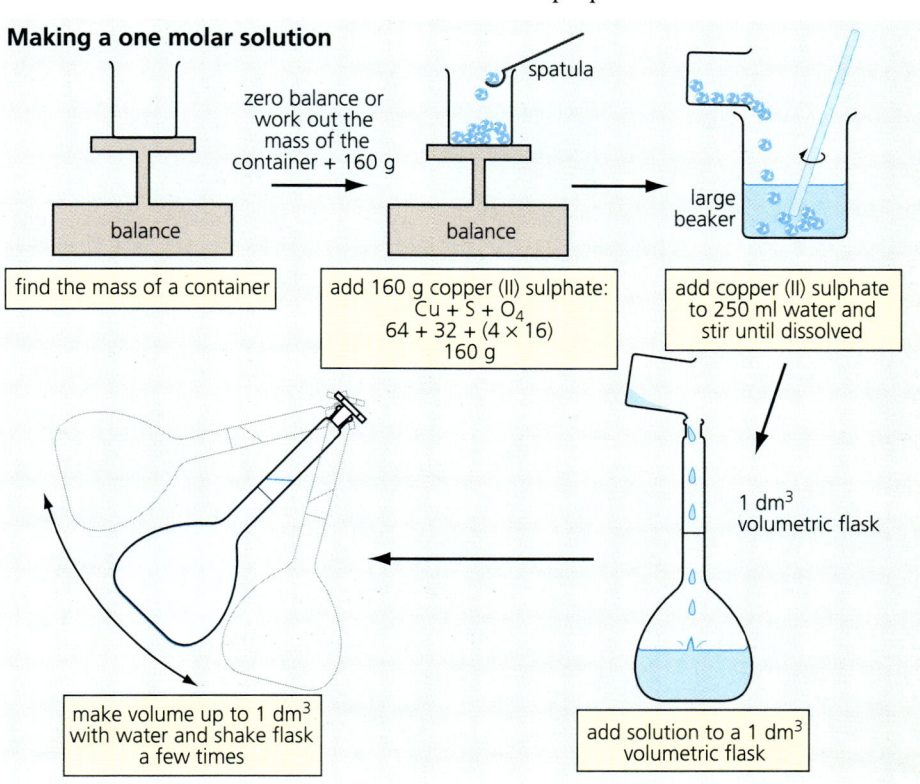

Making a one molar solution

find the mass of a container

zero balance or work out the mass of the container + 160 g

add 160 g copper (II) sulphate:
Cu + S + O$_4$
64 + 32 + (4 × 16)
160 g

add copper (II) sulphate to 250 ml water and stir until dissolved

1 dm^3 volumetric flask

add solution to a 1 dm^3 volumetric flask

make volume up to 1 dm^3 with water and shake flask a few times

123

Measuring in chemistry

The following equation can be used to find the number of moles of substance in an aqueous solution:

$$\text{number of moles} = \frac{\text{volume of solution (cm}^3\text{)} \times \text{molarity}}{1000}$$

this can be rearranged to give

$$\text{volume of solution (cm}^3\text{)} = \frac{\text{moles} \times 1000}{\text{molarity}}$$

or

$$\text{molarity} = \frac{\text{moles} \times 1000}{\text{volume}}$$

Making solutions of different concentrations

copper (II) sulphate
Cu + S + O$_4$
64 + 32 + (4 × 16)
160 g = M$_r$

crystals dissolved in water and made up to 1 dm^3

if 160 g (1 mole) added

if 80 g (0.5 mole) added

if 16 g (0.1 mole) added

1 dm^3 of this solution contains one mole of copper (II) sulphate

this is a 1.0 M solution

1 dm^3 of this solution contains 0.5 moles of copper (II) sulphate

this solution has a molarity of 0.5 M

1 dm^3 of this solution contains 0.1 moles of copper (II) sulphate

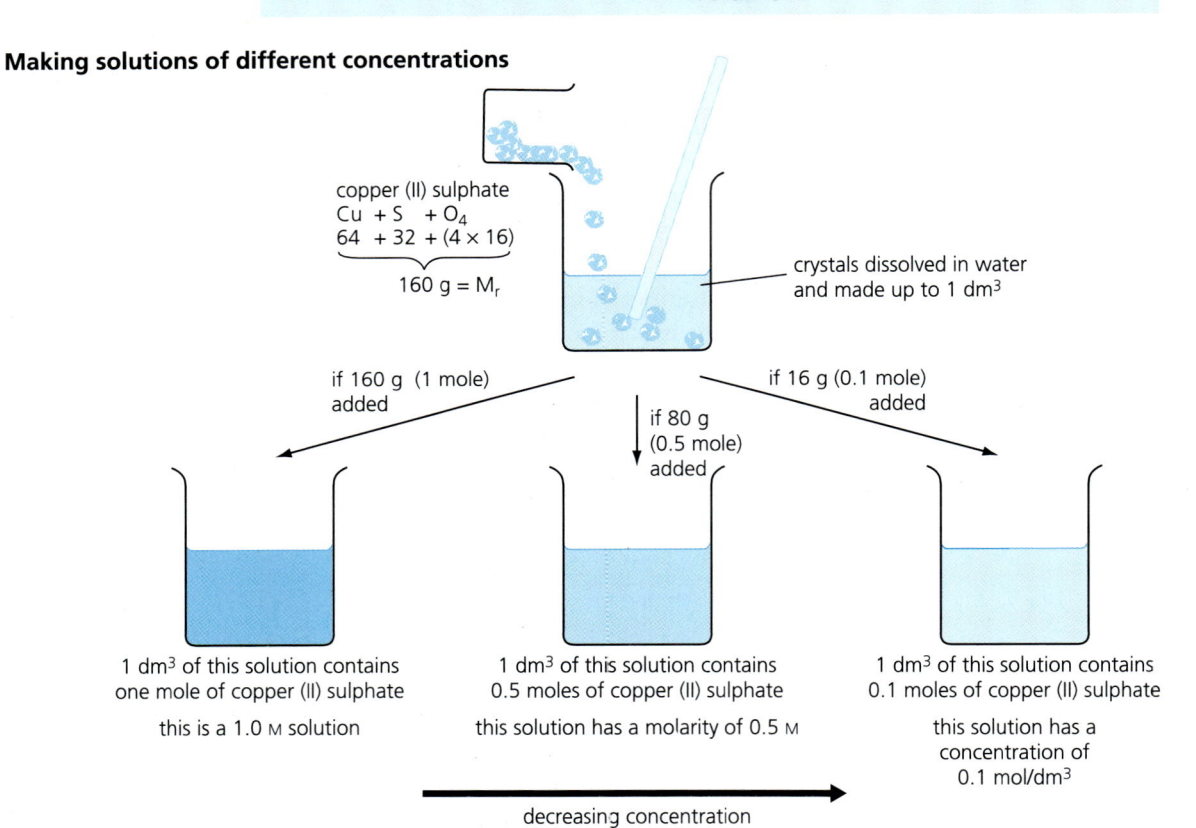

this solution has a concentration of 0.1 mol/dm^3

decreasing concentration

Figure 7

WORKED EXAMPLES

1 How many moles are present in 200 cm^3 of a 2.0 M solution of hydrochloric acid?

$$\text{moles} = \frac{\text{volume} \times \text{molarity}}{1000}$$

$$= \frac{200 \times 2.0}{1000}$$

$$= 0.4 \text{ moles}$$

2 What volume of 0.25 M copper (II) sulphate solution would contain 0.5 moles?

$$\text{volume} = \frac{\text{moles} \times 1000}{\text{molarity}}$$

$$= \frac{0.5 \times 1000}{0.25}$$

$$= 2000 \text{ cm}^3 \text{ or } 2 \text{ dm}^3$$

3 What is the molarity of 100 cm³ of a solution of sodium chloride containing 0.04 moles?

$$\text{molarity} = \frac{\text{moles} \times 1000}{\text{volume}}$$

$$= \frac{0.04 \times 1000}{100}$$

$$= 0.4 \text{ M}$$

4 What is the molarity of 200 cm³ of an aqueous solution containing 2.02 g of potassium nitrate (KNO_3)?

First find the number of moles of potassium nitrate:

M_r: K   N O_3
      $\underbrace{39 + 14 + (3 \times 16)}_{101}$

$$\text{moles} = \frac{\text{mass}}{M_r}$$

$$= \frac{2.02}{101}$$

$$= 0.02 \text{ moles}$$

$$\text{molarity} = \frac{\text{moles} \times 1000}{\text{volume}}$$

$$= \frac{0.02 \times 1000}{200}$$

$$= 0.1 \text{ M}$$

---

12 Work out how many moles are present in the following aqueous solutions:
    a 500 cm³ 1.0 M sodium hydroxide
    b 1000 cm³ 0.2 M hydrochloric acid
    c 250 cm³ 0.04 M copper (II) sulphate
    d 5 dm³ 2 M potassium nitrate.

13 Find the molarity of the following aqueous solutions:
    a 250 cm³ potassium chlorate solution containing 0.1 moles
    b one litre of sucrose solution containing 0.5 moles
    c 50 cm³ copper (II) chloride solution containing 0.0015 moles
    d 6 dm³ sodium chloride solution containing 0.2 moles.

Measuring in chemistry

14 Find the molarity of the following aqueous solutions:
   a 7.35 g sodium chloride (NaCl) in 100 cm^3 solution
   b 9.45 g nitric acid (HNO$_3$) in 200 cm^3 solution
   c 2.64 g ammonium sulphate ((NH$_4$)$_2$SO$_4$) in 250 cm^3 solution
   d 360 cm^3 ammonia gas (NH$_3$) dissolved in 2000 cm^3 solution at room temperature and pressure.

Summary of the mole in gases and solutions

- One mole of any gas contains 6.023×10^{23} particles.
- At STP one mole of any gas occupies 24.4 dm^3.
- The molarity of a solution is the number of moles of a substance dissolved in each litre.
- A one molar solution contains one mole of solute dissolved in a litre of solution.
- Moles of a gas = $\dfrac{\text{volume (cm}^3)}{22\,400}$ (STP) or $\dfrac{\text{volume (cm}^3)}{24\,000}$ (room temperature and pressure)
- At room temperature and pressure, one mole of any gas occupies 24 dm^3.
- Avogadro's law states that equal volumes of all gases at the same temperature and pressure will contain equal numbers of molecules.
- For a solution: moles = $\dfrac{\text{volume (cm}^3) \times \text{molarity}}{1000}$

9.4 Chemical equations

A chemical equation sums up what is happening in a reaction.
For example, when hydrogen and oxygen react together to make water, the equation is as follows:

| 2H$_2$(g) | + | O$_2$(g) | → | H$_2$O(l) |

This shows *which* chemicals are reacting:

| hydrogen | + | oxygen | → | water |

and *how many moles* are involved:

| 2 moles hydrogen molecules | 1 mole oxygen molecules | 2 moles water molecules |

State symbols show solid (s), liquid (l), gas (g) or aqueous solution (aq). This equation shows that hydrogen and oxygen are gases and that water is a liquid.

Chemists from different countries can communicate with each other by chemical equations.

Mg(s) + 2HCl(aq) → MgCl$_2$(aq) + H$_2$(g)

How does the mole help us to write equations?

The mole can be used to help write chemical equations from measurements made during a reaction. You can see how this is done in figure 8.
Once a chemical equation is known, it can be used to make predictions about the substances involved in the reaction.

Moles and equations

Decomposition of copper carbonate

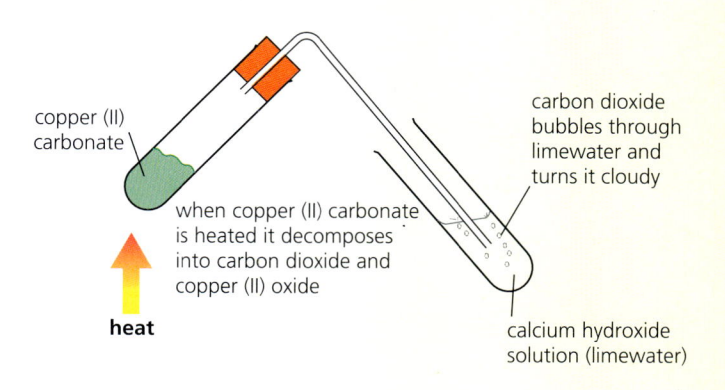

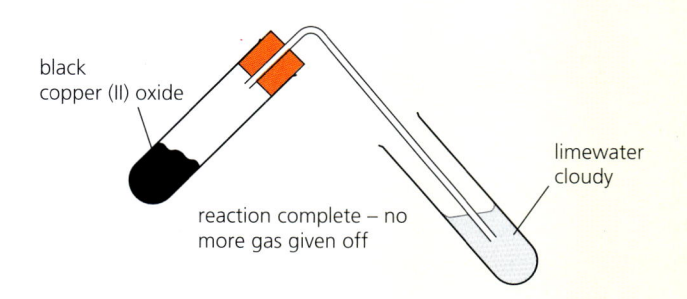

To write a balanced equation for this reaction the number of moles of each substance must be found

Example measurements:
mass of copper (II) carbonate = 1.86 g
mass of copper (II) oxide remaining = 1.20 g
by subtraction, mass of carbon dioxide given off = 0.66 g

Calculation:

M_r values:
Cu C O_3 Cu O   C O_2
64 + 12 + (3 × 16)   64 + 16   12 + (2 × 16)
     124   80   44

Masses measured: 1.86 g   1.20 g   0.66 g

moles = $\frac{mass}{M_r}$: $\frac{1.86}{124}$ $\frac{1.20}{80}$ $\frac{0.66}{44}$

            0.015   0.015   0.015

molar ratio   1   :   1   :   1

The equation is therefore balanced as it is, and the experimental results show that:

one mole of copper (II) carbonate → one mole of copper (II) oxide + one mole of carbon dioxide

$CuCO_3$ → CuO + CO_2

Figure 8

What happens when silver carbonate decomposes?

All compounds of silver break down easily to give the metal. Silver carbonate decomposes when heated:

$$2Ag_2CO_3(s) \rightarrow 4Ag(s) + 2CO_2(g) + O_2(g)$$

This equation can be used to find the mass of silver that would be formed when, for example, 11.04 g of silver carbonate is heated (Ag = 108, C = 12, O = 16)

M_r of silver carbonate:
Ag_2 C O_3
(2 × 108) + 12 + (3 × 16)
           276

select the relevant substances from the equation:
molar ratio:
$2Ag_2CO_3 \rightarrow 4Ag$
2 moles → 4 moles
   1   :   2

moles of silver carbonate used (= $\frac{mass}{M_r}$): $\frac{11.04}{276}$ = 0.04

use molar ratio to find moles of silver formed:
0.04 moles silver carbonate : 0.08 moles silver

find mass of silver (mass = moles × A_r): = 0.08 × 108
= 8.64 g

127

Measuring in chemistry

What predictions can be made in reactions involving gases?

Avogadro's law states that equal numbers of moles of any gas will always occupy the same volume at the same temperature and pressure. This means that calculations involving gases can often involve simple deduction rather than lengthy calculations.

For example, ammonia reacts with hydrogen chloride as follows:

$$NH_3(g) + HCl(g) \rightarrow NH_4Cl(s)$$

Since this equation shows that one mole of hydrogen chloride gas reacts with one mole of ammonia, the volumes of the two gases reacting will also be equal.

How can molarity be calculated using titration?

Sulphuric acid can be neutralised by alkalis such as sodium hydroxide as follows:

$$H_2SO_4(aq) + 2NaOH(aq) \rightarrow Na_2SO_4(aq) + 2H_2O(l)$$

The exact volumes of sodium hydroxide needed to neutralise a particular volume of sulphuric acid can be measured by **titration** (figure 9). When the molarity of one solution is known, a titration can be used to find the molarity of the other solution.

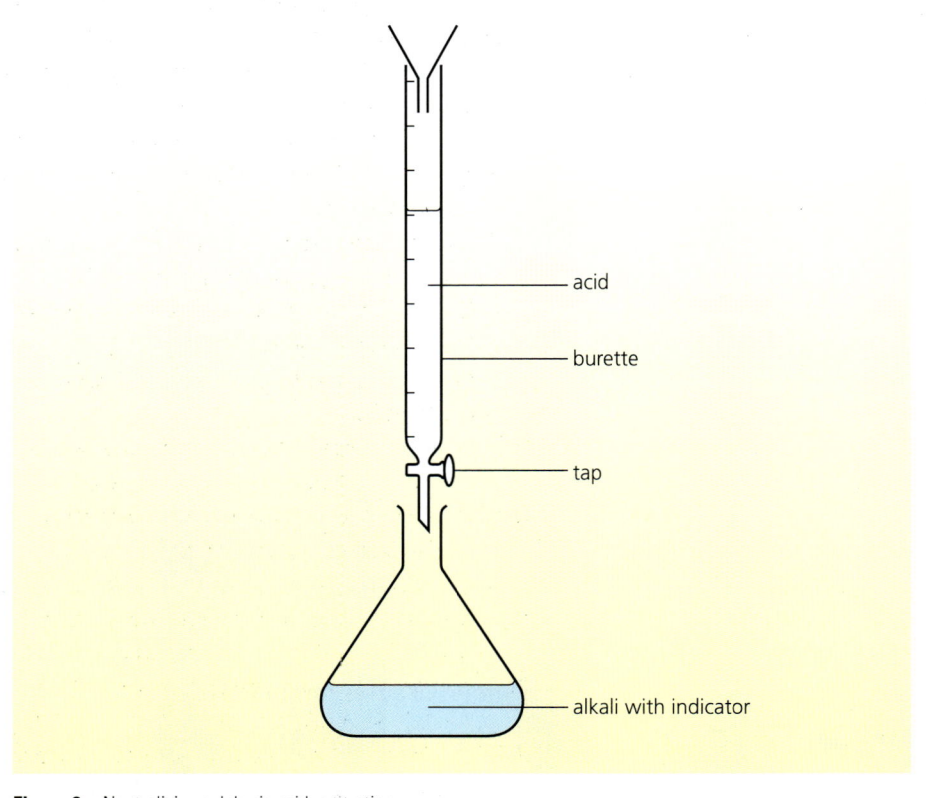

Figure 9 Neutralising sulphuric acid: a titration.

Moles and equations

WORKED EXAMPLE

25.0 cm³ of sodium hydroxide solution was neutralised by 15.0 cm³ 0.10 M sulphuric acid. Use this information to find the molarity of the alkali.

select relevant substances from equation: H_2SO_4 → $2NaOH$

molar ratio: 1 : 2

find moles of acid: moles = $\dfrac{\text{volume} \times \text{molarity}}{1000}$

$= \dfrac{15.0 \times 0.1}{1000}$

$= 0.0015$ moles

use molar ratio to find moles of alkali: 0.0015 moles H_2SO_4 → 0.003 moles NaOH

find molarity of alkali: molarity = $\dfrac{\text{moles} \times 1000}{\text{volume}}$

$= \dfrac{0.003 \times 1000}{25}$

$= 0.12$ M

---

15 Write balanced symbol equations, including the state symbols, for the reactions below.

  a 7.35 g concentrated sulphuric acid (H_2SO_4) reacts with 8.82 g of sodium chloride crystals (NaCl) to give 10.695 g solid sodium sulphate (Na_2SO_4) and 3600 cm³ of hydrogen chloride gas (HCl)

  b 2.872 g of solid lead dioxide powder (PbO_2) was reduced by 576 cm³ of hydrogen gas (H_2) to give 2.484 g of solid lead and 0.432 g water

  c 1.066 g of sodium carbonate powder (Na_2CO_3) was reacted with 40 cm³ 0.5 M hydrochloric acid (HCl). 40 cm³ of 0.5 M sodium chloride solution was formed, together with 0.18 g water and 240 cm³ of carbon dioxide gas

  d 0.25 g zinc metal reacted with 40 cm³ of 0.2 M nitric acid (HNO_3) to give 96 cm³ hydrogen gas and a solution containing 0.756 g zinc nitrate ($Zn(NO_3)_2$)

  e 72 cm³ ammonia gas (NH_3) was broken down by heat to give 36 cm³ of nitrogen gas (N_2) and 108 cm³ of hydrogen gas (H_2)

  f 0.762 g iodine crystals (I_2) reacted with 72 cm³ of chlorine gas (Cl_2) to give 0.975 g of liquid iodine monochloride (ICl).

16 What mass of copper metal could be obtained by reducing 4.0 g copper (II) oxide:

  $CuO(s) + H_2(g) \rightarrow Cu(s) + H_2O(l)$

17 What volume of carbon dioxide gas (measured at room temperature and pressure) could be obtained by completely breaking down 5.0 g calcium carbonate:

  $CaCO_3(s) \rightarrow CaO(s) + CO_2(g)$

18 What volume of 0.2 M hydrochloric acid would exactly react with 2.1 g magnesium carbonate:

  $MgCO_3(s) + 2HCl(aq) \rightarrow MgCl_2(aq) + CO_2(g) + H_2O(l)$

19 What mass of lead metal would be obtained if 4.46 g of lead (II) oxide is heated in a stream of methane:

  $4PbO(s) + CH_4(g) \rightarrow 4Pb(s) + CO_2(g) + 2H_2O(l)$

20 What volume of sulphur dioxide gas will be formed when 1 g of sulphur is burned:

  $S(s) + O_2(g) \rightarrow SO_2(g)$

21 What volume of 0.2 M sodium hydroxide solution would be needed to neutralise 25 cm³ of 0.1 M sulphuric acid:

  $H_2SO_4(aq) + 2NaOH(aq) \rightarrow Na_2SO_4(aq) + 2H_2O(l)$

Measuring in chemistry

Summary of chemical equations

- A chemical equation shows which chemicals are reacting and how many moles are involved.
- Measurements can be made during reactions, and the information used to write equations.
- Chemical equations can be used to make predictions about the amounts of substances involved in a reaction.
- A titration involves using a solution of a known molarity to find the molarity of another solution.

Examination style questions

1 Copper (II) oxide is a black powder that, when heated in a stream of hydrogen gas, reacts in the following way: copper (II) oxide + hydrogen → copper + water
In an experiment to verify the formula of copper (II) oxide, 4.0 g of the oxide were heated in a stream of hydrogen. After the reaction had finished, 3.2 g of an orange–pink powder was left.
  a What is the orange–pink powder?
  b Calculate:
    i the mass of copper metal **ii** the mass of oxygen that reacted with hydrogen in this experiment.
  c Using relative atomic mass values find the moles of copper and oxygen reacting.
  d From the mole ratio of the values calculated in **c** deduce the formula of copper (II) oxide.
  e It was found that if the final residue was not properly cooled at the end of the experiment, the pink powder turned black and increased in mass. What has caused this?
  f Particular care must be taken during this experiment in handling the hydrogen gas. Suggest one hazard associated with this, and the precautions that should be taken.

2 Use relative atomic mass values to help answer these questions.
  a What mass of copper (II) oxide is formed when 6.2 g of copper (II) carbonate decompose
    $CuCO_3(s) \rightarrow CuO(s) + CO_2(g)$
  b How much iron (II) sulphide is formed when 11.2 g of iron react completely with sulphur
    $Fe(s) + S(s) \rightarrow FeS(s)$
  c Limestone can be heated in a furnace and decomposed to quicklime (calcium oxide)
    $CaCO_3(s) \rightarrow CaO(s) + CO_2(g)$
  How many tonnes of quicklime would be formed when 20 tonnes of limestone are roasted in this way?

3 Hydrogen peroxide decomposes as follows:
    $2H_2O_2(aq) \rightarrow 2H_2O(l) + O_2(g)$
  a Find the relative molar mass of hydrogen peroxide.
  b How many moles are present in 6.3 g of hydrogen peroxide?
  c How many moles of oxygen molecules are formed when 6.8 g of hydrogen peroxide decompose?
  d Calculate the volume of oxygen that this represents at STP.

4 Baking powder makes cakes rise because when the sodium hydrogen carbonate it contains is heated carbon dioxide gas is given off
    $2NaHCO_3(s) \rightarrow Na_2CO_3(s) + H_2O(l) + CO_2(g)$
  a Describe a chemical test that could be carried out to prove that the gas produced is carbon dioxide.
  b What volume of carbon dioxide (measured at STP) would be produced when 1.686 g of sodium hydrogen carbonate decompose?

Acids, bases and salts 10

Learning objectives

By the end of this chapter you should be able to:
- **describe** the pH scale and how it measures acidity
- **explain** how some common indicators work
- **describe** the properties of acids and bases
- **distinguish** a base from an alkali
- **explain** how the concentration of an acid or base is different from its strength
- **explain** how bases and acids neutralise each other
- **describe** ways of following neutralisation
- **describe** different ways that salts can be prepared in the laboratory

Acids, bases and salts are groups of chemicals that surround us in daily life and which have many uses. The acid in fruit adds to its taste and nutritional value. Acid in our stomachs helps digest food. Bases are useful in the house and garden. Common salt – sodium chloride – is essential for life.

10.1 pH and indicators

How can you tell the pH of a solution?

The pH of a solution is measured on the **pH scale**. This is a series of numbers from 0 to 14. Solutions with a pH less than 7 are **acidic**, those with pH more than 7 are **alkaline**, and the middle number indicates a **neutral** substance, which is neither acid nor alkaline.

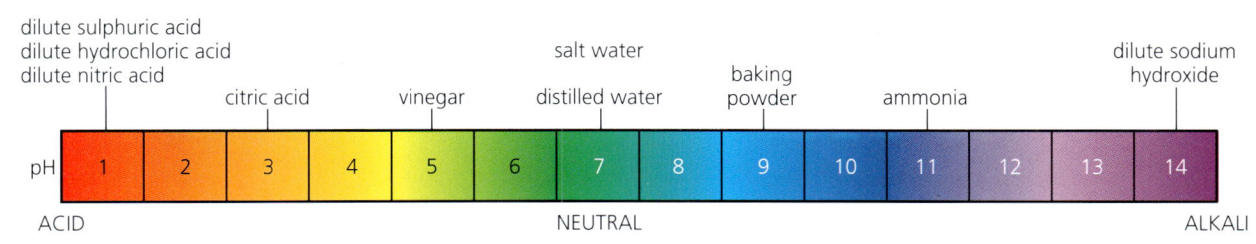

pH	1	2	3	4	5	6	7	8	9	10	11	12	13	14
	dilute sulphuric acid, dilute hydrochloric acid, dilute nitric acid		citric acid		vinegar		salt water, distilled water		baking powder		ammonia			dilute sodium hydroxide

ACID — NEUTRAL — ALKALI

Figure 1 Some common household substances on the pH scale.

Some natural colours in plants change when placed in acidic or alkaline solutions. The one most commonly used is litmus, which is red in acids and blue in alkalis. Chemicals that change their colour depending on the acidity of a solution are called **indicators**.

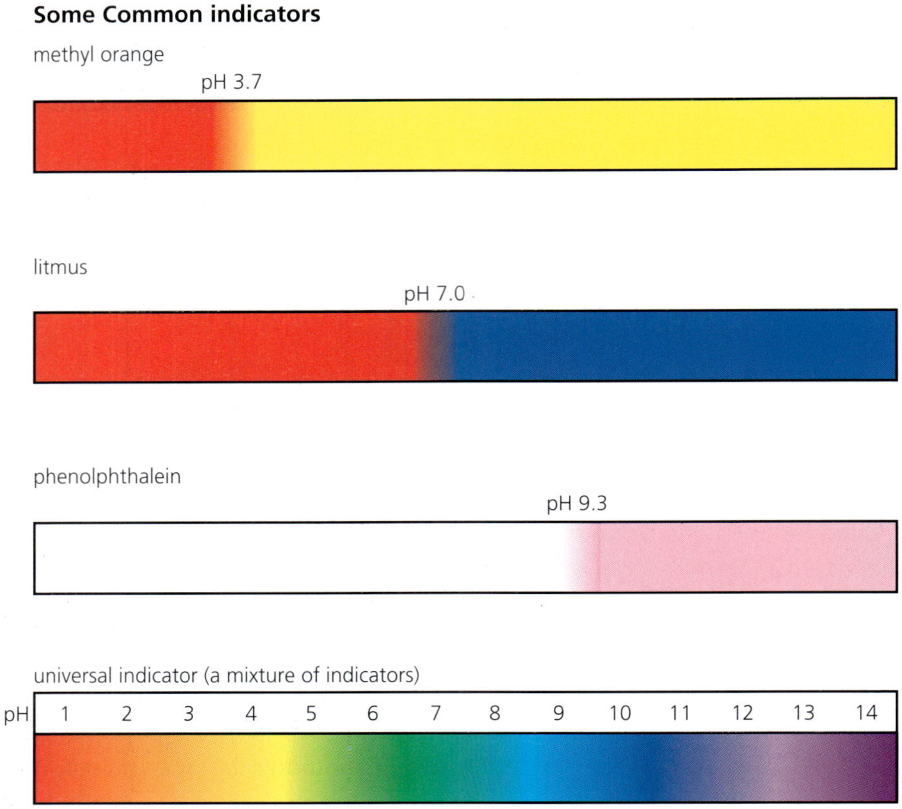

Using chemistry in everyday life

Some Common indicators

methyl orange — pH 3.7

litmus — pH 7.0

phenolphthalein — pH 9.3

universal indicator (a mixture of indicators)
pH 1 2 3 4 5 6 7 8 9 10 11 12 13 14

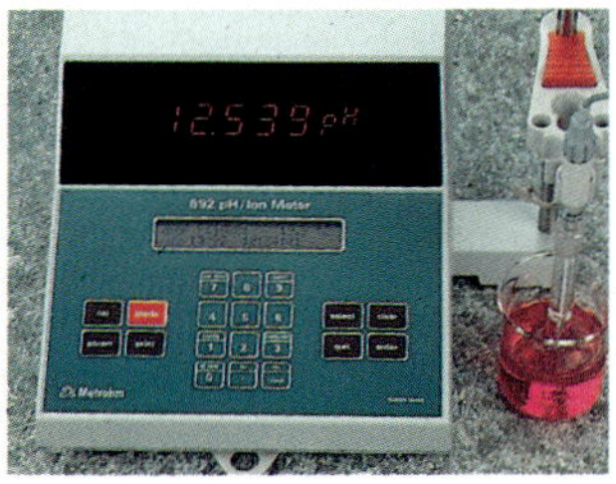

The pH of a solution can be measured very accurately using a pH meter.

Figure 2

Summary of pH and indicators

- The pH scale shows whether a solution is acid, alkali or neutral.
- An indicator is a chemical that changes colour with changes in pH.

10.2 Acids
What are acids?

Acids are chemicals that dissolve in water to release hydrogen ions, H^+. The hydrogen ion is very reactive. When this ion dissolves in water, it joins onto a water molecule to form the much more stable hydroxonium ion, H_3O^+. Hydroxonium ions can be are represented by writing the (aq) state symbol after a hydrogen ion: $H^+(aq)$. These ions give acids their unique properties.

Acids, bases and salts

Table 1 Some common acids

Name	Formula	Description	Where found
citric acid	$C_6H_8O_7$	white solid	citrus fruits such as lemons and limes
ethanoic acid (acetic acid)	$C_2H_4O_2$	colourless liquid	vinegar
hydrochloric acid	HCl	colourless gas	stomach acid (dissolved in water), also manufactured as a useful chemical
nitric acid	HNO_3	colourless liquid	a constituent of 'acid rain', also a useful chemical
sulphuric acid	H_2SO_4	dense colourless liquid	constituent of 'acid rain', also a useful chemical

Important points about acids

- All acids need to be dissolved in water before they will show acidic properties.

- All metals react with at least one acid. The general pattern for this is:
  metal + acid → salt + hydrogen
  For example, zinc reacts with sulphuric acid:
  $Zn(s) + 2HCl(aq) \rightarrow ZnSO_4(aq) + H_2(g)$
  The only exception to this pattern is that nitric acid reacts with many metals to give oxides of nitrogen instead of hydrogen. For example, copper metal can react with nitric acid in one of two ways:
  $Cu(s) + 4HNO_3(aq) \rightarrow Cu(NO_3)_2(aq) + 2H_2O(l) + 2NO_2(g)$
  $3Cu(s) + 8HNO_3(aq) \rightarrow 3Cu(NO_3)_2(aq) + 4H_2O(l) + 2NO(g)$

- All acids react with metal oxides and hydroxides in a general pattern like this:
  metal oxide or hydroxide + acid → salt + water
  For example, copper (II) oxide reacts with sulphuric acid:
  $CuO(s) + H_2SO_4(aq) \rightarrow CuSO_4(aq) + H_2O(l)$
  Calcium hydroxide reacts with hydrochloric acid:
  $Ca(OH)_2(aq) + 2HCl(aq) \rightarrow CaCl_2(aq) + 2H_2O(l)$

- All acids react with carbonates:
  carbonate + acid → salt + water + carbon dioxide
  For example, calcium carbonate reacts with hydrochloric acid:
  $CaCO_3(s) + 2HCl(aq) \rightarrow CaCl_2(aq) + H_2O(l) + CO_2(g)$
  This reaction is a useful test for acids. When any acid is dropped onto a carbonate carbon dioxide gas is given off.

- Aqueous solutions of acids will always conduct electricity. This is because acidic solutions always contain ions, which can move through the water and carry the electric current.

Using chemistry in everyday life

1. Complete and balance the following symbol equations.
   a Mg(s)   + HCl(aq)   →
   b Al$_2$O$_3$(s)   + HNO$_3$(aq) →
   c K$_2$CO$_3$(aq)   + HCl(aq)   →
   d ZnO(s)   + HNO$_3$(aq) →

What is acid strength?

The strength of an acid refers to the extent to which the acid molecules can be split up into ions. A **strong acid** will be almost totally split up, or **'dissociated'**, into ions. In a **weak acid** only a few ions are present.

Hydrochloric acid is said to be a strong acid, because in aqueous solution it is almost entirely split up into ions. Ethanoic acid is a weak acid, because in aqueous solution most of it remains as molecules, with only a few ions formed.

Table 2 *Properties of strong and weak acids*

	Strong acid	Weak acid
example	hydrochloric acid	ethanoic acid
formula	HCl	CH$_3$COOH
electrical conductivity of aqueous solution	very good	poor
pH of 0.1 M solution	1	5
	the acid splits up almost entirely into ions	the acid forms only a few ions, most of it remaining as molecules

Is strength the same as concentration?

It is important to distinguish between the strength of an acid and its concentration. Acid **strength** is to do with how well an acid is dissociated into ions. The **concentration** of an acid refers to *how much* of the acid is dissolved in a certain volume of water – a 0.001 M solution of nitric acid (a strong acid) is quite dilute, a 5.0 M solution is quite concentrated.

2. Citric acid, which is found in many fruits, is known to be a **weak acid.** It may be used in low **concentrations** as an additive to fruit drinks.
   Explain as clearly as you can the meaning of the words in bold type.

Summary of Acids

- Acids dissolve in water to form hydrogen ions.
- Acids react with metals, bases and carbonates.
- All acids conduct electricity in aqueous solution.

10.3 Bases and alkalis
What is the difference between a base and an alkali?

A **base** is a substance that reacts with an acid to neutralise it. When this happens, a new substance called a salt is formed. Some bases dissolve in water and others do not. A base that is water soluble is called an **alkali**. When a base does not dissolve in water, its pH cannot be measured. When bases do dissolve in water, they form alkaline solutions with a pH greater than 7. All alkaline solutions contain hydroxide ions, OH⁻, dissolved in water. These ions give alkalis their unique properties.

Table 3 Some common bases

Name	Formula	Uses
ammonia	NH_3	in household cleaners, as a breakdown product of urine (nappies and stables sometimes smell of ammonia)
calcium hydroxide	$Ca(OH)_2$	lime to neutralise soil
magnesium hydroxide	$Mg(OH)_2$	indigestion remedies to neutralise excess stomach acid
sodium hydroxide	NaOH	'caustic soda' in oven cleaners

Ammonia is a stable gas

3 The following table shows the pH of various solutions:

Name	Formula	pH of aqueous solution
ammonia	NH_3	10
ethanoic acid	$C_2H_4O_2$	4
hydrochloric acid	HCl	1
sodium hydrogen carbonate	$NaHCO_3$	9
sodium hydroxide	NaOH	14

Which of these solutions is best to:

a use to neutralise a spill of very alkaline oven cleaner?
b swallow as an indigestion remedy to neutralise excess stomach acid?
c use, with care, as a very alkaline substance to clean baked-on grease from an oven?
d spray onto soil to counteract excess acidity?

Important points about bases

- All bases react with acids to neutralise them and form a salt, in the following general pattern:

    base + acid → salt + water

    For example, insoluble magnesium oxide is neutralised by sulphuric acid:

    $MgO(s) + H_2SO_4(aq) → MgSO_4(aq) + H_2O(l)$

    Similarly, sodium hydroxide is neutralised by nitric acid:

    $NaOH(aq) + HNO_3(aq) → NaNO_3(aq) + H_2O(l)$

- Alkaline solutions always conduct electricity. This is because they contain ions, which can move through the water and carry the electric current.

4 Complete and balance the following symbol equations:
 a $NaOH(aq) + H_2SO_4(aq) →$
 b $CaO(s) + HNO_3(aq) →$
 c $Al(OH)_3(aq) + HCl(aq) →$

What is alkaline strength?

Alkalis, like acids, can be described as strong or weak. This refers to the extent to which the alkali can split up into ions. A **strong alkali** will be almost totally dissociated into ions, a **weak alkali** will mostly exist as whole molecules.

Sodium hydroxide is said to be a strong alkali, because in aqueous solution it is almost entirely split up into $Na^+(aq)$ ions and $OH^-(aq)$ ions. Ammonia solution is said to be weakly alkaline, because in aqueous solution it is mostly in the form of molecules and only a few of these molecules split up into ions.

Table 4 Strong and weak alkalis

	Strong alkali	Weak alkali
example	sodium hydroxide	ammonia solution
formula	NaOH	NH_3
electrical conductivity of aqueous solution	very good	poor
pH of 0.1 M solution	14	10
	the base has split up almost entirely into ions	only a few ions are formed, most of the base remaining as molecules

Are oxides acids or bases?

Oxygen reacts with almost all other metallic and non-metallic elements to form oxides. An oxide is a compound of oxygen with another element. Oxides can behave as acids or bases, and some act as both.

Non-metal oxides are acidic. They will react directly with bases to form salts. Sulphur dioxide is an acidic oxide which can be neutralised by reacting it with calcium carbonate (limestone):

$$SO_2(g) + CaCO_3(s) \rightarrow CaSO_3(s) + CO_2(g)$$

Most non-metal oxides will dissolve in water to form acidic solutions. The nitrogen dioxide formed during any combustion process will dissolve in rainwater to make two different nitric acids:

$$2NO_2(g) + H_2O(l) \rightarrow HNO_3(aq) + HNO_2(aq)$$

Most metal oxides and hydroxides are bases. They neutralise acids in a variety of ways. For example, copper (II) oxide neutralises hydrochloric acid:

$$CuO(s) + 2HCl(aq) \rightarrow CuCl_2(aq) + H_2O(l)$$

Similarly, calcium hydroxide will neutralise nitric acid:

$$Ca(OH)_2(s) + 2HNO_3(aq) \rightarrow Ca(NO_3)_2(aq) + 2H_2O(l)$$

What are amphoteric oxides?

Amphoteric oxides react with both acids and bases. Aluminium oxide is amphoteric. It will react with acids as follows:

$$Al_2O_3(s) + 6HCl(aq) \rightarrow 2AlCl_3(aq) + 3H_2O(l)$$
aluminium chloride

It will also react with alkalis:

$$Al_2O_3(s) + 2NaOH(aq) \rightarrow 2NaAlO_2(aq) + H_2O(l)$$
sodium aluminate

Aluminium is sometimes described as a 'weak' metal. This is not to do with its physical strength, but its chemical properties. In the periodic table, aluminium is next to the non-metallic element silicon. Some of its chemical properties are between those of metals and non-metals. One example of this is having an oxide that is amphoteric.

A few oxides are sometimes described as **neutral**. These do not react readily with either acids or bases. One example of a neutral oxide is carbon monoxide.

Name	Formula
aluminium oxide	Al_2O_3
calcium oxide	CaO
nitrogen dioxide	NO_2
phosphorus (V) oxide	P_2O_5
sodium oxide	NaO
sulphur trioxide	SO_3

5 Study the table opposite. Find the position of the elements involved on the periodic table and use this information to determine whether the oxide is likely to be basic, acidic or amphoteric.

Summary of bases and alkalis

- A base is a substance that neutralises an acid, forming a salt.
- An alkali is a water-soluble base.
- All alkaline solutions contain hydroxide ions.
- All acids and alkalis conduct electricity in aqueous solution.
- Oxides may be basic, acidic or neutral.

Using chemistry in everyday life

10.4 Neutralisation

What happens when a base reacts with an acid?

An acid and a base react together in a process known as **neutralisation**. All acids in aqueous solution contain hydrogen ions, H⁺(aq). Similarly all alkalis in aqueous solution contain hydroxide ions, OH⁻(aq). During the process of neutralisation, these ions cancel react together.

Hydrochloric acid and sodium hydroxide react together like this:

$$NaOH(aq) + HCl(aq) \rightarrow NaCl(aq) + H_2O(l)$$

During this reaction the chloride ions from the acid and the sodium ions from the alkali don't actually take part in the reaction – they are present before and afterwards. This can be shown by rewriting the equation to show the ions and molecules present:

$$Na^+(aq)OH^-(aq) + H^+(aq)Cl^- \rightarrow Na^+(aq)Cl^-(aq) + H_2O(l)$$

Figure 3

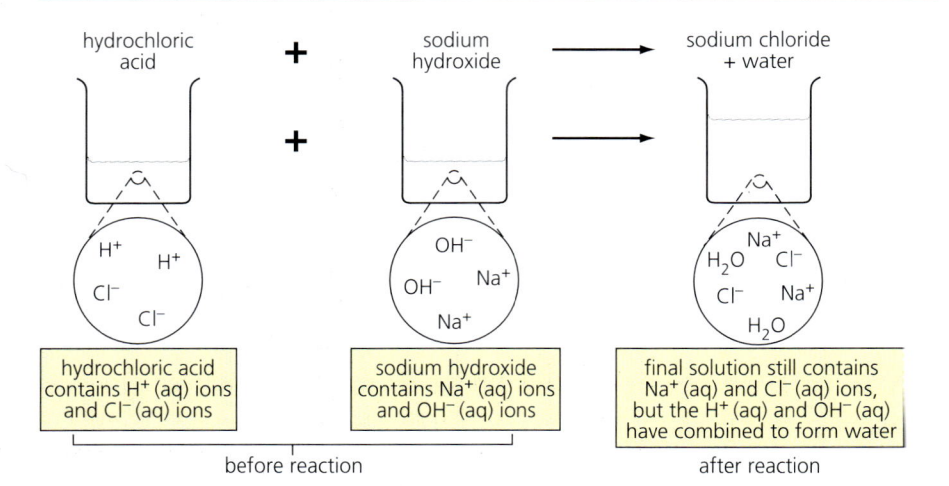

hydrochloric acid + sodium hydroxide → sodium chloride + water

hydrochloric acid contains H⁺ (aq) ions and Cl⁻ (aq) ions

sodium hydroxide contains Na⁺ (aq) ions and OH⁻ (aq) ions

final solution still contains Na⁺ (aq) and Cl⁻ (aq) ions, but the H⁺ (aq) and OH⁻ (aq) have combined to form water

before reaction — after reaction

6 a Explain what the process of neutralisation involves.
b Write a balanced symbol equation for the reaction between sodium hydroxide and nitric acid.
c What is a spectator ion? Study the equation that you have written and write down the names and symbols of the spectator ions in this reaction.
d Write an ionic equation for this neutralisation reaction.

In this reaction the ions that take no part in the process are called **spectator ions**. If spectator ions are removed from the equation, an **ionic equation** can be written. This shows only the ions that take part in the reaction – in this case the hydrogen ions from the acid and the hydroxide ions from the alkali combine to make water:

$$H^+(aq) + OH^-(aq) \rightarrow H_2O(l)$$

This happens every time any acid is neutralised by any alkali. Whatever acid is involved it will always contain hydrogen ions. Whatever alkali is involved it will always contain hydroxide ions. When they react together, a molecule of water is always formed.

How can you follow neutralisation in the laboratory?

In a titration a solution of a known concentration can be used to find the concentration of a second solution.

Acids, bases and salts

Change in temperature

thermometer or temperature probe

The neutralisation reaction gives out heat - it is **exothermic**. As the reaction continues the temperature rises

When neutralisation is complete the temperature stops rising

As more acid is added, the temperature will start to fall

Using a pH meter

pH meter

pH electrode

At start, the solution is alkaline

At neutralisation point, the pH suddenly changes

When too much acid has been added the solution becomes acidic

basic apparatus for titration

0.1M hydrochloric acid

conical flask

burette

tap

white tile (to see colour change)

sodium hydroxide solution of unknown molarity

solutions that contain ions conduct electric current

Change in conductivity

conductivity meter

as neutralisation proceeds, H$^+$ and OH$^-$ ions combine to form water molecules and ions are removed from solution. The conductivity goes down

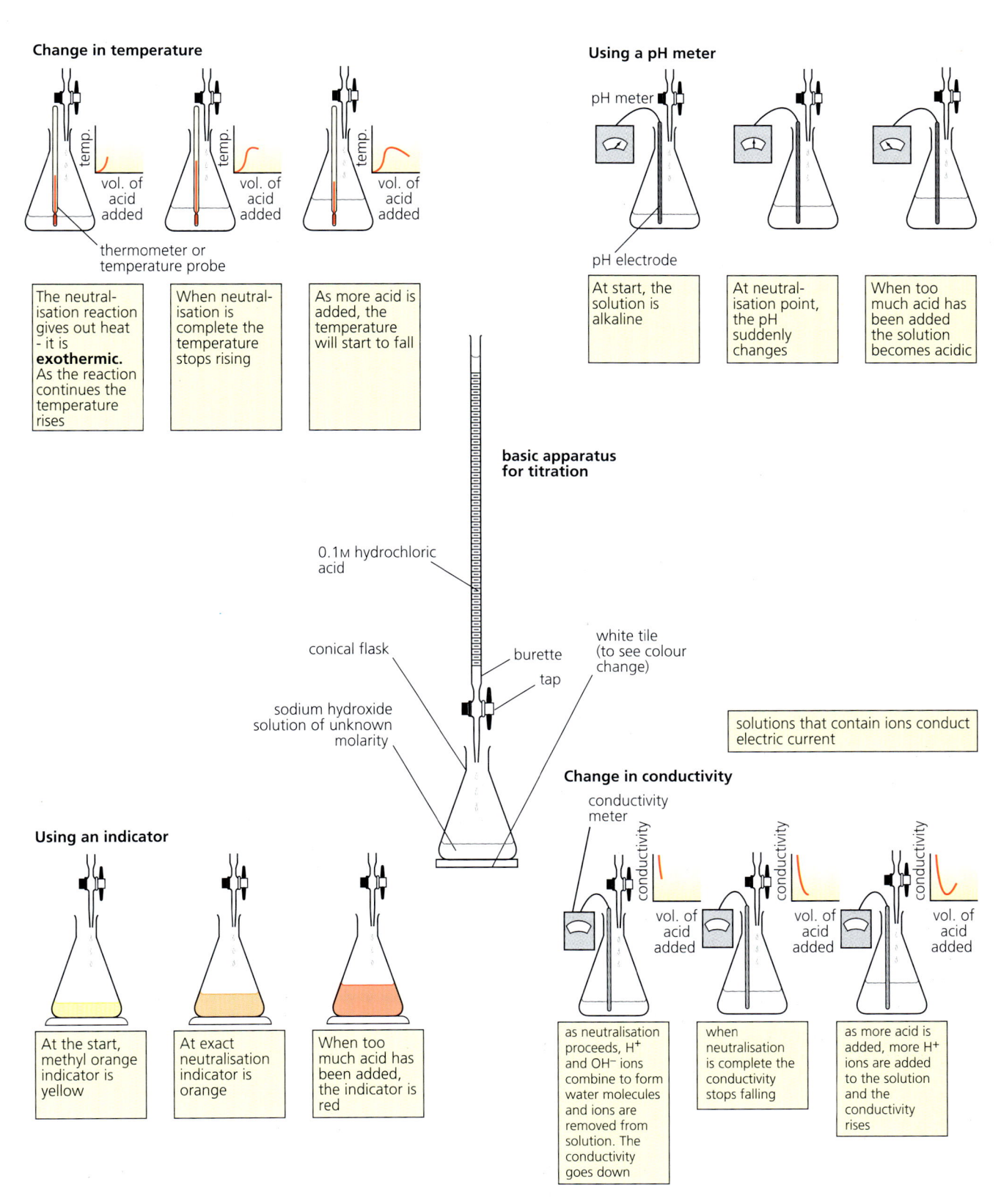

when neutralisation is complete the conductivity stops falling

as more acid is added, more H$^+$ ions are added to the solution and the conductivity rises

Using an indicator

At the start, methyl orange indicator is yellow

At exact neutralisation indicator is orange

When too much acid has been added, the indicator is red

Figure 4 The process of neutralisation can be followed in a number of ways.

139

Using chemistry in everyday life

Summary of neutralisation

- The process that happens when an acid and a base react together is called neutralisation.
- The ionic equation for neutralisation is written $H^+(aq) + OH^-(aq) \rightarrow H_2O(l)$
- The concentration of an acid or base can be found using titration.

10.4 Salts
How are salts formed?

When an acid and a base react together a salt is formed.

| general reaction: | base + acid → salt + water |

The actual salt produced will depend on the 'parent' acid and base.

| NaOH(aq) + HCl(aq) → NaCl(aq) + H₂O(l) |
| sodium hydroxide + hydrochloric acid → sodium chloride + water |

The salt formed here is sodium chloride (NaCl). The positive sodium ion comes from the base, sodium hydroxide, and the negative chloride ion comes from the hydrochloric acid. All simple salts have a **cation** and an **anion** that come from a base and acid in this way. When the salt is formed, one or more hydrogen atoms on the acid are replaced by a positive ion from the base.

Figure 5 Ions in salts.

positive ions from a base   and   negative ions from an acid

e.g. sodium hydroxide + hydrochloric acid
NaOH   HCl
  ↓ contains   ↓ contains
Na⁺   Cl⁻
         ↘   ↙
        NaCl
salt formed is   sodium chloride

hydrochloric acid forms salts called **chlorides**

e.g. copper (II) oxide + sulphuric acid
CuO   H₂SO₄
  ↓ contains   ↓ contains
Cu²⁺   SO₄²⁻
         ↘   ↙
        CuSO₄
salt formed is   copper (II) sulphate

sulphuric acid forms salts called **sulphates**

e.g. magnesium oxide + nitric acid
MgO   2HNO₃
  ↓ contains   ↓ contains
Mg²⁺   NO₃⁻ + NO₃⁻
         ↘   ↙
        Mg(NO₃)₂
salt formed is   magnesium nitrate

nitric acid forms salts called **nitrates**

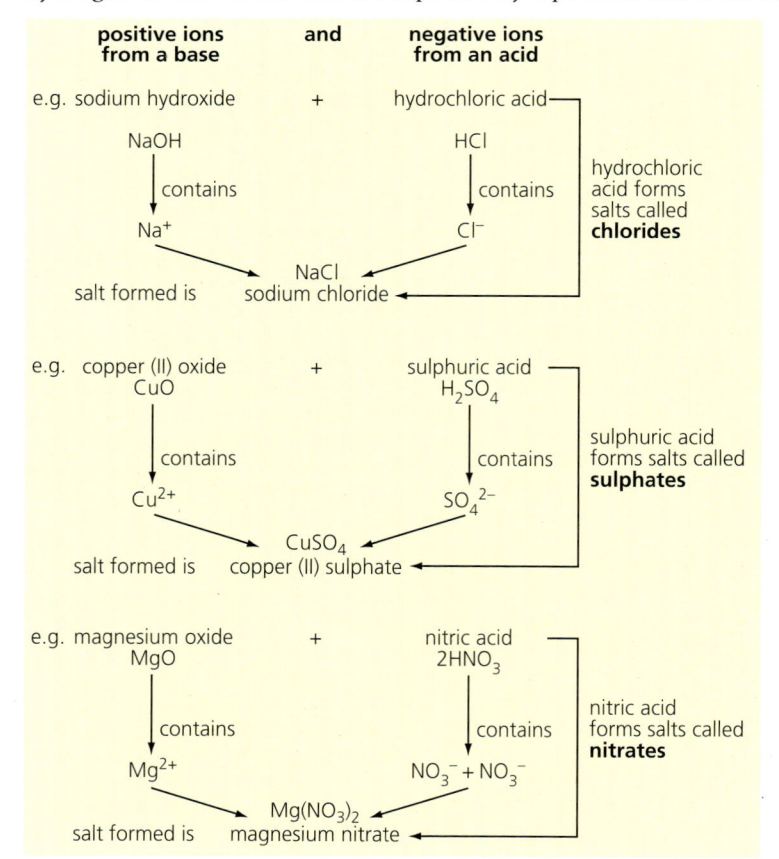

7 Look back at table 2 on page 100. Use the information in the table to write formulae for the following compounds:
  a silver chloride
  b sodium nitrate
  c lead sulphate
  d calcium carbonate
  e potassium chloride.

8 Which of the substances in the last question do you think is soluble in water?

Acids, bases and salts

Making sodium nitrate

$$NaOH(aq) + HNO_3(aq) \rightarrow NaNO_3(aq) + H_2O(l)$$

- burette
- dilute nitric acid
- known volume of sodium hydroxide with indicator
- white tile

Dilute acid added to a known volume of sodium hydroxide until the indicator changes colour. The volume of nitric acid used is measured

The volume calculated is then added to the same volume of sodium hydroxide without indicator

Making zinc sulphate

$$Zn(s) + H_2SO_4(aq) \rightarrow ZnSO_4(aq) + H_2O(l)$$

- zinc powder
- dilute sulphuric acid
- excess zinc
- zinc sulphate solution

Zinc powder added to dilute sulphuric acid until reaction stops – there is then excess zinc

Excess zinc is filtered off

Making copper (II) sulphate

$$CuO(s) + H_2SO_4(aq) \rightarrow CuSO_4(aq) + H_2O(l)$$

- copper (II) oxide
- warm dilute sulphuric acid
- copper (II) sulphate solution
- heat

Copper (II) oxide added to warm dilute sulphuric acid until there is an excess of the insoluble oxide

Solution boiled to ensure the reaction is complete

Excess copper oxide is filtered off

Making nickel (II) chloride

$$NiCO_3(s) + 2HCl(aq) \rightarrow NiCl_2(aq) + H_2O(l) + CO_2(g)$$

- nickel carbonate powder
- dilute hydrochloric acid
- excess nickel carbonate
- nickel (II) chloride solution
- heat

Nickel (II) carbonate powder added to dilute hydrochloric acid until there is excess of the insoluble carbonate

Solution is boiled to ensure reaction is complete

Excess nickel carbonate filtered off

---

heat

The solution is heated to drive off excess water until it is saturated

Solution is left to cool and crystallise

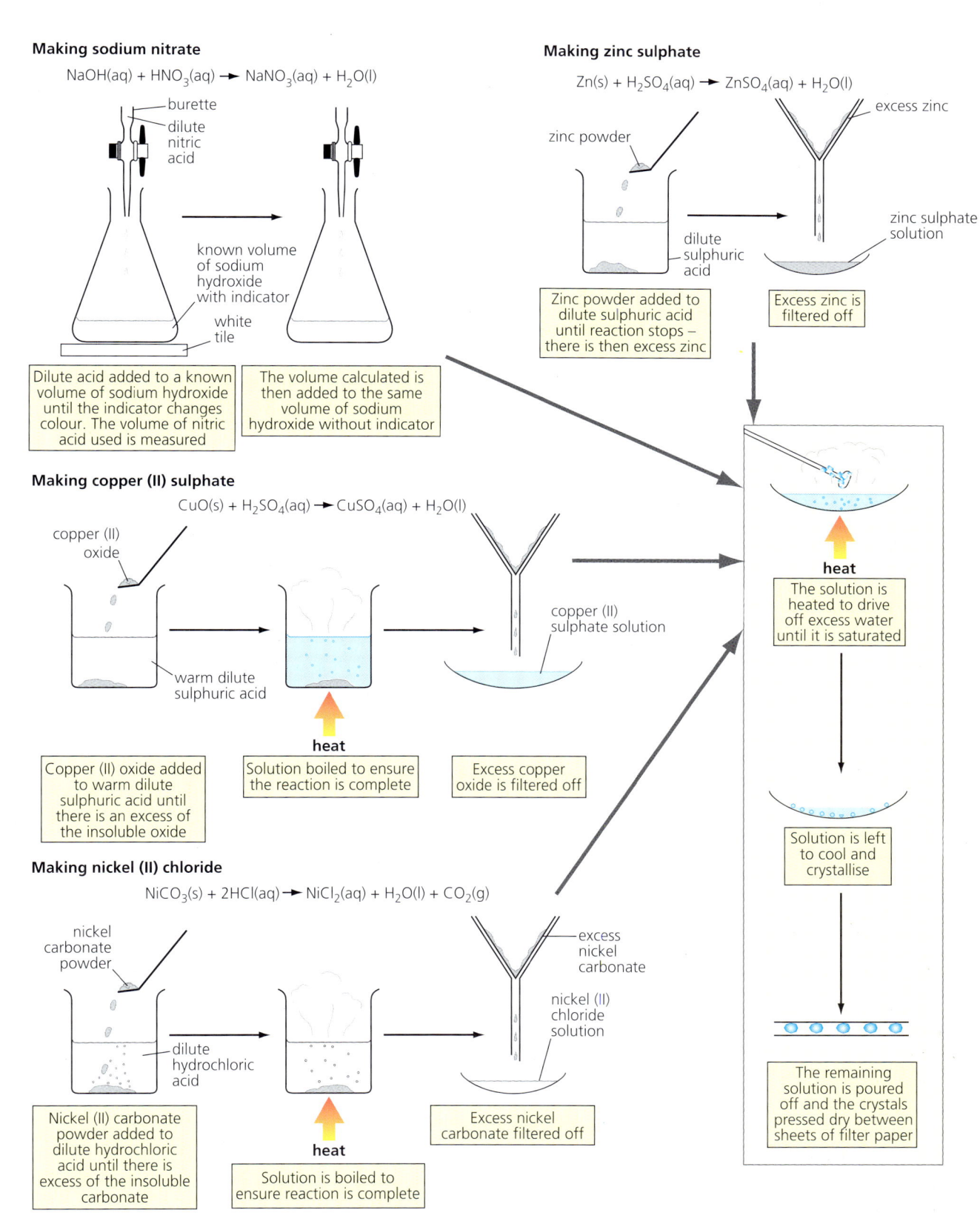

The remaining solution is poured off and the crystals pressed dry between sheets of filter paper

Figure 6 There are several ways of preparing salts in the laboratory.

141

Using chemistry in everyday life

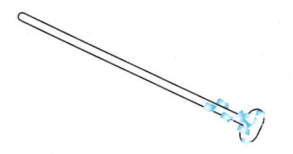

Figure 7 Crystallising a solution. A small amount of solution is removed on the end of a cold, dry, stirring rod. If crystals form on the rod then the rest of the solution will also form crystals when cooled.

Reacting a metal with an acid

All metals react with at least one acid, so many different salts could be made by dissolving various metals in acids. This is a good method for making salts from moderately reactive metals like zinc or magnesium. It is not suitable for very unreactive metals, since the acid would have to be dangerously concentrated for a reaction to take place. It is also not suitable for very reactive metals like sodium or potassium, as these are dangerously reactive with acids.

Reacting a base and an acid

When a metal is either very unreactive or dangerously reactive it is safer to use the metal oxide or hydroxide to prepare the salt.

Reacting carbonates and acids

All carbonates react with acids to make salts.

Making insoluble salts by precipitation

The three methods just described are only suitable for preparing salts that are soluble in water. To prepare salts that are insoluble in water, a different process must to be used. Solutions of two soluble salts are added together to make an insoluble salt in a **precipitation** reaction.

Preparing an insoluble salt from soluble salts by precipitation

$AgNO_3(aq) + NaCl(aq) \rightarrow AgCl(s) + NaNO_3(aq)$

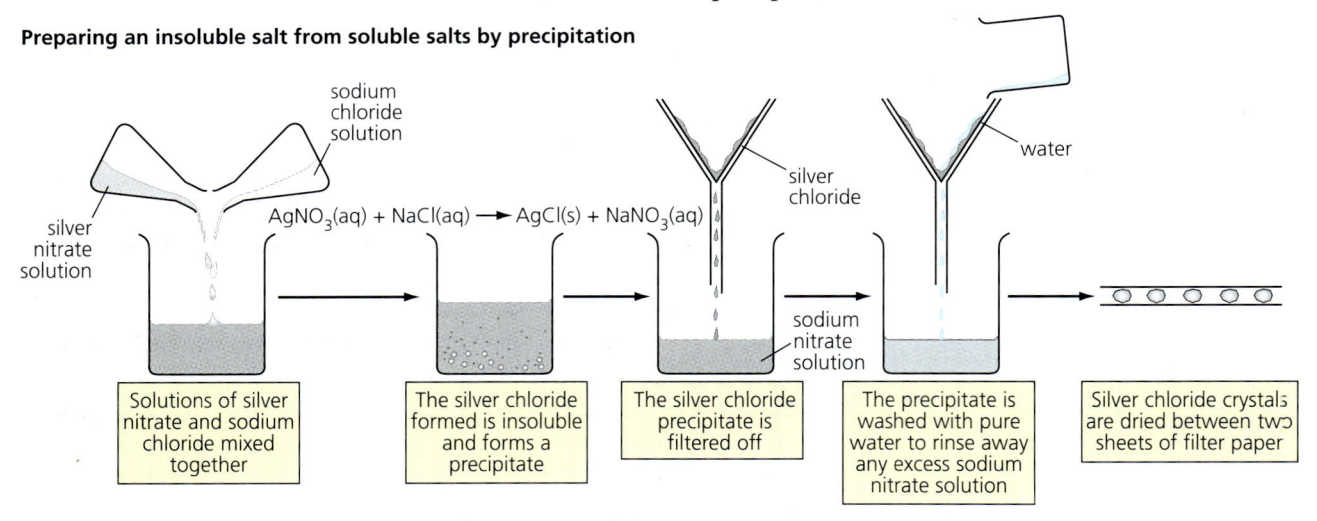

| Solutions of silver nitrate and sodium chloride mixed together | The silver chloride formed is insoluble and forms a precipitate | The silver chloride precipitate is filtered off | The precipitate is washed with pure water to rinse away any excess sodium nitrate solution | Silver chloride crystals are dried between two sheets of filter paper |

Figure 8 The insoluble salt, silver chloride, can be prepared by reacting two soluble salts together.

9 Table 5 contains information about various compounds. Which compounds would you use to prepare:
 a barium sulphate
 b lead chloride (in a cold solution)
 c magnesium carbonate
 d silver bromide?
 Write a balanced symbol equation for each reaction.

Acids, bases and salts

Table 5 *Solubility of various salts in water*

Name	Formula	Solubility in water
ammonium sulphate	$(NH_4)_2SO_4$	soluble
barium carbonate	$BaCO_3$	insoluble
barium chloride	$BaCl_2$	soluble
barium sulphate	$BaSO_4$	insoluble
lead chloride	$PbCl_2$	insoluble (in cold)
lead nitrate	$Pb(NO_3)_2$	soluble
magnesium carbonate	$MgCO_3$	insoluble
magnesium nitrate	$MgNO_3$	soluble
potassium bromide	KBr	soluble
silver bromide	$AgBr$	insoluble
silver nitrate	$AgNO_3$	soluble
silver sulphate	Ag_2SO_4	insoluble
sodium carbonate	Na_2CO_3	soluble
sodium chloride	$NaCl$	soluble

Summary of salts

- The general reaction for forming a salt is:
  base + acid → salt + water
- Salts can be prepared in the laboratory by reacting metals, bases or carbonates with acids.
- Insoluble salts can be precipitated out of a reaction between two soluble salts.

Examination style questions

1 a Describe how you could prepare a sample of pure magnesium sulphate crystals ($MgSO_4.7H_2O$) in the laboratory, starting with magnesium oxide and dilute sulphuric acid.

b Write a balanced symbol equation for this reaction.

c Calculate the maximum mass of magnesium sulphate crystals that could be prepared starting from 8.0 g of magnesium oxide.

d Explain why a sample of lead sulphate could not be prepared in a similar way using lead oxide and sulphuric acid.

e Briefly outline a way in which lead sulphate could be prepared in the laboratory.

f Write a balanced symbol equation for the reaction you described in **e**.

2 A titration was carried out to determine the molarity of a sample of sodium hydroxide solution. A burette was filled with 0.150 M sulphuric acid, and this was added to exactly 25.0 cm³ of sodium hydroxide solution in a conical flask. The pH of the solution in the flask was plotted throughout the experiment, and the results are shown in figure 9.

a Use the graph to determine the pH of the sodium hydroxide at the start of the reaction.

b What is the pH at the end of the experiment?

c Write a balanced symbol equation, including state symbols, for this reaction.

d Use the graph to determine the volume of sulphuric acid which exactly neutralised the sodium hydroxide.

e Calculate the molarity of the sodium hydroxide solution used in this experiment.

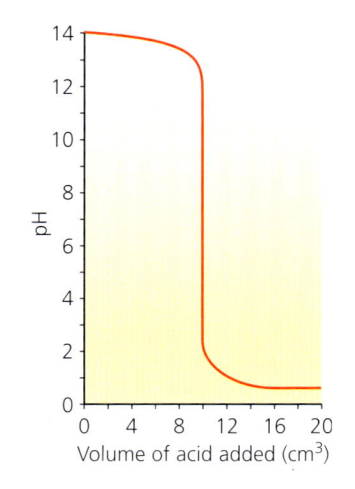

Figure 9

143

Water and aqueous solutions 11

Learning objectives

By the end of this chapter you should be able to:
- **describe** the water cycle
- **explain** how water supplies and sewage are treated to make them safe to use
- **explain** how water becomes hard and how hardness can be removed
- **recognise** the difference between temporary and permanent hardness
- **list** some of the unusual properties of water
- **define** water of crystallisation
- **interpret** solubility curves
- **describe** some of the chemical tests for common ions

11.1 Obtaining clean water

Why is pure water rare in nature?

Roughly 80% of the surface of the Earth is covered by water but about 97% of this water is unfit to drink. Most of it is sea water, which contains too many dissolved solids to make it suitable for drinking. A number of natural processes occur on the Earth which endlessly recycle vital elements and compounds. One example of these cycles is the **water cycle**, described in figure 1.

Because water is such a good solvent it is often called a **universal solvent**. When water passes over various rocks and minerals, it dissolves small amounts of many substances. Various gases present in the atmosphere also dissolve in water. For this reason water is seldom found in a completely pure state in the natural world.

What do we use water for?

People in the developed world use hundreds of litres of water in their homes each day. Most of this is used for flushing the toilet and for washing and cleaning. Only a relatively small proportion is used for drinking.

Industry also uses large amounts of water – to wash raw materials such as wood pulp, coal and metal ores or for cooling. The food processing industry uses a lot of water to clean and prepare foods.

Water and aqueous solutions

Many industries use water for cooling and the water downstream from a power station like this can be several degrees warmer as a result of passing through the cooling towers. This can cause 'thermal pollution', in which the level of oxygen dissolved in the water is reduced. The species of plants and fish living in the area will change as the environment is altered.

Water cycle

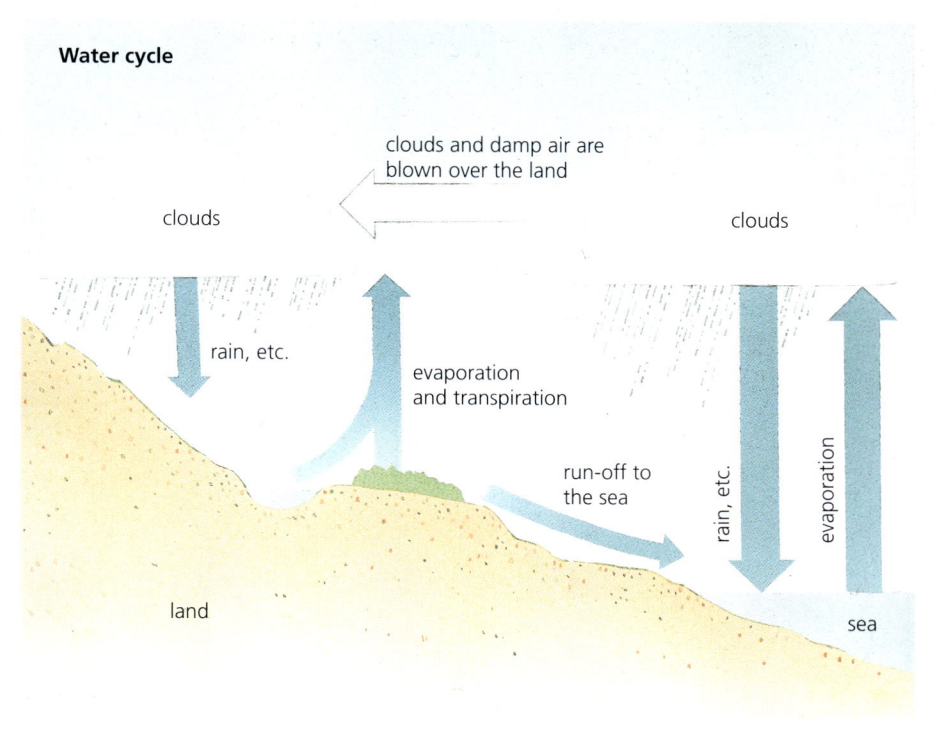

clouds and damp air are blown over the land

clouds — clouds

rain, etc.

evaporation and transpiration

run-off to the sea

rain, etc.

evaporation

land — sea

Figure 1 The water cycle is essential to provide us with supplies of fresh water.

How is the water supply treated?

Most of the water we use come from rivers, lakes or underground water-bearing rocks called **aquifers**. It must be treated before it can be used.

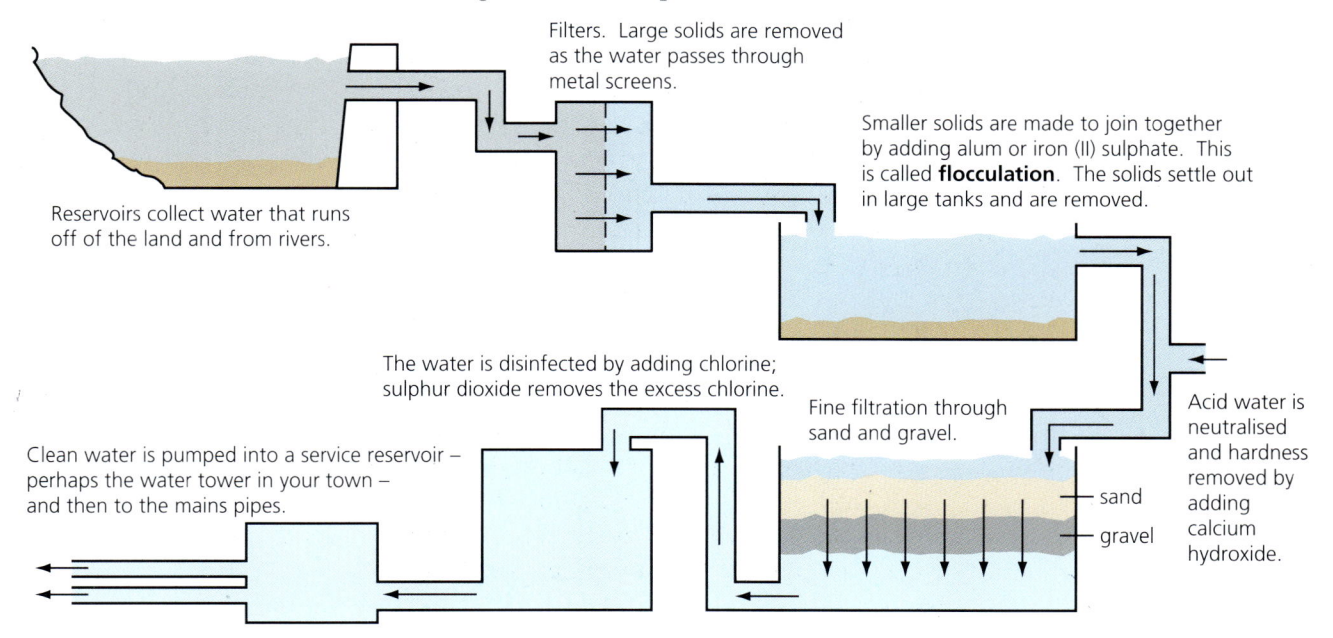

Reservoirs collect water that runs off of the land and from rivers.

Filters. Large solids are removed as the water passes through metal screens.

Smaller solids are made to join together by adding alum or iron (II) sulphate. This is called **flocculation**. The solids settle out in large tanks and are removed.

The water is disinfected by adding chlorine; sulphur dioxide removes the excess chlorine.

Fine filtration through sand and gravel.

Acid water is neutralised and hardness removed by adding calcium hydroxide.

Clean water is pumped into a service reservoir — perhaps the water tower in your town — and then to the mains pipes.

sand
gravel

Figure 2 Water obtained from streams, rivers and aquifers must be purified before it is fit for human consumption.

145

Water and aqueous solutions

1. Why is it important to treat drinking water before it reaches the home?
2. Give two uses for water in the home and two uses in industry.
3. Do you think that the water filtered from a gravel bed like that in figure 2 is safe to drink? Give reasons for your answer.

4. Do you think that fluoride should be added to drinking water by the water company, or do you think people should make their own choices? Discuss your reasons.

Sometimes water companies add compounds containing fluorine to the water supply if levels are naturally low. Such fluoride compounds are known to help prevent tooth decay. However, some people are unhappy that chemicals are added to their drinking water. These people feel that they should be allowed to choose for themselves whether or not to add fluoride to their water.

What happens to sewage?

Whenever you flush the toilet, empty the bath or sink, or run a washing machine or dishwasher, the water 'disappears' down the drain and is often forgotten. Rainwater from roofs, roads and pavements and waste water from industry also flows through the drains. The waste water is collected into a network of underground **sewers**, which channel it to a sewage treatment plant.

Treatment of sewage follows the same pattern as the preparation of fresh water (figure 3).

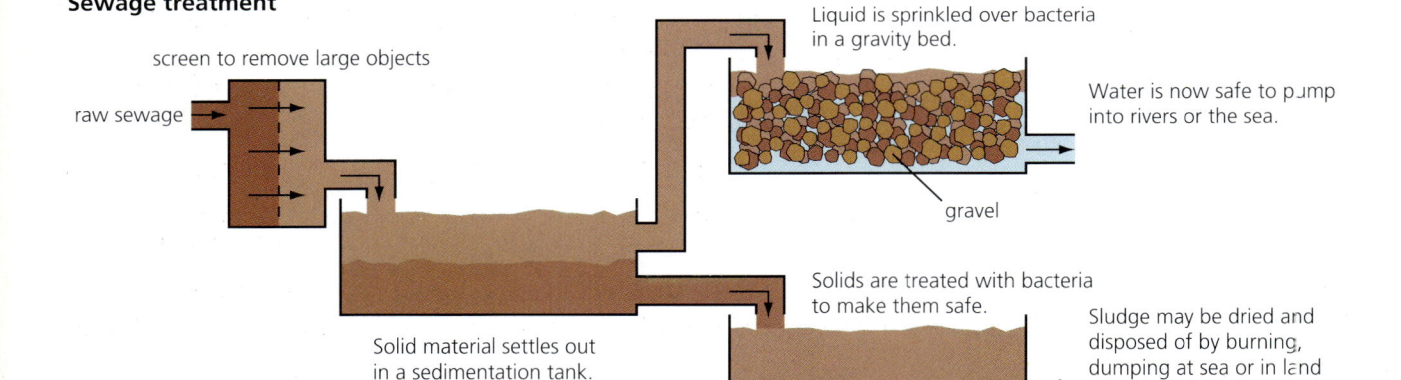

Figure 3

Sewage treatment

- raw sewage → screen to remove large objects
- Solid material settles out in a sedimentation tank.
- Liquid is sprinkled over bacteria in a gravity bed.
- Water is now safe to pump into rivers or the sea.
- gravel
- Solids are treated with bacteria to make them safe.
- Sludge may be dried and disposed of by burning, dumping at sea or in land reclamation. Some may be used as fertiliser.

5. Suggest some of the uses for the sludge from a sewage treatment works.
6. In some coastal areas sewage is discharged directly into the sea. Do you think this is a suitable way of disposal? Give reasons for your answer.

Summary of obtaining clean water

- Water is sometimes called a universal solvent because it dissolves many substances.
- Water is recycled naturally in the water cycle.
- Water supplies are treated to make them safe to drink.
- Sewage and waste water are usually treated to make them safe before being discharged into rivers or the sea.

11.2 Hardness in water

What is the difference between 'hard' and 'soft' water?

Supplies of water are sometimes described as 'soft' or 'hard'. **Soft water** contains very few dissolved solids. Rainwater collected directly, for example in a garden water butt, is usually quite soft. If water has flowed only over relatively insoluble rocks such as granite it dissolves very few solids, so it is also quite soft.

Hard water contains dissolved solids. These are present because rainwater has flowed over minerals such as gypsum (calcium sulphate, $CaSO_4$) or limestone (calcium carbonate, $CaCO_3$). Small amounts of compounds of calcium, magnesium or iron dissolve in the water, making it hard.

How does water become hard?

Solids can be dissolved in water and make it hard in several ways. One way is that the solid, such as the calcium sulphate present in gypsum, simply dissolves into the water:

$$CaSO_4(s) + aq \longrightarrow Ca^{2+}(aq) + SO_4^{2-}(aq)$$

this shows water is present as a solvent — solution of calcium sulphate in water

Once calcium sulphate has dissolved in water, it cannot easily be removed – for example it is not changed by boiling. This type of solution is therefore known as **permanent hardness**.

Rainwater is naturally slightly acidic. If this water falls on limestone the following chemical reaction occurs:

$$CaCO_3(s) + H_2O(l) + CO_2(g) \rightarrow Ca(HCO_3)_2(aq)$$

calcium carbonate (limestone) — rainwater — calcium hydrogencarbonate

The product of this reaction dissolves in water and is washed away. When limestone is **eroded** like this, spectacular underground caves and tunnels can be formed.

The calcium hydrogencarbonate in the water makes it hard. This particular solution is not very stable, however. When it is left to evaporate, or is boiled, the process shown in the equation above is reversed, and calcium carbonate is deposited:

$$Ca(HCO_3)_2(aq) \xrightarrow{\text{evaporation or boiling}} CaCO_3(s) + H_2O(l) + CO_2(g)$$

This is why such a solution is referred to as having **temporary hardness**. When drips of this solution evaporate on the roof or floor of a cave, it gives rise to stalactites and stalagmites. These are made from the precipitated calcium carbonate formed in this reaction.

When acidic rainwater falls on areas of limestone the calcium carbonate in the rock reacts with the acid to form soluble calcium hydrogencarbonate. This process has given rise to underground caves and tunnels in limestone areas.

Water and aqueous solutions

What effects does hard water have?

When temporary hard water is boiled in kettles or boilers, the hardness is removed from the water and is deposited as a **scale** of solid calcium carbonate.

Hard water reacts with soap to form **scum**, a white insoluble solid called calcium stearate. Instead of the soap forming a foamy lather and being able to clean well, it is wasted by being turned to scum. This problem can be avoided by using 'soapless' detergents in hard water areas. These are compounds very similar to soap, but they do not react with the hardness in water to form a scum and so are more effective and economical to use.

Hard water can also be useful. The taste is generally thought to be better, and hard water is favoured by brewers in beer making. The dissolved compounds of calcium, magnesium and iron are also good for general health, such as growth of healthy bones and teeth.

When temporary hard water is boiled, calcium carbonate is deposited as scale. This can eventually block the pipe. It also wastes energy, since heat cannot be efficiently transferred to the water.

7 Limescale is formed wherever temporary hard water is heated. Temporary hard water is a weak solution of calcium hydrogencarbonate ($Ca(HCO_3)_2$).
   a How does this get into the water supply?   **b** How can you tell if you live in a hard water area?

Can hardness be removed from water?

Ion-exchange resins remove the ions that cause hardness and replace them with other ions such as sodium (Na^+) or hydrogen (H^+). The water that comes out of the column has been 'softened'.

The compounds of calcium and magnesium that cause hardness in water can be removed.

Washing soda (a name sometimes given to sodium carbonate) can be added to water, for example for washing clothes. It is also present in many bath salts. This reacts to remove dissolved calcium in hard water as a precipitate of calcium carbonate:

$Ca^{2+}(aq)$	+	$CO_3^{2-}(aq)$	→	$CaCO_3(s)$
calcium ions in hard water		carbonate ions in sodium carbonate (washing soda)		hardness removed as a precipitate of calcium carbonate

Another way of removing hardness is to use an ion-exchange resin.

8 Table 1 shows an analysis of various samples of mineral water.

Table 1 *Concentration of various ions in mineral waters (mg/l)*

Ion	Sample A	Sample B	Sample C	Sample D
calcium	55	78	64	75
magnesium	19	24	23	25
sodium	24	5	34	12
potassium	1	1	5	2
hydrogen carbonate	248	357	149	370
chloride	42	4.5	51	6
sulphate	23	10	27	6
nitrate	<0.1	3.8	22	0.5
total dissolved solids at 180°C	280	309	366	320
pH	7.4	7.2	7.9	5.4

a Which sample of water is the most acidic?
b Which sample of water is the most alkaline?
c A patient suffering from high blood pressure had been advised to go on a low sodium diet. Which sample of water might help them fulfil this?
d A reasonable level of calcium in drinking water helps contribute to healthy bones and teeth. Which sample of water contains the most calcium?
e Which sample contains the most dissolved solids?
f Name one compound which could be present in all these samples that gives rise to permanent hardness in water.
g Name one compound which could be present in all these samples that gives rise to temporary hardness in water.

Summary of hardness in water

- Water becomes hard due to the presence of dissolved compounds of calcium, magnesium and iron.
- Permanent hardness cannot be removed by boiling, but temporary hardness can.
- Hard water wastes soap by turning it into scum and can coat pipes and boilers with scale.
- Hardness in water can be removed by precipitation or by ion-exchange resins.

11.3 Water pollution

What do we mean by 'water pollution'?

Rain and rivers have always been a natural way of washing away small amounts of waste materials in the air and on land. In the natural course of things organic matter from plants or animals is broken down by bacteria into harmless products, many of which are nutrients for plants. An excess of any one waste product can overwhelm the natural processes of breakdown. When this natural balance is upset the water has become **polluted**. The water supply can be polluted by humans in several ways.

Fertilisers

These are used in intensive farming to increase the yield of crops. If water-soluble fertilisers like ammonium nitrate are used in excess they can be washed out of the soil by rainwater and enter rivers. An excess of dissolved fertiliser in river water results in **eutrophication**, which causes a number of problems:
- Water plants, especially green algae, reproduce rapidly and clog up the waterways.
- A thick layer of algae forms on the surface of the water, stopping sunlight reaching the plants at the bottom of the waterway. As a result, these plants die.
- Some of the algae die and bacteria develop to feed on them. These bacteria use up the oxygen supply in the water.
- The fish and other forms of life that need this oxygen to breathe will die and decay, leaving putrid, poisonous water.

Water and aqueous solutions

Distance downstream (m)	Dissolved oxygen (mg/l)
0	16
10	9
20	5.5
30	5.1
40	6.8
50	8.2
60	10
70	11.2
80	12.4
90	13.2
100	14.5
1100	14.5

Sewage

If excess human or animal sewage enters a river it can cause eutrophication. In most places this is now prevented by anti-pollution laws, and rivers are becoming cleaner and less polluted.

9 a Use the data in the table opposite to draw a graph to show the amount of oxygen dissolved in the river water downstream from the sewage outlet.
   b Explain the shape of the oxygen graph you have drawn.

Detergents

Most detergents are biodegradable and so are broken down before they can cause too much pollution. However, many modern detergents contain phosphates, which can cause eutrophication.

10 a How is the natural balance in a river upset by an excess of fertiliser or organic matter? What is this process called?
   b Suggest two ways in which such pollution could be reduced or prevented.
11 Why does the presence of sewage in a river cause eutrophication?

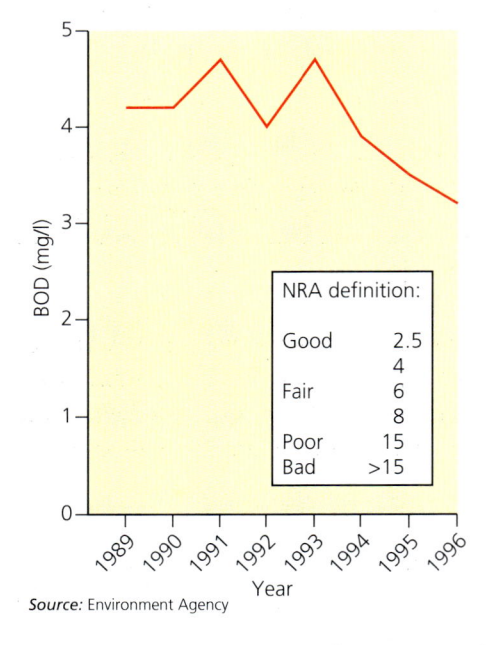

(Graph: BOD (mg/l) vs Year 1989–1996, showing values around 4.2 rising to ~4.7 in 1991 and 1993, then falling to ~3.2 by 1996. NRA definition: Good 2.5, Fair 4, Poor 6, Bad 8, 15, >15. Source: Environment Agency)

Pesticides

Pesticides, fungicides and herbicides can all easily be washed into rivers and streams by rainwater. Some of these chemicals are non-biodegradable and will last quite a long while in the water supply. Water treatment does not remove all of these substances, and drinking water sometimes contains small amounts of pesticides and herbicides.

Industrial wastes

In the past, many companies discharged their waste into river water. Waste from breweries, paper mills or slaughterhouses added a great deal of organic matter to rivers and caused eutrophication. Chemical industries discharged waste materials containing toxic chemicals such as compounds of the metals mercury, cadmium or nickel.

New laws which make industries responsible for the safe disposal or recycling of polluting waste material have done much to improve the health of rivers and lakes.

Figure 4 The river Aire has been one of the most polluted rivers in the country because of pollution from the textile and chemical industries. Several water treatment plants have been built in the last few years in the worst affected areas, and this is improving the water quality. The figure showing this best is the biochemical oxygen demand (BOD). The lower the value, the better the water quality.

Summary of water pollution

- Pollution of fresh water happens if the natural processes of breakdown of waste products are overwhelmed.
- Humans pollute their water supply with fertilisers, sewage, pesticides, detergents and industrial waste.
- Many pollutants cause the problem of eutrophication.

11.4 Unusual properties of water

Figure 5 The structure of ice.

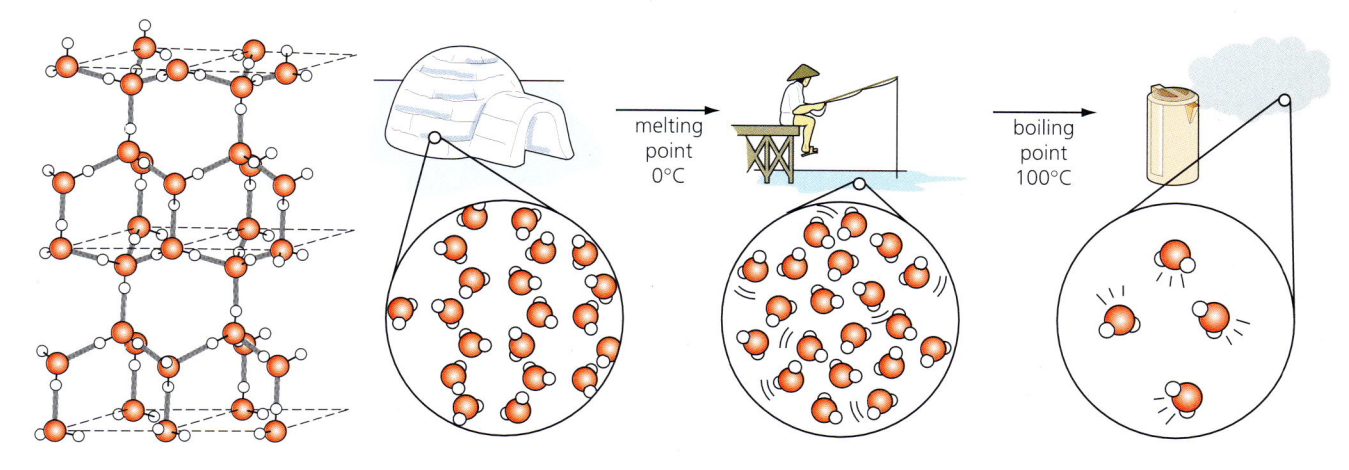

Water is the only common substance that exists as a solid, liquid and a gas in the Earth's environment.

Table 2 Unusual properties of water

Property	Explanation
Water is a **liquid** at room temperature. Other molecules of a similar M_r such as ammonia (NH_3) or carbon monoxide (CO) are gases	The forces between molecules in water are quite strong compared with those in other similar small molecules
Water **expands** as it freezes. This makes ice less dense than water	When ice forms, water molecules are held quite far apart in a rigid open structure
Water is an excellent **solvent** for many solids, liquids and gases	Water is a molecule, and can therefore dissolve many other substances made from molecules. Water molecules are also polar – they have a negative and positive end to the molecule. This means that water is a good solvent for many ionic compounds

What is water of crystallisation?

Table 3 Some compounds containing water of crystallisation

Name	Formula
barium chloride	$BaCl_2 \cdot 2H_2O$
calcium chloride	$CaCl_2 \cdot 6H_2O$
copper (II) sulphate	$CuSO_4 \cdot 5H_2O$
sodium carbonate	$Na_2CO_3 \cdot 10H_2O$
zinc sulphate	$ZnSO_4 \cdot 7H_2O$

Many solids, when heated, will eventually melt. However, when some solids are gently heated they first give off clouds of steam. This is because these substances contain **water of crystallisation**. This is water that is chemically joined inside the structure of a crystal. Heating the crystals drives off the water of crystallisation.

Figure 6

Water of crystallisation

$$CuSO_4 \cdot 5H_2O \rightarrow CuSO_4(s) + 5H_2O(g)$$

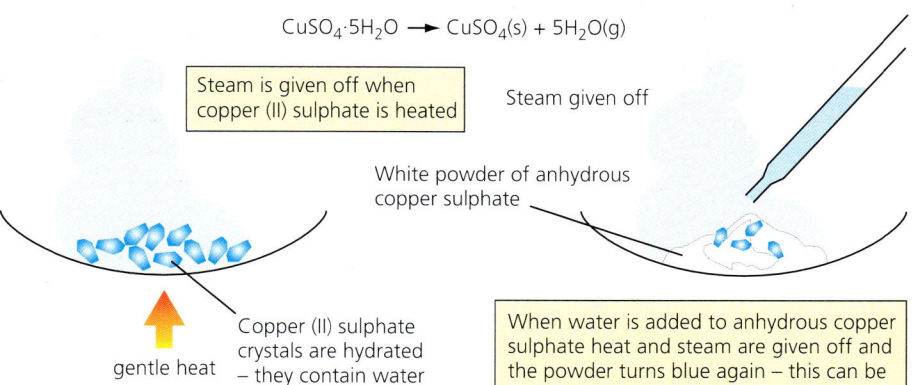

Steam is given off when copper (II) sulphate is heated

Steam given off

White powder of anhydrous copper sulphate

Copper (II) sulphate crystals are hydrated – they contain water of crystallisation

gentle heat

When water is added to anhydrous copper sulphate heat and steam are given off and the powder turns blue again – this can be used as a test for water

12 Why does ice float on water?

151

Water and aqueous solutions

Summary of unusual properties of water

- Water is a unique compound with many unusual properties.
- Water of crystallisation is loosely held in the structure of some crystals.

11.5 Water as a solvent

Why is water so useful?

Water is sometimes known as a 'universal solvent' because many substances are at least slightly soluble in it. Many chemical reactions in the laboratory are carried out in aqueous solution. Water is also vital for all plant and animal life. It dissolves and transports nutrients around organisms and helps to remove waste products. Water contributes towards plants and animals being flexible and able to move, rather than rigid.

Words used to describe the process of dissolving

Word	Meaning
decant	to pour off a liquid, leaving a solid in the bottom of the container
solubility	the number of grams of a solid that will dissolve in 100 g of water at a particular temperature
solute	the substance being dissolved
solvent	the substance dissolving the solute
solution	a solution is formed when a solute dissolves in a solvent
saturated solution	when no more solute will dissolve at a particular temperature

How can solubility be measured?

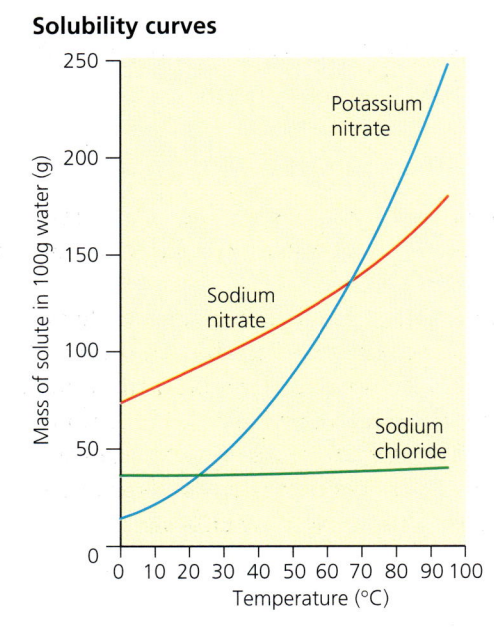

Solubility curves

Chemists often need to know the **solubility** of a given substance in water. You can do this by preparing a graph known as a **solubility curve**. This measures how the solubility of a substance alters with changes in temperature. The solubility curves plotted in figure 10 show that changes in solubility with temperature are quite varied. The solubility of a compound such as sodium chloride hardly alters as the temperature changes, whereas that of potassium nitrate rises steeply.

Once such a curve has been prepared the solubility of a substance at a particular temperature can be discovered by reading it off the graph. For example, from the curve in figure 7 you can see that the solubility of potassium nitrate at 70 °C is 135 g in 100 g water.

It is possible to use solubility curves to make predictions about what will happen as a solution is cooled. An example is shown in figure 8.

Figure 7

Figure 8 A solubility curve can be used to deduce information about a substance.

Solubility curve for copper (II) sulphate

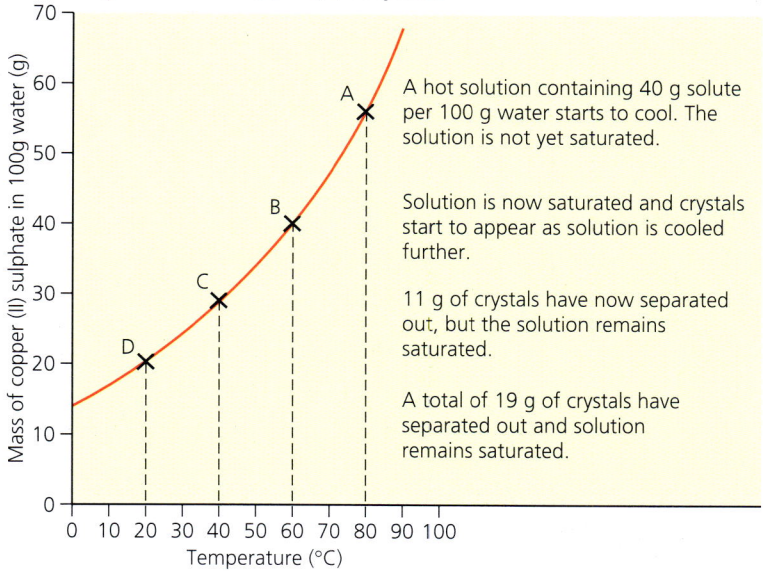

- A: A hot solution containing 40 g solute per 100 g water starts to cool. The solution is not yet saturated.
- B: Solution is now saturated and crystals start to appear as solution is cooled further.
- C: 11 g of crystals have now separated out, but the solution remains saturated.
- D: A total of 19 g of crystals have separated out and solution remains saturated.

Temperature (°C)	Solubility (g per 100 g water)
0	3.3
10	5.1
20	7.3
30	10.1
40	14.0
50	18.5
60	24.0
70	30.2
80	37.4
90	46.0
100	56.2

13 Write a sentence to explain the meaning of each of the following words:
  a anhydrous   **c** solubility   **e** solute   **g** solvent
  b saturated solution   **d** solubility curve   **f** solution   **h** water of crystallisation

14 The data in the table shows how the solubility of potassium chlorate (KClO$_3$) changes with temperature.
  a Plot a solubility curve for potassium chlorate from the table.
  b From your graph find the solubility of potassium chlorate at
    i 45°C   **ii** 65°C
  c A solution containing 14.9 g of potassium chlorate in 100 g water is heated to 65°C.
    i Mark these conditions on your graph with a cross and label it A.
    ii The solution at point A is left to cool. Mark B on the graph the temperature at which crystals will first start to form.
    iii The solution is now cooled to room temperature (20°C). Mark this point C on your graph. What mass of crystals will be formed between points B and C?

Do gases dissolve in water?

Water is a good solvent for gases. Some gases, such as oxygen, are only slightly soluble in water, yet this dissolved oxygen is used by fish and water plants for respiration. Other gases dissolve readily in water.

Unlike many solids, gases become less soluble as the temperature increases. This can be clearly seen if a glass of water is left on a sunny windowsill. As the water warms, bubbles of air will appear in the water. In hot dry weather this can cause problems for fish – as the water warms, less oxygen is dissolved in the water and respiration can become difficult.

Gas solubility

Some gases dissolve slightly in water…	Other gases react chemically with water …
For example:	For example:
100 g water at 20°C will dissolve	100 g water at 20°C will dissolve
2 cm^3 of hydrogen or	75 litres of ammonia or
3 cm^3 of oxygen or	48 litres of hydrogen chloride or
1.6 cm^3 of nitrogen	4.2 litres of sulphur dioxide or
	92 cm^3 of carbon dioxide

Water and aqueous solutions

How may aqueous solutions be analysed?

Many laboratory chemicals are used as aqueous solutions. It is useful to know how to test such solutions to find out what is present – this is called **chemical analysis**. Table 4 describes some of the tests for various ions in aqueous solution.

Table 4 Tests for ions in aqueous solution

Ion	Formula	Test	Result	Equation
hydrogen	H^+	drop solution onto a carbonate, such as calcium carbonate, $CaCO_3$	carbon dioxide gas evolved	$H^+(aq) + CO_3^{2-}(aq) \rightarrow H_2O(l) + CO_2(g)$
hydroxide	OH^-	add solution to a solution of an ammonium salt, such as ammonium chloride (NH_4Cl) and warm	ammonia gas evolved (alkaline pH, forms white smoke with concentrated HCl)	$NH_4^+(aq) + OH^-(aq) \rightarrow NH_3(g) + H_2O(l)$
calcium	Ca^{2+}	flame test: hold aqueous solution in hot blue flame	brick-red flame	
potassium	K^+	flame test	lilac flame	
sodium	Na^+	flame test	orange flame	
aluminium	Al^{3+}	add dilute sodium hydroxide solution until in excess	white gelatinous precipitate formed, which dissolves in excess alkali	$Al^{3+}(aq) + 3OH^-(aq) \rightarrow Al(OH)_3(s)$
ammonium	NH_4^+	warm with dilute sodium hydroxide solution	ammonia gas evolved (alkaline pH, forms white smoke with concentrated HCl)	$NH_4^+(aq) + OH^-(aq) \rightarrow NH_3(g) + H_2O(l)$
copper	Cu^{2+}	add dilute ammonia solution until in excess	turquoise gelatinous precipitate forms, which dissolves in excess to give a royal blue solution	$Cu^{2+}(aq) + 2OH^-(aq) \rightarrow Cu(OH)_2(s)$
iron (II)	Fe^{2+}	add sodium hydroxide solution	green precipitate, which slowly turns brown at the surface	$Fe^{2+}(aq) + 2OH^-(aq) \rightarrow Fe(OH)_2(s)$
iron (III)	Fe^{3+}	add sodium hydroxide solution	rust-brown precipitate	$Fe^{3+}(aq) + 3OH^-(aq) \rightarrow Fe(OH)_3(s)$
chloride	Cl^-	add dilute HNO_3 followed by silver nitrate solution	white precipitate of silver chloride	$Ag^+(aq) + Cl^-(aq) \rightarrow AgCl(s)$
bromide	Br^-	add dilute HNO_3 followed by silver nitrate solution	cream-coloured precipitate of silver bromide	$Ag^+(aq) + Br^-(aq) \rightarrow AgBr(s)$
iodide	I^-	add dilute HNO_3 followed by silver nitrate solution	pale yellow precipitate of silver iodide	$Ag^+(aq) + I^-(aq) \rightarrow AgI(s)$
nitrate	NO_3^-	boil with dilute sodium hydroxide solution then add aluminium powder	ammonia gas evolved (alkaline pH, forms white smoke with concentrated HCl)	$3NO_3^-(aq) + 5OH^-(aq) + 2H_2O(l) + 8Al(s) \rightarrow 3NH_3(g) + 8AlO_2^-(aq)$
sulphate	SO_4^{2-}	add dilute HCl followed by barium chloride solution	white precipitate of barium sulphate	$Ba^{2+}(aq) + SO_4^{2-}(aq) \rightarrow BaSO_4(s)$
carbonate	CO_3^{2-}	add a dilute acid, for example HCl	carbon dioxide gas evolved	$H^+(aq) + CO_3^{2-}(aq) \rightarrow H_2O(l) + CO_2(g)$

15 Why do fizzy drinks, which contain carbon dioxide dissolved under pressure, go 'flat' quickly on a warm day?

16 The labels of four bottles of laboratory chemicals have fallen off. To find out what they contained the contents were subjected to the tests shown in this table.

Test	Solid A	Solid B	Solid C	Solid D
dilute hydrochloric acid added	CO_2 evolved	no reaction	no reaction	CO_2 evolved
dilute nitric acid added, followed by silver nitrate solution	no reaction	white precipitate	no reaction	no reaction
boiled with sodium hydroxide solution then aluminium powder added	no reaction	no reaction	ammonia gas evolved	no reaction
flame test	orange flame	orange flame	no colour	blue–green flame
sodium hydroxide solution added and warmed	no reaction	no reaction	ammonia gas evolved	no reaction
dilute ammonia solution added	no reaction	no reaction	no reaction	turquoise precipitate formed, then royal blue solution

    a Which solid(s) were compounds of sodium?
    b Which solid(s) could have been used as a fertiliser?
    c Solid D was a green powder, and the other three solids were colourless. What could solid D be?
    d Suggest identities for A, B and C.

Summary of water as a solvent

- A solubility curve shows how the solubility of a substance varies with temperature.
- The solubility of some substances increases with temperature.
- The solubility of gases in water decreases as temperature rises.
- The presence of various ions in solution can be detected by chemical tests.

Examination style questions

Temperature (°C)	Solubility (g per 100 g water)
0	0.34
10	0.24
20	0.17
30	0.13
40	0.10
50	0.08
60	0.06

1 Gases such as oxygen and carbon dioxide dissolve in water. The solubility of these gases varies with temperature. Why are such dissolved gases important to plants and animals?

2 The table shows how the solubility of carbon dioxide gas in water changes as temperature increases.
    a Plot a solubility curve for carbon dioxide.
    b What happens to the solubility of carbon dioxide as the temperature rises?
    c Use your graph to find the solubility of carbon dioxide
        i at 15°C   **ii** at 35°C

Electrolysis

12

Learning objectives

By the end of this chapter you should be able to:
- **describe** the process of electrolysis
- **write** simple ion–electron equations
- **describe** oxidation and reduction in terms of electron transfer
- **calculate** the quantity of electricity used in an experiment
- **calculate** the charge on an ion from suitable data
- **list** applications of electrolysis

12.1 Explaining electrolysis

What is electrolysis?

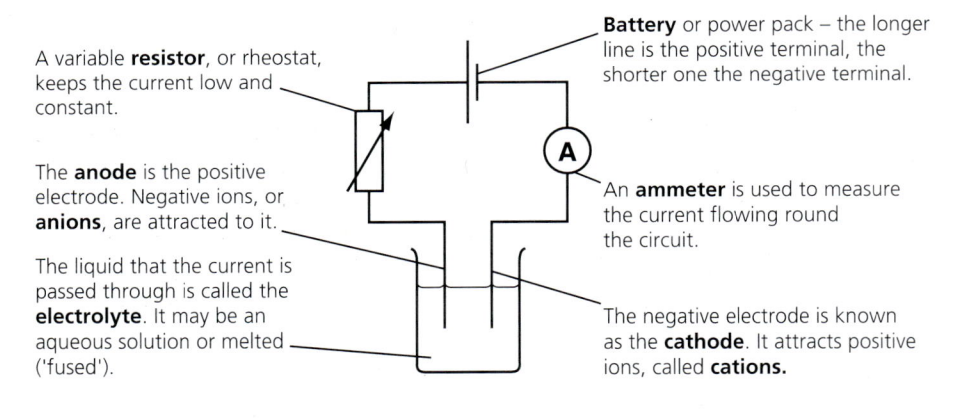

A variable **resistor**, or rheostat, keeps the current low and constant.

The **anode** is the positive electrode. Negative ions, or **anions**, are attracted to it.

The liquid that the current is passed through is called the **electrolyte**. It may be an aqueous solution or melted ('fused').

Battery or power pack – the longer line is the positive terminal, the shorter one the negative terminal.

An **ammeter** is used to measure the current flowing round the circuit.

The negative electrode is known as the **cathode**. It attracts positive ions, called **cations**.

The word 'electrolysis' means 'splitting with electricity'. In this process, an ionic compound is dissolved in water or melted. An electric current is then passed through the solution or melt. This breaks down the compound.

Figure 1 Simple electrolysis.

How do ionic compounds behave when electrolysed?

Solid ionic compounds consist of a regular lattice of ions arranged in a giant structure. When the compound is melted, this ordered structure breaks down to give an irregular mass of ions that are free to move. When the electric current is switched on, the ions **migrate** to the electrode of opposite charge because opposite charges attract. Positive ions are attracted to the negative cathode, and negative ions are attracted to the positive anode. As they do so, the ions carry the current across the electrolyte. This is why ionic compounds conduct an electric current when liquid.

1 What is the general name of positive ions that are attracted to the cathode?
2 What is the general name for negative ions that are attracted to the anode?

Electrolysis

Electrolysing molten lead bromide

Figure 2 Electrolysis of lead bromide.

Negative bromide ions are drawn to the anode by electrostatic attraction. Each of two bromide ions loses an electron to the anode:
$2Br^-(l) \rightarrow Br_2(l) + 2e^-$
The bromide ions are **discharged** and two bromine atoms join together to become a molecule of bromine.

The fumes of bromine and the compounds of lead formed are toxic, so this experiment must be performed in a fume cupboard.

Positive lead ions are drawn to the cathode by electrostatic attraction. Each ion gains two electrons from the cathode:
$Pb^{2+}(l) + 2e^- \rightarrow Pb(l)$
The lead ion loses its charge – it is **discharged** and becomes a lead atom.

The equations shown in figure 2 are known as **ion–electron equations**. Note that the number of electrons gained from the cathode is the same as the number of electrons lost to the anode. This maintains an electrical balance in the process. Electrons lost at the anode are continually 'pumped' by the battery or power pack round to the cathode.

3 Zinc chloride is a compound known to have a giant ionic structure. One method of making the element zinc is to electrolyse liquid zinc chloride.
   a From your knowledge of the charge on ions, deduce the formula of zinc chloride.
   b Write an ion–electron equation for the process that happens at the cathode.
   c Write an ion–electron equation for what happens at the anode.

Another example of the electrolysis of a fused or melted compound is that of sodium chloride. When solid sodium chloride is melted and electrolysed, it is broken down to sodium and chlorine. This process is the only practicable way of manufacturing sodium metal. Because both sodium and chlorine are very reactive elements, it is important that once they are discharged at the electrodes, they are kept apart to prevent them reacting together again.

What happens during electrolysis in an aqueous solution?

In the laboratory, it is difficult to heat a compound until it is liquid and electrolyse it at the same time. Most laboratory investigations of electrolysis are therefore carried out in aqueous solutions in an electrolysis cell like the one in figure 3.

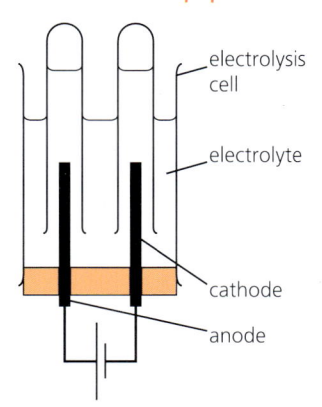

Figure 3 An electrolysis cell.

Electrolysis

Electrolysis of dilute hydrochloric acid
This acid contains positive hydrogen ions, $H^+(aq)$ and negative chloride ions, $Cl^-(aq)$.

At the cathode, hydrogen gas is formed:
$$2H^+(aq) + 2e^- \rightarrow H_2(g)$$

At the anode, chlorine gas is formed:
$$2Cl^-(aq) \rightarrow Cl_2(g) + 2e^-$$

Electrolysing copper (II) chloride solution
This solution contains $Cu^{2+}(aq)$ and $Cl^-(aq)$ ions.

At the cathode, copper metal is deposited:
$$Cu^{2+}(aq) + 2e^- \rightarrow Cu(s)$$

At the anode, chlorine gas is formed:
$$2Cl^-(aq) \rightarrow Cl_2(g) + 2e^-$$

Electrolysing dilute sulphuric acid
When dilute sulphuric acid is electrolysed it behaves as if it were simply water being broken down into its elements. Water itself contains some ions because the following process happens to a small proportion of water molecules:

$$H_2O(l) \rightarrow H^+(aq) + OH^-(aq)$$

At the cathode, hydrogen gas is formed:
$$4H^+(aq) + 4e^- \rightarrow 2H_2(g)$$

At the anode, oxygen gas is formed:
$$4OH^-(aq) \rightarrow O_2(g) + 2H_2O(l) + 4e^-$$

It is important that the number of electrons lost and gained is the same in the two ion–electron equations. When this happens two volumes of hydrogen gas are formed for every one volume of oxygen gas. This can be used as a simple piece of evidence that the formula of water (H_2O) indicates that it contains twice as many hydrogen atoms as oxygen atoms.

4 An electrolysis cell was used to investigate the products formed when an electric current was passed through various electrolytes. Suggest a suitable inert material from which to make the electrodes.

Does the electrode material affect the outcome?
When copper (II) sulphate solution is electrolysed using carbon electrodes, the following processes occur.

At the anode
Sulphate ions do not discharge. However, hydroxide ions from the water are attracted to the anode and discharged as oxygen gas:

$$4OH^-(aq) \rightarrow O_2(g) + 2H_2O(l) + 4e^-$$

Electrolysis

At the cathode

Copper metal is deposited. Discharge of hydroxide ions involves four electrons, so to maintain an electrical balance two copper (II) ions must be discharged:

$$2Cu^{2+}(aq) + 4e^- \rightarrow 2Cu(s)$$

Using copper electrodes

When copper (II) sulphate is electrolysed using copper electrodes, a different process happens.

At the anode, copper on the anode dissolves away into solution:
$$Cu(s) \rightarrow Cu^{2+}(aq) + 2e^-$$

At the cathode, copper is deposited:
$$Cu^{2+}(aq) + 2e^- \rightarrow Cu(s)$$

What is formed when reactive metal compounds are electrolysed?

When aqueous solutions of compounds of very reactive metals like sodium are electrolysed, the products are not what might be expected. For example, in electrolysing aqueous sodium chloride, chlorine is discharged from the anode:

$$2Cl^-(aq) \rightarrow Cl_2(g) + 2e^-$$

At the cathode, sodium metal should be deposited but it is too reactive to be formed in aqueous solution, so hydrogen ions present in the water are discharged as hydrogen gas instead:

$$2H^+(aq) + 2e^- \rightarrow H_2(g)$$

The process may be summed up as follows:

sodium chloride: $Na^+(aq)$ + $Cl^-(aq)$
  sodium ions remain in aqueous solution
  chloride ions are discharged as chlorine gas

water: $H_2O(l)$ → $H^+(aq)$ + $OH^-(aq)$
  hydrogen ions discharged as hydrogen gas
  hydroxide ions remain in aqueous solution

As a result of this process, sodium ions and hydroxide ions build up in aqueous solution, which therefore becomes alkaline.

5 Copy out and complete table 1.

Table 1

Electrolyte	Product formed at anode	Product formed at cathode
aqueous copper (II) chloride	chlorine	
molten sodium chloride		sodium
concentrated aqueous sodium chloride		
dilute sulphuric acid		

Electrolysis

Oxidation and reduction

O oxidation
I is
L loss (of electrons)
R reduction
I is
G gain

One way to consider oxidation and reduction is in terms of gaining or losing oxygen. Another way, which is relevant in electrolysis, is to consider what is happening to the electrons in a given reaction. Reduction is defined as a gain of electrons and oxidation as a loss of electrons. One way of remembering this is to use the acronym OIL RIG.

6 Which of the following ion–electron equations involves oxidation and which reduction?

a $Zn^{2+}(l) + 2e^- \rightarrow Zn(l)$
b $2I^-(l) \rightarrow I_2(l) + 2e^-$
c $2K^+(l) + 2e^- \rightarrow 2K(l)$
d $2Cl^-(l) \rightarrow Cl_2(g) + 2e^-$
e $2H^+(aq) + 2e^- \rightarrow H_2(g)$
f $4OH^-(aq) \rightarrow O_2(g) + 2H_2O(l) + 4e^-$
g $Al^{3+}(l) + 3e^- \rightarrow Al(l)$

Summary of explaining electrolysis

- Electrolysis involves splitting an ionic compound into its elements by passing an electric current through it.
- Ionic compounds can be electrolysed when melted or when dissolved in water.
- During electrolysis, ions migrate to the electrode of opposite charge, where they are discharged.
- An ion–electron equation shows the electron transfer happening at a particular electrode.
- The electrode material can affect the products of electrolysis.
- Oxidation can be defined as loss of electrons and reduction as gain of electrons.

12.2 Measuring in electrolysis

What can be calculated?

Electrolysis experiments can be followed quantitatively (i.e. being measured) and used to predict how much of a given element will be formed during electrolysis.

In the nineteenth century, the scientist Michael Faraday found that the mass of substance liberated in electrolysis is proportional to the quantity of electricity which passes through the electrolyte. The quantity of electricity passing in any experiment (Q) is measured in **coulombs**. One coulomb (1 C) is the amount of electricity flowing when 1 ampere (1 A) is passed in 1 second:

| quantity of electricity = current in amperes × seconds |
| Q = I × t |

This can be rearranged to give:

| current (A) = coulombs / seconds   or   I = Q/t |

or

| seconds = coulombs / current (A)   or   t = Q/I |

WORKED EXAMPLE

When silver nitrate solution is electrolysed using silver electrodes, silver dissolves from the anode and is deposited onto the cathode.

Sample measurements:

Mass of cathode (at start)	=	20.013 g
Mass of cathode (at finish)	=	20.445 g
Mass of silver deposited	=	0.432 g
Current flowing	=	0.20 A
Time	=	1930 seconds
Quantity of electricity (I × t)	=	0.20 × 1930
	=	386 C

Once this information has been obtained, the quantity of electricity needed to deposit one mole of silver (108 g) can be calculated.

In this experiment,

0.432 g of silver was deposited by	386 C
so 1.0 g silver would need	$\dfrac{386}{0.432}$
and one mole of silver (108 g) would need	$\dfrac{386}{0.432} \times 108$
=	96 500 C

In experiments like this, it would be expensive and impractical to perform an experiment using one mole of silver. Instead, the results of using a small amount of the metal are multiplied up to find out how much electricity would be needed to deposit one mole of the metal.

One mole of electrons will always liberate one mole of a singly charged ion. One mole of electrons is sometimes known as one **Faraday** (1 F).

1 Faraday = 96 500 coulombs

1 F = 96 500 C

Sometimes this is also called the **Faraday constant**.

---

7 Calculate the quantity of electricity (in coulombs) when:
   a 0.02 amps are passed for 200 seconds
   b 0.04 amps are passed for 500 seconds
   c 0.05 amps are passed for 10 minutes
   d 0.04 amps are passed for 2 hours.

8 It is very important to keep the products of electrolysis of sodium chloride or magnesium chloride apart, or they will react violently together. Write balanced equations for the reactions that would take place if the products were allowed to come together.

Electrolysis

How many Faradays are needed to discharge ions with multiple charges?

9 In an experiment to electrolyse copper (II) sulphate solution using copper electrodes, 0.24 g of copper was deposited at the cathode when a current of 0.1 A was passed for 2 hours.
  a Draw a labelled diagram to show the apparatus that could be used in this experiment.
  b Calculate the charge on a copper ion.
  c Write ion–electron equations to show what happens at the anode and the cathode.

When copper (II) sulphate solution is electrolysed using copper electrodes, copper metal dissolves off the anode and is deposited onto the cathode. Copper is a 2+ ion, so each ion needs two electrons to be discharged to produce one copper atom:

$Cu^{2+}(aq)$	+	$2e^-$	$\rightarrow$	$Cu(s)$
one copper (II) ion	gains	two electrons	to give	one copper atom
one mole of copper (II) ions	gains	two moles of electrons (i.e. two Faradays)	to give	one mole of copper atoms

When one mole of copper atoms are deposited in this experiment, two moles of electrons are needed. This is equal to two Faradays:

$$2 \text{ Faradays} = 2 \times 96\,500$$
$$= 193\,000\,C$$

Table 2 Moles of electrons

One mole of 1+ or 1– ions (e.g. Ag^+, Na^+, K^+, H^+, OH^-, Cl^-, Br^-)	is discharged by	1 Faraday or 96 500 C
One mole of 2+ or 2– ions (e.g. Mg^{2+}, Ca^{2+}, Cu^{2+}, Pb^{2+}, O^{2-})	is discharged by	2 Faradays or 193 000 C
One mole of 3+ or 3– ions (e.g. Al^{3+}, Cr^{3+})	is discharged by	3 Faradays or 289 500 C

WORKED EXAMPLE

In an experiment electrolysing copper (II) sulphate solution, 0.1 A was passed for 3860 seconds. During this time, the mass of the copper cathode increased by 0.128 g. Calculate **a** the amount of electricity needed to deposit one mole of copper atoms and **b** the charge on a copper ion.

a Using the equation $Q = I \times t$:
$$Q = 0.1 \times 3860$$
$$= 386\,C$$

0.128 g copper was deposited by 386 C, so 1.0 g copper would be deposited by: $\frac{386}{0.128}$ C

and 64 g copper would be deposited by: $\frac{386}{0.128} \times 64$ C

Amount of electricity needed to deposit 1 mole of copper = 193 000 C

b Number of Faradays used = $\frac{193\,000}{96\,500}$ = 2 F

Copper was deposited on the cathode, so it must have been a positive ion ...

so the charge on a copper ion is 2+

Summary of measuring in electrolysis

- The quantity of electricity flowing is measured in coulombs:
  $Q = I \times t$
- One Faraday is one mole of electrons and is equal to 96 500 coulombs.
- One Faraday will discharge one mole of singly charged ions in electrolysis.

12.3 Electrolysis in industry

The principles of electrolysis are used in industry to make a wide variety of chemicals that in turn are used to make many everyday materials.

What happens when brine is electrolysed?

One of the earliest applications of electrolysis was that of sodium chloride solution. In places where underground salt deposits were discovered, this was dissolved, pumped to the surface and electrolysed. Because of the many useful chemicals that can be produced in this process, several sites where such salt deposits occur have evolved into large complexes for the chemical industry.

Electrolysis of brine is usually carried out in a **diaphragm cell**, where the electrodes are arranged in layers. The diaphragm that separates the layers also helps prevent the hydrogen and chlorine gases from mixing and reacting together.

Electrolysis of brine in a diaphragm cell

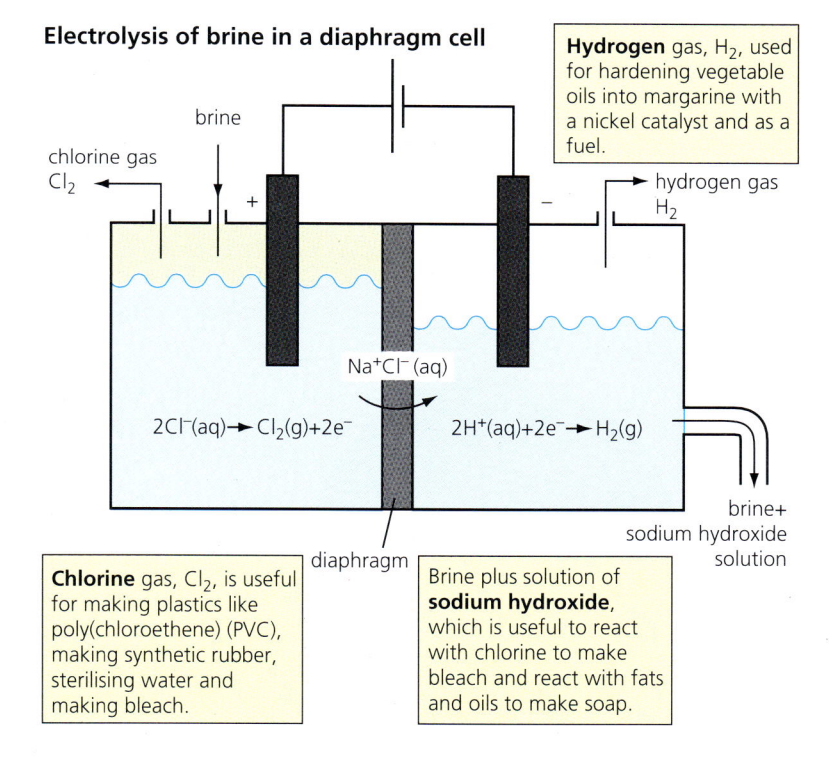

Hydrogen gas, H_2, used for hardening vegetable oils into margarine with a nickel catalyst and as a fuel.

$2Cl^-(aq) \rightarrow Cl_2(g) + 2e^-$

$2H^+(aq) + 2e^- \rightarrow H_2(g)$

$Na^+Cl^-(aq)$

Chlorine gas, Cl_2, is useful for making plastics like poly(chloroethene) (PVC), making synthetic rubber, sterilising water and making bleach.

Brine plus solution of **sodium hydroxide**, which is useful to react with chlorine to make bleach and react with fats and oils to make soap.

Figure 4

10 a When brine is electrolysed, the solution around the cathode becomes alkaline. Explain, with the aid of an equation, how this happens.
b Give the chemical name and formula of the three products formed by electrolysis of brine.
c Write ion–electron equations to show the processes that occur at the anode and cathode.
d The prices of the products of this electrolysis are much higher than the cost of the brine used as the starting material. Suggest three reasons for this.

How are reactive metals extracted?

Many metals are too reactive to be discharged by electrolysis in aqueous solution. For such metals, often the only practicable way to extract them is by melting a suitable metal compound and electrolysing it. **Magnesium** and **sodium** are extracted by electrolysing the melted chloride and **aluminium** is extracted by electrolysis of melted aluminium oxide (see Chapter 13, *Metals*).

11 Electrolysis of sodium chloride (melting point 801°C) and magnesium chloride (melting point 714°C) needs to be carried out with the chlorides melted. Why do you think these melting points are so high?

Electrolysis

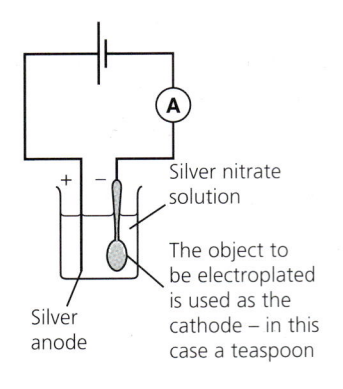

What is electroplating?

Electroplating involves using electrolysis to coat an object with a thin film of metal. Often this is done for economic reasons, with a fairly cheap metal like steel being coated with more expensive metals like silver, gold or chromium.

Electroplating can also be used to modify the chemical reactivity of the object plated. One example of this is that steel cans for food containers can be plated with a thin layer of tin inside. Tin itself is too soft and expensive to use for the can, but it is fairly unreactive, and prevents the food from causing the steel to rust.

Diagram labels: Silver nitrate solution; The object to be electroplated is used as the cathode – in this case a teaspoon; Silver anode

Figure 5 Electroplating involves plating a thin layer of a valuable metal like silver onto a less valuable metal like steel.

How is electrolysis used to purify metals?

Often at the end of a chemical process the metal extracted is still impure. Copper is needed for precision electrical equipment and works better if it is very pure. Copper can be purified by making a large impure block of copper the anode, and a thin piece of very pure copper the cathode. The two electrodes are then immersed in copper (II) sulphate solution. Copper metal dissolves off the anode and is deposited onto the cathode. However, any impurities either remain in solution or are left behind at the bottom of the container as a 'sludge'.

Figure 6 Purifying metals. Impure copper is made into the anode in a bath of copper (II) sulphate. During electrolysis pure copper is deposited on the copper cathode and impurities are left behind.

Purifying metals using electrolysis

Diagram labels: Anode made of a block of impure copper; Copper (II) sulphate solution; Cathode made of pure copper; Impurities remain in solution or deposit as a 'sludge'; Copper dissolves from the anode and pure copper deposits on the cathode.

Summary of electrolysis in industry

- The electrolysis of brine produces hydrogen, chlorine and sodium hydroxide, which in turn can be made into many useful chemicals.
- Very reactive metals can be extracted by electrolysis of their melted compounds.
- Electroplating coats a thin layer of a metal onto another cheaper metal so as to modify its physical or chemical properties.
- Metals can be obtained in a high state of purity using electrolysis.

Examination style questions

1. In an experiment involving nickel plating, a teaspoon (acting as the cathode) increased in mass from 10.005 g to 10.123 g when a current of 0.1 A was passed through the solution for 3860 seconds.
   a Deduce whether nickel ions are positively or negatively charged. State how you arrive at your conclusion.
   b Calculate the quantity of electricity (in coulombs) that is passed through the solution in this experiment.
   c Calculate the quantity of electricity needed to deposit one mole of nickel.
   d Deduce the charge on a nickel ion.

2. a Draw a labelled diagram to show the apparatus that you would use to electroplate some jewellery with silver metal.
   b Suggest modifications that would be needed if the jewellery were to be plated with gold instead of silver.

3. When electrolysis and electroplating are carried out, an electric current flows around the entire circuit. Name the particles that carry the current in
   a the wires   b the electrolyte.

4. Aluminium is extracted by electrolysing a melted mixture of alumina and cryolite, using carbon electrodes. Data on these two minerals are given in the table below.

Mineral	Chemical name	Formula	Melting point (°C)
alumina	aluminium oxide	Al_2O_3	2047
cryolite	sodium aluminium fluoride	Na_3AlF_6	1000

In the melted mixture the aluminium occurs in the form of Al^{3+} and O^{2-} ions.
   a Pure alumina is too expensive to use in this process. Give one reason for this.
   b Write ion-electron equations for the process that happens at the anode and the cathode.
   c The anode is eroded away during this process, and needs to be replaced from time to time. Suggest a reason for this.
   d It is very much cheaper to produce aluminium cans from recycled aluminium. Suggest one reason for this.

5. Alumina is known to be amphoteric.
   a What is an amphoteric compound?
   b How would you demonstrate this in the laboratory?

6. Aluminium is used to make cans for soft drinks. Suggest two reasons why it is suitable for this purpose.

7. The following equation shows the overall change that takes place when copper (II) chloride solution is electrolysed using carbon electrodes:
   $CuCl_2(aq) \rightarrow Cu(s) + Cl_2(g)$
   a Which substance would be formed at the cathode? Write an ion–electron equation for this process.
   b Which substance would be formed at the anode? Write an ion–electron equation for this process.
   c Describe a chemical test for the substance formed at the anode.
   d Write ion–electron equations for the processes happening at each electrode if the carbon rods were replaced by copper strips.

8. During an experiment (conducted at room temperature and pressure) to electrolyse some copper (II) chloride solution, a current of 0.5 A was passed for 4825 seconds. Calculate:
   a the mass of copper
   b the volume of chlorine gas formed in this time.

Metals

13

Learning objectives

By the end of this chapter you should be able to:
- **describe** the characteristic physical and chemical properties of metals
- **explain** how the physical properties of metals can be altered
- **explain** how various metals are extracted from their ores
- **describe** similarities and trends in the properties of metals in Groups I and II of the periodic table
- **list** the properties of the transition metals
- **explain** the importance of recycling metals

13.1 Physical properties of metals

How many elements are metals?

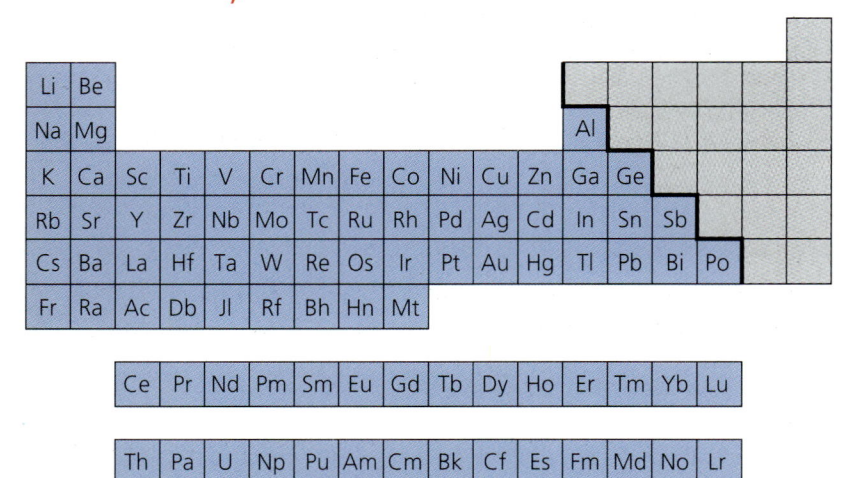

Of the 109 elements known at present, 87 of these are metals. Humans have used metals for thousands of years, because of their physical and chemical properties. Some metals are quite rare in the Earth's crust, and others are highly radioactive or short-lived. For this reason, a relatively small proportion of all metals are widely known and used.

Figure 1 Metals are found on the left and to the bottom of the periodic table. Electron shells in metals are only partially filled.

What physical properties are special to metals?

A quick glance at a substance may often be enough to suggest that it is a metal – all metals have a characteristic appearance. Most metals have similar physical properties.

Metals like the steel used in the construction of this suspension bridge have physical properties that make them suitable for a wide range of purposes.

Although metals such as aluminium are hard, they are malleable and can be beaten into sheets, which is used to wrap foodstuffs.

- **Metals are shiny.** Light rays are reflected off the surface of a metal, so its surface has a characteristic shine or 'lustre'.
- **Metals conduct electricity.** All metals conduct an electric current when solid and when liquid. This is due to the presence of electrons in the lattice of metal atoms which are free to move and carry the electrical current (see Chapter 8, *Chemical bonding*).
- **Metals conduct heat.** All metals conduct heat well. This makes them useful for many objects such as saucepans and boilers, where they help conduct heat to the water or other substance being heated.
- **Metals are strong.** Substances may be strong under tension (have high **tensile strength**) or strong under compression (have high **compressive strength**). Many metals show both types of strength, and this makes them useful for a wide range of construction and manufacturing purposes.
- **Metals are hard.** Many metals are quite hard, and this makes them useful for making tools.
- **Metals are malleable.** A malleable substance can be easily beaten into sheets, bent or changed into different shapes without being broken. This property is unique to metals, and it enables them to be formed into a wide variety of shapes.
- **Metals have high melting and boiling points.** All metals (except mercury) are solid at room temperature. This is because metal atoms are held together by strong **metallic bonds** (see Chapter 8, *Chemical bonding*).
- **Density of metals.** Many metals are quite dense, because their atoms are fairly small and form a close-packed structure. This makes them useful for heavy stable objects and structures. However, metals with a low density can also be quite useful.

1. Name a metal that is a liquid at room temperature and pressure.
2. Which metal is used to line the inside of metal food containers?
3. Give the name and symbol for a metal that is used to galvanise iron.
4. Name a metal that floats on water.

5. The melting point of tungsten is 3410 °C. Comment on how this is connected to the use of tungsten for the filament in light bulbs.
6. Mercury is used inside thermometers. List two physical properties of mercury that make it suitable for this purpose.

Metals

Do metals form crystals?

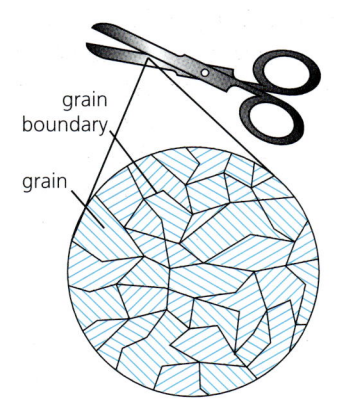

When hot liquid metals are cooled, they crystallise as they turn to a solid. Solid metals contain a mass of interlocking crystals or '**grains**'. Each grain contains a fairly regular arrangement of metal atoms, but its structure is separate from that of surrounding grains.

When metals solidify, a regular **giant structure** of atoms is formed. In places where this lattice is perfectly formed the metal will be strong. However, often atoms are 'missing' from the lattice. Such faults in the structure are called **dislocations**, and they make the metal weaker.

Figure 2 All metals form tiny interlocking crystals or 'grains'. The size of each grain affects the physical properties of the metal.

Can the properties of a metal be altered?

If a metal is required for a special use, it is helpful to be able to change its physical properties. Some of these changes are explained here.

Working metals

Beating, rolling or hammering a metal into different shapes is known as **working** the metal. When a metal is 'cold-worked' it is forced into new shapes at, or just above, room temperature. As the metal is worked, the dislocations become more and more interlocked and the metal gains strength as well as a new shape. However, if a metal is cold-worked for too long it may become brittle and fracture. Metals can also be 'hot-worked' or **forged**. This needs less force because the metal is softer when it is hot.

Suddenly cooling a hot metal by immersing it in cold water or cold oil is called **quenching**. This leads to rapid formation of very small grains, which make the metal harder but more brittle. Metals used in cutting tools, or as the teeth of gear wheels, are treated in this way to make them very hard.

When metals are heated up they become soft and easier to work. Hot-working a metal is known as forging.

7 The table below shows the properties of five elements.

Element	Melting point (°C)	Boiling point (°C)	Density (g/cm³)
A	−218	−183	0.0013
B	419	908	7.1
C	3550	4830	3.5
D	−7	58	3.1
E	63	766	0.86

   a Which two of these elements could be made from simple molecules?
   b List two of these elements that might be metals.
   c Which one of these elements might be a metal that floats on water?

8 A pure metal will not resist bending forces very well. How could the grain structure of the metal be changed to increase its strength?

Alloying metals

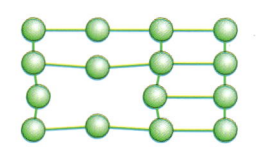

Dislocations weaken the structure of a metal.

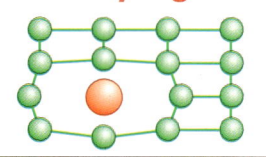

The presence of atoms of a different metal or non-metal will strengthen the structure.

Figure 3 Atoms of another metal or non-metal can prevent dislocations from weakening a metal.

An **alloy** is a mixture of metals. The physical properties of an alloy will depend on its composition. Metallurgists (scientists who work with metals) often design new alloys to suit particular purposes.

Alloying a metal makes it stronger and more durable, because it prevents dislocations from weakening the metal.

Table 1 Composition of some alloys

Alloy	Composition	Properties/uses
brass	60% copper, 40% zinc	shiny metal with a low melting point, which makes it easy to work and mould
coinage bronze	95% copper, 3.5% tin, 1.5% zinc	used for 'copper' coins because it is harder and more durable than pure copper
cupronickel	75% copper, 25% nickel	used for 'silver' coins because it is cheaper and more durable than silver
duralumin	95% aluminium, 4% copper, 1% magnesium	used for making aircraft because it is much stronger than pure aluminium
invar	64% iron, 36% nickel	used in making watch parts to help them keep good time, because it expands and contracts only a little with changes in temperature
permalloy	78% nickel, 21% iron, 1% carbon	used to make electromagnets because it rapidly gains and loses magnetic properties
solder	63% tin, 37% lead	used to join two metals in electrical connections because it has a low melting point

Summary of physical properties of metals

- Metals are shiny, good conductors of heat and electricity, strong, of variable hardness and density and are malleable.
- Solid metals contain grains, which are a mass of interlocking crystals.
- Weaknesses in the grain structure of a metal are called dislocations.
- Metals can be worked into new shapes when hot or cold.
- Alloys are solid mixtures of metals with useful properties.

13.2 Chemical properties of metals

What chemical properties do metals have?

All metals have some chemical properties in common. For example:
- they all react with oxygen to form metal **oxides**
- nearly all metal oxides are **bases**
- metals will react in a similar way with non-metals to form **salts** such as chlorides, nitrates or sulphates
- nearly all metal compounds formed in this way are **ionic**
- all metals will lose electrons to form **positive** ions.

Metals

How are pure metals obtained?

A few metals such as copper and gold occur naturally in some places in the Earth's crust. Such metals are said to occur in a 'native' state. Most metals are fairly reactive, and are therefore found only as compounds, chemically joined to other elements.

A mineral or mixture of minerals that contains enough of a particular metal for it to be economically worthwhile to extract is known as an **ore**.

When a deposit of an ore is discovered in amounts to make it worth extracting, it needs to be **mined**. Mines may be underground or open cast. Unfortunately, mining rocks and minerals always causes environmental problems.

Mining often extracts substances containing a high proportion of waste material. This is sometimes dumped in unsightly spoil heaps

When metal ores are taken from the ground they contain large quantities of impurities, such as rocks, sand or mud. Extracting the ore and removing these impurities can create environmental problems.

Metals can be extracted from their ores in a number of ways.
- A fairly unreactive metal forms compounds that are easily decomposed. It is sometimes possible simply to heat a compound like this, and the metal will be formed.
- The more reactive the metal, the more stable its compounds, and the harder it will be to reduce the ore to the metal. Many ores must be reacted with a **reducing agent** such as carbon or carbon monoxide to extract the metal. Examples of metals that are extracted like this are zinc, iron, tin and lead.
- Some very reactive metals (such as sodium, magnesium or aluminium) can be extracted only by electrolysis.

How is lead extracted from galena?

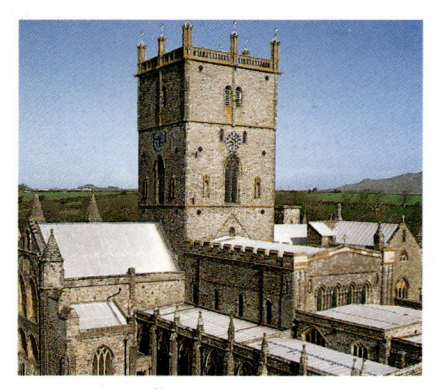

One way in which the metal is extracted from the purified ore is to roast it in air to form lead (II) oxide:

$$2PbS(s) + 3O_2(g) \rightarrow 2PbO(s) + 2SO_2(g)$$

The lead oxide formed in this reaction is then heated with carbon to reduce it to lead:

$$\overset{\text{reduction}}{2PbO(s) + C(s)} \rightarrow 2Pb(l) + CO_2(g)$$

Lead can be used as a roofing material on large buildings. Lead is flexible, impermeable to water and fairly unreactive.

How is zinc extracted?

Zinc is found as the ore **zinc blende**, which is impure zinc sulphide. This is roasted in air to turn it to zinc oxide:

$$2ZnS(s) + 3O_2(g) \rightarrow 2ZnO(s) + 2SO_2(g)$$

The oxide is then reduced to the metal by heating it with carbon:

$$\overset{\longleftarrow \text{reduction} \longrightarrow}{ZnO(s) + C(g) \rightarrow Zn(l) + CO(g)}$$

The carbon monoxide is burned off at the mouth of the furnace:

$$2CO(g) + O_2(g) \rightarrow 2CO_2(g)$$

Zinc is used to galvanise iron and prevent its corrosion. It is also used for the outer casing of some dry batteries.

---

9 Lead metal can be extracted from lead sulphide, PbS, by heating it in air to produce lead (II) oxide and then reducing the oxide by heating with carbon.
  a Explain why this process is known as reduction.
  b Write a balanced symbol reaction for the reaction of lead (II) oxide and coke.
  c State two uses for lead metal.
  d Fumes from lead compounds are poisonous, and can cause brain damage. Heating lead sulphide can produce sulphur dioxide, which is an irritating acidic gas. Suggest two ways of preventing pollution with lead and sulphur dioxide.

How is tin extracted?

Tin is found as the ore **cassiterite** or 'tinstone', which is impure tin (IV) oxide, SnO_2. Tin is extracted by heating the purified oxide strongly with carbon. The oxide is reduced to tin metal:

$$\overset{\longleftarrow \text{reduction} \longrightarrow}{SnO_2(s) + C(s) \rightarrow Sn(l) + CO_2(g)}$$

Tin can be used to plate steel to prevent it rusting ('tinplate'). It is also used in several important alloys.

---

10 When some metal oxides are heated with carbon, they are reduced to the metal. The table below shows the results of heating various metal oxides with carbon.

Oxide	Formula	Result
aluminium oxide	Al_2O_3	white powder, which is unchanged by heating
copper (II) oxide	CuO	black powder quickly turns orange on heating
lead (II) oxide	PbO	orange powder forms shiny silvery globules

  a Which oxides have been reduced to the metal?
  b Write balanced symbol equations for these reactions.
  c Describe how you would demonstrate that a metal has been formed in these reactions.
  d Which of these three metals is the most reactive?

Metals

How is iron extracted from its ores?

Nearly 5% of the Earth's crust is made from iron compounds. The core of the Earth is also thought to consist of hot iron (see Chapter 4, *Rocks and minerals*). Iron is extracted from ores such as **haematite** in a **blast furnace**.

When the iron is run off from a blast furnace it is still impure and quite brittle. At this stage it is known as **cast iron**. Cast iron can be used as it is for some purposes where high tensile strength is not required – for example metal drainpipes and gutters, covers for drains and inspection pipes in the road.

Iron is purified by blasting oxygen gas through the hot liquid metal. Impurities such as carbon and sulphur are removed as their oxides.

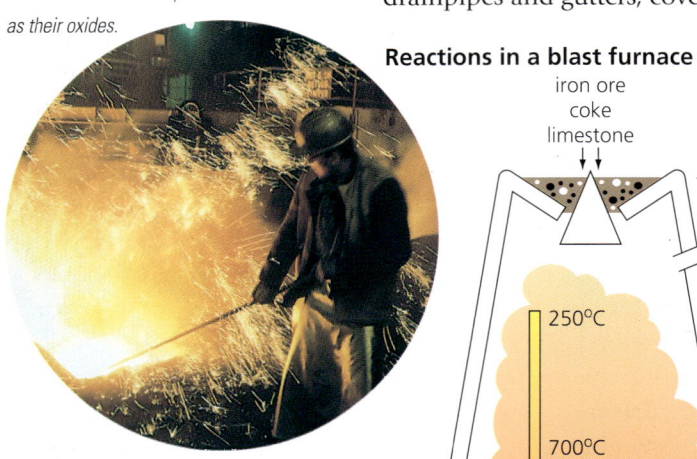

Figure 4

Reactions in a blast furnace

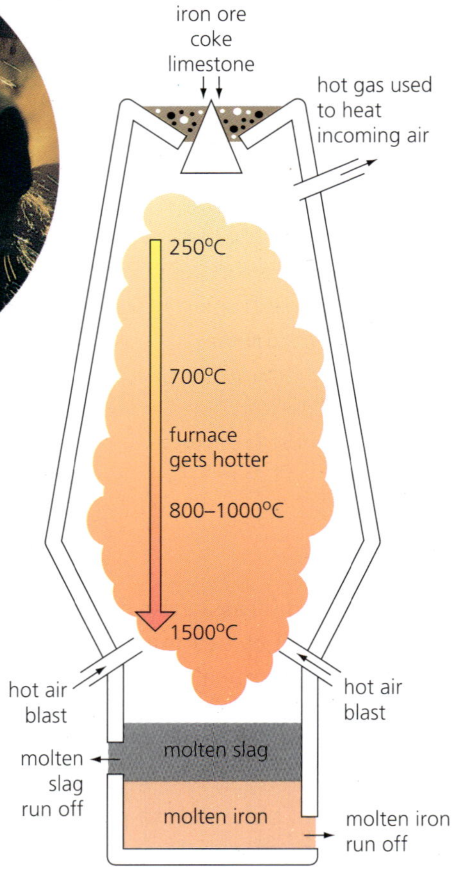

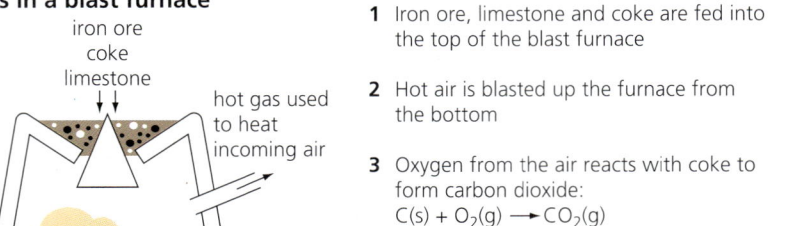

iron ore
coke
limestone

hot gas used to heat incoming air

250°C

700°C

furnace gets hotter

800–1000°C

1500°C

hot air blast

molten slag run off

molten slag

molten iron

molten iron run off

1. Iron ore, limestone and coke are fed into the top of the blast furnace

2. Hot air is blasted up the furnace from the bottom

3. Oxygen from the air reacts with coke to form carbon dioxide:
$C(s) + O_2(g) \rightarrow CO_2(g)$

4. Carbon dioxide reacts with more coke to form carbon monoxide:
$CO_2(g) + C(s) \rightarrow 2CO(g)$

5. Carbon monoxide is a reducing agent. Iron (III) oxide is reduced to iron:
⌐ reduction = loss of oxygen ⌐
$Fe_2O_3(s) + 3CO(g) \rightarrow 2Fe(l) + 3CO_2(g)$

6. Dense molten iron runs to the bottom of the furnace and is run off. There are many impurities in iron ore. The limestone helps to remove these as shown in 7 and 8.

7. Limestone is broken down by heat to calcium oxide:
$CaCO_3(s) \rightarrow CaO(s) + CO_2(g)$

8. Calcium oxide reacts with impurities like sand (silicon dioxide) to form a liquid called 'slag':
$CaO(s) + SiO_2(s) \rightarrow CaSiO_3(l)$
   impurity   slag
The liquid slag falls to the bottom of the furnce and is tapped off.

Pure iron on its own is rather soft, and not very useful. When it is alloyed with carbon and various metals, it is known as **steel**. There are hundreds of possible alloys of iron, each with its own particular properties.

- **Mild steel** contains iron alloyed with 0.3% carbon, which gives the metal extra strength.
- **Stainless steel** contains up to 20% chromium and 10% nickel, together with a little carbon. This makes the metal stronger and prevents it from rusting.
- **High-speed steels** contain iron alloyed to tungsten and chromium. These are used in drill bits, as they are hard and maintain a good cutting edge at high temperatures.

11 Name a mineral that contains iron (III) oxide.

12 Iron and aluminium are both extracted from their oxides, iron (III) oxide and aluminium oxide.
   a From your knowledge of the charges on ions, write down the formulae of these two oxides.
   b Both of these oxides are found naturally as ores. What is an ore?
   c What type of chemical process happens when the oxides are turned into the metals?

13 When iron is alloyed with chromium, stainless steel is produced. Give two advantages that this alloy has over pure iron.

How is aluminium extracted?

14 Iron is extracted by reacting the oxide with carbon monoxide in a blast furnace. Suggest a reason why this method does not work for aluminium.

Aluminium is extracted from the ore **bauxite**, which is impure aluminium oxide. The metals described in this chapter so far are extracted using a chemical reducing agent – carbon or carbon monoxide. Aluminium is a more reactive metal, which means that its compounds are quite stable. Carbon does not react with aluminium oxide and a more powerful reduction process is needed. Aluminium is therefore extracted from its ore by **electrolytic reduction** – the electrolysis of its melted oxide.

Figure 5

Electrolysis of bauxite

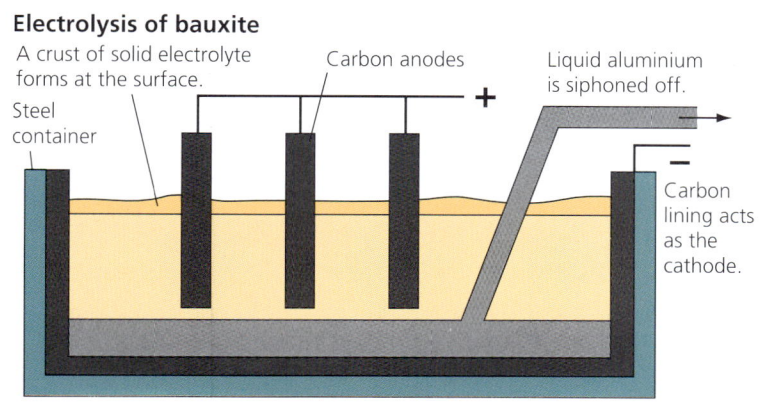

- A crust of solid electrolyte forms at the surface.
- Steel container
- Carbon anodes
- Liquid aluminium is siphoned off.
- Carbon lining acts as the cathode.

Aluminium is formed at the cathode and can be siphoned away.

Electrolyte of melted bauxite (Al_2O_3) and cryolite (Na_3AlF_6) at about 950°C.

Aluminium oxide has a very high melting point (2047°C), which would require a lot of energy to keep it as a liquid. So during the electrolysis another aluminium compound called **cryolite** (or sodium aluminium fluoride, Na_3AlF_6) is added. This lowers the melting point of the mixture to about 950°C.

As the electrolysis proceeds, the oxygen produced at the anode reacts with the carbon electrode and oxidises it away as a mixture of carbon monoxide and carbon dioxide. The anode therefore needs to be replaced from time to time.

Extracting aluminium from bauxite needs a great deal of energy. The electrolyte must be heated constantly, and large amounts of electrical energy are needed for the electrolysis. For this reason the site where aluminium is electrolysed is often near sources of cheap electrical energy such as hydroelectric power.

What is aluminium used for?

Aluminium is a shiny metal with a fairly low density (2.7 g/cm^3). Although aluminium itself is quite reactive, the outside of the metal develops a thin layer of aluminium oxide, which makes it quite stable and unreactive, and keeps its surface shiny even when exposed to air or water.

Aluminium can be used in doors, window frames and greenhouses, because its resistance to corrosion means that it is fairly easy to maintain.

When the QE2 was built 1200 tonnes of aluminium were built into its superstructure. Because aluminium has such a low density, the shipbuilders were able to build an extra passenger deck without affecting the stability of the ship.

Aluminium is coated in a thin layer of oxide that makes it resistant to corrosion. It can be used to make doors, window frames and greenhouses.

Metals

How can the resistance of aluminium to corrosion be improved?

15 Many everyday objects are made from aluminium.
   a Suggest two uses for this metal. State which properties of the metal make it particularly useful for each purpose.
   b Aluminium objects may be anodised. What does this involve?
   c List two advantages that anodising can bring.

The resistance of aluminium to corrosion can be greatly improved by **anodising** the metal. An aluminium object is made into the anode in a bath of chromic acid. The oxygen evolved at the aluminium anode reacts with the metal to make the oxide layer even thicker. This thick layer of aluminium oxide makes the metal shiny and even more resistant to corrosion. In addition, because aluminium oxide adsorbs dyes, anodised objects made from aluminium can be attractively coloured.

Summary of chemical properties of metals

- All metals react with oxygen to form metal oxides, which are nearly all bases.
- Metals react with many non-metals to form ionic salts.
- When a metal is extracted from its compound, reduction takes place.
- An ore is a mineral containing enough metal to make extraction economically worthwhile.
- Carbon or carbon monoxide can be used to reduce many ores to the metal.
- The ores of very reactive metals such as aluminium, magnesium and sodium are reduced by electrolysis.
- Anodising aluminium gives it a protective coat of oxide that makes the metal shiny and durable.

13.3 Metals and the periodic table

Metals have many physical and chemical properties in common. Various groups of metals in different positions in the periodic table have distinctive properties. Elements in the same group of the periodic table often have similar properties, and there is often a trend in properties as you go down a group.

16 Using only the symbols shown in the figure below, write out the symbols for:
   a a metal
   b a non-metal
   c two metals in the same group
   d two metals in the same period
   e a solid
   f a liquid
   g a gas

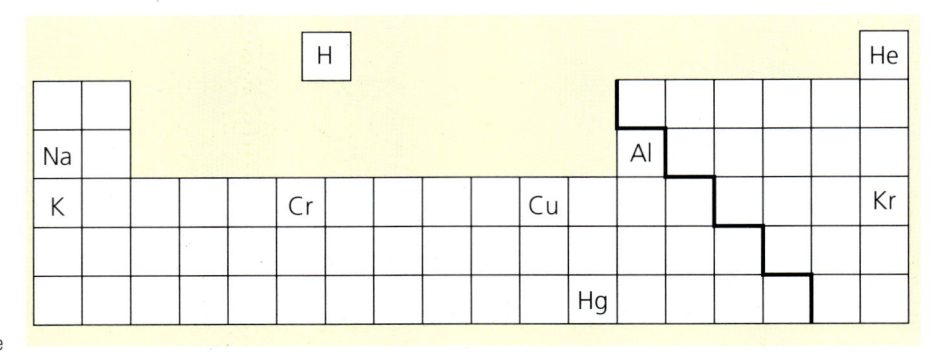

Figure 6 Elements in the same group behave like a chemical family. Each member of the family is different, but there are always 'family likenesses' within a group.

Metals

What are the properties of the metals in Group I?

Group I in the periodic table contains the most chemically reactive metals. Some of their properties are shown in table 2.

Table 2 *Group I elements*

Name	Symbol	Melting point (°C)	Boiling point (°C)	Density (g/cm^3)
lithium	Li	180	1330	0.53
sodium	Na	98	890	0.97
potassium	K	64	774	0.86
rubidium	Rb	39	688	1.53
caesium	Cs	29	690	1.90

The metals themselves are so reactive that in the Earth's crust they are only ever found as compounds. Sea water and salt deposits contain large amounts of Group I compounds such as sodium chloride.

Physical properties

All Group I metals are:
- soft and shiny when freshly cut
- good electrical conductors
- low in density.

Chemical properties

- All Group I metals react with the oxygen in air and must be stored under oil to prevent them being oxidised in air. They are only shiny for a moment when freshly cut, before a dull layer of oxide forms on the surface:

$$4Na(s) + O_2(g) \rightarrow 2Na_2O(s)$$

The metals burn in air and oxygen with brightly coloured flames.

- All Group I metals react well with water. The heat from the reaction melts most of these metals, which moves over the surface of the water on a cushion of hydrogen and steam:

$$2Na(l) + H_2O(l) \rightarrow 2NaOH(aq) + H_2(g)$$

The reaction of potassium with water is so vigorous that the hydrogen produced catches fire, and sometimes explodes:

$$2K(l) + H_2O(l) \rightarrow 2KOH(aq) + H_2(g)$$

The metal hydroxides produced in these reactions are strongly alkaline. For this reason, Group I elements are sometimes called the **alkali metals**.

- All Group I metals react readily with halogens such as chlorine:

$$2Li(s) + Cl_2(g) \rightarrow 2LiCl(s)$$
$$2Na(s) + Cl_2(g) \rightarrow 2NaCl(s)$$
$$2K(s) + Cl_2(g) \rightarrow 2KCl(s)$$

Note

As you go down the group, this reaction becomes more vigorous. The salts produced are all stable compounds made from ions.

Metals

Table 3 Group I compounds

Metal	Chloride	Bromide	Nitrate	Sulphate	Carbonate
lithium	LiCl	LiBr	LiNO$_3$	Li$_2$SO$_4$	Li$_2$CO$_3$
sodium	NaCl	NaBr	NaNO$_3$	Na$_2$SO$_4$	Na$_2$CC$_3$
potassium	KCl	KBr	KNO$_3$	K$_2$SO$_4$	K$_2$CO$_3$

Similarities and trends

These metals are all soft and of low density. When they do react, they form compounds with similar formulae (table 3).

Group I metals get more reactive going down the group. The reason for this is that when Group I metals react they always lose an electron to form a 1+ ion.

For example, lithium reacts with chlorine:

$$2Li(s) + Cl_2(g) \rightarrow 2LiCl(s)$$

lithium contains metal atoms — lithium chloride contains ions

When this reaction happens, each lithium atom loses an electron to a chlorine atom. The metal atom becomes a 1+ lithium ion, and each chlorine atom becomes a 1– chloride ion. Going down Group I, the metal atoms become larger as successive electron shells are added. The outer electron gets further from the positive nucleus, and is held on less strongly. As this outer electron becomes easier to lose, the metals become more reactive.

Sodium is used in the photo-electric cells of some burglar alarms.

Salt is used to season food.

Rock salt is spread on roads in winter to melt the ice and grit the road. However, the salt can increase the rate of corrosion of the steel used in vehicles and bridges.

Sodium and other Group I hydroxides are strong alkalis. They can be used in making soap, paper and many other substances.

The characteristic orange glow of street lamps is due to sodium vapour in the lamp.

17 When the element caesium is reacted with water an alkaline solution, A, is formed and a colourless gas, B, is given off.
   a Suggest a chemical name and formula for solution A.
   b What do you think the pH of solution A is?
   c Would the chemical reactivity of caesium be greater than, the same as, or less than that of other Group I metals? Why?
   d What is gas B?
   e How would you test for gas B?

How are the elements in Group II similar?

Group II elements are also reactive metals, but not as reactive as those in Group I. These metals are not found directly in the Earth's crust, only as compounds. Sea water contains large amounts of magnesium chloride, and much of the Earth's crust contains deposits of calcium carbonate in the form of chalk, limestone or marble.

Table 4 Group II elements

Name	Symbol	Melting point (°C)	Boiling point (°C)	Density (g/cm³)
beryllium	Be	1280	2477	1.85
magnesium	Mg	650	1110	1.74
calcium	Ca	850	1487	1.54
strontium	Sr	768	1380	2.62
barium	Ba	714	1640	3.51

Physical properties

Group II metals:
- are silvery and shiny when kept away from air
- have fairly high melting and boiling points
- are good electrical conductors
- have fairly low density, but are more dense than Group I metals.

Chemical properties

- Group II metals all react with the oxygen in air. They tarnish when left out as a dull layer of oxide forms. When heated in air the metals burn with a bright flame:

$$2Mg(s) + O_2(g) \rightarrow 2MgO(s)$$
$$2Ca(s) + O_2(g) \rightarrow 2CaO(s)$$

Going down Group II, this reaction becomes increasingly vigorous.

- All Group II metals react well with water or steam. Magnesium reacts only slowly with water, but burns brightly when heated in steam:

$$Mg(s) + H_2O(g) \rightarrow MgO(s) + H_2(g)$$

Note that magnesium forms the oxide here and not the hydroxide.
Calcium is more reactive, and when put in cold water reacts to produce bubbles of hydrogen gas:

$$Ca(s) + 2H_2O(g) \rightarrow Ca(OH)_2(s) + H_2(g)$$

The metal oxides and hydroxides produced in these reactions are all strong bases.

Similarities and trends

Group II metals are all reactive metals with fairly high melting points and low densities. They form ionic compounds with similar formulae.

Table 5 Group II compounds

Metal	Chloride	Bromide	Nitrate	Sulphate	Carbonate
magnesium	$MgCl_2$	$MgBr_2$	$Mg(NO_3)_2$	$MgSO_4$	$MgCO_3$
calcium	$CaCl_2$	$CaBr_2$	$Ca(NO_3)_2$	$CaSO_4$	$CaCO_3$

The metals in Group II get more reactive further down the group, although they are not as reactive as Group I elements.

Metals

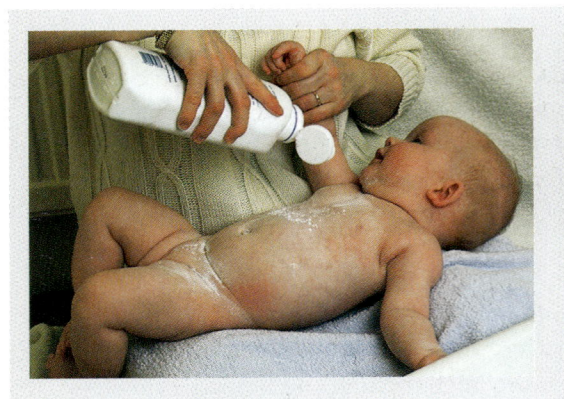

Cement is made by strongly heating limestone (calcium carbonate, CaCO$_3$) and clay. When cement is mixed with sand and water it forms mortar, which is used to bind bricks and stone blocks together.

Talc is made from magnesium silicate powder.

Calcium phosphate, Ca$_3$(PO$_4$)$_2$, is an essential part of bones and teeth. Calcium compounds are an essential part of a healthy diet.

Magnesium oxide suspended in water is called 'magnesia'. It neutralises excess stomach acid without generating any gases.

Figure 7 Reactions of calcium and it's compounds.

Plaster of Paris is a form of calcium sulphate, CaSO$_4$. When mixed with water it expands and then sets hard in a few minutes. It can be used to protect broken bones. The walls inside a building can also be 'plastered' with a mixture of calcium sulphate and water.

Patients needing an X-ray of their digestive system are given a 'barium meal'. This contains barium sulphate (BaSO$_4$) and the large Ba^{2+} ions show up well on an X-ray. Most barium compounds are poisonous, but barium sulphate is so insoluble in water that is safe to consume.

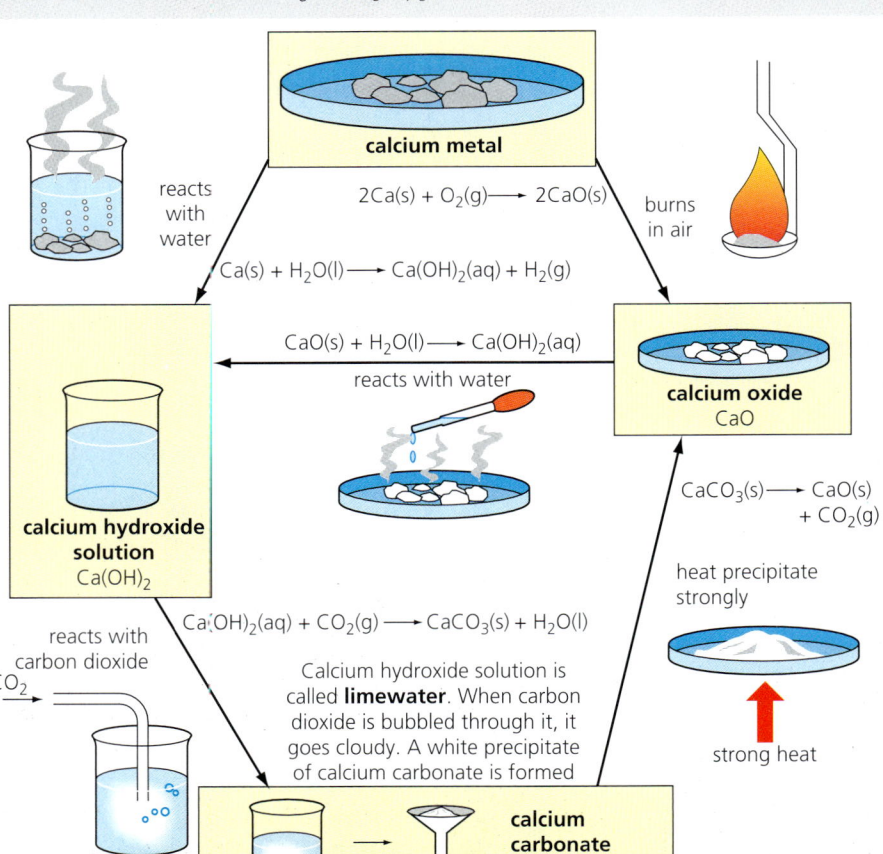

calcium metal

reacts with water

$2Ca(s) + O_2(g) \longrightarrow 2CaO(s)$

burns in air

$Ca(s) + H_2O(l) \longrightarrow Ca(OH)_2(aq) + H_2(g)$

$CaO(s) + H_2O(l) \longrightarrow Ca(OH)_2(aq)$

reacts with water

calcium oxide CaO

$CaCO_3(s) \longrightarrow CaO(s) + CO_2(g)$

calcium hydroxide solution Ca(OH)$_2$

heat precipitate strongly

reacts with carbon dioxide

CO$_2$

$Ca(OH)_2(aq) + CO_2(g) \longrightarrow CaCO_3(s) + H_2O(l)$

Calcium hydroxide solution is called **limewater**. When carbon dioxide is bubbled through it, it goes cloudy. A white precipitate of calcium carbonate is formed

strong heat

calcium carbonate CaCO$_3$

178

What are the properties of the transition metals?

The transition metals are found in the central block of the periodic table. They have many similar physical and chemical properties and so are studied together. They are sometimes known as the **heavy metals**, because of their high densities. There are three rows of transition metals in the periodic table, but only some of the first row metals will be studied here.

Figure 8 The transition metals.

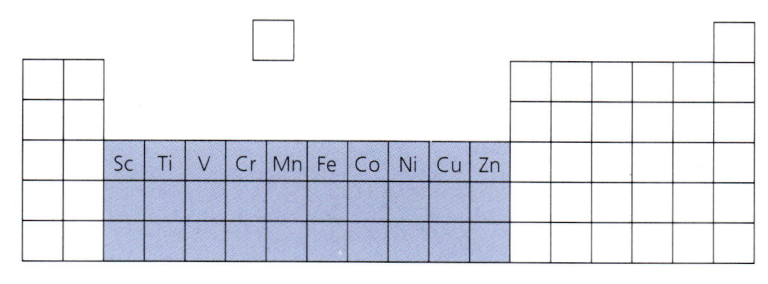

Table 6 The first row of the transition metals

Name	Symbol	Melting point (°C)	Boiling point (°C)	Density (g/cm³)
scandium	Sc	1540	2730	3.0
titanium	Ti	1675	3260	4.5
vanadium	V	1900	300	6.0
chromium	Cr	1890	2482	7.2
manganese	Mn	1240	2100	7.2
iron	Fe	1535	3000	7.9
cobalt	Co	1492	2900	8.9
nickel	Ni	1453	2730	8.9
copper	Cu	1083	2595	8.9
zinc	Zn	420	907	7.1

Table 7 Colours of some transition metal compounds

Compound	Formula	Colour
chromium sulphate	$Cr_2(SO_4)_3$	green
potassium chromate	K_2CrO_4	yellow
potassium dichromate	$K_2Cr_2O_7$	orange
potassium manganate (VII)	$KMnO_4$	purple
iron (II) sulphate	$FeSO_4$	green
iron (III) chloride	$FeCl_3$	brown
nickel nitrate	$NiNO_3$	green
copper (II) sulphate	$CuSO_4$	blue

Physical properties

The transition metals
- are shiny metals of various colours
- have high melting points, due to strong metallic bonds
- have high densities, due to fairly small atoms being packed closely together
- form coloured compounds of great variety.

The different colours of hair are due to the presence of transition metal compounds. Blonde hair contains titanium compounds, red hair contains molybdenum compounds and brown hair contains compounds of iron, cobalt and copper.

Transition metal compounds cause the colours in jewels such as rubies, sapphires, emeralds and amethysts.

Metals

- are good **catalysts**. They increase the rate of some chemical reactions, and help industrial processes happen faster and more economically. For example **iron** is a catalyst in the Haber process used to make ammonia:

$$N_2(g) + 3H_2(g) \xrightarrow[\text{catalyst}]{\text{iron}} 2NH_3(g)$$

vanadium (V) oxide catalyses part of the processes to make sulphuric acid:

$$2SO_2(g) + O_2(g) \xrightarrow[\text{catalyst}]{V_2O_5} 2SO_3(g)$$

manganese (IV) oxide is a catalyst in the decomposition of hydrogen peroxide solution:

$$2H_2O_2(aq) \xrightarrow[\text{catalyst}]{MnO_2} 2H_2O(l) + O_2(g)$$

Chemical properties

- When transition metals react to form compounds, they can form ions with **variable charges**.
- Transition metals vary in their **reaction** with **oxygen**. Chromium is very resistant to this reaction, and it maintains a shiny silver surface. Iron, on the other hand, reacts quite readily, if moisture is present, to form **rust**. The rate of rusting is increased by increase in temperature and by the presence of carbon dioxide or dissolved metal salts. Rusting is a complex chemical process, but rust itself is 'hydrated' iron (III) oxide. This means that the iron (III) oxide is associated with a variable amount of water within the structure. The formula for rust can be written $Fe_2O_3 \cdot nH_2O$, where the letter 'n' represents a variable number of molecules of water.

Rusting: the corrosion of iron.

The steel frame of a bicycle can be protected by several coats of tough paint which will keep air and moisture away from the metal. The bicycle chain is protected by a layer of oil or grease, which is impervious to air and water and protects the metal. The wheel rims of many bicycles are made from steel. One way to protect this is to chrome plate the metal. Chromium is a shiny, unreactive metal and the thin layer protects the steel underneath. Another way in which chromium can be used is to alloy it to make stainless steel.

Many food containers are made from steel, because of its strength and low price. The steel can be protected from the moisture in the food inside by a thin layer of an unreactive metal like tin (this is why they're called 'tins' even though they are not made of tin), or by a thin layer of plastic

Zinc is more reactive than iron, and can be used to prevent rusting. Zinc is known as a sacrificial metal, because when it is in contact with iron it corrodes more readily than the iron, and stops the iron rusting. The zinc can be coated in a thin layer onto steel – this is known as galvanised iron. Another method is to attach blocks of zinc to areas of steel that are particularly likely to rust (such as a ship's hull or under the wheel arches of cars). The zinc reacts and dissolves away in preference to the iron, and will have to be replaced occasionally.

18 a What is the chemical name and formula for rust?
  b Which two substances must be present for rusting to occur?
  c State two ways of increasing the rate of rusting of iron.
  d List three ways of preventing iron from rusting.
19 Explain why objects made of aluminium show few signs of corrosion, even though aluminium is a much more reactive metal than iron.

Why recycle metals?

Many metals that are widely used in the developed world today are in short supply. New reserves might be discovered, but in the end there is only a finite amount of any element on the planet. While there is a large supply of the ores of metals such as aluminium, iron and chromium, others are in short supply. The ores of metals such as tungsten, tin, zinc or gold may last for less than 50 years at the present rate of mining. In the face of this problem, one way forward is to **recycle** metals.

If people realise that metals are valuable, they will think twice before throwing them away. One metal which can be profitably recycled is aluminium.

Although there are only limited reserves of gold in the Earth's crust, a very high proportion of the gold we use is recycled. This is because very few people will throw away something made of gold – it is usually sold or recycled.

Recycling aluminium is a highly efficient way of saving energy. Dealers will pay at least 30p per kilogram of aluminium cans (about 50 cans), and since over 2000 million aluminium cans are produced each year, that would be worth £20 000 000 if it were all recycled!

Summary of metals and the periodic table

- Group I metals are all soft metals with a low density, are very reactive and need to be stored under oil.
- Group II metals all have fairly low density (but higher than Group I) and are quite reactive. They can be stored in dry air.
- Group II metals are less reactive than Group I metals.
- Metals in Group I and Group II become more reactive going down the group because as the atoms get larger electrons are lost more easily.
- Metals and compounds of Groups I and II have a wide variety of uses.

- The elements in the central block of the periodic table are known as the transition metals.
- Transition metals are all shiny metals with high melting and boiling points, have high density, are good catalysts and produce coloured compounds.
- Transition metals form ions with variable charges. Some react with oxygen and corrode away while others are resistant to corrosion.
- Recycling is an important way to conserve resources and save energy.

Metals

Examination style questions

1 Limestone is mined from the ground, broken into lumps then heated in a kiln together with coke. This process of heating limestone to make 'quicklime' has been carried out for hundreds of years.
  a Suggest two ways in which a limestone quarry might be an environmental hazard. How could these problems be overcome?
  b What is the chemical name and formula for limestone?
  c Write a balanced equation for the reaction that happens when limestone is heated strongly in a kiln. Where does the heat energy needed for this process come from?
  d Quicklime is turned into 'slaked' lime by adding water. What is the chemical name and formula for slaked lime?
  e Write a symbol equation for the reaction of water with slaked lime.
  f Give one use for limestone and one for slaked lime.

2 a Describe three observations you would make if a small piece of sodium is added to some water in a trough.
  b Write a balanced symbol equation for the reaction that occurs.
  c One of the products of the reaction of sodium with water is a gas. What is this gas, and how would you confirm its presence?

3 Aluminium and iron both occur as minerals in many places in the Earth's crust. Iron is extracted using a blast furnace by reduction with carbon monoxide. Aluminium is extracted by electrolysis. Reduction using electrolysis is much more expensive than reduction with carbon monoxide.
  a Why must aluminium be extracted by electrolysis?
  b One way of reducing the cost of aluminium is to recycle used metal. Suggest three advantages of recycling aluminium.
  c Give equations for the reaction at the anode and cathode when aluminium is electrolysed.

4 Aluminium can be made into several useful alloys.
  a What is an alloy?
  b Name an alloy of aluminium.
  c Give one advantage the use of an alloy can have over a pure metal.

5 The figure opposite sums up the extraction of iron in a blast furnace.
At point A a mixture of iron ore and two other substances is loaded into the blast furnace.
  a Give the name and formula of one ore of iron.
  b Give the name and formula of the other two substances loaded into the top of the furnace.
  c Write a balanced symbol equation for the reaction that happens in the furnace when iron ore forms iron metal.
  d What is substance B and why is it used here?
  e What is substance C?
  f What is substance D?
  g State one impurity present in substance D and state what effect it has on D.

6 a Name two elements in the same group as sodium.
  b Sodium reacts readily with oxygen in the air, both at room temperature and when heated. How should sodium be stored to prevent this happening?
  c Sodium oxide, Na_2O, is formed when sodium metal is burned in air. Write a balanced equation for this reaction.

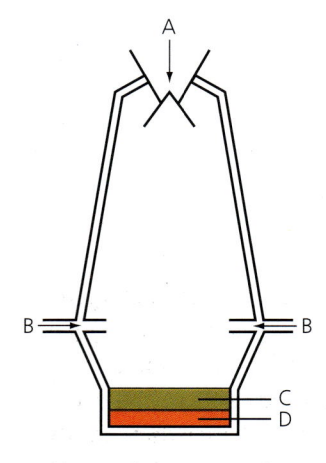

Metals, redox reactions and cells 14

Learning objectives

By the end of this chapter you should be able to:
- **explain** how oxidising and reducing agents work
- **describe** some redox reactions
- **describe** how metals react with oxygen, water and acids
- **predict** whether certain reactions will occur using the reactivity series of metals
- **describe** displacement reactions
- **describe** some simple cells and their uses

14.1 Oxidation and reduction

The chemical processes of reduction and oxidation happen all around us every day. For example:
- All living things stay alive by respiration – a process that involves oxidation.
- Much of the energy to power our homes or move vehicles comes from burning fuels – another oxidation process.
- The metals that we use to construct everyday objects have been produced by reduction reactions.

---

1 In each of the following equations state which substance is oxidised and which is being reduced. Explain briefly your reasoning.
  a $Fe_2O_3(s) + 3CO(g) \rightarrow 2Fe(l) + 3CO_2(g)$
  b $2Mg(s) + CO_2(g) \rightarrow 2MgO(s) + C(s)$
  c $2Fe^{2+}(aq) + Cl_2(g) \rightarrow 2Fe^{3+}(aq) + 2Cl^-(aq)$
2 State and explain an everyday reaction that involves oxidation.
3 State and explain an everyday reaction that involves reduction.

What are oxidising agents?

A chemical that brings about oxidation is known as an **oxidising agent**. Oxygen itself is a good oxidising agent. Other chemicals that can easily 'give away' oxygen are also good oxidising agents. Some substances with several oxygen atoms chemically joined within their structure will often make good oxidising agents.

Oxidation is also defined as loss of electrons, so any substance that readily gains electrons will also be a good oxidising agent. Non-metals in Groups VI and VII of the periodic table (such as fluorine, chlorine and oxygen) are one or two electrons short of a full shell. They therefore readily gain electrons to form a stable full shell of electrons and will be good oxidising agents.

183

Metals, redox reactions and cells

What is a reducing agent?

A chemical that brings about reduction is known as a **reducing agent**. Hydrogen and carbon are well known reducing agents. Other chemicals that readily gain oxygen are also good reducing agents.

Reduction is also defined as gain of electrons, so any substance that readily loses electrons is also a good reducing agent. Metals in Groups I and II of the periodic table (such as sodium, magnesium or calcium) readily lose their outer electrons. They therefore easily lose electrons and form a stable full shell of electrons.

Table 1 Oxidising and reducing agents

Oxidising agents with 'available oxygen'	Reducing agents that readily gain oxygen
oxygen, O_2	carbon, C
potassium chlorate (V), $KClO_3$	carbon monoxide, CO
potassium chlorate (VII), $KClO_4$	hydrogen, H_2
potassium manganate, $KMnO_4$	
sodium nitrate, $NaNO_3$	
Oxidising agents that readily gain electrons	**Reducing agents that readily lose electrons**
fluorine, F_2	aluminium, Al
chlorine, Cl_2	magnesium, Mg
	sodium, Na
	zinc, Zn

How may redox reactions be explained?

4 Write one sentence to explain:
   a oxidation
   b reduction
   c an oxidising agent
   d a reducing agent
   e a redox reaction.

5 Silver nitrate solution reacts with iron (II) sulphate solution as follows:
$AgNO_3(aq) + FeSO_4(aq) \rightarrow Ag(s) + Fe_2(SO_4)_3(aq)$
   a Write an ionic equation for this reaction.
   b State which substance is being reduced and which oxidised.

Oxidation and reduction nearly always happen at the same time – when one substance is reduced another will be oxidised. One substance gains electrons from another substance that has lost electrons. A chemical reaction that involves both reduction and oxidation at the same time is known as a **redox** reaction.

For example, copper (II) sulphate solution reacts with zinc metal:

$$\text{reduction}$$
$$CuSO_4(aq) + Zn(s) \rightarrow Cu(s) + ZnSO_4(aq)$$
$$\text{oxidation}$$

copper ions gain two electrons

ionic equation: $Cu^{2+}(aq) + Zn(s) \rightarrow Cu(s) + Zn^{2+}(aq)$

zinc atoms lose two electrons

In this reaction each zinc atom gives away two electrons to a Cu^{2+} ion. The zinc acts as a reducing agent – it reduces the copper ions to copper metal. The zinc metal is itself oxidised to Zn^{2+} ions.

Electrolysis can also be regarded as a redox process. For example, when melted sodium chloride is electrolysed the Na⁺ ions migrate to the negative cathode and the Cl⁻ ions migrate to the positive anode.

Reduction always happens at the cathode – sodium ions are discharged:

reduction = gain of electrons

$$2Na^+(l) + 2e^- \longrightarrow 2Na(l)$$

Oxidation always happens at the anode – chloride ions are discharged:

oxidation = loss of electrons

$$2Cl^-(l) \longrightarrow Cl_2(g) + 2e^-$$

During the electrolysis of sodium chloride a redox process takes place. Sodium ions gain electrons and are reduced to sodium metal. Chloride ions lose electrons and are oxidised to chlorine gas.

How do metals react with oxygen?

Oxygen is a very reactive non-metal, and it will react with metals to form compounds called **oxides**. For example:

copper + oxygen → copper (II) oxide
$$2Cu(s) + O_2(g) \rightarrow 2CuO(s)$$

Some metals (potassium, for example) react very readily with oxygen and will burn brightly in the oxygen in air. Other metals (such as copper) will gradually tarnish in air, slowly forming a thin layer of oxide on the surface of the metal. Very unreactive metals (like gold) will stay bright and shiny in air for long periods of time.

Table 2 Reacting metals with oxygen

	Metal	Symbol	Reaction with oxygen
most reactive	potassium	K	burns brightly in air with a purple flame: $4K(s) + O_2(g) \rightarrow 2K_2O(s)$
↓	sodium	Na	burns in air with an orange flame: $4Na(s) + O_2(g) \rightarrow 2Na_2O(s)$
	calcium	Ca	burns in air with a brick-red flame: $2Ca(s) + O_2(g) \rightarrow 2CaO(s)$
	magnesium	Mg	burns in air with a bright white flame: $2Mg(s) + O_2(g) \rightarrow 2MgO(s)$
least reactive	copper	Cu	does not burn, but slowly forms a black oxide layer: $2Cu(s) + O_2(g) \rightarrow 2CuO(s)$

The **reactivity series of metals** (table 3) is a list comparing how readily metals react with oxygen.

Table 3 The reactivity series of metals

potassium	sodium	lithium	calcium	magnesium	aluminium	(carbon)	zinc	iron	tin	lead	(hydrogen)	copper	mercury	silver	gold	platinum
K	Na	Li	Ca	Mg	Al	C	Zn	Fe	Sn	Pb	H	Cu	Hg	Ag	Au	Pt

← most reactive   least reactive

Metals, redox reactions and cells

Sometimes carbon and hydrogen are shown in the reactivity series of metals. Metals that are less reactive than carbon may be extracted from their oxides by reduction with carbon. Metals that are less reactive than hydrogen may also be extracted from their oxides by reduction with hydrogen.

What happens when metals react with water?

When metals react with water a competition goes on to see which element can 'win' the oxygen.

Very reactive metals like potassium or calcium easily win the oxygen in water. The oxide produced goes on to form a hydroxide.

Less reactive metals like lead lose the competition for water and the hydrogen and oxygen in water stay joined together

Figure 1 When metals react with water a competition takes place to see which element can 'win' the oxygen.

Some metals react with water or steam to form a metal hydroxide or oxide, and hydrogen gas is given off. For example,

$$\text{calcium} + \text{water} \rightarrow \text{calcium hydroxide} + \text{hydrogen}$$
$$Ca(s) + H_2O(l) \rightarrow Ca(OH)_2(s) + H_2(g)$$

However, not all metals react with water. Very unreactive metals like copper, silver and gold will not react with water at all. This is why copper is used for pipes and containers for water.

When metals react with water, a redox reaction is happening. This can be seen as a competition for the oxygen in water. When metals such as sodium and calcium react with water, the metals 'win' the competition and take oxygen from the water, leaving hydrogen gas. Metals such as copper and silver 'lose' the competition and oxygen remains joined to hydrogen in water.

How do metals react with acids?

All metals react with at least one acid to form a salt. Usually hydrogen gas is also given off. For example,

$$\text{magnesium} + \text{sulphuric acid} \rightarrow \text{magnesium sulphate} + \text{hydrogen}$$
$$Mg(s) + H_2SO_4(aq) \rightarrow MgSO_4(aq) + H_2(g)$$

Metals react with acids in the same order of reactivity as in their reaction with oxygen and with water.

Table 4 Reactivity of metals

Metal	Symbol	Reaction with water	Reaction with acid
potassium	K	violent reaction in cold water, forming hydrogen which then burns: $2K(s) + 2H_2O(l) \rightarrow 2KOH(aq) + H_2(g)$	very violent and dangerous reaction, which should never be tried in the laboratory: $2K(s) + 2HCl(aq) \rightarrow 2KCl(aq) + H_2(g)$
sodium	Na	vigorous reaction in cold water: $2Na(s) + 2H_2O(l) \rightarrow 2NaOH(aq) + H_2(g)$	dangerously violent reaction: $2Na(s) + H_2SO_4(aq) \rightarrow Na_2SO_4(aq) + H_2(g)$
calcium	Ca	reacts well with cold water, forming a precipitate of calcium hydroxide: $Ca(s) + 2H_2O(l) \rightarrow Ca(OH)_2(s) + H_2(g)$	very vigorous reaction: $Ca(s) + 2HNO_3(aq) \rightarrow Ca(NO_3)_2(aq) + H_2(g)$
magnesium	Mg	little or no reaction with water, but burns readily in steam: $Mg(s) + H_2O(g) \rightarrow MgO(s) + H_2(g)$	vigorous reaction: $Mg(s) + 2HCl(aq) \rightarrow MgCl_2(aq) + H_2(g)$
copper	Cu	no reaction	little reaction with sulphuric or hydrochloric acid, but will react with nitric acid: $Cu(s) + 8HNO_3(aq) \rightarrow 3Cu(NO_3)_2(aq) + 4H_2O(l) + 2NO(g)$

Metals, redox reactions and cells

Do metals react with solutions of salts?

Metals will react, under certain circumstances, with solutions of the salts of other metals. For example, when a strip of zinc metal is suspended in some copper (II) sulphate solution a reaction occurs after a few minutes. Crystals of copper metal start to grow on the zinc strip, the solution becomes warm and the strong blue colour of the copper (II) sulphate becomes paler. Zinc is more reactive than copper and is higher in the reactivity series of metals. In this reaction, zinc **displaces** copper from the solution in a **displacement reaction**. This happens when a more reactive metal displaces a less reactive one from a solution of its salt:

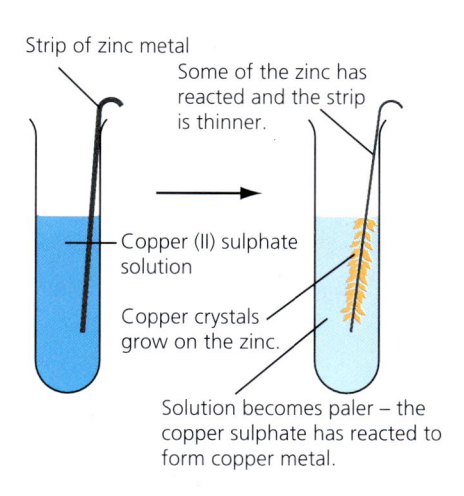

Figure 2 A displacement reaction.

Before reaction:
The copper and sulphate are quite 'happy' together – nothing is there to compete.

When zinc is added:
Zinc is more reactive than copper. Zinc wins the competition and copper is displaced or 'thrown out' on its own.

Figure 3 Zinc and copper sulphate – a displacement reaction.

$$Zn(s) + CuSO_4(aq) \rightarrow ZnSO_4(aq) + Cu(s)$$

Displacement reactions also involve redox processes. Here the zinc is oxidised to zinc ions in the zinc sulphate solution. Copper ions in the copper (II) sulphate are reduced to copper metal.

The reactivity series can be used to make predictions as to which metals will react in displacement reactions and which will not.

6 Various mixtures of metals and metal oxides were heated to see whether any reaction took place.

Metal	aluminium oxide	calcium oxide	magnesium oxide	iron oxide	lead oxide	zinc oxide
aluminium	–	✗	✗	✓	✓	✓
calcium	✓	–	✓	✓	✓	✓
magnesium	✓	✗	–	✓	✓	✓
iron	✗	✗	✗	–	✓	✗
lead	✗	✗	✗	✗	–	✗
zinc	✗	✗	✗	✓	✓	–

✓ = reaction occurs
✗ = no reaction

a Use the information in the table to deduce the order of reactivity of these metals and list them, with the most reactive metal first.

b Use your knowledge of the charge on ions to deduce the formulae of each of these metal oxides.

c Suggest, with a reason in each case, which metal would be most suitable for making:

 i a waterproof seal on a roof
 ii the main bodywork of a car
 iii greenhouse and window frames
 iv a weighted belt for divers to wear.

7 Write down three observations you would expect if an excess of powdered zinc metal was shaken with some copper (II) sulphate solution.

Metals, redox reactions and cells

Summary of oxidation and reduction

- Oxidation is gain of oxygen and loss of electrons.
- Reduction is loss of oxygen and gain of electrons.
- An oxidising agent brings about oxidation. Oxidising agents are themselves reduced.
- A reducing agent brings about reduction. Reducing agents are themselves oxidised.
- In a redox reaction oxidation and reduction happen at the same time.
- Electrolysis is a redox process – oxidation happens at the anode and reduction happens at the cathode.
- Metals react with varying degrees of reactivity with oxygen to make oxides.
- Only some metals react with water or steam to give metal hydroxides or oxides and hydrogen gas.
- All metals react with at least one acid to give a salt and usually hydrogen gas.
- In a displacement reaction a more reactive metal displaces a less reactive metal from a solution of its salt.
- The reactivity series of metals arranges metals in order of reactivity.

14.2 Electricity from chemical reactions

Many chemical reactions involve energy changes, and often heat or light is given off. It is possible in some cases to arrange the apparatus and chemicals so that much of this energy is turned into an electric current. A **cell** is a simple device to turn chemical energy into electrical energy. A simple cell was invented by Daniell to use the reaction between zinc metal and copper (II) sulphate solution to provide electrical energy. When this reaction is carried out in a test tube, a displacement reaction happens and heat is given off.

Symbol equation: $Zn(s) + CuSO_4(aq) \rightarrow ZnSO_4(aq) + Cu(s)$
ionic equation: $Zn(s) + Cu^{2+}(aq) \rightarrow Zn^{2+}(aq) + Cu(s)$

Each zinc atom gives away two electrons to a Cu^{2+} ion. Zinc has a greater tendency to give away electrons than copper, which makes it a better reducing agent. Copper ions are reduced to copper metal and zinc atoms are oxidised to Zn^{2+} ions.

When copper and zinc are used as electrodes in a Daniell cell and the two solutions have a concentration of 1.0 M, then a potential difference of about 1.1 V is set up.

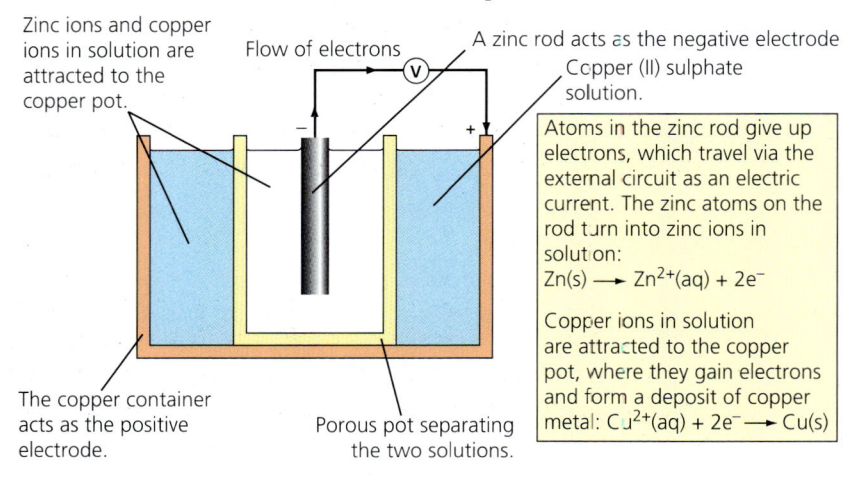

Other pairs of metals can be used to form similar cells. The more reactive metal of the pair will lose electrons to the ions of the less reactive metal. When metals are near each other on the reactivity series, the potential difference set up is small. For example, a cell using zinc and iron (which have similar reactivities) will set up a potential difference of only 0.32 V but a cell involving magnesium and silver (which have very different reactivities) would set up a potential difference of 3.2 V.

Figure 4 A Daniell cell.

Zinc ions and copper ions in solution are attracted to the copper pot.

Flow of electrons

A zinc rod acts as the negative electrode

Copper (II) sulphate solution.

Atoms in the zinc rod give up electrons, which travel via the external circuit as an electric current. The zinc atoms on the rod turn into zinc ions in solution:
$Zn(s) \rightarrow Zn^{2+}(aq) + 2e^-$

Copper ions in solution are attracted to the copper pot, where they gain electrons and form a deposit of copper metal: $Cu^{2+}(aq) + 2e^- \rightarrow Cu(s)$

The copper container acts as the positive electrode.

Porous pot separating the two solutions.

Metals, redox reactions and cells

How are cells used?

Lead–acid battery

A **battery** is a series of individual cells that are combined. The battery that provides electrical energy for vehicles is known as a **lead–acid accumulator**. When the vehicle is started the battery provides an electric current to help start the engine. Once the engine is running it drives a small dynamo which produces an electric current to recharge the battery. The battery itself consists of a series of plates of lead alternating with a grid of lead packed with lead (IV) oxide. The plates dip into dilute sulphuric acid.

Vehicles powered by rechargeable batteries are quiet and do not produce polluting gases. The batteries must be recharged from time to time by connecting them to an electricity supply.

Car batteries are very heavy because they contain a series of plates made from lead and lead (IV) oxide dipping into dilute sulphuric acid.

These batteries are very heavy, and one of the problems of electric-powered vehicles is the mass of the batteries. However, electric vehicles are quiet and do not produce harmful exhaust fumes. Although lead and its compounds are poisonous, used batteries do not usually cause pollution problems. Since lead is a valuable metal, nearly all the lead in old discarded batteries is recovered and recycled.

8 The batteries for cars and other vehicles contain plates of lead and lead (IV) oxide dipping into an electrolyte of dilute sulphuric acid.
  a What is an electrolyte?
  b List two precautions that must be taken when dealing with this particular electrolyte.
9 Describe how a car battery works.
10 Give one advantage and one disadvantage of using lead–acid accumulators in vehicles.

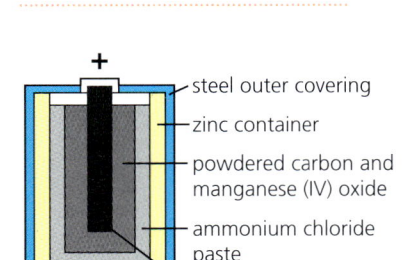

Zinc–carbon dry cells

The everyday 'batteries' that we use to power calculators or torches are often **zinc–carbon dry cells**. The electrolyte in a dry cell is kept just moist, and there is no risk of spilling aqueous solutions. In this cell, the zinc casing acts as the negative electrode and is gradually dissolved away. When the battery is flat, the zinc is nearly all used up. It is important at this stage to remove the battery from electrical equipment, or the wet paste inside may leak out and cause damage. Once the battery has gone flat it must be thrown away.

Figure 5 (steel outer covering, zinc container, powdered carbon and manganese (IV) oxide, ammonium chloride paste, carbon rod)

11 a Draw a labelled diagram of a cell that uses magnesium and lead electrodes, together with aqueous solutions of magnesium sulphate and lead nitrate.
  b Suggest a disadvantage of using a cell containing aqueous salts like this. How is this disadvantage overcome in the small cells sold for everyday use?

Silver oxide cells

The tiny 'button' cells in watches and cameras are also a type of dry cell, containing zinc and silver oxide. The high price of silver and its compounds makes these rather expensive but they do last for a long time, because generally watches and cameras need only a small current.

189

Alkaline cells
'Alkaline' cells are similar to zinc–carbon dry batteries, but the electrolyte contains alkaline potassium hydroxide and the zinc electrode is made slightly porous. Alkaline cells provide a greater current and last longer than zinc–carbon cells.

Rechargeable cells
One type of rechargeable cell contains cadmium and nickel compounds. A redox reaction occurs to produce an electric current when the cell is in use. When the cell is connected to a recharger an electric current is passed through. This reverses the reaction and recharges the cell.

Fuel cells
Fuel cells use the energy from fuels to provide electrical energy. A fuel such as hydrogen or methane is passed into the cell together with oxygen. These are made to react via the external circuit to provide an electric current. Although fuel cells are expensive to construct, provided the fuel is continually passed in, the cell will continue to provide an electric current. Fuel cells are used in spacecraft to provide a constant source of electrical energy.

12 Suggest a use for a fuel cell for which it is particularly suited. Give a reason for your answer.

13 Briefly describe how a fuel cell works.

Summary of electricity from chemical reactions

- A cell is a device for turning chemical energy into electrical energy.
- In the redox reaction of a cell the negative electrode is oxidised and the positive electrode is reduced.
- The greater the difference in reactivity of two metals in a cell, the greater the potential difference set up.
- A lead–acid vehicle battery is very heavy, but the battery is recharged while the vehicle is running.
- Dry cells contain electrodes and chemicals in an electrolyte paste. Once the reaction is finished the cell is thrown away.
- Rechargeable cells are expensive to buy but can be used many times.
- A fuel cell provides a continual source of electrical energy, provided the fuel and oxygen are supplied constantly.

Examination style questions

1 Crystals of lead metal can be grown when a strip of zinc metal is suspended in dilute lead nitrate solution.
  a Draw a labelled diagram of the apparatus and chemicals you could use to demonstrate this process.
  b Write a balanced equation for this reaction.
  c Write an ionic equation for this reaction, stating which are the spectator ions.
  d Explain briefly, in terms of electron transfer, which particles are oxidised and which reduced in this reaction.

2 A simple cell was set up, using the apparatus shown on the left.
  a Name the piece of apparatus labelled V.
  b What is the purpose of the pieces of filter paper soaked in saturated potassium nitrate solution?
  c When a student set up a cell using copper as metal A and zinc as metal B, they measured a potential difference of 1.1 V.
    i Write an ion-electron equation to show the formation of copper metal from copper (II) ions in aqueous solution.
    ii Write an ion-electron equation for the formation of zinc ions in aqueous solution from the zinc metal electrode.
  d Suggest a metal that could be used instead of copper in this cell to produce a greater potential difference. Give a reason for your choice.

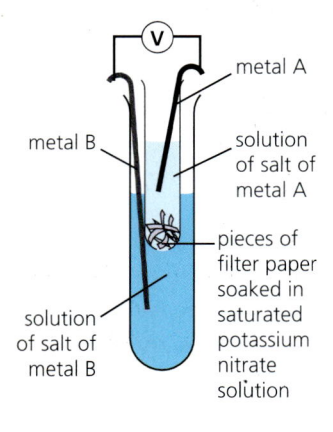

Non-metals 15

Learning objectives

By the end of this chapter you should be able to:

- **list** some of the physical and chemical properties of non-metals
- **describe** some of the properties and uses of hydrogen
- **describe** the carbon cycle
- **describe** the nitrogen cycle
- **explain** how ammonia is manufactured from nitrogen
- **describe** how nitric acid is manufactured
- **calculate** the percentage of elements by mass in a fertiliser
- **describe** the Contact process
- **discuss** the trends in physical and chemical properties of Group VII elements

15.1 Properties of non-metals

What are the physical properties of non-metals?

Non-metals exist in the Earth's environment both as elements and as a wide variety of compounds. Non-metallic elements come in a variety of forms, and can have very different physical properties.

Figure 1 Only 22 of the known elements are non-metals. They are found on the right and to the top of the periodic table. This indicates that the electron shells are fairly well filled. In the noble gases the outer electron shells are full.

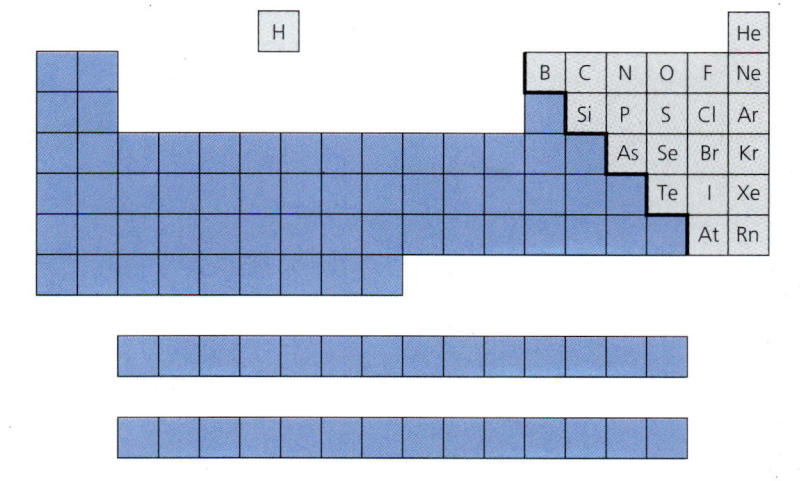

- **Variable melting and boiling points** Most non-metals are either solids or gases. At room temperature bromine is the only liquid non-metal.
- **Non-metals are dull** Most non-metals have a dull surface when they are solid (except for diamond, which has a brilliant shine).

Using chemicals in everyday life

1 Give the name and symbol of one non-metal that is:
  a a solid
  b a liquid
  c a gas
  at room temperature and pressure.

2 Chlorine is a non-metal that forms a variety of compounds. Give the name and formula of a chlorine compound that is
  a ionic
  b covalently bonded.

3 Many non-metal oxides react with water to form acidic solutions. Explain, with the help of a balanced equation, how nitric acid (HNO_3) might be formed in this way.

- **Non-metals are brittle** Many non-metals have very little strength in the solid state (except diamond, which is very hard and strong).
- **Electrical conductivity** Most non-metals are poor electrical conductors. Some, like silicon, are semi-conductors. Graphite is the only non-metal that is a good electrical conductor.
- **Thermal conductivit** Non-metals are poor conductors of heat.

Table 1 Physical properties of some of the non-metals

Name	Symbol	Melting point (°C)	Boiling point (°C)	Density (g/cm³)
carbon	C	sublimes at 3730	4830	graphite 2.3, diamond 3.5
nitrogen	N	−210	−96	gas
oxygen	O	−218	−83	gas
fluorine	F	−220	−188	gas
silicon	Si	1410	2360	2.3
phosphorus	P	44	280	1.82
sulphur	S	113	445	2.07
chlorine	Cl	−101	−35	gas
germanium	Ge	937	2830	5.4
bromine	Br	−7	59	3.12
iodine	I	114	184	4.93

Do non-metals have similar chemical properties?

With the exception of the noble gases, all non-metals have various properties in common. Non-metallic elements have electron shells that are nearly full. When non-metals react to form compounds, they gain a stable full outer shell of electrons by forming either ionic or covalent compounds (see Chapter 8, *Chemical bonding*).

When non-metals react with metals they form **ionic** compounds. The non-metal atoms gain electrons from the metal and form stable negatively charged ions.

When non-metals react with other non-metals they form **covalent** compounds by sharing electrons and forming a stable outer shell of electrons. Most non-metals react with oxygen to form **oxides**, which are covalently bonded compounds.

Non-metal oxides react with water to form **acidic** solutions. Many common acids are associated with non-metals – for example, hydrochloric acid, nitric acid, phosphoric acid and sulphuric acid.

Summary of properties of non-metals
- Non-metals have similar physical properties.
- Non-metals have many chemical properties in common.

15.2 Hydrogen

Why is hydrogen unique?

Since hydrogen atoms have only a single electron, the element has unique properties which mean it is placed on its own at the top of the periodic table. Hydrogen *could* be placed in either Group I or Group VII, as it has some properties in common with both these groups. Like Group I elements it has a single electron in its outer shell, which it can lose to form an H^+ ion. Like Group VII elements, it can also gain an electron to acquire a full outer shell and form an H^- ion. It will also form a diatomic H_2 molecule in a similar way to the halogens of Group VII.

Where is hydrogen found?

The main element in the Sun is hydrogen. The energy the Sun emits is mostly caused by hydrogen atoms fusing at very high temperatures to produce atoms of helium. In this thermogram of the Sun, the lighter colours represent hotter areas.

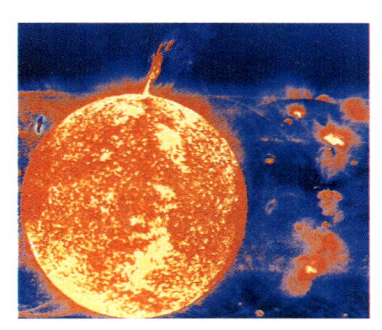

Hydrogen is one of the most common elements, found in space as part of stars.

In the Earth's atmosphere there is almost no free hydrogen, although there are more compounds of hydrogen than of any other element – more than two million are known. Some of the most common hydrogen compounds on Earth are water and hydrocarbons like methane.

How is hydrogen manufactured?

Hydrogen can be extracted from hydrocarbons in various ways. For example, if methane is heated with steam in the presence of a limited amount of oxygen, the following reactions happen:

$$CH_4(g) + H_2O(g) \xrightarrow[900°C]{\text{nickel catalyst}} CO(g) + 3H_2(g)$$

$$2CH_4(g) + O_2(g) \longrightarrow 2CO(g) + 4H_2(g)$$

The carbon monoxide is removed by reacting it with steam:

$$CO(g) + H_2O(g) \xrightarrow[450°C]{\text{iron catalyst}} CO_2(g) + H_2(g)$$

The remaining carbon dioxide is removed by dissolving it in water under pressure.

Using chemicals in everyday life

Hydrogen can be produced from **water** by the electrolysis of brine, or of water itself. Hydrogen gas is discharged at the cathode from hydrogen ions present in water:

$$2H^+(g) + 2e^- \rightarrow H_2(g)$$

Large amounts of hydrogen gas are also produced during the refining of crude oil.

In the laboratory, hydrogen can be prepared by the action of a moderately reactive metal such as zinc with a dilute acid.

Making hydrogen in the laboratory   Figure 2

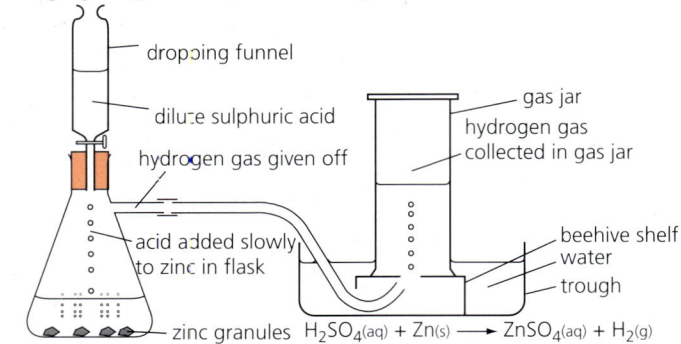

Diagram labels: dropping funnel; dilute sulphuric acid; hydrogen gas given off; acid added slowly to zinc in flask; zinc granules; gas jar; hydrogen gas collected in gas jar; beehive shelf; water; trough

$$H_2SO_4(aq) + Zn(s) \rightarrow ZnSO_4(aq) + H_2(g)$$

What properties does hydrogen possess?

- Hydrogen is a colourless gas.
- It has very low density – it is the lightest gas known.
- Hydrogen has no smell.
- Hydrogen burns in air or oxygen:

$$2H_2(g) + O_2(g) \rightarrow 2H_2O(g)$$

A mixture of hydrogen and oxygen will explode with a squeaky 'pop'. This is used as a **test for hydrogen**. A jet of hydrogen gas will also burn quietly in air.
- Hydrogen reacts with chlorine to make hydrogen chloride gas:

$$H_2(g) + Cl_2(g) \rightarrow 2HCl(g)$$

This reaction can occur explosively if the gases are mixed and exposed to ultra-violet light. A jet of burning hydrogen will also continue to burn quietly in chlorine to produce hydrogen chloride.
- Hydrogen gas is a good **reducing agent**. Hydrogen is sometimes placed in the reactivity series of metals. When oxides of metals less reactive than hydrogen are heated in a stream of hydrogen gas, they are reduced to the metal.

Summary of hydrogen

- Hydrogen has a unique position in the periodic table.
- Hydrogen can be made from hydrocarbons and from water.
- Hydrogen is a colourless, odourless gas with a very low density.
- Hydrogen is a good fuel.
- Hydrogen is a good reducing agent.

Non-metals

15.3 Elements in Group IV

What are the Group IV elements?

Group IV is situated in the centre of the periodic table. This group contains both non-metals and metals. Germanium, which is half-way down the group, has some properties of both – it is therefore sometimes known as a **metalloid**.

Where are Group IV elements found?

All living things – both plant and animal – are made from compounds of **carbon**. This is most obvious when food is burned. Overcooked food, whether meat or vegetables, will burn and turn black, leaving impure deposits of carbon behind. Carbon also has a number of unique properties. One is its ability to form large molecules containing long chains of carbon atoms. Because there are so many different molecules containing carbon, these are usually studied in organic chemistry (see Chapter 16 *Organic chemistry*).

Compounds of **silicon** are widely found in rocks and minerals. About 26% of the Earth's crust consists of silicon in the form of its compounds. These include sandstone, sand and clay. **Metals** such as tin and lead occur in the earth's crust as metal ores.

What is the carbon cycle?

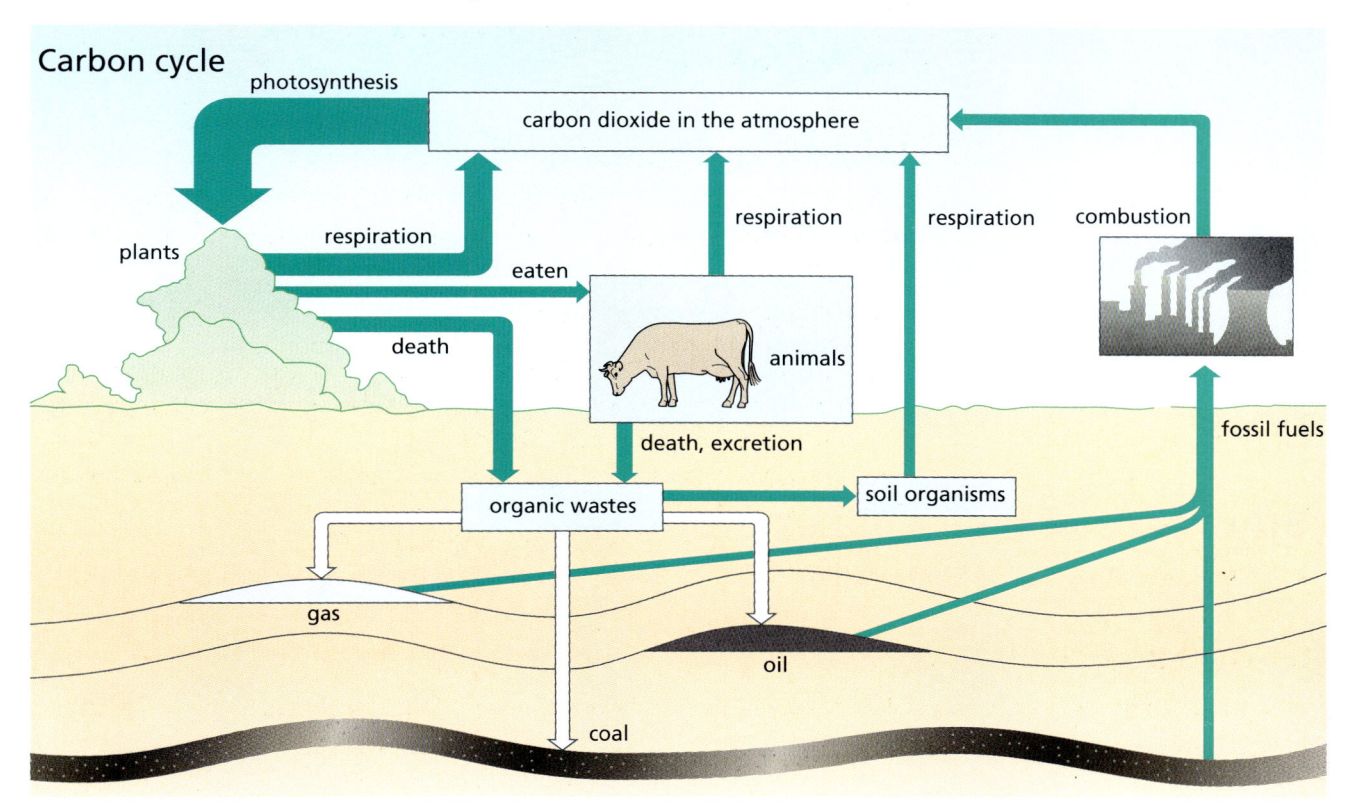

Figure 3

195

Using chemicals in everyday life

4 Where do
  a plants   b animals
  get their carbon from?
5 Describe how the carbon inside an organism may be released back into the air.

The carbon cycle is a complex series of chemical reactions in which compounds of carbon circulate in the Earth's environment. Like other cycles (such as the water cycle), it is finely balanced so that various compounds are constantly being used up and reformed. One of the main balances in this cycle is between **animals**, which release carbon dioxide into the air during respiration, and **plants**, which use up atmospheric carbon dioxide during photosynthesis.

Does carbon exist in only one form?

The element carbon can exist in several forms, two of which are diamond and graphite. Different physical forms of an element are known as **allotropes**. A third series of allotropes of carbon, the fullerenes, have recently been discovered. Diamond and graphite have very different properties because the atoms within their structures are arranged differently.

Table 2 Properties of diamond and graphite

6 Which allotrope of carbon is used
  a in jewellery
  b on the bits of drills
  c as a lubricant
  d in pencil leads?

Diamond	Graphite
The three-dimensional giant structure of carbon atoms makes it the hardest structure known	The two-dimensional structure of layers of atoms gives graphite a soft, slippery feel as the layers slide over each other
Density of 3.5 g/cm^3 (atoms packed more closely in diamond)	Density 2.3 g/cm^3
Clear and brilliantly shiny when polished	Dull grey and opaque
Does not conduct electricity	Good electrical conductor (the only non-metal that conducts well)

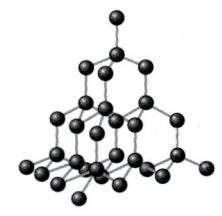

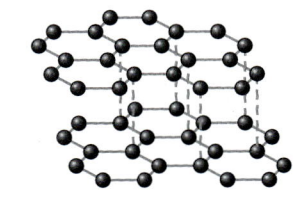

Although diamond and graphite are very different in appearance, they have similar chemical properties. The main reaction of carbon is that it burns well:

$$C(s) + O_2(g) \rightarrow CO_2(g)$$

Summary of elements in Group IV

- Group IV elements contain both metals and non-metals.
- The carbon cycle describes how carbon and its compounds circulate in the Earth's environment.
- Carbon can exist as several allotropes.

15.4 Elements in Group V

What are the Group V elements?

Group V contains two very important elements – nitrogen and phosphorus. Compounds of these elements are essential for all plant and animal life. This group also contains the notorious poison arsenic and two elements that are less well known – antimony and bismuth.

Where are Group V elements found?

Four-fifths of the Earth's atmosphere is nitrogen gas. Because it is so unreactive, it is one of the few elements that occurs naturally in the Earth's environment. You will find more about the properties of nitrogen gas in Chapter 3, *The air*. Compounds of both nitrogen and of phosphorus are widely found in minerals and are essential to all living things.

How is nitrogen recycled in the atmosphere?

The element and its compounds are constantly being used up and formed in a number of processes that occur in the natural world. This circulation is known as the **nitrogen cycle** and is described in figure 4.

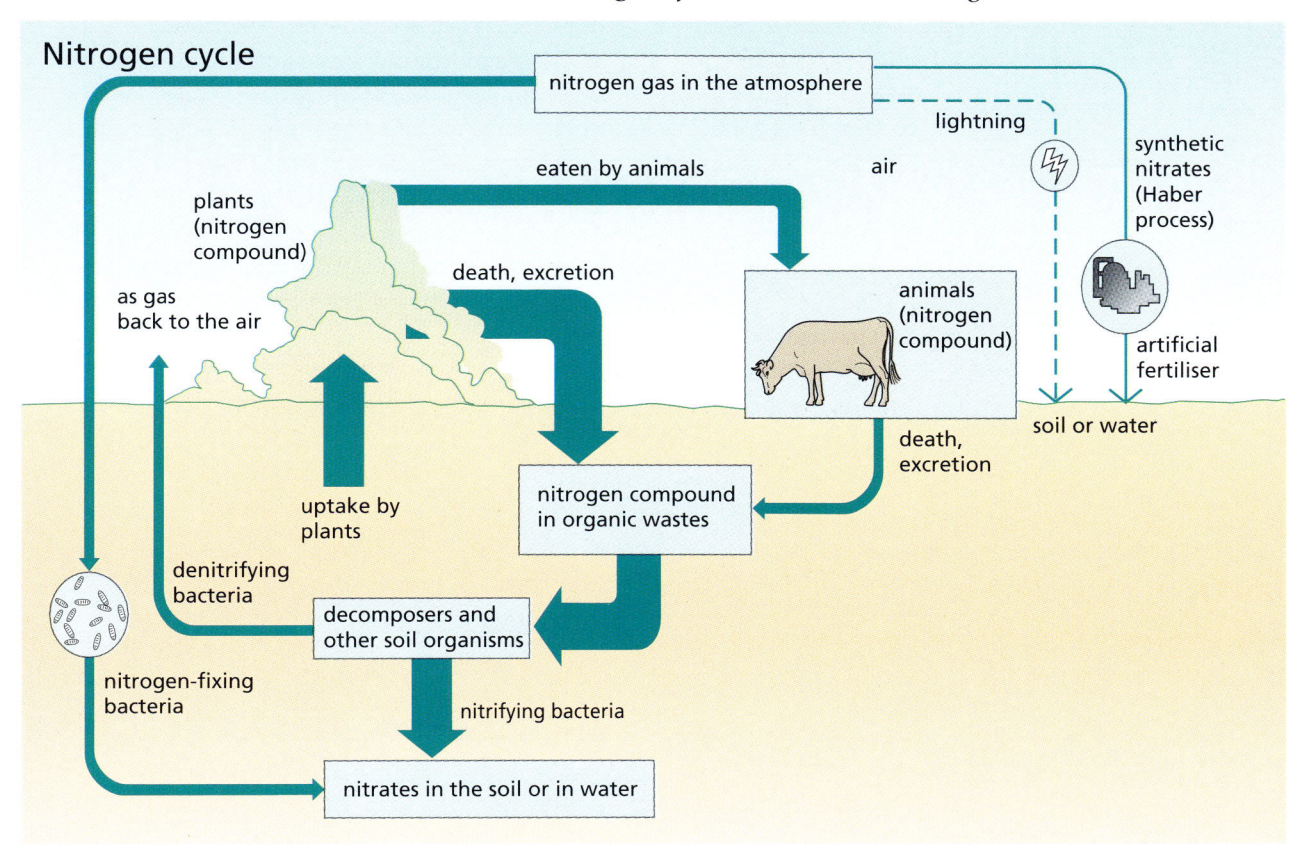

Figure 4

Using chemicals in everyday life

What is produced by the Haber process?

An important use of nitrogen gas from the air is the production of ammonia in the **Haber process**. The plant needed to make ammonia from hydrogen and nitrogen is varied and complex. The high pressures involved mean that all the pumps and pipes must be made very strong. It is also important to insulate the pipework to keep some parts hot and other areas cool.

The raw materials for this process are air, methane and water. The hydrogen gas used in the Haber process is obtained by reacting methane or other hydrocarbons with steam and the nitrogen gas is obtained from the air. The nitrogen and hydrogen are allowed to mix in a ratio of 1:3. The following reaction occurs:

$$N_2(g) + 3H_2(g) \rightleftharpoons 2NH_3(g)$$

The reaction rate is increased greatly by using finely divided iron as a **catalyst**.

The temperature must be kept between 350°C and 500°C. If the temperature is any lower than 350°C, the reaction proceeds too slowly to allow economic production of ammonia. If the temperature is higher than 500°C, much of the ammonia formed decomposes into nitrogen and hydrogen. The actual temperature used is an 'optimum' – a compromise somewhere between these extremes.

The pressure is kept between 80 and 200 atmospheres. The higher the pressure, the more easily nitrogen and hydrogen molecules combine to form ammonia. However, as the pressure is increased the high engineering standards needed to construct the plant become more and more expensive. So the pressure used is also a compromise level that allows ammonia to be produced economically. Further details about some of the principles behind reversible reactions are given in Chapter 20, *Reversible reactions*.

Note

The arrow ($\rightleftharpoons$) in the equation means that a reaction is reversible – it can proceed in either direction.

Temperature (°C)	Percentage yield
0	82
100	54
200	34
300	22
400	14
500	8

7 Chemical companies want to get the highest percentage yield when they produce chemicals. But percentage yield may change with a change in temperature or with a change in pressure. Draw a graph using the information in the table for a reaction which was followed at different temperatures but at a constant pressure.
   a Which temperature must the plant operate at to get a 60% yield?
   b If the plant operated at 250°C what percentage yield would be obtained?

How is nitric acid manufactured?

One major use of ammonia is to make nitric acid. This process is carried out as shown in figure 5.

Non-metals

Manufacture of nitric acid

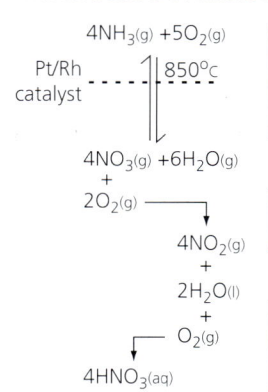

$4NH_3(g) + 5O_2(g)$

Pt/Rh catalyst ---- 850°C

$4NO_3(g) + 6H_2O(g)$
+
$2O_2(g)$

$4NO_2(g)$
+
$2H_2O(l)$
+
$O_2(g)$

$4HNO_3(aq)$

A mixture of air and ammonia is heated and passed through a metal gauze of platinum and rhodium. This acts as a catalyst.

The nitrogen monoxide formed reacts with more oxygen in the air.

The nitrogen dioxide formed dissolves in water with more oxygen in the air to produce nitric acid.

Figure 5

Nearly all explosives require nitric acid as one of the reagents.

Nitric acid is neutralised by various bases to make salts, which are useful fertilisers.
$NH_3(aq) + HNO_3(aq) \rightarrow NH_4NO_3(aq)$

Synthetic fibres such as nylon and polyester are made using nitric acid.

Many modern textile dyes need nitric acid as a starting material.

Nitric acid is a useful laboratory chemical.

Figure 6 Uses of nitric acid.

---

8 Ammonia can be converted to nitric acid in the following overall reaction:

$NH_3(g) + 2O_2(g) \rightarrow HNO_3(l) + H_2O(g)$

Calculate the mass of nitric acid that could be obtained from 51 tonnes of ammonia.

9 In the Haber process nitrogen from the air is combined with hydrogen to make ammonia. The table gives the percentage yield of ammonia at different temperatures and pressures.

Temperature (°C)	Percentage yield at a pressure (MPa) of:				
	2.5	5.0	10	20	40
100	91.7	94.5	96.7	98.4	99.4
200	63.6	73.5	82.0	89.0	94.6
300	27.4	39.6	53.1	66.7	79.7
400	8.7	15.4	25.4	38.8	55.4
500	2.9	10.5	15.6	18.3	31.9

a Which of the following terms best describes the most productive combination of pressure and temperature?

i High pressure with high temperature
iii Low pressure with high temperature
ii High pressure with low temperature
iv Low pressure with low temperature.

b High-pressure compressors are very expensive to buy and use, so a manufacturer thinks about using a cheaper compressor which can produce 20 MPa only. What percentage yield would they expect to get at a temperature of 100°C?

c The manufacturer decides to operate at a low pressure – and then their research experts tell them that at 100°C the reaction would go so slowly that the production wouldn't be economical. They suggest that a temperature of 450°C would be much better. Why is the reaction rate likely to be so much quicker at this higher temperature?

d The experts also point out that at 450°C they could use a catalyst to speed the reaction further (the only catalysts available won't work below 400°C). What is a catalyst?

Using chemicals in everyday life

> **e** The manufacturer takes the advice and builds a pilot plant. They find that when they pump the mixture through it at a reasonable rate only about 13% of the gases combine to make ammonia, even with a catalyst present.
> **i** What percentage yield does the table say they should have obtained?
> **ii** Suggest what the manufacturer could do improve the yield – without changing the catalyst or the temperature and pressure.

Nitrogen and fertilisers

Compounds of nitrogen are essential to plant growth – they help in the development of green leaves and new shoots. Plants also combine nitrogen with carbon compounds to form proteins, which are important foods for many animals. Although nitrogen is present in large quantities in the atmosphere, plants and animals can't use the gas directly from the air. Plants must take in nitrate ions, dissolved in water, through their roots. Animals can use nitrogen only when it is in the form of protein.

When crops are grown and harvested, the nutrients that they have taken from the soil are removed, and the soil becomes depleted in the minerals needed to sustain healthy plant growth. It is vital to replace essential elements lost from the soil in this way.

How does nitrogen get into the soil?

Figure 7 Adding nitrogen to the soil.

Ammonia can be injected directly into the soil either as a gas or in solution in water. It must be placed deep in the soil below the level of plant roots, so they are not damaged by its alkaline pH.

Ammonium nitrate and ammonium sulphate are very soluble in water and quickly dissolve in the soil to add soluble nitrogen.

Fertilisers containing soluble compounds of nitrogen can be spread onto farmland to encourage the growth of crops.

Some plants, like peas, beans and clover, have clusters of bacteria in nodules in their roots. These bacteria are able to turn atmospheric nitrogen into nitrates. This is known as 'fixing' nitrogen.

The high temperature in a lightning bolt causes gases in the air to combine and form oxides of nitrogen. These dissolve in rainwater to form very dilute nitric acid. This can help to add soluble nitrogen compounds to the soil.

Non-metals

Synthetic 'NPK' compound fertilisers are often added to farmland. The numbers on the pack show how much of each element the fertiliser contains.

A traditional way of replacing soil nutrients has been to allow farm animals to trample their manure into their bedding and then to leave it to decay. The resulting 'farmyard manure' is rich in many nutrients and can be spread onto fields to enrich the soil. Unlike very soluble fertilisers like ammonium nitrate, farmyard manure will break down slowly in the soil and gradually release nutrients.

'Slow-release' fertilisers dissolve slowly over a period of weeks or months. This prevents the fertiliser being washed away too quickly.

Organic materials (rotted plants or animal excrement) have been used as fertilisers for centuries. They break down slowly in the soil and release nitrogen compounds to the plant roots.

Plants also need phosphorus compounds for good root growth and potassium compounds to help produce fruit. A **compound fertiliser** contains compounds of each of these essential elements, and sometimes compounds of other important nutrients. Compound fertilisers are often called **'NPK'** – after the symbols for the elements nitrogen, phosphorus and potassium.

How do you calculate the amount of a particular element in a fertiliser?

The amount of nitrogen in a fertiliser will indicate how much nitrogen it can make available to the plant. This can be calculated from the formula of the compound.

WORKED EXAMPLE

Find the percentage by mass of nitrogen present in ammonium sulphate, $(NH_4)_2SO_4$.

Calculate the M_r of the compound:

$(NH_4)_2$	S	O_4
$(14 + 4) \times 2$	32	(16×4)
36	32	64

$M_r =$ 132

One mole of the compound has a mass of 132 g. The formula shows that two nitrogens are present, so out of the 132 g, $(14 \times 2) = 28$ g is due to the presence of nitrogen. This can be expressed as a percentage:

percentage of nitrogen present $= \dfrac{28 \times 100}{132}$

$= 21.2\%$

201

Using chemicals in everyday life

What problems can fertilisers cause?

Nitrates are excellent fertilisers. However, all nitrates (and a number of other fertilisers) are soluble in water and can be washed away by heavy rainfall. Apart from the waste of money and loss of the fertiliser, the nutrients can enter river water and cause **eutrophication** (see Chapter 11, *Water and aqueous solutions*). Once nitrates have entered river water they are very difficult to remove.

10 Calculate the percentage by mass of nitrogen in the following compounds:
  a Ammonium nitrate, NH_4NO_3
  b Ammonium sulphate $(NH_4)_2SO_4$
  c Urea, CON_2H_4
  d Ammonia, NH_3

Summary of elements in Group V

- The nitrogen cycle describes how nitrogen and its compounds circulate in the Earth's environment.
- Ammonia is manufactured from nitrogen and hydrogen by the Haber process.
- Ammonia can be reacted with water and air to make nitric acid.
- Compounds of nitrogen, phosphorus and potassium can be used as fertilisers.

15.5 Group VI elements

Which elements are in Group VI?

Group VI elements are non-metallic and include the important elements oxygen and sulphur. Oxygen is abundant in the atmosphere and in compounds in the Earth's crust. Its properties are described in more detail in Chapter 3, *The air*. Sulphur also occurs naturally in the Earth's crust. Compounds of sulphur are found in a number of minerals as sulphides and sulphates. Sulphur is also an important part of the structure of some proteins.

How many allotropes of sulphur are there?

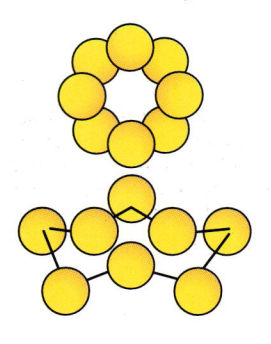

At room temperature, sulphur is a yellow solid. Since it is made from small molecules with weak forces between them, it has a relatively low melting point. Solid sulphur can exist as two allotropes, known as **rhombic** and **monoclinic** sulphur. The sulphur molecules are packed together differently in each allotrope. This leads to the two forms having different crystal shapes and different physical properties.

Figure 8 A sulphur molecule is a ring of eight atoms.

Non-metals

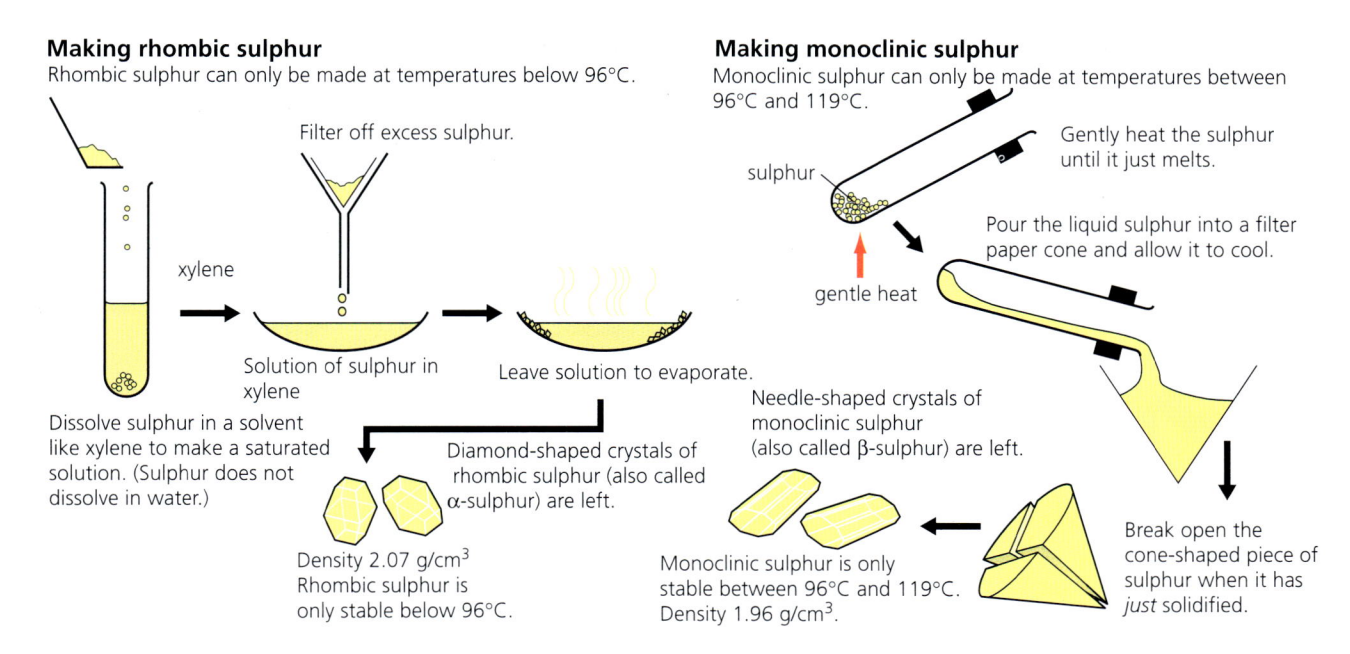

Making rhombic sulphur
Rhombic sulphur can only be made at temperatures below 96°C.

Dissolve sulphur in a solvent like xylene to make a saturated solution. (Sulphur does not dissolve in water.) → Solution of sulphur in xylene → Filter off excess sulphur. → Leave solution to evaporate. → Diamond-shaped crystals of rhombic sulphur (also called α-sulphur) are left.

Density 2.07 g/cm^3
Rhombic sulphur is only stable below 96°C.

Making monoclinic sulphur
Monoclinic sulphur can only be made at temperatures between 96°C and 119°C.

Gently heat the sulphur until it just melts. → Pour the liquid sulphur into a filter paper cone and allow it to cool. → Break open the cone-shaped piece of sulphur when it has *just* solidified. → Needle-shaped crystals of monoclinic sulphur (also called β-sulphur) are left.

Monoclinic sulphur is only stable between 96°C and 119°C. Density 1.96 g/cm^3.

Figure 9 The two allotropes of sulphur have different densities because the S$_8$ molecules are packed more closely in rhombic sulphur than in monoclinic.

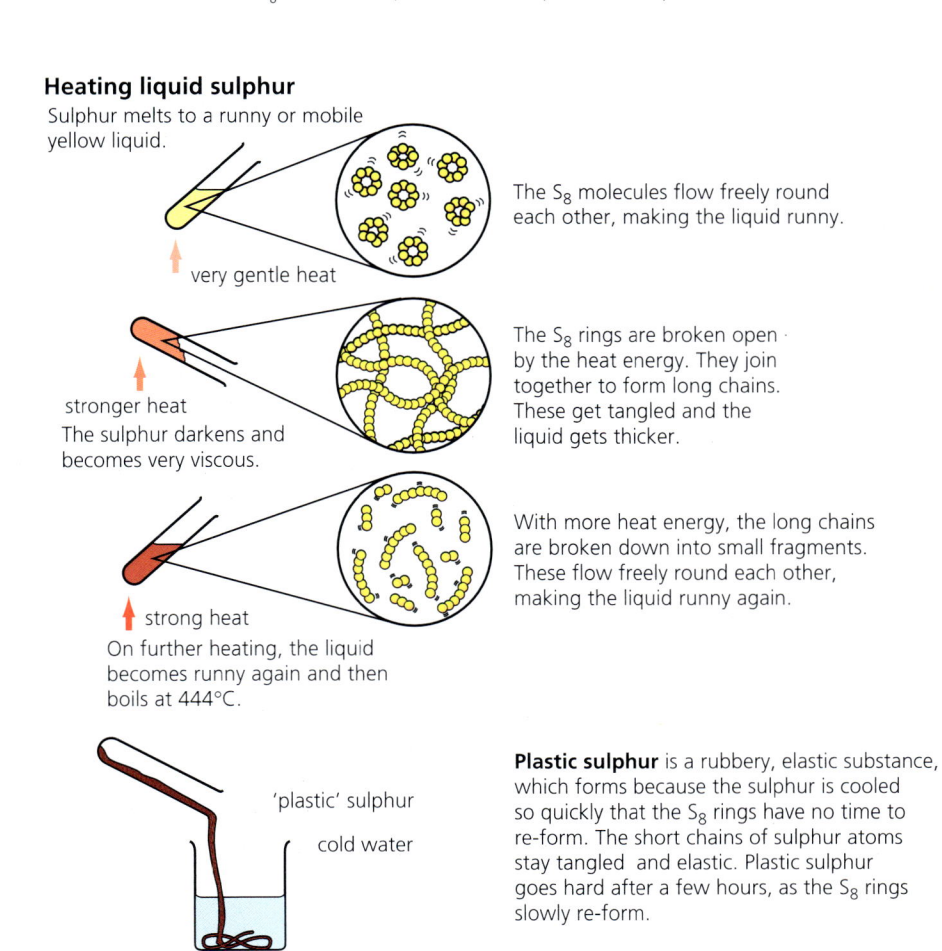

Heating liquid sulphur

Sulphur melts to a runny or mobile yellow liquid.

very gentle heat — The S$_8$ molecules flow freely round each other, making the liquid runny.

stronger heat — The sulphur darkens and becomes very viscous. The S$_8$ rings are broken open by the heat energy. They join together to form long chains. These get tangled and the liquid gets thicker.

strong heat — On further heating, the liquid becomes runny again and then boils at 444°C. With more heat energy, the long chains are broken down into small fragments. These flow freely round each other, making the liquid runny again.

'plastic' sulphur / cold water

Plastic sulphur is a rubbery, elastic substance, which forms because the sulphur is cooled so quickly that the S$_8$ rings have no time to re-form. The short chains of sulphur atoms stay tangled and elastic. Plastic sulphur goes hard after a few hours, as the S$_8$ rings slowly re-form.

Figure 10 Sulphur goes through some unusual changes as it is heated.

Using chemicals in everyday life

How is sulphuric acid made from sulphur?

Figure 11 The Contact process for making sulphuric acid.

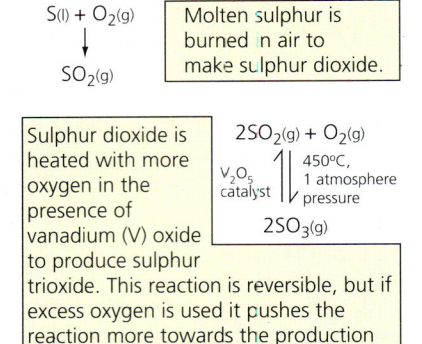

$S(l) + O_2(g) \rightarrow SO_2(g)$

Molten sulphur is burned in air to make sulphur dioxide.

Sulphur dioxide is heated with more oxygen in the presence of vanadium (V) oxide to produce sulphur trioxide. This reaction is reversible, but if excess oxygen is used it pushes the reaction more towards the production of sulphur trioxide.

$2SO_2(g) + O_2(g) \rightleftharpoons 2SO_3(g)$
V_2O_5 catalyst, 450°C, 1 atmosphere pressure

$SO_3(g) + H_2O(l) \rightarrow H_2SO_4(l)$

Sulphur trioxide is added to a solution of 98% sulphuric acid and 2% water. It reacts with the small amount of water to make the pure acid.

The industrial process used to make sulphuric acid from the raw materials of air, sulphur (or an ore containing sulphur) and water is called the **Contact process**. It is outlined in figure 11. The reaction is reversible and the conditions must be carefully adjusted to give the optimum yield. The catalyst vanadium (V) oxide increases the rate of reaction and the temperature is kept at about 450°C so that the sulphur trioxide formed doesn't break down again.

The process takes place at just above atmospheric pressure. Increasing the pressure would increase the yield of sulphur trioxide. However, since the oxygen used as one raw material is obtained from the air, it is more economic to use a large excess of air in this process rather than to build the expensive plant needed to withstand high pressures.

What uses does sulphuric acid have in the laboratory?

Concentrated sulphuric acid is a dense oily liquid that must be handled with great care. It is useful in several areas.

- As a *dehydrating* agent. The acid has a great affinity for water and can be used to dry gases because it absorbs any moisture they contain. It cannot be used to dry alkaline gases such as ammonia, as it reacts with them. It will react with plant or animal tissue or materials to extract water, leaving only charcoal behind.
- As an *acid*. Diluted sulphuric acid can be used in a number of neutralisation reactions to make sulphates. For example:

$$CuO(s) + H_2SO_4(aq) \rightarrow CuSO_4(aq) + H_2O(l)$$

- As an *oxidising* agent. Hot concentrated sulphuric acid will oxidise a number of substances. For example, carbon is oxidised to carbon dioxide:

$$C(s) + H_2SO_4(l) \rightarrow CO_2(g) + 2SO_2(g) + 2H_2O(g)$$

Summary of Group VI elements

- Sulphur and oxygen are two important Group VI elements.
- Sulphur exists in two physical forms – rhombic and monoclinic.
- The Contact process manufactures sulphuric acid from sulphur, water and air.
- Sulphuric acid has many uses in industry and in the laboratory.

15.6 Elements in Group VII

Why are the Group VII elements called halogens?

Group VII contains some very reactive non-metallic elements. None of the elements in this group occur naturally, but their compounds are widespread, especially dissolved in sea water. Group VII elements are sometimes called **halogens**. This comes from a Greek word meaning 'salt-makers', since all halogens react with metals to form a variety of salts.

What properties do the halogens share?

The halogens are all non-metals with low melting and boiling points. They are all made from small diatomic molecules, the two atoms being joined by covalent bonds. At room temperature and pressure, chlorine is a poisonous dense green gas. Bromine is a dense, poisonous, red–brown liquid. It is very **volatile**, which means it easily turns into a gas. Iodine is a solid. It is dense and consists of shiny metallic-looking crystals. When gently warmed it sublimes into a purple vapour.

Figure 12 The halogens all react in similar ways.

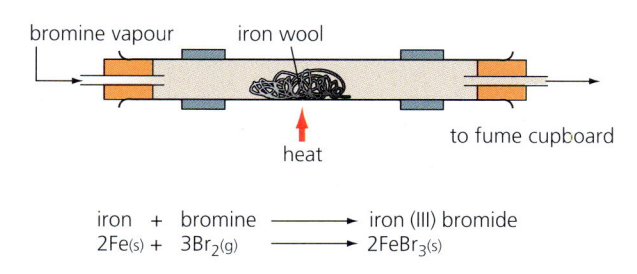

iron + bromine ⟶ iron (III) bromide
$2Fe_{(s)} + 3Br_{2(g)} \longrightarrow 2FeBr_{3(s)}$

Halogens react with most metals to make salts. The ions formed by the halogens in these reactions always carry a 1– charge.

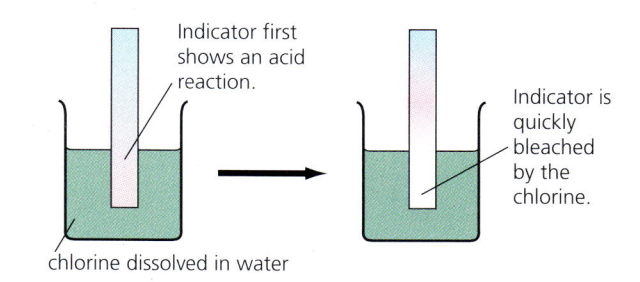

Chlorine dissolves in water to make a strong bleach.

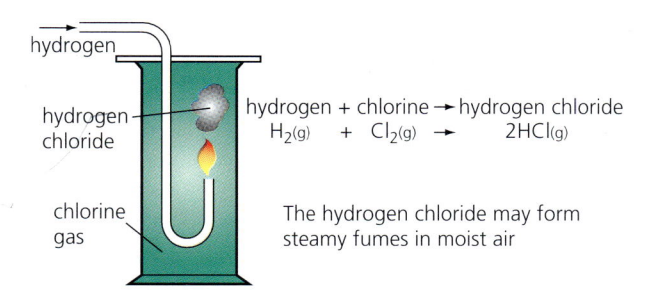

hydrogen + chlorine ⟶ hydrogen chloride
$H_{2(g)} + Cl_{2(g)} \longrightarrow 2HCl_{(g)}$

The hydrogen chloride may form steamy fumes in moist air

A hydrogen flame continues to burn in a gas jar of chlorine, making hydrogen chloride gas.

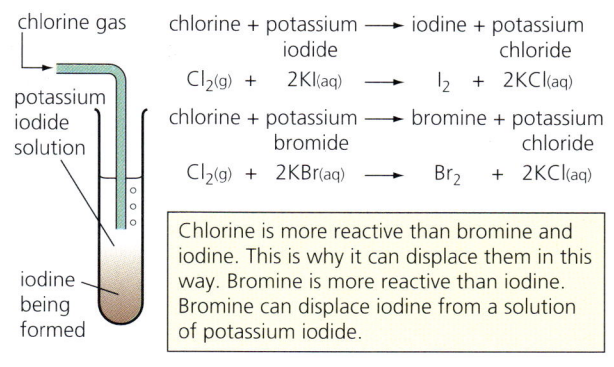

chlorine + potassium iodide ⟶ iodine + potassium chloride
$Cl_{2(g)} + 2KI_{(aq)} \longrightarrow I_2 + 2KCl_{(aq)}$

chlorine + potassium bromide ⟶ bromine + potassium chloride
$Cl_{2(g)} + 2KBr_{(aq)} \longrightarrow Br_2 + 2KCl_{(aq)}$

Chlorine is more reactive than bromine and iodine. This is why it can displace them in this way. Bromine is more reactive than iodine. Bromine can displace iodine from a solution of potassium iodide.

Chlorine can displace bromine and iodine from a solution of their salts.

Using chemicals in everyday life

When halogens undergo chemical reactions there is a **trend** in properties. Halogens react either to gain an electron to form a 1− ion or by sharing an electron pair to form a covalent bond. Going down the group the halogen atoms increase in size. This is because the outer electrons are further from the electrostatic attraction of the nucleus. Going down the group it becomes more difficult for the atom to gain or share an electron, and the elements become less reactive.

11 Use your knowledge of the physical properties of chlorine, bromine and iodine to predict:
   a the colour and state of matter of fluorine
   b the colour and state of astatine
   c whether fluorine is more or less reactive than chlorine
   d whether astatine is more or less reactive than iodine
   all at room temperature and pressure. Give a reason for each of your predictions.

12 From your knowledge of the reactivity of the halogens, predict whether a solution of potassium bromide will react with chlorine gas or with iodine solution. For any reaction that you predict will occur write a balanced equation, and state which substances are being oxidised and which are being reduced.

How is chlorine manufactured?

In industry, chlorine is made on a large scale by the electrolysis of brine (see Chapter 12, *The sea*). In the laboratory, chlorine can be prepared by reacting an oxidising agent with concentrated hydrochloric acid. The preparation must be carried out in a fume cupboard because chlorine is poisonous.

Making chlorine in the laboratory

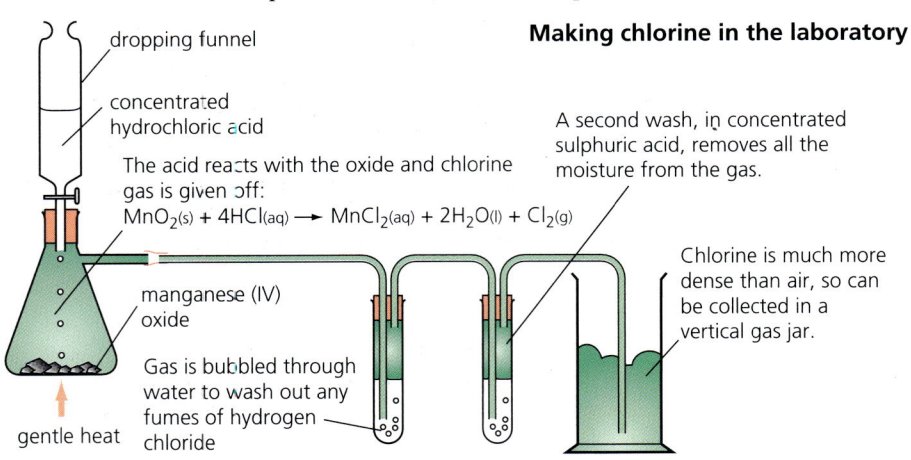

- dropping funnel
- concentrated hydrochloric acid
- The acid reacts with the oxide and chlorine gas is given off:
  $MnO_2(s) + 4HCl(aq) \rightarrow MnCl_2(aq) + 2H_2O(l) + Cl_2(g)$
- manganese (IV) oxide
- gentle heat
- Gas is bubbled through water to wash out any fumes of hydrogen chloride
- A second wash, in concentrated sulphuric acid, removes all the moisture from the gas.
- Chlorine is much more dense than air, so can be collected in a vertical gas jar.

Teflon is a polymer containing compounds of fluorine. It has a non-stick surface and is used in cookware and on the base of skis to stop sticking

Figure 13 In the laboratory, chlorine must be made in the fume cupboard.

Chlorine is used to kill harmful bacteria in swimming pools and domestic water supplies

Non-metals

Hydrogen chloride is a useful compound of chlorine that has a wide variety of uses. It is a dense colourless gas with a choking smell. It forms cloudy fumes in moist air, and dissolves readily in water to make hydrochloric acid.

Figure 14 Hydrogen chloride can be made in the laboratory – but only in a fume cupboard!

Making hydrogen chloride in the laborarory

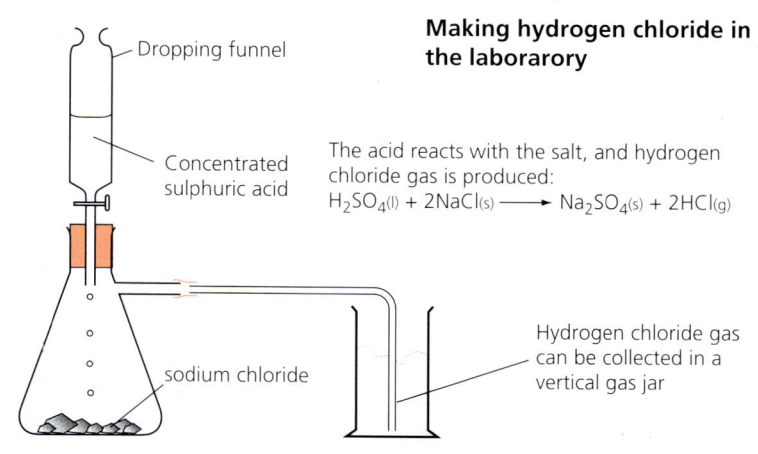

The acid reacts with the salt, and hydrogen chloride gas is produced:
$H_2SO_4(l) + 2NaCl(s) \longrightarrow Na_2SO_4(s) + 2HCl(g)$

Hydrogen chloride gas can be collected in a vertical gas jar

Figure 15 Properties of hydrogen chloride.

Hydrogen chloride reacts with ammonia

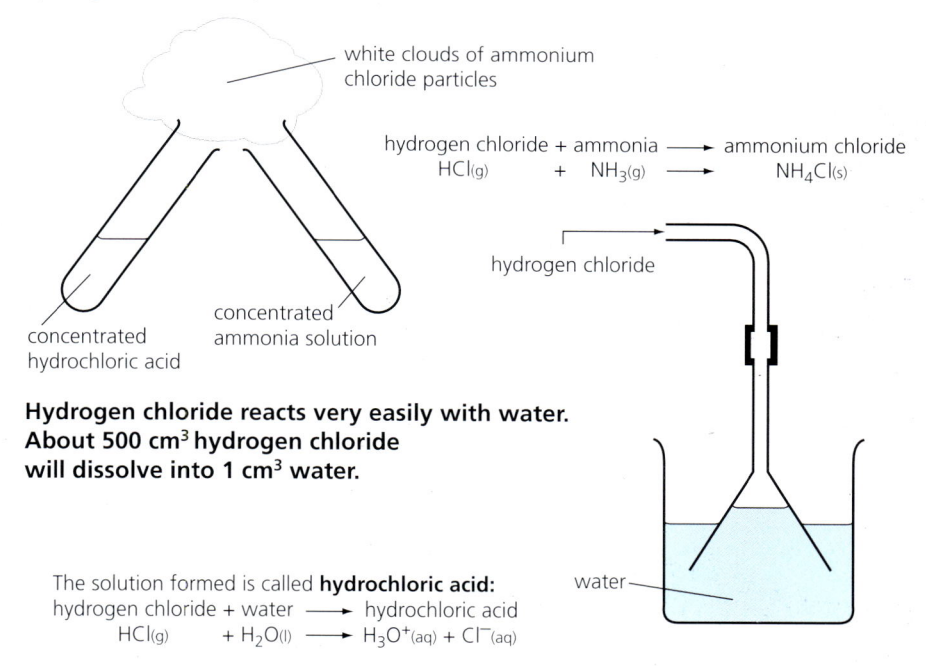

white clouds of ammonium chloride particles

hydrogen chloride + ammonia $\longrightarrow$ ammonium chloride
$HCl(g)$ + $NH_3(g)$ $\longrightarrow$ $NH_4Cl(s)$

Hydrogen chloride reacts very easily with water. About 500 cm³ hydrogen chloride will dissolve into 1 cm³ water.

The solution formed is called **hydrochloric acid**:
hydrogen chloride + water $\longrightarrow$ hydrochloric acid
$HCl(g)$ + $H_2O(l)$ $\longrightarrow$ $H_3O^+(aq) + Cl^-(aq)$

Summary of elements in Group VII

- The elements in Group VII are known as the halogens.
- The halogens have low melting and boiling points, but these rise going down the group.
- All halogens react with both metals and non-metals.
- A more reactive halogen will displace a less reactive one from a solution of its salt.
- Reactivity decreases as you go down the group.
- Hydrogen chloride gas can be reacted with water to make hydrochloric acid.

Using chemicals in everyday life

EXAMINATION style questions

1 The map illustrates an area of land where the river water is thought to be polluted. Investigations have shown high levels of nitrates in the river water.

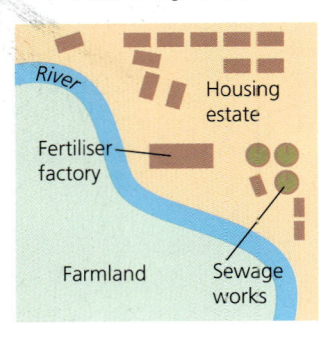

   a Name three possible sources of nitrate pollution.
   b What effect might high levels of nitrate have on the life in the river?
   c Suggest ways in which such pollution might be minimised.

2 The figure shows part of the nitrogen cycle.
   a What is the formula of
      i   nitrogen gas
      ii ammonia?
   b Where does the nitrogen used in the Haber process come from?
   c Ammonium nitrate (NH_4NO_3) is widely used as a fertiliser. Calculate the percentage by mass of nitrogen in this compound.
   d Why are fertilisers containing nitrogen added to the soil?
   e What problems may be caused when excess fertilisers are washed into river water?

3 The percentage of ammonia formed in the Haber process can vary, according to the conditions applied. The effect of temperature and pressure on the amount of ammonia produced is illustrated in the graph.
   What happens to the percentage of ammonia produced when:
   a the pressure is increased
   b the temperature is increased?
   c Which conditions of temperature and pressure combine to produce the highest yield of ammonia?

4 In the Contact process for the manufacture of sulphuric acid, sulphur dioxide (SO_2) is reacted with oxygen in the air (O_2) to make sulphur trioxide (SO_3).
   a Write a balanced equation for this reaction.
   b Suggest a suitable catalyst for this reaction, giving its name and formula.
   c Sulphur dioxide can also be used to help preserve some foods. Describe how it acts in this way.

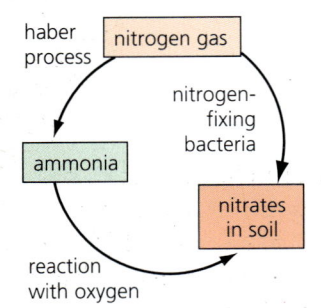

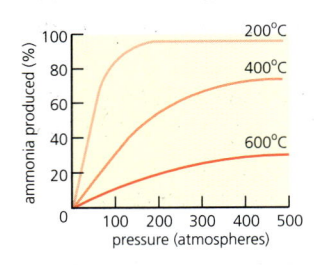

Organic chemistry 16

Learning objectives

By the end of this chapter you should be able to:
- **describe** how fossil fuels were formed
- **describe** fractional distillation of crude oil
- **recognise** saturated and unsaturated molecules
- **explain** the terms isomerism and homologous series
- **draw** simple alkanes, alkenes, alcohols and carboxylic acids and list their properties
- **explain** how soaps and detergents work
- **describe** some polymers and their properties

16.1 Organic chemistry

Why is carbon unique?

Carbon is found in Group IV of the periodic table. This indicates that carbon has four electrons in its outer shell available for bonding. It can therefore form up to four single covalent bonds. Carbon atoms are fairly small. When they form covalent bonds the atoms are close together and the bonds formed quite strong. Many carbon compounds are therefore fairly stable and carbon can form compounds containing thousands of atoms. Covalent compounds of carbon are called **organic** compounds.

The carbon atom can also join to atoms of other elements in a great variety of ways. Organic molecules can therefore be found in many different shapes and sizes – long straight chains, branched chains and rings of atoms. Over two million carbon compounds are known, and they are studied in **organic chemistry**.

All living things contain organic molecules, some of them very large and complex. Organic chemicals are also widely used in everyday life. Lighting a gas fire to keep warm or a Bunsen burner in a laboratory involves burning a simple organic chemical – methane. Camping gas cookers burn another organic chemical – butane. Car engines are powered by petrol or diesel, which are mixtures of organic chemicals. These organic chemicals are good fuels.

Some fuels are highly flammable and need to be handled with great care – this Formula One car was engulfed in flames after an accident.

209

Using chemicals in everyday life

How did the fossil fuels form?

Coal, crude oil and natural gas are known as **fossil fuels** because they were formed from the fossilised remains of plants or animals. They are also useful as raw materials from which a large range of organic chemicals can be manufactured.

Much of the coal in use today was formed about 250 million years ago, when many parts of the world were covered with subtropical swamps and vegetation. As the vegetation died, it was covered in layers of sand and mud which were compressed to form sedimentary rocks (see Chapter 4, *Rocks and minerals*). Over millions of years the organic remains turned into coal. Much coal can be mined and burned with little further processing.

Crude oil and natural gas are often found together in underground deposits. Most of these deposits are over 150 million years old. They were formed from the fossilised remains of very small sea creatures. When these died, their remains fell to the sea bed and they became covered in layers of sand and mud. In time, these became porous sedimentary rocks. The temperature of underground rocks often rises at greater depths. Over millions of years, the combination of raised temperatures (90–120°C), and the absence of oxygen slowly changed the organic remains into crude oil and natural gas.

Note

Hydrocarbons are compounds of hydrogen and carbon.

Many deposits of oil and gas are found underground off the coast. Offshore drilling rigs are expensive to construct and maintain but the high prices obtained for the products makes them economically worth while.

One of the most common geological features where crude oil and natural gas are found is called an anticline. The oil and gas are trapped under pressure in porous rocks. They often rise up until they reach a non-porous layer of rock, where they remain trapped. When a hole is drilled in the non-porous rock the oil and gas will often come shooting out under the effect of the high pressure.

Natural gas is mostly methane (CH_4) and is widely used as a fuel in homes and power stations. Crude oil comes out of the ground as a dark brown liquid with an unpleasant smell. It is a mixture of hundreds of different molecules, most of which are **hydrocarbons**.

Organic chemistry

How are the components of crude oil separated?

Crude oil is transported by pipeline or tanker to a refinery, where the various chemicals present are separated from each other by **fractional distillation**. Each hydrocarbon in crude oil has its own boiling point. Small molecules with a low relative molar mass have quite low boiling points; larger, heavier molecules have higher boiling points.

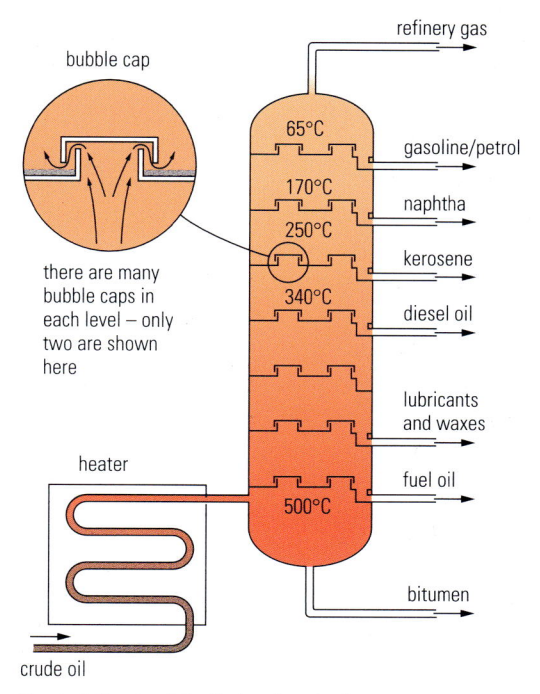

Figure 1 Fractional distillation of crude oil.

1 The following table shows an analysis of various gases that are used as fuels.

Gas	% hydrogen	% nitrogen	% methane	% propane	% carbon monoxide
A	100	0	0	0	0
B	50	0	0	0	50
C	0	0	100	0	0
D	0	0	0	100	0

   a Which of these fuels would burn to form only water?
   b Which fuel most resembles natural gas?
   c Write the letter of the gas that would be most suitable for a portable supply of bottled gas.

2 Five of the fractions from the distillation of crude oil are refinery gases, gasoline, kerosene, diesel and fuel oil. Which of these
   a could be used as a fuel for jet engines?
   b could be used as a fuel for motor cars?
   c is most viscous?
   d has the highest boiling range?

How long will the fossil fuels last?

There are limited supplies of coal, oil and natural gas in the Earth's crust. Although new deposits are being discovered all the time, the supply is not infinite and it will eventually run out. What has taken millions of years to form is currently being used up at such a rate that most supplies of these fuels will be used up in a relatively short time.

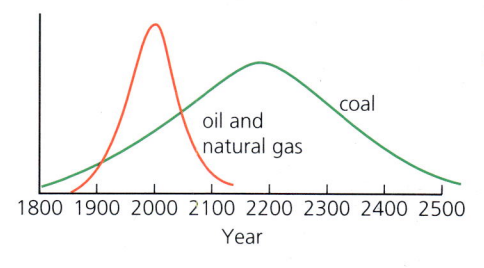

Figure 2 If we continue to use the fossil fuels at our current rates, they will run out in only a few centuries.

211

Using chemicals in everyday life

Eventually we will have to find alternative sources of energy. Many people think that it is wasteful to use up such large amounts of fossil fuel by burning when they are so useful to make materials such as plastics, paints, dyes and medicines.

When hydrocarbons are burned they give off heat energy. This is an exothermic reaction. The energy produced is either used directly for heat or converted into other types of energy. When hydrocarbons are burned in an excess of oxygen, they always produce carbon dioxide and water. For example:

3 Suggest three changes people may need to make as fossil fuel supplies start to be used up.

4 Write a balanced equation for the complete combustion of propane gas (C_3H_8) in a good supply of air. What might happen if propane is burned with a limited supply of oxygen, and why might this be dangerous?

carbon in methane forms carbon dioxide

$$CH_4(g) + 2O_2(g) \rightarrow CO_2(g) + H_2O(g)$$

hydrogen in methane forms water vapour

Burning hydrocarbons in a limited supply of oxygen can form poisonous fumes of carbon monoxide. This happens inside car engines, where there is only a limited supply of air. It can also happen when gas heaters operate without adequate ventilation.

Summary of organic chemistry

- Carbon can form a variety of molecules of different shapes and sizes.
- Organic chemistry is the study of covalent compounds of carbon.
- Coal, oil and natural gas are all fossil fuels.
- Crude oil can be separated out into groups of compounds with similar boiling points by fractional distillation.
- Fossil fuels are all finite resources.

16.2 Alkanes

What are alkanes?

The many different organic compounds can be classified into a number of 'families', depending on their composition. The simplest of these families is a group of hydrocarbons known as the **alkanes**. They all contain carbon joined to hydrogen with single covalent bonds.

Any organic compound can be written down in various ways. The **molecular formula** simply shows the number of atoms of each element present. More information is given by the **structural formula**, which shows all the covalent bonds present and which atoms are joined to which within the molecule. The structural formula does not show the exact shape of a molecule.

Organic chemistry

Table 1 Naming organic compounds

Name of molecule starts with	Number of carbon atoms in the molecule
meth-	1
eth-	2
prop-	3
but-	4
pent-	5
hex-	6
hept-	7
oct-	8
non-	9
dec-	10

Table 2 The alkanes are the simplest of the hydrocarbons

Name	Molecular formula	Structural formula	Boiling point (°C)
methane	CH_4	H–C(H)(H)–H	−164
ethane	C_2H_6	H–C(H)(H)–C(H)(H)–H	−87
propane	C_3H_8	H–C(H)(H)–C(H)(H)–C(H)(H)–H	−42
butane	C_4H_{10}	H–C(H)(H)–C(H)(H)–C(H)(H)–C(H)(H)–H	0
pentane	C_5H_{12}	H–C(H)(H)–C(H)(H)–C(H)(H)–C(H)(H)–C(H)(H)–H	36

The simplest alkane is methane. Each successive alkane has an extra —CH_2— group added on. Any family of organic compounds with similar structures that get larger in this way is known as a **homologous series.** All the chemicals in a series have similar sounding names. The names of all the alkanes end with '-ane'. A homologous series will also have a similar **general formula**. The general formula for the alkanes is C_nH_{2n+2}.

What is isomerism?

5 Draw the molecular and structural formulae for:
  a methane
  b propane
  c 2-methylbutane.

6 Draw out the structural formula of a straight chain molecule of pentane. Then draw as many isomers of this structure as you can.

Carbon has a unique ability to join to itself and form not only straight chains of atoms but also a variety of other shapes. The carbon atoms in the first three alkanes can only join in a straight line but the atoms in butane and larger molecules can be arranged in several different ways. Each different arrangement is a separate chemical compound known as an **isomer**. Isomers have the same molecular formula but different structural formulae.

Table 3 The same number of atoms can join together in different ways known as isomers

Name	Structural formula	Boiling point (°C)
butane	H–C(H)(H)–C(H)(H)–C(H)(H)–C(H)(H)–H	0
2-methylpropane	H–C(H)(H)–C(H)–C(H)(H)–H with –C(H)(H)–H below middle C	−12

Using chemicals in everyday life

Do alkanes all have similar properties?

The following trends can be seen in the physical properties of the alkanes as they get larger.
- They are all colourless gases, liquids and solids.
- The melting and boiling points rise as the M_r rises.
- Liquid alkanes become more viscous as the M_r rises.

All the alkanes have the following chemical properties.
- They all burn in air, especially the smaller molecules, which burn with a clean blue–yellow flame. For example:

$$CH_4(g) + 2O_2(g) \rightarrow CO_2(g) + H_2O(g)$$
$$C_3H_8(g) + 5O_2(g) \rightarrow 3CO_2(g) + 4H_2O(g)$$

Alkanes are mostly used as fuels in combustion reactions.
- Alkanes react slowly with halogens in the presence of ultra-violet light. For example:

methane + chlorine $\xrightarrow{\text{ultra-violet light}}$ chloromethane + hydrogen chloride

$$CH_4(g) + Cl_2(g) \xrightarrow{\text{ultra-violet light}} CH_3Cl(l) + HCl(g)$$

H–C(H)(H)–H + Cl–Cl $\xrightarrow{\text{ultra-violet light}}$ H–C(H)(H)–Cl + H–Cl

ethane + bromine $\xrightarrow{\text{ultra-violet light}}$ bromoethane + hydrogen bromide

$$C_2H_6(g) + Br_2(l) \xrightarrow{\text{ultra-violet light}} C_2H_5Br(l) + HBr(g)$$

H–C(H)(H)–C(H)(H)–H + Br–Br $\xrightarrow{\text{ultra-violet light}}$ H–C(H)(H)–C(H)(H)–Br + H–Br

These processes are known as **substitution reactions** because one or more of the hydrogen atoms on the alkane is substituted by a halogen atom.

7 Plot a graph of the boiling point of the first five straight chain alkanes (y axis) against their M_r values (x axis). What trend do you see in the graph? Can you think of an explanation for this trend?

8 The hydrocarbon with the molecular formula C_4H_{10} can form two different structures.
  a What is the name given to molecules that can form two or more structures with the same formula?
  b What is a homologous series?
  c Which homologous series do these come from?

Summary of alkanes

- A molecular formula shows the number of atoms of each element present in a compound.
- The structural formula shows the arrangement of atoms within a molecule.
- A homologous series of compounds contain molecules with similar structures and increasing M_r values.
- Isomers are compounds that have the same molecular formula, but different structural formulae.
- The simplest example of a homologous series is the alkanes.

16.3 Alkenes

What makes alkenes different from alkanes?

The alkenes are another important homologous series. They are also hydrocarbons, but at least two of the carbon atoms present are joined to each other with a double covalent bond. The simplest alkene, ethene, has two carbon atoms. Other members of the homologous series follow on from this.

Table 4 The alkenes

Name	Molecular formula	Structural formula	Boiling point (°C)
ethene	C_2H_4	H₂C=CH₂	−104
propene	C_3H_6	CH_3−CH=CH$_2$	−48
but-1-ene	C_4H_8	CH_3−CH_2−CH=CH$_2$	−6
pent-1-ene	C_5H_{10}	CH_3−CH_2−CH_2−CH=CH$_2$	30

The names of the alkenes all have the ending '-ene'. The general formula of the alkenes is C_nH_{2n}.

Figure 3 Saturated and unsaturated molecules.

In all the alkanes, each carbon atom is joined to four other atoms by covalent bonds. This is the maximum number of atoms carbon can join to. The molecule is said to be **saturated**.

In all the alkenes, at least two of the carbon atoms are joined by a double covalent bond. These atoms are joined to only three other atoms, and the molecule is said to be **unsaturated**.

9 Study the following structures of molecules. For each one say whether the molecule is saturated or unsaturated.

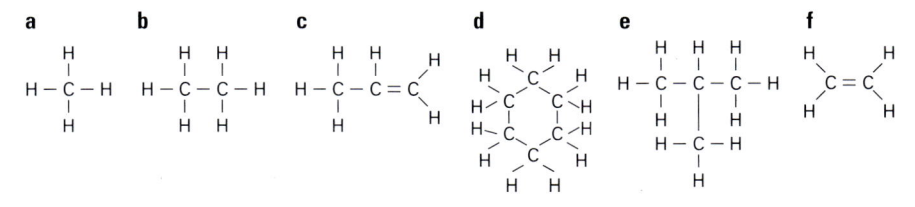

a b c d e f

215

Using chemicals in everyday life

How are alkenes manufactured?

When crude oil is fractionally distilled, the various fractions all have important uses. One of the fractions in greatest demand is the gasoline fraction, which is used to make petrol for cars. The demand for this fraction is greater than the supply from crude oil. The demand is met by taking larger molecules from other fractions (for which there is less demand) and breaking them down into smaller ones. This process is called **cracking**.

Cracking paraffin oil
paraffin vapour passes over catalyst
porous pot acts as a catalyst
gas containing smaller molecules, including some alkenes
water
gentle heat
strong heating
mineral wool soaked in paraffin

Cracking is carried out at 400–700 °C and in the presence of an aluminium oxide catalyst. It is therefore sometimes known as catalytic cracking (or 'cat-cracking').

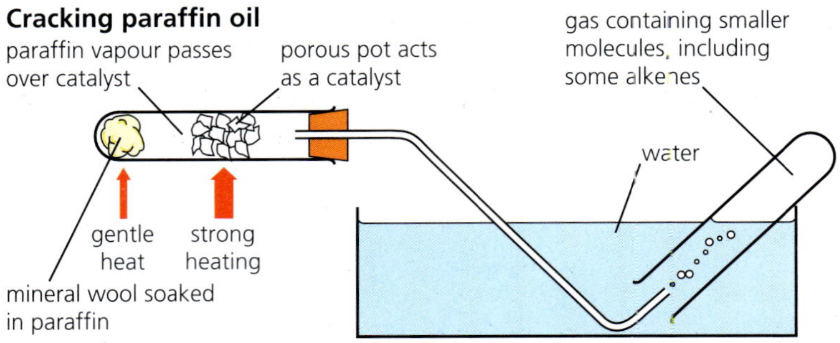

Figure 4 Cracking crude oil in the laboratory.

What are the properties of alkenes?

Like the alkanes, the members of the alkene family have similar physical properties.
- They are all colourless gases, liquids or solids, depending on the M_r.
- The melting and boiling points rise as the M_r rises.
- Liquid alkenes become more viscous as the M_r rises.

The alkenes also have similar chemical properties.
- They burn well in air, with a yellow smoky flame. For example:

| ethene | + | oxygen | → | carbon dioxide | + | water |
| $C_2H_4(g)$ | + | $3O_2(g)$ | → | $2CO_2(g)$ | + | $2H_2O(g)$ |

- Alkenes react well with both bromine and bromine water. The red–brown colour of the bromine quickly disappears:

ethene + bromine → 1,2-dibromoethane

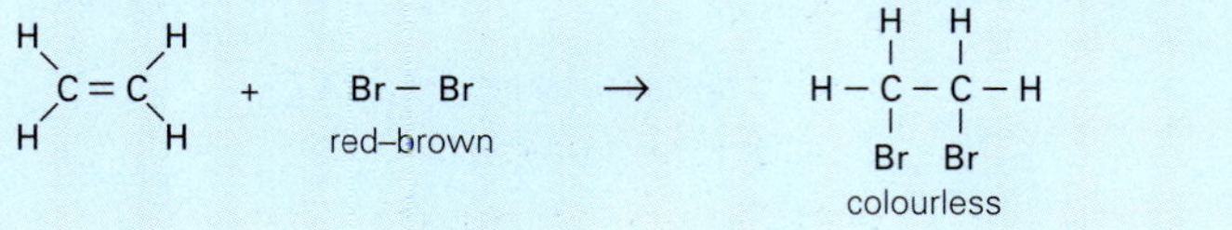

$H_2C=CH_2$ + Br–Br (red-brown) → H–C(H)(Br)–C(H)(Br)–H (colourless)

Note

Bromine or bromine water is often used as a **test for a double bond**. Any molecule with a carbon–carbon double bond will decolorise bromine water.

The double bond in alkenes makes them very reactive. When the bromine is added, the double bond opens up to allow the bromine atoms to add onto the carbon atoms. This is known as an **addition reaction**.

- Alkenes react with hydrogen, when heated in the presence of a nickel catalyst.

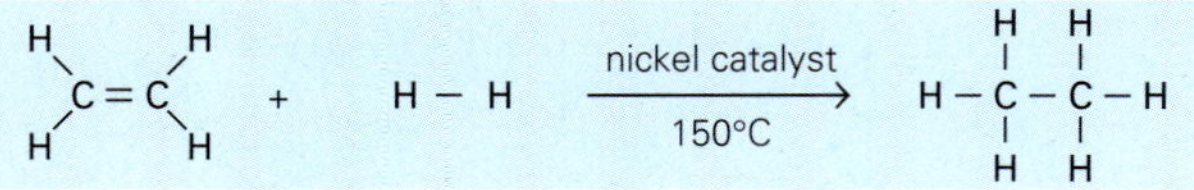

$H_2C=CH_2$ + H–H $\xrightarrow[150°C]{\text{nickel catalyst}}$ H–C(H)(H)–C(H)(H)–H

This reaction is used to manufacture margarine from vegetable oils, which are liquids that contain long hydrocarbon chains. One or more of the carbon–carbon bonds in these chains are double bonds, so the molecule is unsaturated. Fat molecules are similar to oils, but they contain single bonds in the hydrocarbon chain. The different shape of these saturated molecules means that fats are soft solids at room temperature. When margarine is made, hydrogen is added to the hot oil in the presence of a nickel catalyst. The hydrogen adds across the double bond, making the molecule saturated. As more double bonds are saturated the liquid gradually solidifies. Soft margarines have been only partly '**hydrogenated**' in this way. The more hydrogen is added, the more saturated and harder the fat becomes. Margarine or any other foodstuff containing unsaturated molecules will decolorise bromine water.

- Ethene can be made to react with steam, in an important industrial process to make ethanol. Moderate heating, together with increased pressure and a catalyst are needed.

$$CH_2=CH_2 + H_2O \xrightarrow[300°C, 70 \text{ atmospheres}]{\text{solid acid catalyst}} CH_3-CH_2-OH$$

The reaction is known as **hydration**, since water adds on to the ethane molecules. It is an important way of making ethanol.

10 Ethene and ethane will both react with bromine. Describe each of these reactions, with the help of equations showing the name and structural formulae of the substances involved. Describe any differences in the ways these reactions occur.

11 The table gives some information about some organic compounds.

Compound	Molecular formula	Melting point (°C)	Boiling point (°C)
A	C_2H_4	−169	−104
B	C_2H_6	−183	−89
C	C_3H_8	−188	−42
D	$C_{10}H_{22}$	−30	174
E	$C_{30}H_{62}$	37	343

Which substances are:
- **a** alkenes?
- **b** alkanes?
- **c** solids at room temperature (20°C)?
- **d** liquids at room temperature?
- **e** gases at room temperature?
- **f** able to decolorise bromine water rapidly?

Summary of alkenes

- The alkenes are a homologous series containing carbon–carbon double bonds.
- Saturated compounds contain only single carbon–carbon bonds.
- A molecule containing double or triple bonds is said to be unsaturated.
- The double bond in alkenes makes them very reactive.
- Alkenes are produced in large quantities by cracking fractions from the distillation of crude oil.

Using chemicals in everyday life

16.4 Alcohols

What are the alcohols?

Alcohols have the general formula $C_nH_{2n+1}OH$. The best known alcohol is **ethanol**, which is the alcohol present in alcoholic drinks. Like other homologous series, the alcohols have similar names, and usually have the ending '-ol'. The special feature of alcohols is the –OH group present. This is known as a **functional group**, and it gives alcohols their particular properties.

Table 5 The alcohols

Name	Molecular formula	Structural formula	Boiling point (°C)
methanol	CH_3OH	H–C(H)(H)–O–H	65
ethanol	C_2H_5OH	H–C(H)(H)–C(H)(H)–O–H	79
propanol	C_3H_7OH	H–C(H)(H)–C(H)(H)–C(H)(H)–O–H	97
butan-1-ol	C_4H_9OH	H–C(H)(H)–C(H)(H)–C(H)(H)–C(H)(H)–O–H	117
pentan-1-ol	$C_5H_{11}OH$	H–C(H)(H)–C(H)(H)–C(H)(H)–C(H)(H)–C(H)(H)–O–H	138

How is ethanol manufactured?

Ethanol can be made in two main ways. In the chemical industry, most of the ethanol used is made by reacting ethene with steam, as described in the last section. This produces ethanol that is quite pure and useful for many industrial and chemical processes.

The second way of making ethanol is by **fermentation** of carbohydrates from plants. Fermentation is caused by an enzyme present in yeast. When carbohydrates such as glucose are fermented, they break down into ethanol and carbon dioxide:

$$\text{glucose} \xrightarrow[\text{yeast}]{\text{fermentation}} \text{ethanol} + \text{carbon dioxide}$$

$$C_6H_{12}O_6(aq) \longrightarrow 2C_2H_5OH(aq) + 2CO_2(g)$$

The containers and conditions must be kept very clean to keep out bacteria which could alter the fermentation reaction. Cleanliness is also essential when

Fermentation is used by both brewers and bakers. In the brewery, the yeast produces ethanol in the drink. When bread is baked the carbon dioxide gas produced makes the bread rise.

Organic chemistry

The ethanol produced by fermentation is a dilute solution in water. It can be concentrated by fractional distillation.

the process is used to make food or drink products. Air must be kept away from fermentation reactions, otherwise the ethanol will be further oxidised to form ethanoic acid (this is present in vinegar). Yeast is a living organism, and it needs to be kept warm to work well. If it is too cold the fermentation will be very slow. However, if the reaction is too hot, the yeast will be killed. Fermentation is an exothermic process – heat energy is given off.

In some breweries, where beer is produced on a large scale, the fermentation tanks must be cooled to prevent the reaction overheating and killing the yeast.

12 a Write balanced equations for two possible ways of making ethanol.
   b Why is fermentation useful to both baker and brewer?
   c Give two uses for ethanol.

13 The table below shows the contents of several alcoholic drinks.

Drink	Volume (cm³)	Percentage alcohol in drink
beer	568	5
wine	200	12
sherry	50	20
gin	25	40

   a Which drink contained the highest concentration of alcohol?
   b Calculate the volume of alcohol in one litre of each drink.

What properties does ethanol have?

Ethanol has the following physical and chemical properties.
- It is a colourless, volatile liquid.
- It dissolves easily in water – it is water-miscible.
- Ethanol is a good fuel, and burns easily in air with a clean blue flame to give carbon dioxide and water:

$$C_2H_5OH(l) + 3O_2(g) \rightarrow 2CO_2(g) + 3H_2O(g)$$

'Methylated' spirits is sold as a fuel and solvent. It is mostly ethanol, with up to 10% of poisonous methanol added to make it unfit to drink. Usually a bitter-tasting substance and a purple dye are also added.

- Ethanol can be **dehydrated**. Water is removed from the ethanol molecule, leaving ethene gas. This reaction can be made to happen by passing ethanol vapour over hot aluminium oxide:

$$C_2H_5OH(g) \xrightarrow[300°C]{Al_2O_3} C_2H_4(g) + H_2O(g)$$

Using chemicals in everyday life

- Ethanol can be oxidised to give ethanoic acid, which is the acid present in vinegar. If dilute alcoholic drinks such as beer, cider or wine are left in the open air, bacteria act with oxygen in the air to turn the ethanol into vinegar:

$$C_2H_5OH(aq) + O_2(g) \xrightarrow{\text{action of bacteria}} CH_3COOH(aq) + H_2O(l)$$

A similar oxidation reaction can be made to occur with other oxidising agents such as acidified potassium dichromate solution.

Gasohol – the fuel of the future?

14 Why is gasohol likely to become more important in the future?

Most cars run on petrol obtained from the gasoline fraction of crude oil distillation. However, crude oil is a finite resource, and eventually alternative fuels will be needed. The cost of crude oil adds considerably to the import bill of nations with no resources of their own. In response to this, some nations that have the land and a suitable climate have started to grow sugar cane. They ferment this to produce ethanol, which is then mixed with petrol to produce gasohol. Car engines burn this fuel well without alterations.

Summary of alcohols

- A functional group is an atom, or group of atoms, that gives a homologous series its particular properties.
- The alcohols are a homologous series containing the –OH functional group.
- Ethanol is the alcohol found in alcoholic drinks.
- Ethanol can be produced by fermentation of carbohydrates.

16.5 Carboxylic acids

What is a carboxylic acid?

The sharp taste of vinegar is an important addition to many foods. Similarly the distinctive taste of lemons and limes makes them useful in cooking. Each of these substances contains an organic acid. There are a number of such acids that form a separate homologous series known as the carboxylic acids.

These acids all have names ending in '-oic acid'. They also have the same general formula, $C_nH_{2n+1}COOH$. The functional group that gives these acids their particular properties is the **carboxyl group**, —COOH.

Organic chemistry

Table 6 *The carboxylic acids*

Name	Molecular formula	Structural formula	Boiling point (°C)
methanoic acid	HCOOH	H–C(=O)(O–H)	101
ethanoic acid	CH₃COOH	H–C(H)(H)–C(=O)(O–H)	118
propanoic acid	C₂H₅COOH	H–C(H)(H)–C(H)(H)–C(=O)(O–H)	141
butanoic acid	C₃H₇COOH	H–C(H)(H)–C(H)(H)–C(H)(H)–C(=O)(O–H)	164

What are the properties of ethanoic acid?

- Ethanoic acid is a colourless liquid with a pungent smell.
- The pure acid is known as 'glacial' ethanoic acid. This is because it has a melting point of 17°C, and freezes to ice-like crystals on cold days. In the laboratory it is usually used in diluted form.
- Ethanoic acid is a weak acid. In aqueous solution the acid exists mostly in the form of molecules, with only a relatively small proportion dissociated into ions:

$$CH_3COOH(aq) \rightleftharpoons CH_3COO^-(aq) + H^+(aq)$$

The hydrogen ions that are present give acid properties, and a 0.1 M solution of ethanoic acid will have a pH of abut 5.

- Ethanoic acid reacts with alkalis and bases to give salts called **ethanoates**. The hydrogen on the carboxyl group is replaced by a metal ion to make the salt. Ethanoates are written in an unusual way, with the negative anion first and the positive metal cation second. For example:

$$\text{ethanoic acid} + \text{potassium hydroxide} \rightarrow \text{potassium ethanoate} + \text{water}$$
$$CH_3COOH(aq) + KOH(aq) \rightarrow CH_3COOK(aq) + H_2O(l)$$

- Dilute ethanoic acid will react with some metals to give a salt and hydrogen. For example:

$$\text{magnesium} + \text{ethanoic acid} \rightarrow \text{magnesium ethanoate} + \text{hydrogen}$$
$$Mg(s) + 2CH_3COOH(aq) \rightarrow (CH_3COO)_2Mg + H_2(g)$$

- Dilute ethanoic acid reacts with carbonates to give a salt, carbon dioxide and water. For example:

$$\text{sodium carbonate} + \text{ethanoic acid} \rightarrow \text{sodium ethanoate} + \text{carbon dioxide} + \text{water}$$
$$Na_2CO_3(aq) + 2CH_3COOH(aq) \rightarrow CH_3COONa(aq) + CO_2(g) + H_2O(l)$$

- Glacial ethanoic acid reacts with alcohols to produce sweet smelling liquids called **esters**. Esters are responsible for many of the sweet smells of flowers or fruits. Synthetic esters are often added to foods to improve their flavour. Some esters are also used as solvents in adhesives. The sale of these is often restricted, because some people inhale the solvent. This can be very dangerous as it causes disorientation, and can lead to death.

15 The following structures represent various organic compounds:

A: CH_4 (methane)
B: $CH_3-CH=CH_2$ (propene)
C: CH_3-CH_2-OH (ethanol)
D: $CH_3-CH_2-CH_2-CH_2-CH_2-CH_2-CH_2-CH_3$ (octane)
E: CH_3-OH (methanol)
F: CH_3-COOH (ethanoic acid)

a Two of these compounds are alcohols. Which ones?
b Which compounds are alkanes?
c Name one compound that might be found in petrol.
d Which compound would react with sodium carbonate to produce carbon dioxide gas?
e Give the letter of the compound present in alcoholic drinks.

Summary of carboxylic acids

- The carboxylic acids are a homologous series containing the –COOH functional group.
- Ethanoic acid is found in vinegar.
- Ethanoic acid is used as a raw material to make polymers.

16.6 Soaps, detergents and polymers

What gives soaps their properties?

Oils and fats contain long organic molecules that are esters. When these are boiled with an alkali, such as sodium hydroxide, they are broken down into soap and glycerol:

fat	+	sodium hydroxide	→	soap	+	glycerol
octadecanoic acid (stearic acid)				sodium octadecanoate (sodium stearate)		

This reaction is known as **saponification**, which literally means 'soap-making'.
Soap molecules are shaped rather like a tadpole, with a 'head' consisting of an electrically charged ion and a long 'tail' made of a long hydrocarbon chain. Soap lowers the surface tension of water and enables it to penetrate and thoroughly 'wet' substances. It also acts by helping to loosen and remove particles of grease and dirt.

Organic chemistry

One of the disadvantages of using soap is that it forms a scum when used in hard water. One way this problem can be dealt with is to use **soapless detergents**. These have a similar structure to soap and work in the same way. The main difference is that they remain dissolved in hard water, and do not react to form a scum.

Figure 5 Soaps and detergents.

A soap molecule – sodium octadecanoate (sodium stearate), $C_{17}H_{35}COO^-Na^+$

This is sometimes represented as:

hydrocarbon 'tail'   ionic 'head'

A soapless detergent – for example $C_{18}H_{29}SO_3^-Na^+$

This can be represented as:

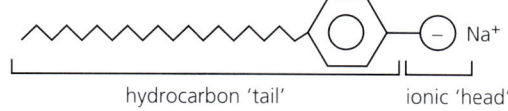

hydrocarbon 'tail'   ionic 'head'

How soaps work

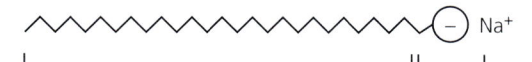

The long hydrocarbon 'tail' can dissolve in fat, but not in water. It is the 'water-hating' end.

This end of the molecule ionises in water, to give it a slight negative charge. It is the 'water-loving' end.

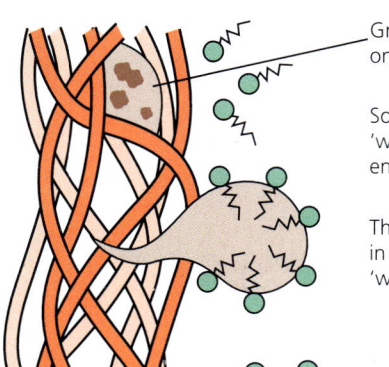

Grease and dirt particles rest on the fibres of the fabric.

Soap molecules contain ions with 'water-hating' and 'water-loving' ends.

The 'water-hating' tails dissolve in the grease, but the 'water-loving' ends stick out.

As the fabric is agitated, the grease and dirt are removed.

Using chemicals in everyday life

What is a polymer?

Polymers are large molecules that are made by joining together many smaller molecules, which are known as **monomers**. **Polymerisation** is the chemical reaction in which many monomer molecules join together to form a polymer.

Polymers have some very useful properties. All living things contain naturally occurring polymers. Once scientists understood the structure and properties of naturally occurring polymers, they started to make similar large molecules – **synthetic polymers**.

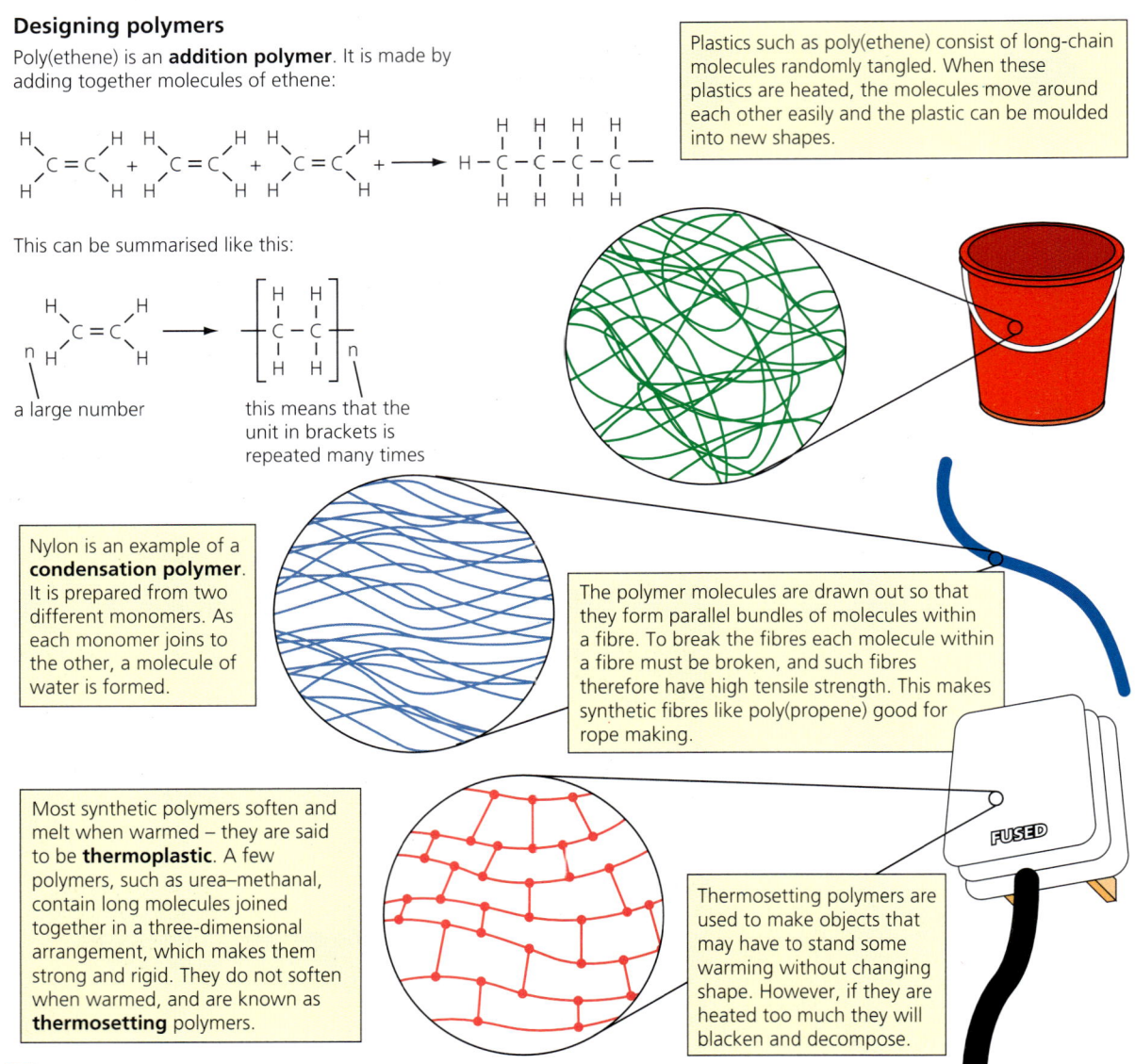

Designing polymers

Poly(ethene) is an **addition polymer**. It is made by adding together molecules of ethene:

Plastics such as poly(ethene) consist of long-chain molecules randomly tangled. When these plastics are heated, the molecules move around each other easily and the plastic can be moulded into new shapes.

This can be summarised like this:

a large number

this means that the unit in brackets is repeated many times

Nylon is an example of a **condensation polymer**. It is prepared from two different monomers. As each monomer joins to the other, a molecule of water is formed.

The polymer molecules are drawn out so that they form parallel bundles of molecules within a fibre. To break the fibres each molecule within a fibre must be broken, and such fibres therefore have high tensile strength. This makes synthetic fibres like poly(propene) good for rope making.

Most synthetic polymers soften and melt when warmed – they are said to be **thermoplastic**. A few polymers, such as urea–methanal, contain long molecules joined together in a three-dimensional arrangement, which makes them strong and rigid. They do not soften when warmed, and are known as **thermosetting** polymers.

Thermosetting polymers are used to make objects that may have to stand some warming without changing shape. However, if they are heated too much they will blacken and decompose.

Note

Monomer: *mono* means *one*, *mer* means *part*

Polymer: *poly* means *many*, *mer* means *parts*

Figure 6 Once chemists understand how the structure of a polymer affects its properties, they can 'design' new polymers to adapt to particular uses.

224

Organic chemistry

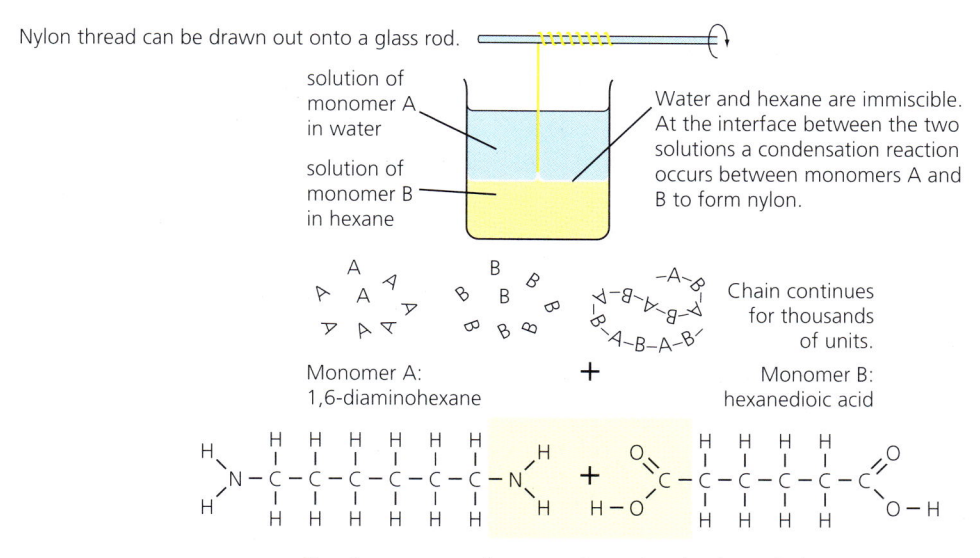

Figure 7 Making nylon in the laboratory.

Nylon thread can be drawn out onto a glass rod.

- solution of monomer A in water
- solution of monomer B in hexane

Water and hexane are immiscible. At the interface between the two solutions a condensation reaction occurs between monomers A and B to form nylon.

Chain continues for thousands of units.

Monomer A: 1,6-diaminohexane + Monomer B: hexanedioic acid

Reaction occurs easily: no catalyst or heating is needed.

+ H₂O

Table 7 Addition polymers and their uses

Monomer	Structure	Polymer	Structure	Uses
ethene	H₂C=CH₂	poly(ethene)	−[CH₂−CH₂]−$_n$	plastic bags, bowls and buckets
propene	H₂C=CH(CH₃)	poly(propene)	−[CH(CH₃)−CH₂]−$_n$	ropes, crates, carpets
phenylethene (styrene)	H₂C=CH(C₆H₅)	poly(phenylethene) (polystyrene)	−[CH(C₆H₅)−CH₂]−$_n$	insulation, kitchen utensils, toys
chloroethene (vinyl chloride)	H₂C=CHCl	poly(chloroethene) (poly vinyl chloride – 'PVC')	−[CHCl−CH₂]−$_n$	insulating electrical wiring, packaging, sheeting, pipes and gutters
tetrafluoroethene	F₂C=CF₂	poly(tetrafluoroethene) ('PTFE')	−[CF₂−CF₂]−$_n$	non-stick surfaces
methylmethacrylate	H(COOH)C=CH(CH₃)	poly(methylmethacrylate) ('perspex')	−[C(CH₃)(COOH)−CH₂]−$_n$	clear plastic sheeting

Using chemicals in everyday life

How can synthetic polymers be disposed of?

Naturally occurring polymers like starch, cellulose, silk or protein are all **biodegradable** – they are readily broken down into simpler substances by the action of bacteria. Most synthetic polymers are not biodegradable and will remain as they are when left in the open air, causing problems with litter.

One effective way to dispose of some polymers is to incinerate them. When an incinerator is operating properly at high temperatures, polymers such as poly(ethene) can be broken down into carbon dioxide and water. However, other polymers, such as PVC, can produce harmful pollutant gases when incinerated.

It is also helpful to recycle polymers. There are some problems to this because there are so many different types of polymers that it is quite difficult to sort them out for recycling.

Polymer chemists are developing biodegradable synthetic polymers. Some scientists are even researching into making crops that will yield polymer molecules at harvest time instead of food!

16 a Explain what is meant by 'biodegradable' and 'non-biodegradable' polymers.
  b Give an example of each type of polymer.
  c Suggest one use to which each of the polymers you have listed may be put.

17 a Name the main raw material from which most synthetic polymers are made.
  b What is the name given to a plastic that can be softened by heating and moulded into shape? Give an example of such a plastic, and one way it can be used.
  c What name is given to plastics that will not melt when warmed after they have been moulded into shape?

18 The following equations represent the reactions of various organic compounds:

A $6CO_2(g) + 6H_2O(l) \rightarrow C_6H_{12}O_6(aq) + 6O_2(g)$
B $C_6H_{12}O_6(aq) \rightarrow 2C_2H_5OH(aq) + 2CO_2(g)$
C $C_{15}H_{32}(l) \rightarrow C_{11}H_{24}(l) + C_4H_8(g)$
D $nC_2H_4(g) \rightarrow -[CH_2-CH_2]_n-$

  a In which of these reactions are large molecules being broken down into smaller ones?
  b State the type of reaction happening in each of the processes.

Summary of soaps, detergents and polymers

- Soaps and detergents are organic molecules with properties that are useful in cleaning.
- Polymers are long-chain molecules formed by joining together many small monomer molecules.
- Addition polymers are formed simply by adding together monomer molecules.
- Condensation polymers are formed in a reaction that also produces water.
- Thermoplastic polymers soften when heated.
- Thermosetting polymers remain hard when heated.
- Many synthetic polymers are non-biodegradable, so must be disposed of carefully or recycled.

Organic chemistry

EXAMINATION style questions

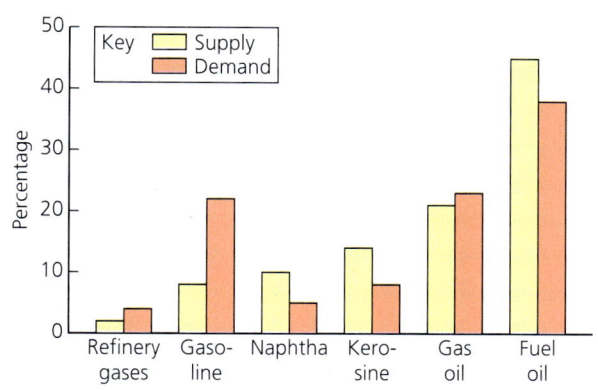

1 Study the following bar chart.

a Which fraction from North Sea crude oil is present in the greatest amount?

b For which fraction/s from this distillation is the demand higher than the supply?

c Briefly outline the process used to break down fractions which are in excess to meet demands for other fractions.

d For which fraction does the demand most exceed the supply? Suggest a reason for this.

2 Which of the following equations involves:

a cracking? **c** fermentation?
b polymerisation? **d** evaporation?

A $C_{15}H_{32}(l) \rightarrow C_{12}H_{26}(l) + C_3H_6(g)$

B $C_4H_{10}(l) \rightarrow C_4H_{10}(g)$

C $nC_2H_4(g) \rightarrow \left[\begin{array}{cc} H & H \\ | & | \\ -C - C - \\ | & | \\ H & H \end{array} \right]_n$ (s)

D $C_6H_{12}O_6(aq) \rightarrow 2C_2H_5OH(aq) + 2CO_2(g)$

3 Hydrocarbon X contains 85.7% carbon and 14.3% hydrogen by mass. Its relative molar mass is 42.

a Calculate:
i the empirical formula
ii the structural formula.
b To which homologous series does X belong?
c Draw a structural formula for X
d Suggest how X would react with oxygen, and write a balanced chemical equation

4 The table shows details about various addition polymers.

Monomer	Structure	Polymer	Structure
ethene	$H_2C=CH_2$	poly(ethene)	$\left[\begin{array}{cc} H & H \\ | & | \\ -C-C- \\ | & | \\ H & H \end{array} \right]_n$
chloroethene	$\begin{array}{c} H \\ \end{array} C=C \begin{array}{c} Cl \\ H \end{array}$		
		poly(tetrafluoroethene)	$\left[\begin{array}{cc} F & F \\ | & | \\ -C-C- \\ | & | \\ F & F \end{array} \right]_n$

a Copy out the table and complete the missing information.
b Explain what the term 'addition polymer' means.
c Suggest one use for each of these three polymers.

Materials science 17

Learning objectives

By the end of this chapter you should be able to:
- **explain** what materials science involves
- **describe** some of the physical and chemical properties of substances that are relevant to their use
- **list** some of the ways in which materials can be classified

17.1 Properties of materials

What is materials science?

For thousands of years humans have used naturally occurring materials – such as wood, stone, animal skins, wool, cotton or silk – to make useful, everyday objects. Materials science is the study of how the structure and properties of a particular material can be related to possible uses. A new material may be made, and materials scientists will search for a use to which it can be put. At other times a material might be needed for a particular purpose, and materials scientists will try to make something to meet this demand.

Flints are naturally occurring minerals consisting of nearly pure silica (silicon dioxide, SiO_2). They are very hard, and can be chipped to form shapes with very sharp edges. This property made flints very useful for cutting and for weapons for people living in the stone age. Flints also generate sparks when struck against some metals – a property which can be used to light fires or fire some guns.

What physical properties can be related to use?

- **Electrical conductivity** measures how well a substance conducts an electrical current. This property varies greatly between different materials. Some metals, such as silver and copper, are excellent conductors. Metalloids, like silicon, are semi-conductors. Non-metals, plastics and ceramics are poor electrical conductors.
- **Thermal conductivity** measures how well a substance conducts heat, and it varies greatly between materials. Most metals are good thermal conductors.

Materials science

Table 1 *Moh's scale of hardness compares all substances to the hardness of diamond, the hardest substance known*

Hardness	Example
10.0	diamond
9.7	silicon carbide
7.0	quartz
6.0	steel
5.5	glass
4.5	concrete
2.0	wood
1.0	talc

- The **density** of a material is the mass of a given volume. Gases such as hydrogen and helium have very low densities, liquids have intermediate densities, and some solids have high densities.
- **Elasticity** – when a force is applied to a material, it will change shape. When that force is released an **elastic** material will return to its initial shape. A **plastic** material will retain the new shape.
- The **flexibility** of a material. A flexible material can be easily bent while still retaining its shape.
- **Hardness** – a hard material is difficult to dent or scratch and will stand up to impact without changing shape. A hard substance can always be used to cut or scratch a softer one. Hardness is usually measured on Moh's scale, which is a relative scale from 1 to 10 (this is shown in table 1).
- **Malleability** – a malleable substance can be hammered or pressed into new shapes without breaking or returning to its original shape. Many metals are quite malleable and can be formed into a variety of shapes.
- The **melting and boiling points,** both measured at one atmosphere of pressure.
- Several measurements are relevant to the **optical properties** of a substance. For example, if a substance is **opaque** light cannot pass through it. Light can pass through a **transparent** material without being diffused, so that objects can be clearly seen through it. A **translucent** substance transmits light, but is not transparent.
- The **solubility** of a substance usually varies with temperature.
- Strength is a measure of how difficult a substance is to break when a force is applied. **Tensile** strength measures how well something stands up to being stretched. **Compressive** strength measures how much it can be crushed under a force.
- **Toughness** – a material is said to be tough when it is hard to break or cut. Materials that break and shatter very easily are **brittle**.

These high-voltage electric cables are good electrical conductors. They are usually made from an alloy that has a fairly low density, so the supporting structures do not have to be too large. The ceramic blocks are very good electrical insulators.

A domestic cat has three different types of fur. These all trap air, which is a poor thermal conductor. This helps to keep the cat warm.

The steel used in buildings is strong under tension and compression. The bricks used for the outer wall are strong under compression, and are also quite good thermal insulators.

229

Using chemistry in everyday life

1. It is important to know the properties of a material when deciding a use for it. For each of the following, suggest some properties to investigate.
   a A metal to be used in a saucepan.
   b A synthetic fur fabric to line a jacket.
   c A plastic used to make garden furniture.
   d A ceramic used to make a casserole dish.
2. Study the following passage and give the meaning of the words in italics.

   In the construction of a house, many different materials are used. Bricks are *strong under compression* and are useful in walls. They can be very *brittle*, however, and are *weak under tension*. The windows are made from double-glazed glass – most of which is *transparent*, except for the bathroom window, which is *translucent*.

What chemical properties of materials are considered?

When considering the use to which a material can be put, its chemical properties should also be taken into account. Relevant questions might include:
- does it burn when heated in air?
- does it rust?
- does it react with acids or alkalis?

Summary of properties of materials

- Materials science studies how the structure and properties of a substance are related to its use.
- When finding a use for a new material its physical and chemical properties should be taken into account.

17.2 Classifying materials

How are materials classified?

Materials can be classified in a number of ways.
- Metals and non-metals.
- Ceramics and glasses.
- Colloids.
- Plastics and/or fibres.
- Composite materials.

How are metals and non-metals different?

Elements are divided into metals and non-metals. Generally, they each have special properties that make them useful for various purposes. The particular properties of metals are discussed in more detail in Chapter 13, and you will find more about non-metals in Chapter 15. Table 2 summarises the properties.

Table 2 Properties of metals and non-metals

Metals	Non-metals
usually have high melting and boiling points	most have low melting and boiling points
have a shiny surface	have a dull surface
can be hammered, bent or stretched into shape	are brittle when solid
good conductors of heat and electricity	poor conductors of heat and electricity

What are the properties of ceramics and glasses?

Table 3 Properties of ceramics

good electrical insulators
high melting points
resistance to heat (they are 'refractory')
opaque
brittle and hard
strong under compression but weak under tension
chemically unreactive

A **ceramic** material is usually made from clay which has been 'fired' at high temperatures in a kiln. This alters the structure of the clay, and gives it a new set of properties (see table 3).

Glass is a mixture of substances that have been melted together and allowed to cool so that the original, ordered structure of the starting materials does not re-form. For example, the glass used in windows is made by melting together glass sand (silicon dioxide, SiO_2), soda ash (sodium carbonate, $NaCO_3$), limestone (calcium carbonate, $CaCO_3$) and dolomite (calcium magnesium carbonate, $CaCO_3 \bullet MgCO_3$) to form a mixture of oxides.

Glass has the same properties as ceramics, except that it is transparent.

Many new uses are being found for glass materials, and new glasses are constantly being developed. Here are some examples.
- **Fibreglass** – glass can be drawn out into thin threads. These can be used for insulation and in fibreoptic cables.
- **Pyrex** is a glass that can withstand high temperatures and temperature changes. It contains oxides of silicon, boron, aluminium and sodium.
- **Photochromic glass** contains silver compounds embedded in the glass. These darken on exposure to light and can be used to make lenses for spectacles.

Why recycle glass?

The raw materials for glass have to be mined out of the ground, and to make glass from these requires energy. A lot of used glass is simply thrown away. Although glass can be crushed into smaller pieces, it is chemically very unreactive and does not easily break down. Discarded glass may remain in landfill sites for thousands of years, causing environmental problems.

To get over these problems we now recycle glass – you are probably familiar with the recycling banks in your town centre. It is collected, sorted according to colour and melted down to make new objects. It takes much less energy to melt and remake glass in this way than to start from the original raw materials.

What are colloids?

Many everyday materials such as milk, mayonnaise, cosmetics and paint are all made from a particular mixture of substances known as a **colloid**. A colloid contains a mixture of two substances, one of which is finely suspended in the other. The substances involved in colloids are known as **phases**, and each phase

Using chemistry in everyday life

Figure 1 Many everyday objects are made of colloids.

may be a solid, liquid or a gas. The suspended substance is called the **dispersed phase** and the substance in which it is suspended is called the **continuous phase**. There are several groups of colloids, as you can see in figure 1.

Types of colloids

Colloid	Dispersed phase	Continuous phase	Example
foam	gas	liquid	dispersed phase: air / continuous phase: beer
foam	gas	solid	dispersed phase: air / continuous phase: meringue
emulsion	liquid	liquid	dispersed phase: butterfat / continuous phase: water
emulsion	liquid	solid	dispersed phase: water / continuous phase: cheese
sol	solid	gas	dispersed phase: smoke / continuous phase: air
sol	solid	liquid	dispersed phase: pigment / continuous phase: water
sol	liquid	gas	dispersed phase: water / continuous phase: air
gel	solid	liquid	dispersed phase: gelatine molecules / continuous phase: water

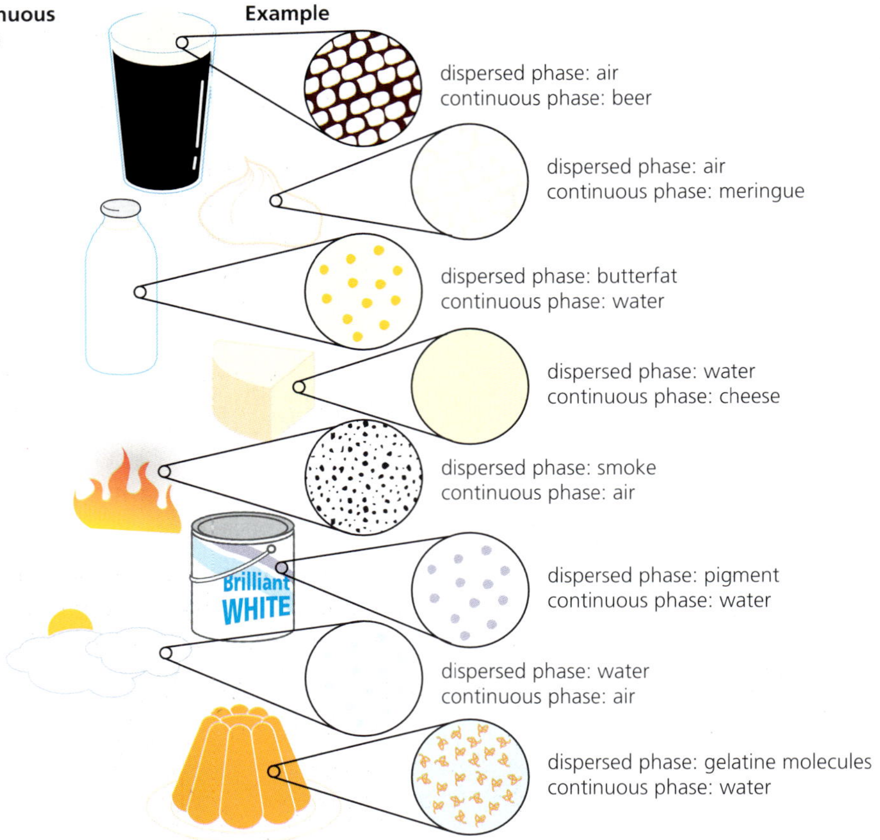

Emulsifiers are substances found in an emulsion. The most common emulsion is between two immiscible liquids such as oil and water. When these are shaken together, they will mix up but then quickly separate into two separate layers. If an emulsifier such as egg yolk or mustard is added, the two liquids do not separate.

How are plastics and fibres useful?

Plastics are synthetic materials made from large molecules and have many useful properties.
- They are flexible.
- Thermoplastics are easily melted and moulded.
- Colourings are easily added.
- They are flexible
- Plastics do not degrade easily.
- Most burn quite easily.

Materials science

Some materials – such as glass, plastics and metals – can be drawn into **fibres**. Other fibres occur naturally – like those in silk, cotton or wool. Fibres are very flexible and can be spun together to make long strands, such as string, cotton or rope. They can also be woven together in strands to make fabrics.

3 'Disposable' glass bottles are made of thin glass and are intended to be thrown away once used. However, some glass bottles are 'returnable'. These need to be able to withstand several trips from the manufacturer to the home and back and are made from thicker glass. They are therefore more expensive to make than disposable bottles. Outline some of the extra costs involved in using returnable bottles. What advantages are there to using these bottles?

4 Classify each of the following colloids:

   a fog
   b salad cream
   c hand cream
   d bread
   e cold custard
   f a jelly baby
   g whipped cream.

5 Some sacks are made from layers of paper and polythene laminated together. What advantages does the paper–polythene laminate have over a sack made just from paper?

What is a composite material?

A composite material is made up of two or more different materials, and combines their properties. Some naturally occurring materials are composites, and many new composite materials are being developed.

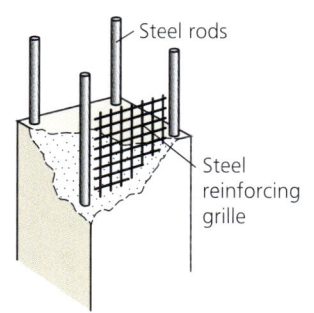

Concrete is a mixture of sand and gravel held together by cement. Although it is strong in compression, it is brittle and weak in tension. Reinforcing the concrete by setting steel mesh and rods into it greatly increases the tensile strength.

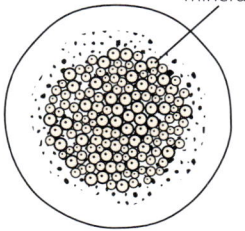

these areas are fibrous tissue saturated with mineral salts

Many boats and canoes are made from polymers and layers of glass fibre. The glass adds strength to the material and the plastic gives it flexibility.

Modern vehicle tyres are made of rubber reinforced with fabric, steel mesh and cable. The rubber is very flexible and the steel adds strength.

Bone is a naturally occurring composite material. It contains a flexible tough fibrous protein called collagen combined with solid mineral salts of mostly calcium phosphate. The mineral gives the bone hardness and strength while the protein gives flexibility. Older people tend to lose collagen and calcium from their bones, which makes them more brittle and liable to break.

Carbon can be drawn into very strong fibres. When these are combined with plastics, they make a very strong, low-density, composite material. Although this material is expensive, it is widely used to make tennis racquets, golf clubs and aircraft parts.

Summary of classifying materials

- All elements are either metals or non-metals.
- Some materials are ceramics or glasses.
- Colloids contain two phases – one suspended in the other.
- Colloids may be foams, emulsions, sols or gels.
- Many natural and synthetic materials can form fibres.
- Composite materials combine the properties of two or more substances.

EXAMINATION style question

1 Match each of the materials in the table with its appropriate use.

Material	Use
carbon fibre	high voltage insulation
ceramic pottery	waterproof sheeting
glass	spinning into fibres to make a strong rope
nylon	reinforcing concrete
polyethene	forming into a crucible to withstand high temperatures
steel	as a matrix in a polymer to make sports equipment

Give reasons for your choices.

Energy

18

Learning objectives

By the end of this chapter you should be able to:
- **describe** the various forms of energy
- **recall** the specific heat capacity of water
- **discriminate** between endothermic and exothermic reactions
- **describe** some chemicals that can be used as fuels
- **calculate** energy changes for various reactions
- **explain** energy changes in terms of making and breaking chemical bonds

18.1 Energy change

How are energy changes useful?

Energy in its various forms is all around us. We need to eat food to provide our bodies with energy. We use the energy from fuels to keep our houses warm and our refrigerators cold. All around us, energy is constantly being changed from one form to another.

Electrical energy from overhead power cables can be used to power trains. The motors on the train convert the electrical energy into kinetic energy to move the train along.

A huge amount of energy is stored inside the atom. This nuclear energy has been used destructively in atom bombs.

Note

When a material is heated, it's particles move faster – they have more **kinetic energy**. Strictly speaking, heat energy is kinetic energy. To distinguish this internal kinetic energy from the kinetic energy of a moving mass we call it heat energy, or more properly, **internal energy**.

Chemical reactions nearly always involve an energy change. You are most likely to observe this as heat energy. Heat energy is often given out during chemical change, and the surroundings get hotter – the reaction is **exothermic**. Sometimes heat energy is taken in by chemicals and the surroundings become cooler – this is an **endothermic** reaction. In combustion reactions, energy may be given out as light and sound as well as heat. In cells, chemical energy is converted into electrical energy.

The changes in heat energy during chemical reactions can give useful information about what is happening during the reaction in terms of the

More chemical ideas

Note

Chemists measure energy in joules (symbol J) or kilojoules (symbol kJ).

1000 J = 1 kJ

chemical bonds being broken and formed. The amount of energy provided by foods is useful to know, and a value of how many kilojoules are available in 100 g of the food often appears on the packaging. It is also useful to know how much energy is released when a measured amount of a fuel is burned.

What energy changes occur when water is heated?

Some of the energy changes involved in heating water are shown in figure 1.

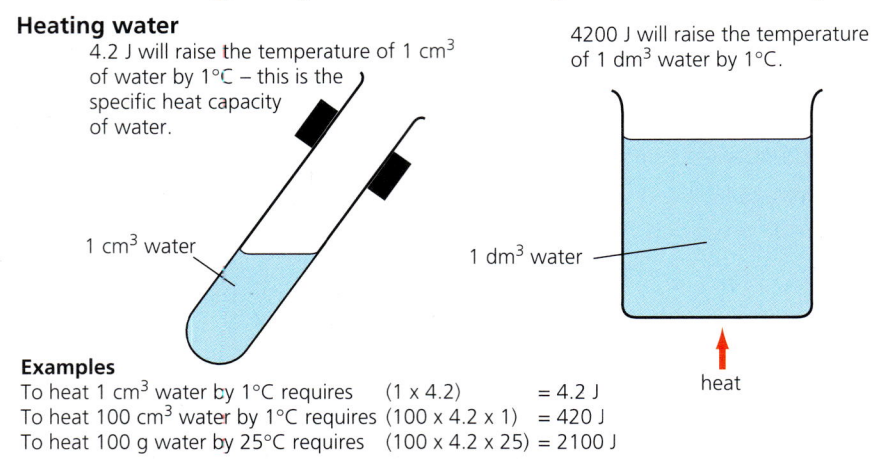

Figure 1

Note

The density of water at room temperature is 1 g/cm^3. This means that the mass in grams of a certain volume of water is the same as the volume. For example, 100 cm^3 water has a mass of 100 g. Since it is often easier to measure the volume of water than its mass, these numbers can be used interchangeably.

Heating water

4.2 J will raise the temperature of 1 cm^3 of water by 1°C – this is the specific heat capacity of water.

4200 J will raise the temperature of 1 dm^3 water by 1°C.

1 cm^3 water

1 dm^3 water

heat

Examples
To heat 1 cm^3 water by 1°C requires   (1 × 4.2)   = 4.2 J
To heat 100 cm^3 water by 1°C requires (100 × 4.2 × 1)   = 420 J
To heat 100 g water by 25°C requires   (100 × 4.2 × 25) = 2100 J

In the example in figure 1 a given mass of water is heated through a known temperature rise. This can be summed up as:

Energy change (J) = mass of water (in grams) × 4.2 × temperature change

WORKED EXAMPLE

How much heat energy is needed to raise the temperature of 200 cm^3 of water from 15°C to 45°C?

Energy needed =   mass of water   ×   4.2   ×   temperature change
              =   200   ×   4.2   ×   (45 − 15)
              =   25 200 J or 25.2 kJ

1. Give an example of an everyday process that is exothermic and one that is endothermic. Say why each process is important.
2. Calculate the amount of energy needed to heat:
   a 100 g water from 15°C to 25°C
   b 250 g water from 20°C to 90°C
   c 1 dm^3 water from 30°C to 50°C
   d 500 cm^3 water from 50°C to 100°C
(specific heat capacity of water = 4.2 J/g/°C).

What types of reaction are exothermic?

Acids and alkalis react together in a neutralisation reaction. As well as new substances being formed, the temperature in the solution involved rises. The heat energy given out in an exothermic reaction can be shown as:

Δ	H	$=$	$-$	x	kJ
'delta' means 'a change'	stands for heat energy		indicates an exothermic reaction: heat is given out	the amount of energy given out	

The amount of energy given out in a particular chemical reaction is often shown after the equation as follows:

$$HCl(aq) + NaOH(aq) \rightarrow NaCl(aq) + H_2O(l) \quad \Delta H = -55 \text{ kJ}$$

WORKED EXAMPLE

When 500 cm^3 of dilute hydrochloric acid (2 M) and 500 cm^3 dilute sodium hydroxide (2 M) react the temperature rises from 15°C to 30°C. How much energy has been given out?

word equation: hydrochloric acid + sodium hydroxide → sodium chloride + water

500 cm^3 2 M   500 cm^3 2 M   1000 cm^3 1 M
(1 mole)   (1 mole)   (1 mole)

symbol equation: HCl(aq) + NaOH(aq) → NaCl(aq) + H$_2$O(l)

ionic equation: H$^+$(aq) + OH$^-$(aq) → H$_2$O(l)

(the sodium ions, Na$^+$, and the chloride ions, Cl$^-$, are spectator ions in this equation.)

Energy change = mass of water × 4.2 × temperature change
            = 1000 × 4.2 × (28 − 15)
            = 54 600 J = 55 kJ (approximately)

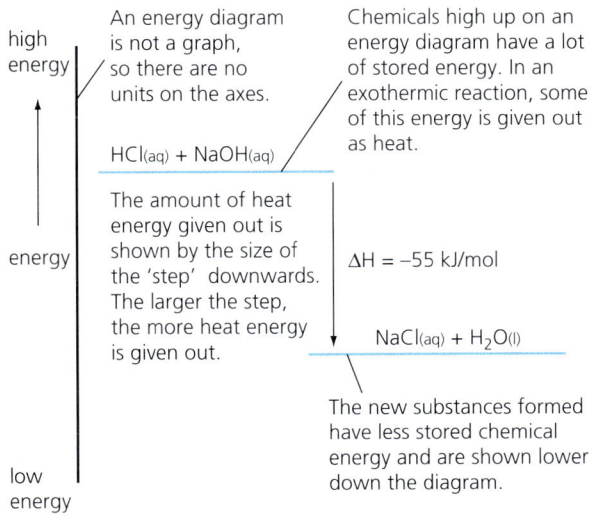

When one mole of an acid is neutralised by a base in this way, the energy change is called the **heat of neutralisation**. The changes involved in this reaction can be summarised by an **energy diagram** like the one in figure 2.

Many **hydration** reactions are exothermic. For example, when water is added to anhydrous copper (II) sulphate so much heat is generated that some of the water being added is boiled away as steam. When concentrated sulphuric acid is diluted with water, a great deal of heat energy is given out. For this process to be safe, the acid must be added to the water slowly, with stirring, so that the heat produced is safely dispersed.

Many **displacement** reactions are also exothermic. For example, zinc powder reacts with copper (II) sulphate solution to give out heat energy:

$$Zn(s) + CuSO_4(aq) \rightarrow ZnSO_4(aq) + Cu(s) \quad \Delta H = -210 \text{ kJ}$$

Figure 2

Energy diagram for a neutralisation reaction

high energy

An energy diagram is not a graph, so there are no units on the axes.

HCl(aq) + NaOH(aq)

The amount of heat energy given out is shown by the size of the 'step' downwards. The larger the step, the more heat energy is given out.

Chemicals high up on an energy diagram have a lot of stored energy. In an exothermic reaction, some of this energy is given out as heat.

$\Delta H = -55$ kJ/mol

NaCl(aq) + H$_2$O(l)

The new substances formed have less stored chemical energy and are shown lower down the diagram.

low energy

237

More chemical ideas

Figure 3 Many displacement reactions are exothermic.

A displacement reaction

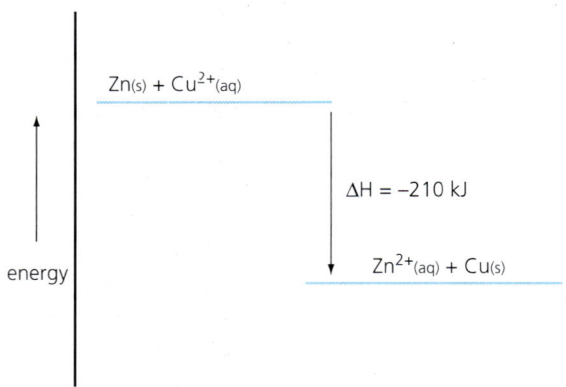

```
Zn(s) + Cu²⁺(aq) ───────────
                              │
                              │ ΔH = −210 kJ
                              ↓
                           Zn²⁺(aq) + Cu(s) ──────
energy
```

What happens in an endothermic reaction?

In an endothermic reaction heat energy is taken in. The amount of heat energy taken in by any endothermic reaction can be shown as follows:

$$\Delta H = + y \text{ kJ}$$
↑indicates an endothermic reaction: heat taken in

WORKED EXAMPLE

When 74.5 g of potassium chloride is dissolved in 1 dm³ water the temperature falls from 15°C to 11°C. What is the energy change?

The process can be summarised as:

KCl(s) + aq → KCl(aq)

('aq' shows that water is acting as a solvent here)

Energy change = mass of water × 4.2 × temperature change
             =   1000   × 4.2 ×   (15 − 11)
             =   16 800 kJ
             =   17 kJ (approximately)

The amount of energy taken in by this process can be shown next to the equation:

KCl(s) + aq → KCl(aq)   H = +17 kJ

Energy diagrams can also be drawn for endothermic reactions – an example is shown in figure 4.

238

Figure 4 An endothermic reaction.

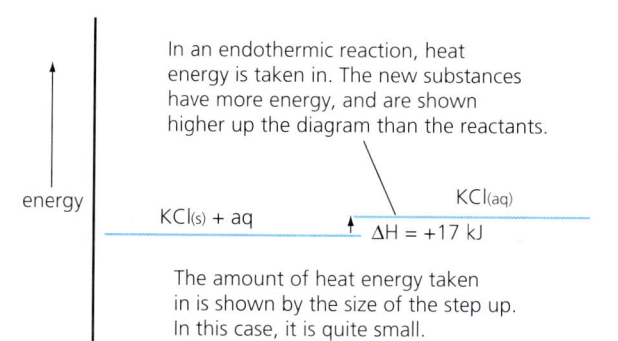

In an endothermic reaction, heat energy is taken in. The new substances have more energy, and are shown higher up the diagram than the reactants.

energy

KCl(s) + aq

KCl(aq)

ΔH = +17 kJ

The amount of heat energy taken in is shown by the size of the step up. In this case, it is quite small.

3 For each of the following equations draw energy diagrams (approximately to scale), showing the reactants, products and the ΔH values:
   a $C(s) + O_2(g) \rightarrow CO_2(g)$ ΔH = –394 kJ
   b $C_2H_5OH(l) + 3O_2(g) \rightarrow 2CO_2(g) + 3H_2O(l)$ ΔH = –1371 kJ
   c $KNO_3(s) + aq \rightarrow KNO_3(aq)$ ΔH = +35 kJ

4 When 0.5 moles of concentrated sulphuric acid was carefully added to water in a beaker to make 500 cm³ of solution, the temperature rose from 15°C to 32°C and the following reaction took place:
   $H_2SO_4(l) + aq \rightarrow H_2SO_4(aq)$
   a Was the reaction endothermic or exothermic?
   b Calculate the amount of energy transferred to the water.
   c Calculate the ΔH for this reaction. Is it positive or negative?
   d Draw an energy diagram for the reaction.

Summary of energy change

- Energy can be changed from one form into another.
- Most chemical reactions involve an energy change, usually in the form of heat.
- The specific heat capacity of water is 4.2 J/g/°C.
- Heat energy changes are given the sign ΔH.
- Exothermic reactions involve a temperature rise, have a negative ΔH sign and involve a 'step down' on an energy diagram.
- Endothermic reactions involve a temperature fall, have a positive ΔH and involve a 'step up' on an energy diagram.

18.2 Chemicals as fuels

What is a fuel?

A fuel is any substance that burns in oxygen to produce heat energy. People burn substances like coal, wood, oil or gas to keep warm or to cook food. Vehicles use fuels such as petrol or diesel, and planes burn kerosene. Another name for burning is combustion. Combustion reactions are always exothermic.

It is useful to be able to measure the heat energy produced by different fuels, so that their efficiency can be compared. One way of comparing liquid fuels in the laboratory is shown in figure 5.

The energy given out when 1 mole of a fuel burns in excess oxygen is known as the **heat of combustion**. Information from data tables shows that for ethanol ΔH = -1371 kJ/mol. This can be shown in the equation for the combustion of ethanol:

$$C_2H_5OH(l) + 3O_2(g) \rightarrow 2CO_2(g) + 3H_2O(g) \quad \Delta H = -1371 \text{ kJ}$$

More chemical ideas

Calculating heat of combustion

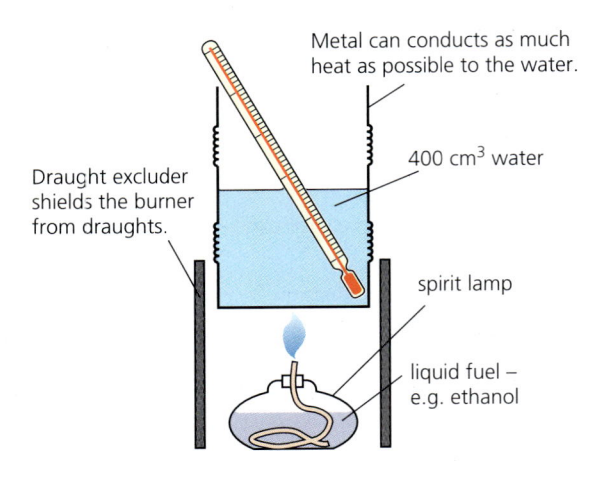

Metal can conducts as much heat as possible to the water.

Draught excluder shields the burner from draughts.

400 cm³ water

spirit lamp

liquid fuel – e.g. ethanol

Example results

Mass of burner + ethanol before experiment = 85.3 g
Mass of burner + ethanol after experiment = 83.8 g
Mass of ethanol burned = 1.5 g
Initial temperature of water = 15°C
Final temperature of water = 34°C
Temperature rise = 19°C

M_r of ethanol: $\underbrace{C_2}_{24} + \underbrace{H_5}_{5} + \underbrace{OH}_{16+1}$
$= 46$

Energy supplied to water = mass of water x 4.2 x temperature change
= 400 x 4.2 x 19
= 31920 J or 31.9 kJ

1.5 g ethanol burned to give 31.9 kJ
so 1 g would burn to give $\frac{31.9 \text{ kJ}}{1.5}$
and 46 g would burn to give $\frac{31.9 \times 46}{1.5}$

= 976 kJ

Figure 5

The value calculated in figure 5 is lower than that recorded in data tables since not all the heat from the spirit burner is transferred to the water. A metal can is used to conduct as much heat as possible to the water, and the burner is shielded from draughts, but even with these precautions some heat energy is lost to the surroundings and some is used up in heating the apparatus.

Table 1 Heats of combustion of some common fuels

Fuel	Formula	Combustion equation	ΔH combustion (kJ/mol)
hydrogen	H_2	$2H_2(g) + O_2(g) \rightarrow 2H_2O(g)$	−286
carbon	C	$C(s) + O_2(g) \rightarrow CO_2(g)$	−394
ethane	C_2H_6	$C_2H_6(g) + 3O_2(g) \rightarrow 2CO_2(g) + 3H_2O(g)$	−1560
ethanol	C_2H_5OH	$C_2H_5OH(l) + 3O_2(g) \rightarrow 2CO_2(g) + 3H_2O(l)$	−1371
butane	C_4H_{10}	$C_4H_{10}(g) + 6O_2(g) \rightarrow 4CO_2(g) + 5H_2O(g)$	−2877
octane	C_8H_{18}	$C_8H_{18}(l) + 12O_2(g) \rightarrow 8CO_2(g) + 9H_2O(g)$	−5512

Are bonds broken or formed in chemical reactions?

Table 2 Some bond energies

Bond	Bond energy (kJ/mol)
H — H	436
C — C	348
C = C	612
O = O	496
C — H	412
O — H	463
C — O	360
C = O	743

The energy changes that happen during a reaction can be understood by thinking about the chemical bonds that are being broken and formed. For example, when ethane burns in oxygen, the following exothermic reaction occurs:

$$C_2H_6(g) + 3O_2(g) \rightarrow 2CO_2(g) + 3H_2O(g) \quad \Delta H = -1560 \text{ kJ}$$

In a chemical reaction, the reactants are used up and new products are formed. For this to happen, the bonds holding the atoms together in the reactant molecules must be broken and new bonds must form to make the products. Breaking bonds requires energy, and is therefore endothermic. As new bonds are formed energy is given out – forming bonds is therefore exothermic.

The bond energy is a measure of the energy needed to break a mole of a particular bond. Since energy is needed to break bonds, all these values will be positive.

The overall energy used or given out in a reaction can be calculated as shown in figure 6.

Figure 6 **Calculating overall energy change when methane burns**

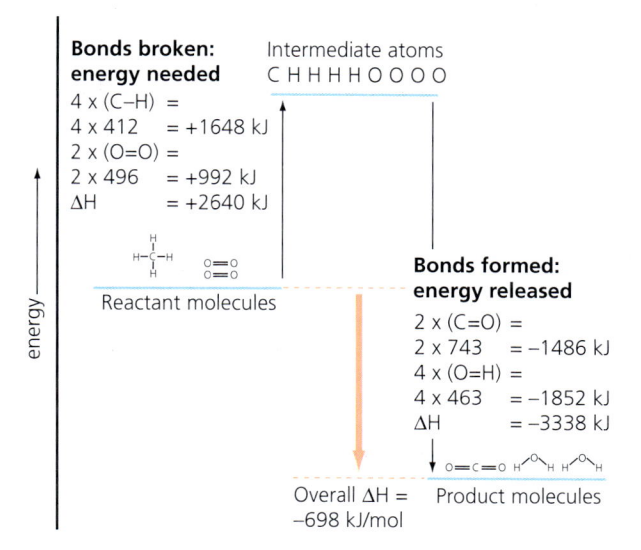

Bonds broken: energy needed
Intermediate atoms
C H H H H O O O O

4 × (C–H) =
4 × 412   = +1648 kJ
2 × (O=O) =
2 × 496   = +992 kJ
ΔH   = +2640 kJ

Reactant molecules

Bonds formed: energy released

2 × (C=O) =
2 × 743   = −1486 kJ
4 × (O=H) =
4 × 463   = −1852 kJ
ΔH   = −3338 kJ

Overall ΔH = −698 kJ/mol

Product molecules

---

5 Give one example of a fuel that is:

   a solid
   b liquid
   c gas.

   Suggest a suitable use for each example you give.

6 The fire triangle shows the three conditions that must be met before combustion can take place.

   Use the fire triangle to explain why the following precautions should be taken if a fire starts.

   a Turn off all gas supplies.
   b Cover a small fire with a wet cloth or blanket.
   c Close all doors and windows.

Summary of chemicals as fuels

- A fuel is a substance that burns in oxygen, giving out heat energy.
- Combustion, or burning, is always exothermic.
- The heat of combustion of a fuel is the energy given out when 1 mol is completely burned in oxygen.
- Energy is needed to break bonds.
- Energy is released when bonds are formed.

More chemical ideas

EXAMINATION style questions

1 Two alternatives for fossil fuels that are being investigated are hydrogen and methanol. The following table gives details of these fuels.

Fuel	Formula	Melting point (°C)	Boiling point (°C)	Heat of combustion (kJ/mol)
hydrogen	H_2	−259	−253	−290
methanol	CH_3OH	−98	65	−730

   a Suggest one advantage of using methanol rather than hydrogen as a fuel in cars.
   b Calculate the heat energy that would be released by burning 1 g of each fuel.

2 An experiment to measure the heat of combustion of ethanol was carried out using the apparatus shown opposite.

The following results were obtained:
Mass of crucible + ethanol at start = 35.74 g
Mass of crucible + ethanol at end = 34.82 g
Initial temperature of water = 15°C
Final temperature of water = 25°C

The specific heat capacity of water is 4.2 J/g/°C.
   a What is the relative molar mass of ethanol, C_2H_5OH?
   b Calculate the amount of energy taken in by the water.
   c How much energy is given out by burning 1 mol of ethanol?
   d Why was a copper container used in this experiment?
   e In tables of data, the value given for the heat of combustion of ethanol is greater than that calculated in **c**. Suggest a reason for this.

3 The table below shows the heat of combustion of some members of the homologous series of alcohols.

Name	Formula	Heat of combustion (kJ/mol)
methanol	CH_3OH	−715
ethanol	C_2H_5OH	−1371
propanol		−2010
butanol	$C_4H_{10}OH$	−2673
pentanol		

   a Write down the formulae for propanol and pentanol.
   b Plot a graph of the heat of combustion (*y* axis) against the number of carbon atoms in each alcohol (*x* axis).
   c Use your graph to predict the heat of combustion of pentanol.
   d Suggest two reasons why some alcohols may be suitable alternatives to fossil fuels.

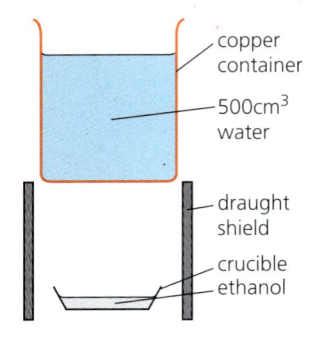

Rates of reaction

19

Learning objectives

By the end of this chapter you should be able to:
- **describe** ways of following a reaction
- **relate** rate of reaction and time
- **interpret** graphs of reaction rates
- **explain** how the rate of a reaction can be altered
- **explain** the difference between a catalyst and an enzyme

19.1 Following reaction rates

How fast do reactions proceed?

Note

Reaction rate and time are inversely proportional to each other. This can be written:

rate $\propto \dfrac{1}{\text{time}}$

Physical and chemical processes can happen at very different rates. The **rate** of a chemical reaction is a measure of how fast it is happening. If the reaction rate is low (that is, the reaction is slow), it will take a long time to finish. If a reaction proceeds quickly, the rate of reaction is high and will be completed in a short time. Reaction rate and time are inversely proportional, so a fast reaction will take a short time and a slow reaction will take a long time. Rusting, for example, usually happens quite slowly, but an explosion is very rapid. Rates can be measured by noting either how rapidly the reactants are being used up or how quickly the products are being formed.

How can you follow the rate of a reaction?

A series of measurements must be made at certain time intervals. What you measure depends on the process being studied.
- If a gas is being given off measure mass, gas volume or pressure.
- If an acid is being formed or used up measure changes in pH.
- If there is a colour change follow it with a colorimeter.

243

More chemical ideas

Figure 1 A reaction can be followed in a number of ways.

Measuring gas volume

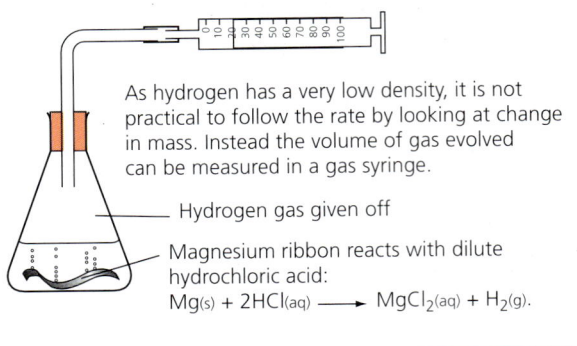

As hydrogen has a very low density, it is not practical to follow the rate by looking at change in mass. Instead the volume of gas evolved can be measured in a gas syringe.

Hydrogen gas given off

Magnesium ribbon reacts with dilute hydrochloric acid:
Mg(s) + 2HCl(aq) ⟶ MgCl$_2$(aq) + H$_2$(g).

Time (seconds)	0	10	20	30	40	50	60	70	80	90	100
Gas volume (cm^3)	0	5	14	27	42	57	72	82	88	90	90

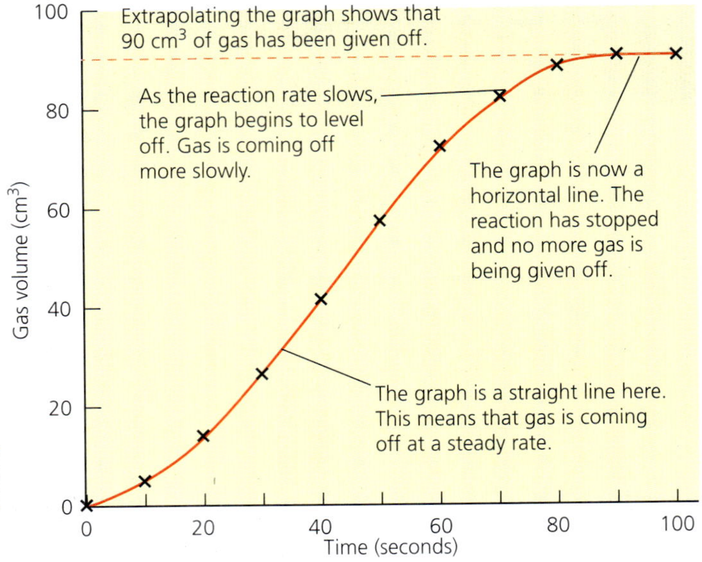

Extrapolating the graph shows that 90 cm^3 of gas has been given off.

As the reaction rate slows, the graph begins to level off. Gas is coming off more slowly.

The graph is now a horizontal line. The reaction has stopped and no more gas is being given off.

The graph is a straight line here. This means that gas is coming off at a steady rate.

Measuring change in mass

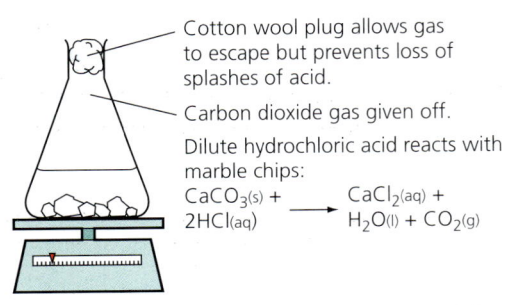

Cotton wool plug allows gas to escape but prevents loss of splashes of acid.

Carbon dioxide gas given off.

Dilute hydrochloric acid reacts with marble chips:
CaCO$_3$(s) + 2HCl(aq) ⟶ CaCl$_2$(aq) + H$_2$O(l) + CO$_2$(g)

As carbon dioxide is quite dense it is possible to follow the reaction rate by looking at the loss in mass as the gas escapes.

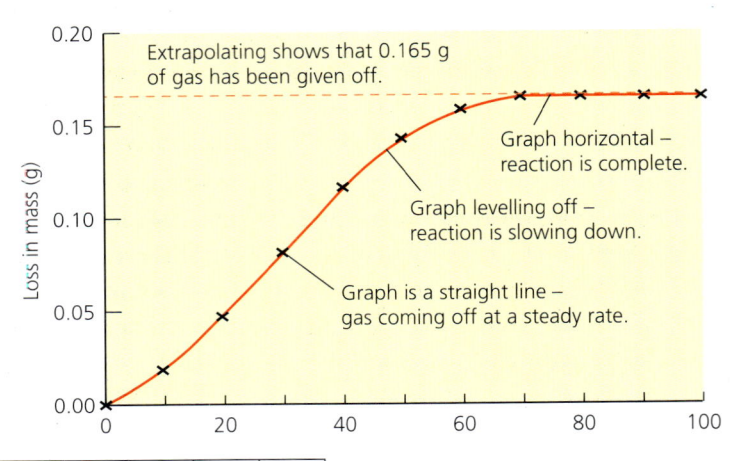

Time (seconds)	0	10	20	30	40	50	60	70	80	90	100
Loss in mass (g)	0	0.018	0.048	0.081	0.116	0.143	0.158	0.165	0.165	0.165	0.165

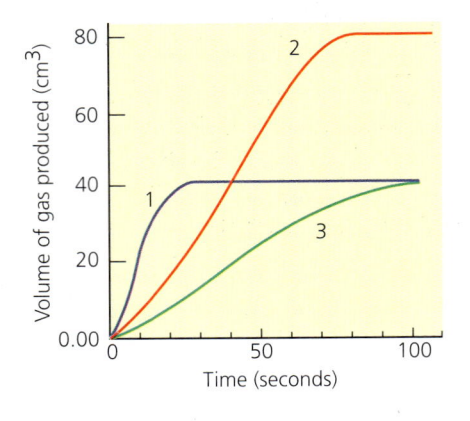

Extrapolating shows that 0.165 g of gas has been given off.

Graph horizontal – reaction is complete.

Graph levelling off – reaction is slowing down.

Graph is a straight line – gas coming off at a steady rate.

1 The graph shows the results of three experiments to follow the reaction between magnesium and dilute hydrochloric acid.
   a Which experiment had the fastest initial rate of reaction?
   b Which experiment produced the greatest final volume of gas?
   c Which experiment used acid with the greatest concentration?
   Give reasons for your answers.

2 Explain briefly the difference between *time* and *rate* in a chemical reaction.

3 Suggest one change in each reaction that could be measured to follow its rate:
   a HCl(aq) + NaOH(aq) → NaCl(aq) + H$_2$O(l)
   b 2Na$_2$S$_2$O$_3$(aq) + I$_2$(aq) → Na$_2$S$_4$O$_6$(aq) + 2NaI(aq)
   c MgCO$_3$(s) + 2HNO$_3$(aq) → Mg(NO$_3$)$_2$(aq) + H$_2$O(l) + CO$_2$(g)

Summary of following reaction rates

- The rates at which physical and chemical processes occur vary.
- Rate and time are inversely proportional to each other – a reaction with a fast rate happens in a short time, and vice versa.
- To follow rate of reaction, some change must be measured at various time intervals.
- Graphs are helpful in understanding changes in reaction rate.

19.2 Factors affecting reaction rates

How does temperature alter reaction rate?

One of the most effective ways of altering the rate of a chemical reaction is to change the temperature. A suitable illustration of this is the reaction between sodium thiosulphate and dilute hydrochloric acid, shown in figure 2.

As temperature is increased, the particles present have more energy. This has two effects:

1. The particles move around faster and collide more often – this slightly increases the reaction rate.
2. Because the particles have more energy, any collisions are more likely to result in the particles reacting – this has a considerable effect on reaction rate.

Effect of temperature on reaction rate

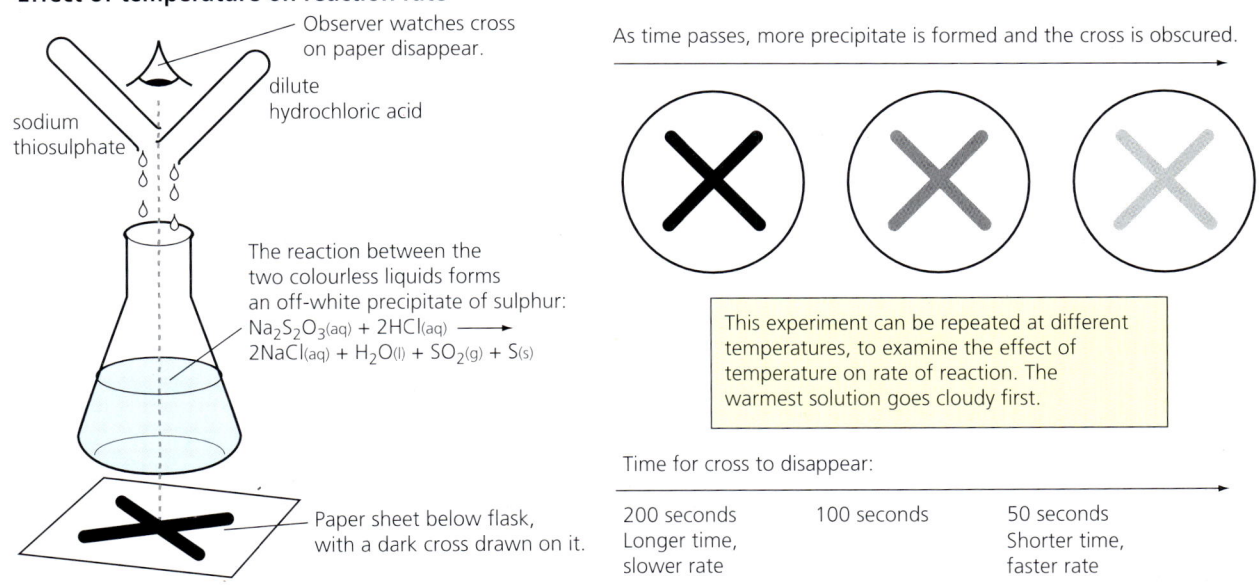

- Observer watches cross on paper disappear.
- sodium thiosulphate
- dilute hydrochloric acid
- The reaction between the two colourless liquids forms an off-white precipitate of sulphur:
  $Na_2S_2O_3(aq) + 2HCl(aq) \longrightarrow 2NaCl(aq) + H_2O(l) + SO_2(g) + S(s)$
- Paper sheet below flask, with a dark cross drawn on it.

As time passes, more precipitate is formed and the cross is obscured.

This experiment can be repeated at different temperatures, to examine the effect of temperature on rate of reaction. The warmest solution goes cloudy first.

Time for cross to disappear:

| 200 seconds | 100 seconds | 50 seconds |
| Longer time, slower rate | | Shorter time, faster rate |

Figure 2 Temperature has a considerable effect on reaction rate. Increasing the temperature by just 10°C can double a reaction's rate.

More chemical ideas

What effects do concentration and pressure have on reaction rate?

The more concentrated a solution, the faster the reaction rate. You can see an example of this in figure 3. When a solution is more concentrated there are more particles of solute present in the same volume of solution. The particles will therefore be closer together and more likely to collide and react. When the solution is diluted with more water the solute particles are more spaced out and so are less likely to collide and react.

Effect of concentration on reaction rate

Reacting magnesium ribbon and dilute hydrochloric acid: $Mg(s) + 2HCl(aq) \longrightarrow MgCl_2(aq) + H_2(g)$

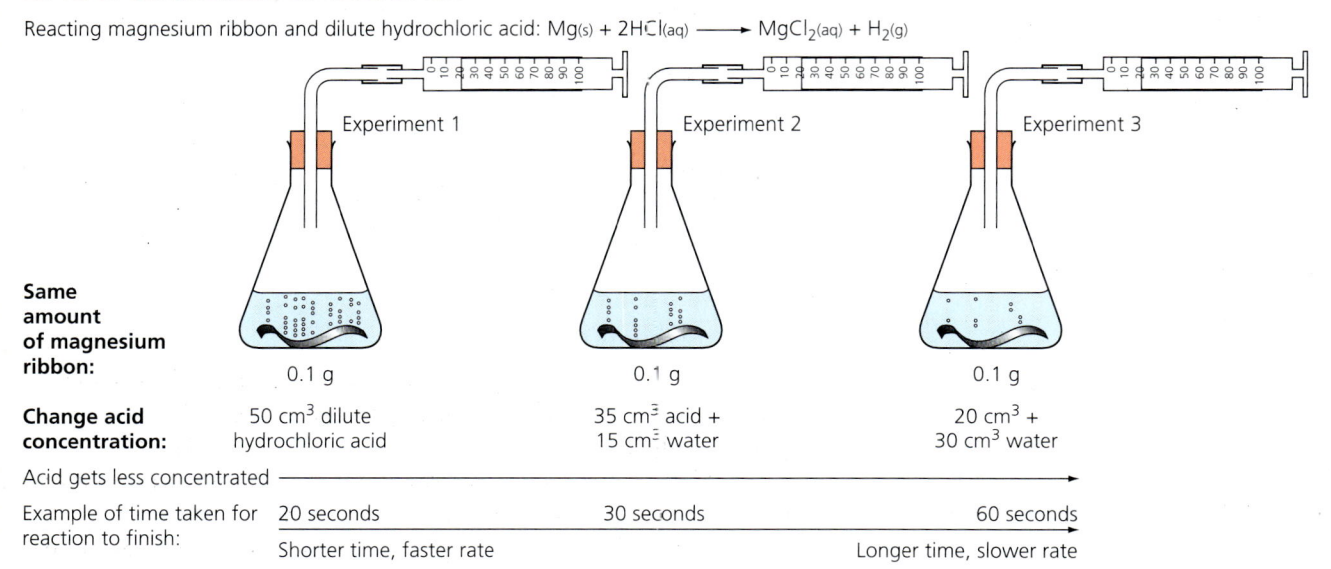

	Experiment 1	Experiment 2	Experiment 3
Same amount of magnesium ribbon:	0.1 g	0.1 g	0.1 g
Change acid concentration:	50 cm³ dilute hydrochloric acid	35 cm³ acid + 15 cm³ water	20 cm³ + 30 cm³ water

Acid gets less concentrated ⟶

Example of time taken for reaction to finish:	20 seconds	30 seconds	60 seconds
	Shorter time, faster rate		Longer time, slower rate

Figure 3

Altering the pressure of gases reacting together has an effect similar to that of changing the concentration of a solution. Increasing the pressure compresses the particles, so that they are closer together and collide more frequently. This increases the reaction rate.

How does surface area affect rate of reaction?

When a solid reacts with a liquid or a gas, the size of the particles of solid will affect the rate of the reaction.

Larger lumps have a smaller surface area than the same mass of smaller pieces. Powders contain small particles of solid, which have a very large surface area and can therefore react very quickly.

Rates of reaction

Effect of surface area on reaction rate

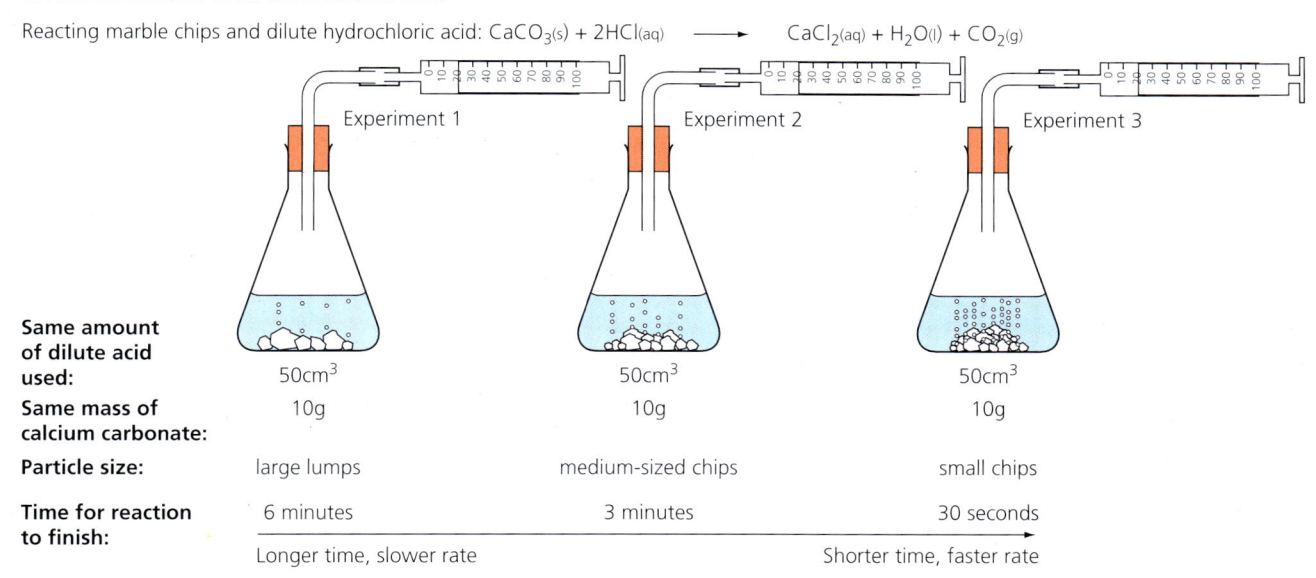

Reacting marble chips and dilute hydrochloric acid: $CaCO_{3}(s) + 2HCl(aq) \rightarrow CaCl_{2}(aq) + H_{2}O(l) + CO_{2}(g)$

	Experiment 1	Experiment 2	Experiment 3
Same amount of dilute acid used:	50cm³	50cm³	50cm³
Same mass of calcium carbonate:	10g	10g	10g
Particle size:	large lumps	medium-sized chips	small chips
Time for reaction to finish:	6 minutes	3 minutes	30 seconds

Longer time, slower rate → Shorter time, faster rate

Figure 4

Why do some reactions need a catalyst?

Catalysts speed up the rate of a chemical reaction without themselves being used up or chemically changed. For example, hydrogen peroxide is a colourless liquid, usually used as an aqueous solution. Under normal circumstances, it is very stable and breaks down only slowly. However, when a small amount of manganese dioxide powder is added, the solution quickly breaks down into water and oxygen gas is given off in an exothermic reaction:

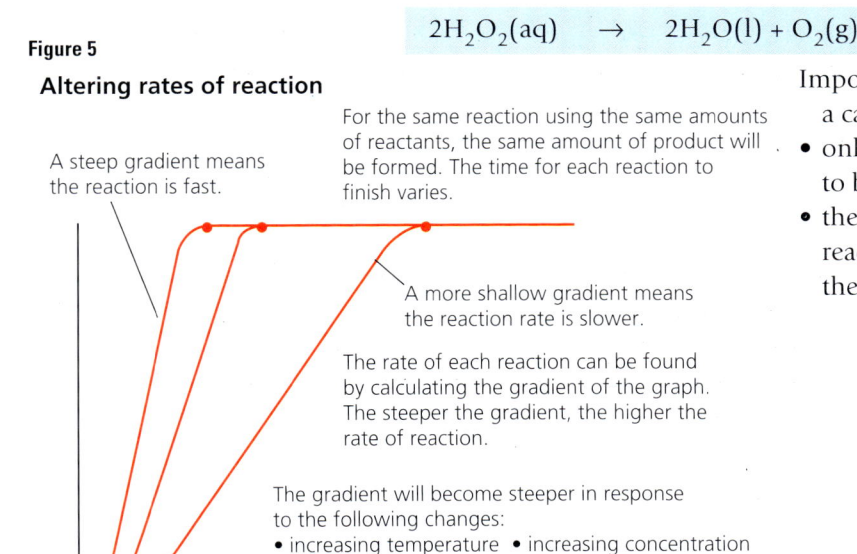

$$2H_{2}O_{2}(aq) \rightarrow 2H_{2}O(l) + O_{2}(g)$$

Figure 5

Altering rates of reaction

A steep gradient means the reaction is fast.

A more shallow gradient means the reaction rate is slower.

For the same reaction using the same amounts of reactants, the same amount of product will be formed. The time for each reaction to finish varies.

The rate of each reaction can be found by calculating the gradient of the graph. The steeper the gradient, the higher the rate of reaction.

The gradient will become steeper in response to the following changes:
- increasing temperature
- increasing concentration
- increasing pressure
- increasing surface area
- adding a catalyst

Important points about the action of a catalyst:
- only a small amount is needed for it to be effective
- the catalyst is not used up during the reaction – the same mass is present at the start and end.

247

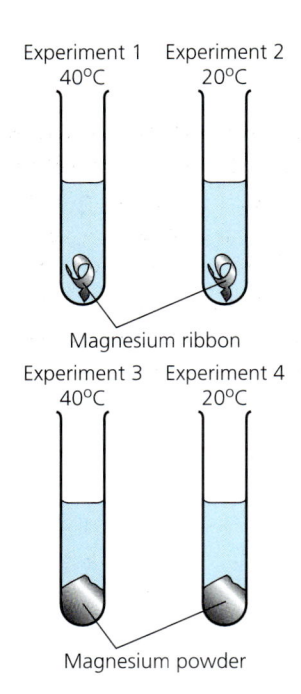

More chemical ideas

Experiment 1 Experiment 2
    40°C   20°C

Magnesium ribbon

Experiment 3 Experiment 4
    40°C   20°C

Magnesium powder

4 The diagrams show the reaction between magnesium ribbon and dilute hydrochloric acid under four different conditions. Which of these would have the fastest reaction rate?

5 The following table lists a series of experiments carried out on the reaction between an excess of marble chips and dilute hydrochloric acid.

Experiment	Marble	Acid
1	20 g large marble chips	40 cm^3 2 M acid
2	20 g small marble chips	20 cm^3 4 M acid
3	20 g powdered marble	20 cm^3 4 M acid
4	20 g small marble chips	80 cm^3 2 M acid

a Which experiment produced the greatest final volume of gas?
b Which experiment had the fastest initial reaction rate?

How do catalysts work?

Chemical reactions very often need energy to start them off. For example, hydrogen will burn in oxygen, but normally only when energy (in the form of a flame) is provided to start the reaction. The minimum energy needed for a reaction to take place is known as the **activation energy**. It acts as a kind of 'energy barrier' – unless the particles reacting have the energy to 'get over' this barrier, a reaction will not take place. A catalyst works by lowering the activation energy barrier. More particles then have the energy needed to react, and the reaction rate is increased.

The chemicals industry uses catalysts to make many large-scale manufacturing processes more economically viable. The Haber process uses finely powdered iron, the Contact process uses vanadium (V) oxide and a platinum/rhodium gauze is used in the manufacture of nitric acid. You will find details of these processes in Chapter 15, *Non-metals*.

Activation energy of burning hydrogen

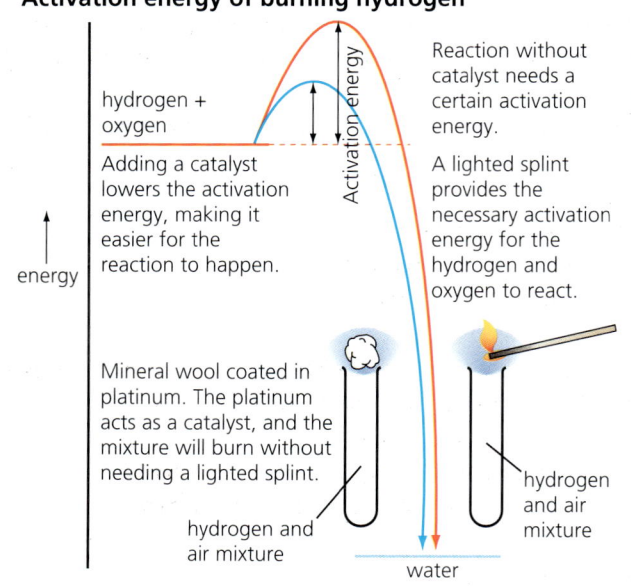

hydrogen + oxygen

Adding a catalyst lowers the activation energy, making it easier for the reaction to happen.

energy

Mineral wool coated in platinum. The platinum acts as a catalyst, and the mixture will burn without needing a lighted splint.

hydrogen and air mixture

Reaction without catalyst needs a certain activation energy.

A lighted splint provides the necessary activation energy for the hydrogen and oxygen to react.

hydrogen and air mixture

water

Figure 6 The action of a catalyst can be shown on an energy diagram.

Rates of reaction

What are enzymes?

The rates of the chemical reactions that occur in living things are controlled by biological catalysts known as **enzymes**. Enzymes are sensitive to the conditions under which the reaction occurs. An inorganic catalyst such as platinum will work over a wide temperature range, but most enzymes will only work over a narrow temperature range. There is often an optimum temperature at which they will function most effectively. Enzymes also will often catalyse only one or two reactions – they are **specific** to a particular reaction. This is in contrast to inorganic catalysts, which will catalyse a wide variety of reactions.

Summary of rates of reaction

- Increasing the temperature increases the rate of a reaction, because particles collide more frequently and with more energy.
- Increasing the concentration of solutions will increase reaction rate, because more particles are present in the same volume and will collide more often.
- Increasing the pressure of reactions involving gases increases the reaction rate, since the gas particles are closer together and collide more often.
- The smaller the particle size, the larger the surface area over which the reaction can occur, and the faster the reaction rate.
- Catalysts increase the rate of a reaction without themselves being used up or chemically changed.
- An enzyme is a biological catalyst.

EXAMINATION style questions

1 Hydrogen peroxide breaks down in the presence of a suitable catalyst as follows:

$$2H_2O_2(aq) \rightarrow 2H_2O(l) + O_2(g)$$

The gas produced can be collected and the reaction rate followed by measuring the volume of gas produced at various times. In the experiment described below, all measurements were made at room temperature and pressure (20°C).

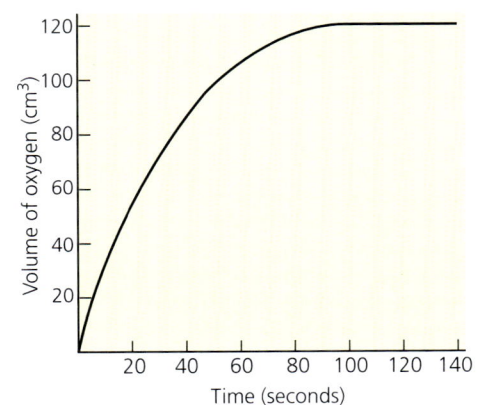

a Draw a fully labelled diagram of the apparatus that you could use to follow the rate of this reaction.

b Use the graph to find:
  i the final volume of oxygen gas formed
  ii the time taken for the reaction to be complete.

c Using the results from this experiment calculate:
  i the number of moles of oxygen gas produced
  ii the number of moles of hydrogen peroxide needed to produce this amount of oxygen
  iii the volume of 0.25 M hydrogen peroxide solution present at the start.

d On the graph, sketch the curve you might expect if:
  i the same volume and concentration of hydrogen peroxide were used at 40°C
  ii 40 cm³ water was added to the original solution at room temperature.

e What is a catalyst?

f Suggest a suitable catalyst for this experiment.

More chemical ideas

Time (seconds)	Volume CO$_2$ produced (cm^3)
0	0
10	8
20	28
30	57
40	78
50	87
60	90
70	90

Time (seconds)	Volume H$_2$ produced (cm^3)
0	0
20	27
40	49
60	68
80	83
100	93
120	99
140	100
160	100
180	100

2 A student studied the rate of the reaction between sodium carbonate and nitric acid:
$$Na_2CO_3(s) + 2HNO_3(aq) \rightarrow 2NaNO_3(aq) + H_2O(l) + CO_2(g)$$
The results are shown in the table.
  a Plot a graph of gas volume (y axis) against time (x axis).
  b When was the reaction rate the fastest:
    i 10 seconds?
    ii 25 seconds?
    iii 45 seconds?
    iv 65 seconds?
  c Use your graph to find the volume of gas produced after:
    i 25 seconds
    ii 45 seconds.
  d After how long did the reaction stop?
  e What was the final volume of gas produced?
  f Suggest two ways of increasing the rate of this reaction.

3 Magnesium ribbon reacts with dilute hydrochloric acid to produce a solution of a salt and hydrogen gas. In an experiment, pieces of magnesium ribbon were added to an excess of dilute acid and the gas volume measured at various times. The results are shown in the table.
  a Write a balanced symbol equation for this reaction.
  b Plot the results on a graph of gas volume (y axis) against time (x axis).
  c Use your graph to find:
    i the volume of gas formed after 50 seconds
    ii the time taken for the reaction to be completed.
  d On your graph, sketch the result you might expect using the same volume of a more concentrated acid.
  e What change would you expect if the magnesium ribbon were replaced with the same mass of magnesium powder? Explain your answer.

Reversible reactions

20

Learning objectives

By the end of this chapter you should be able to:
- **describe** some reversible physical and chemical processes
- **distinguish** between open and closed systems
- **explain** 'dynamic equilibrium'
- **describe** how changes of conditions affect a reaction in equilibrium
- **recall** Le Chatelier's principle

Figure 1 Some reactions tend to proceed in one direction only but others can be reversed quite easily.

Many chemical reactions are 'one-way' processes. The substances present at the start react together to form new products and the reaction then ends. Some other physical and chemical processes can be reversed quite readily. These are known as **reversible reactions**.

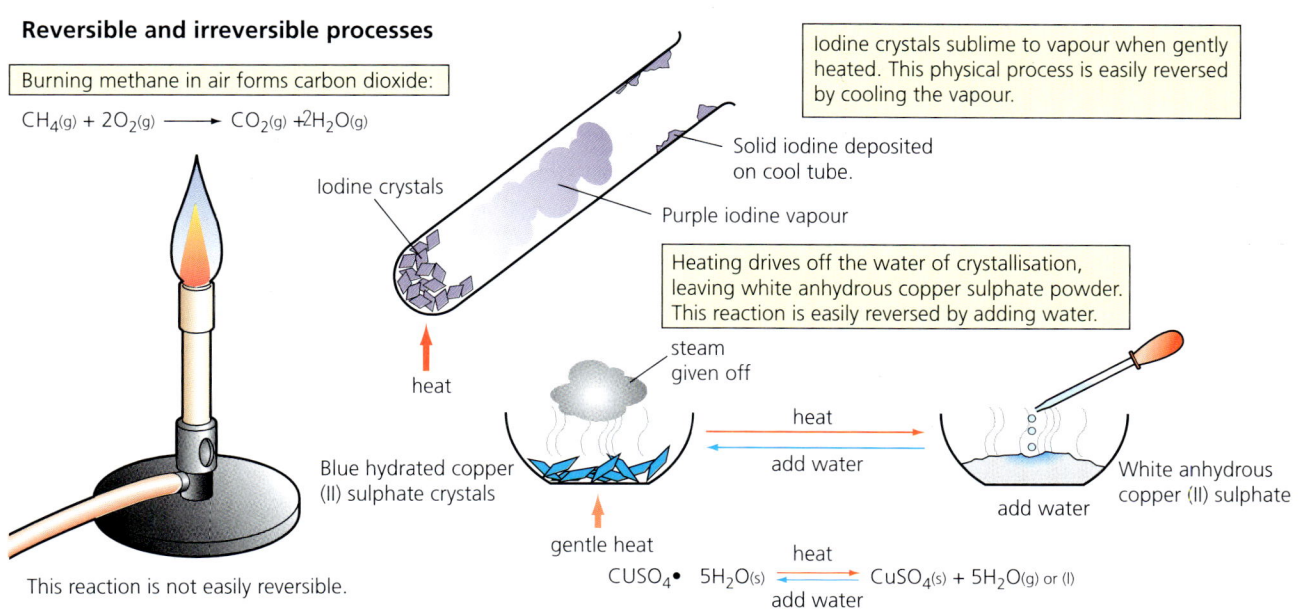

Reversible and irreversible processes

Burning methane in air forms carbon dioxide:

$$CH_4(g) + 2O_2(g) \longrightarrow CO_2(g) + 2H_2O(g)$$

This reaction is not easily reversible.

Iodine crystals sublime to vapour when gently heated. This physical process is easily reversed by cooling the vapour.

Heating drives off the water of crystallisation, leaving white anhydrous copper sulphate powder. This reaction is easily reversed by adding water.

$$CuSO_4 \cdot 5H_2O(s) \underset{\text{add water}}{\overset{\text{heat}}{\rightleftarrows}} CuSO_4(s) + 5H_2O(g) \text{ or } (l)$$

What are open and closed systems?

If ammonium chloride is heated it breaks down to ammonia gas and hydrogen chloride:

$$NH_4Cl(s) \rightarrow NH_3(g) + HCl(g)$$

More chemical ideas

If ammonia and hydrogen chloride vapours are allowed to react in cool conditions they form solid ammonium chloride:

$$NH_3(g) + HCl(g) \rightarrow NH_4Cl(s)$$

When either reaction is allowed to happen in a test tube or basin that is open to the air, the reactants will form products quite readily and the process will be complete. The reaction is said to take place in an **open system**.

If the same reaction is carefully carried out in a sealed container so that the products remain in contact with the reactants, the reaction is said to take place in a **closed system**. When this occurs, two reactions will happen at the same time. This is shown by the $\rightleftharpoons$ sign in place of the usual arrow.

Figure 2 Open and closed systems

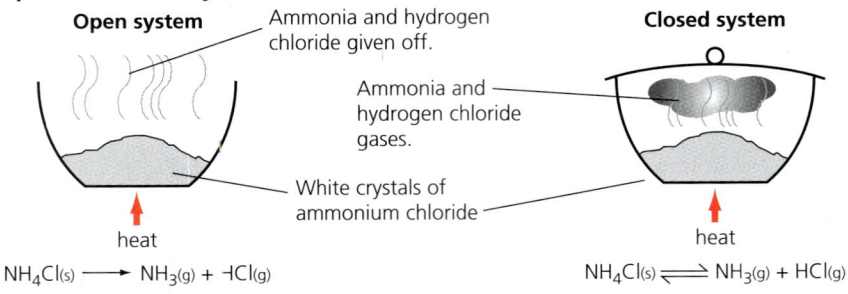

Open system — Ammonia and hydrogen chloride given off.

Closed system — Ammonia and hydrogen chloride gases.

White crystals of ammonium chloride

heat
$NH_4Cl(s) \rightarrow NH_3(g) + HCl(g)$

heat
$NH_4Cl(s) \rightleftharpoons NH_3(g) + HCl(g)$

The reaction $NH_4Cl(s) \rightarrow NH_3(g) + HCl(g)$ is known as the **forward reaction** – the reactants on the left-hand side of the arrow are reacting to form the products on the right-hand side.
The reaction $NH_3(g) + HCl(g) \rightarrow NH_4Cl(s)$ is the **back reaction** – the products on the right-hand side of the equation are reacting to form the reactants on the left-hand side.

What is dynamic equilibrium?

When reversible reactions take place in a closed system, a **dynamic equilibrium** is set up. The word dynamic means 'moving'. Two processes are going on at the same time – the forward and back reactions. The word equilibrium means a 'state of balance'. At equilibrium the concentration of all substances present remains the same because the rates of the forward and back reactions are equal. An example of this is the chromate–dichromate reaction shown in figure 4.

Figure 3 If this girl runs up an escalator at the same rate as the stairs are moving down, she will stay in the same place. This is a dynamic equilibrium.

Reversible reactions

Equilibrium in the chromate–dichromate reaction

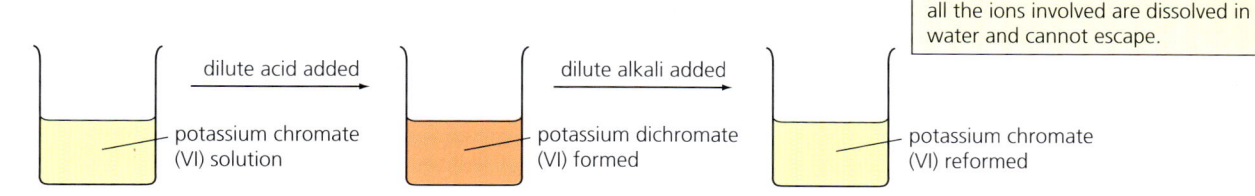

dilute acid added → potassium chromate (VI) solution → potassium dichromate (VI) formed

dilute alkali added → potassium chromate (VI) reformed

This acts as a closed system because all the ions involved are dissolved in water and cannot escape.

In a closed system, two processes are occurring at the same time:

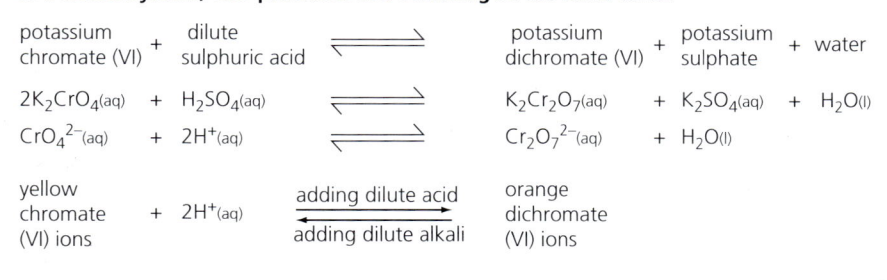

potassium chromate (VI) + dilute sulphuric acid ⇌ potassium dichromate (VI) + potassium sulphate + water

$2K_2CrO_4(aq) + H_2SO_4(aq) \rightleftharpoons K_2Cr_2O_7(aq) + K_2SO_4(aq) + H_2O(l)$

$CrO_4^{2-}(aq) + 2H^+(aq) \rightleftharpoons Cr_2O_7^{2-}(aq) + H_2O(l)$

yellow chromate (VI) ions + $2H^+(aq)$ ⇌ (adding dilute acid / adding dilute alkali) orange dichromate (VI) ions

Dilute acid increases the rate of the forward reaction, producing more $Cr_2O_7^{2-}$ ions. As more are formed, the rate of the back reaction also rises. Eventually the two rates become equal. Dilute alkali neutralises the hydrogen ions present and so slows the rate of the forward reaction. The back reaction continues and eventually the rates of the forward and back reactions become equal.

Figure 4 The reaction between potassium chromate and potassium dichromate is an example of dynamic equilibrium.

How do reaction conditions affect equilibrium?

The reaction conditions – concentration, temperature and pressure – can affect the position of an equilibrium. The way this happens is summed up in **Le Chatelier's principle**:

> When a constraint is placed on a system in equilibrium, then the system responds so as to nullify the effect of the constraint.

The 'constraint' could be a change in concentration, temperature or pressure. The constraint can be brought to nothing in several ways.

- **Increasing the concentration** of a substance leads to that substance being used up faster:

$$A + B \rightleftharpoons C + D$$

The rate of the forward reaction can be increased by adding more A and/or B or removing C and/or D. The rate of the back reaction can be increased by adding more C and/or D or removing A and/or B.

- **Increasing the temperature** favours the endothermic reaction, so that the temperature is reduced.

In exothermic reactions, increasing the temperature makes more A and B, decreasing it makes more C and D:

$$A + B \rightleftharpoons C + D \quad \Delta H = -x \text{ kJ}$$

In endothermic reactions,

$$A + B \rightleftharpoons C + D \quad \Delta H = +y \text{ kJ}$$

Increasing the temperature makes more C and D, decreasing it makes more A and B.

More chemical ideas

- **Increasing the pressure** favours the reaction that involves a decrease in volume, so that the pressure is reduced:

$$2A(g) + B(g) \rightleftharpoons C(g)$$

$\underbrace{2A(g) + B(g)}_{\text{3 moles}}$ ⇌ $\underbrace{C(g)}_{\text{1 mole}}$

increased pressure →
decreased pressure ←

How is Le Chatelier's principle applied in industry?

Some processes used in the manufacture of chemicals involve reversible reactions. By applying some of the factors that can affect reversible reactions the maximum economic yield can be obtained. For example, in the Haber process nitrogen and hydrogen are heated under pressure in the presence of an iron catalyst (see Chapter 15, *Non-metals*, for details of the Haber process). This reaction is reversible:

$$N_2(g) + 3H_2(g) \rightleftharpoons 2NH_3(g) \quad \Delta H = -92 \text{ kJ}$$

The forward reaction is exothermic. Heat could be considered as a 'product' of the reaction. In this case the equation could be written like this:

$$N_2(g) + 3H_2(g) \rightleftharpoons 2NH_3(g) + 92 \text{ kJ}$$

decreasing temperature →
increasing temperature ←

In the back reaction, 92 kJ of heat energy are 'added' to two moles of ammonia molecules, which then split up into nitrogen and hydrogen.

Le Chatelier's principle shows that adding heat energy will favour the back reaction and lowering the temperature will favour the forward reaction. So a high yield of ammonia would be obtained at a low temperature. In practice, the rate at which the ammonia is formed decreases as the temperature is lowered. A compromise or 'optimum' temperature (between 350°C and 500°C) is therefore used to keep the rate at which equilibrium is reached reasonable, but the temperature low enough to give a good yield of ammonia.

In reversible endothermic reactions the opposite applies – increasing the temperature will favour the forward reaction.

Pressure is also an important factor in the Haber process. Increasing the pressure of a gas has an effect similar to the increase in concentration of a solution – more particles are packed into the same volume. Particles therefore collide more frequently, and the rate of reaction increases. This is explained more fully in Chapter 19, *Rates of reaction*.

Reversible reactions

In the Haber process, there are four moles of gas on the left hand side of the equation, but only two on the right:

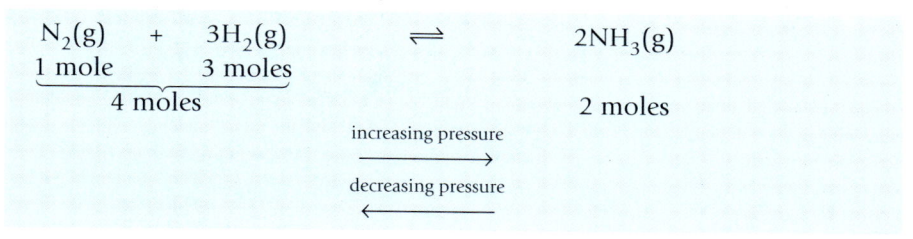

$$N_2(g) + 3H_2(g) \rightleftharpoons 2NH_3(g)$$

1 mole + 3 moles = 4 moles ⇌ 2 moles

increasing pressure →
decreasing pressure ←

If this reaction is carried out at constant pressure, the forward reaction involves four moles of gas 'shrinking' to two moles. In the back reaction, two moles of gas expand to four. Increasing the pressure of a reversible reaction that involves a volume change favours the reaction that involves a decrease in volume. In the Haber process, the higher the pressure, the greater the equilibrium yield of ammonia. However, the machinery and pipework needed for the equipment to function safely becomes very expensive and a compromise must be reached between using a pressure high enough to give a good yield, but not so high that the cost of plant is too expensive.

Pressure changes in reactions involving gases have an effect only when the numbers of moles on either side of the equation are different. When the numbers are equal, a change in pressure will not affect the position of an equilibrium. For example, when hydrogen and iodine are heated together, the following equilibrium is set up:

$$H_2(g) + I_2(g) \rightleftharpoons 2HI(g)$$

1 mole + 1 mole = 2 moles ⇌ 2 moles

Since there are two moles on the left of this equation and two on the right, increasing the pressure will increase the forward and back reaction rates equally. The overall concentrations of each product and reactant are the same. Another way of saying this is that the **position of equilibrium** is unchanged.

A **catalyst** increases the rate of both the forward and back reactions. The position of the equilibrium is not changed by the presence of a catalyst – the amount of products and reactants present at equilibrium is unaffected. However, a catalyst enables a reaction to come to equilibrium more quickly.

1 Which of the following examples are open systems and which are closed systems? Briefly explain your reasoning in each case.
   a A puddle of water outdoors on a warm sunny day.
   b An unopened bottle of a fizzy drink.
   c Sausages cooking on a barbecue.

More chemical ideas

2 In the Contact process, sulphur dioxide is reacted with oxygen in the air to form sulphur trioxide:
$2SO_2(g) + O_2(g) \rightleftharpoons 2SO_3(g)$ $\Delta H = -196$ kJ
Which of the following changes would increase the amount of sulphur trioxide formed at equilibrium?
 a An increase in the overall pressure.
 b Adding more oxygen.
 c Adding more sulphur trioxide.
 d Removing sulphur trioxide.
 e Decreasing the temperature.

Summary of reversible reactions

- A reaction that can go both ways is said to be reversible.
- An open system allows the products of a reaction to escape as they are formed.
- A closed system prevents products escaping, and thus allows a reversible reaction to go in both directions at the same time.
- In a dynamic equilibrium two reactions are going on at the same time – the forward and back reactions.
- The concentrations of reactants and products stay constant in a dynamic equilibrium, because the forward and back reactions are happening at the same rate.
- Changes in reaction conditions, such as concentration, temperature and sometimes pressure, can affect the position of an equilibrium.
- Le Chatelier's principle sums up the effect of changing reaction conditions for reversible processes.

EXAMINATION style questions

1 When bismuth (III) chloride is added to water a white precipitate is formed:
$BiCl_3(aq) + H_2O(l) \rightleftharpoons BiOCl(s) + 2HCl(aq)$
 a What does the $\rightleftharpoons$ sign signify?
 b Suggest one way of reducing the amount of white precipitate formed.
 c Explain why the method you have described reduces the amount of white precipitate.
 d How would adding sodium hydroxide solution to the equilibrium mixture affect the amount of precipitate? Explain your answer.

2 The graph below shows how the conditions under which the Haber process is carried out affect the yield of ammonia formed at equilibrium.
   a How is the yield of ammonia affected by an increase in temperature?
   b How is the yield affected by an increase in pressure?
   c Use the graph to predict the percentage yield of ammonia at 500°C and 250 atmospheres pressure.
   d A catalyst of finely divided iron is used in this process.
      i What is a catalyst?
      ii Why is the iron finely divided?
      iii What effect, if any, does the presence of the catalyst have on the amount of ammonia formed at equilibrium? Explain your answer.

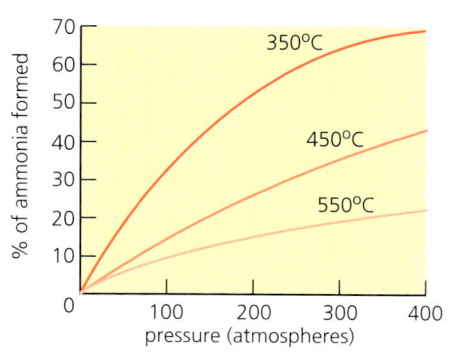

3 Chlorine can be made to react with iodine by passing chlorine gas over some iodine crystals in a fume cupboard. The apparatus used is shown in the figure opposite.
   The reaction takes place in two stages:
   Stage 1: Iodine reacts with the chlorine to form a dark brown liquid called iodine monochloride. This reaction is exothermic.
   $$I_2(s) + Cl_2(g) \rightarrow 2ICl(l)$$
   Stage 2: As more chlorine is passed in, yellow crystals of iodine trichloride appear on the walls of the tube.
   $$ICl(l) + Cl_2(g) \rightleftharpoons ICl_3(s)$$
   If the supply of chlorine is disconnected and the tube turned upside down to pour out the chlorine, the yellow crystals disappear and the brown liquid is reformed. Stage 2 can be repeated many times by adding chlorine, then pouring it away.
   a Why must this experiment be carried out in a fume cupboard?
   b Describe what happens to the forward and back reactions of the equilibrium in stage 2 when chlorine is added and when it is removed.
   c In stage 1, calculate the volume of chlorine gas (at STP) needed to react with iodine to form 0.02 moles of iodine monochloride.

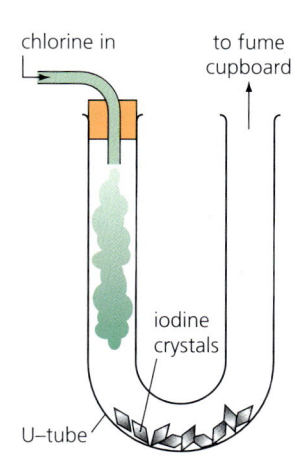

Properties of the elements in alphabetical order

Element	Symbol	Atomic number	Relative atomic mass A_r	MP (°C)	BP (°C)	Density (kg/m³)
Actinium	Ac	89	227	1197	3327	10060
Aluminium	Al	13	27	659	2247	2700
Antimony	Sb	51	122	630	1637	6700
Argon	Ar	18	40	−189	−186	1.66
Arsenic	As	33	75		sublimes at 613	5776
Astatine	At	85	210	300	350	–
Barium	Ba	56	137	710	1637	3600
Beryllium	Be	4	9	1283	2487	1800
Bismuth	Bi	83	209	272	1559	9800
Boron	B	5	11	2027	3927	2500
Bromine	Br	35	80	−7	58	3100
Cadmium	Cd	48	112	321	765	8650
Caesium	Cs	55	133	29	685	1870
Calcium	Ca	20	40	850	1492	1540
Carbon (diamond)	C	6	12	3550	4830	3500
Cerium	Ce	58	140	797	3000	6700
Chlorine	Cl	17	35.5	−101	−34	3.21
Chromium	Cr	24	52	1903	2642	7200
Cobalt	Co	27	59	1495	2877	8800
Copper	Cu	29	64	1083	2582	8930
Dysprosium	Dy	66	163	1407	1407	8500
Erbium	Er	68	167	1497	2600	9000
Europium	Eu	63	152	820	1450	5200
Fluorine	F	9	19	−220	−188	1.7
Francium	Fr	87	223	27	677	–
Gadolinium	Gd	64	157	1312	3000	7900
Gallium	Ga	31	70	30	2237	5905
Germanium	Ge	32	73	937	2827	5400
Gold	Au	79	197	1063	2707	19300
Hafnium	Hf	72	178	2222	5227	13300
Helium	He	2	4	−270	−269	0.17
Holmium	Ho	67	165	1470	2300	8800
Hydrogen	H	1	1	−259	−253	0.08
Indium	In	49	115	156	2047	7300
Iodine	I	53	127	114	183	4950
Iridium	Ir	77	192	2454	4127	22420
Iron	Fe	26	56	1539	2887	7870
Krypton	Kr	36	84	−157	−153	3.46
Lanthanum	La	57	139	920	3367	6150
Lead	Pb	82	207	328	1757	11340
Lithium	Li	3	7	181	1331	534
Lutetium	Lu	71	175	1700	3400	9840
Magnesium	Mg	12	24	650	1117	1740

Manganese	Mn	25	55	1244	2041	7470
Mercury	Hg	80	201	−39	357	13590
Molybdenum	Mo	42	96	2617	4827	10200
Neodymium	Nd	60	144	1024	3100	6960
Neon	Ne	10	20	−248	−246	0.84
Nickel	Ni	28	59	1455	2837	8900
Niobium	Nb	41	93	2497	4927	8580
Nitrogen	N	7	14	−210	−196	1.17
Osmium	Os	76	190	2727	4227	22580
Oxygen	O	8	16	−219	−183	1.33
Palladium	Pd	46	106	1550	3127	12000
Phosphorus (white)	P	15	31	44	281	1820
Platinum	Pt	78	195	1770	3827	21450
Polonium	Po	84	210	254	962	9400
Potassium	K	19	39	63	766	860
Praseodymium	Pr	59	141	935	3000	6800
Promethium	Pm	61	145	1035	2700	–
Protoactinium	Pa	91	231	1200	4000	15400
Radium	Ra	88	226	700	1527	5000
Radon	Rn	86	222	−71	−62	8.9
Rhenium	Re	75	186	3180	5627	20500
Rhodium	Rh	45	103	1966	3727	12440
Rubidium	Rb	37	85	39	701	1530
Ruthenium	Ru	44	101	2427	3727	12400
Samarium	Sm	62	150	1060	1600	7500
Scandium	Sc	21	45	1400	2477	3000
Selenium	Se	34	79	217	685	4810
Silicon	Si	14	28	1410	2677	2300
Silver	Ag	47	108	961	2127	10500
Sodium	Na	11	23.3	98	890	970
Strontium	Sr	38	88	770	1367	2600
Sulphur	S	16	32	119	445	2086
Tantalum	Ta	73	181	2997	5427	16600
Technetium	Tc	43	99	2127	4627	11500
Tellurium	Te	52	128	450	987	6240
Terbium	Tb	65	159	1356		8300
Thallium	Ti	81	204	304	1467	11860
Thorium	Th	90	232	1727	4500	11500
Thulium	Tm	69	169	1545	2000	9300
Tin	Sn	50	119	232	2687	7300
Titanium	Ti	22	48	1677	3277	4540
Tungsten	W	74	184	3377	5527	19250
Uranium	U	92	238	1132	4000	19050
Vanadium	V	23	51	1917	3377	6100
Xenon	Xe	54	131	−111	−108	5.5
Ytterbium	Yb	70	173	824	1500	7000
Yttrium	Y	39	89	1500	3227	4600
Zinc	Zn	30	65	419	908	7140
Zirconium	Zr	40	91	1852	4377	6500

The periodic table

Periodic table of the elements

Groups	I	II												III	IV	V	VI	VII	0
Periods																			
1	1 H hydrogen 1																		2 He helium 4
2	3 Li lithium 7	4 Be beryllium 9												5 B boron 11	6 C carbon 12	7 N nitrogen 14	8 O oxygen 16	9 F fluorine 19	10 Ne neon 20
3	11 Na sodium 23	12 Mg magnesium 24												13 Al aluminium 27	14 Si silicon 28	15 P phosphorus 31	16 S sulphur 32	17 Cl chlorine 35.5	18 Ar argon 40
4	19 K potassium 39	20 Ca calcium 40	21 Sc scandium 45	22 Ti titanium 48	23 V vanadium 51	24 Cr chromium 52	25 Mn manganese 55	26 Fe iron 56	27 Co cobalt 59	28 Ni nickel 59	29 Cu copper 64	30 Zn zinc 65		31 Ga gallium 70	32 Ge germanium 73	33 As arsenic 75	34 Se selenium 79	35 Br bromine 80	36 Kr krypton 84
5	37 Rb rubidium 85.5	38 Sr strontium 88	39 Y yttrium 89	40 Zr zirconium 91	41 Nb niobium 93	42 Mo molybdenum 96	43 Tc technetium 98	44 Ru ruthenium 101	45 Rh rhodium 103	46 Pd palladium 106	47 Ag silver 108	48 Cd cadmium 112		49 In indium 115	50 Sn tin 119	51 Sb antimony 122	52 Te tellurium 128	53 I iodine 127	54 Xe xenon 131
6	55 Cs caesium 133	56 Ba barium 137	57 La lanthanum 139	72 Hf hafnium 178.5	73 Ta tantalum 181	74 W tungsten 184	75 Re rhenium 186	76 Os osmium 190	77 Ir iridium 192	78 Pt platinum 195	79 Au gold 197	80 Hg mercury 201		81 Tl thallium 204	82 Pb lead 207	83 Bi bismuth 209	84 Po polonium 210	85 At astatine 210	86 Rn radon 222
7	87 Fr francium 223	88 Ra radium 226	89 Ac actinium 227	104 Db dubnium 261	105 Jl joliotium 262	106 Rf rutherfordium	107 Bh bohrium	108 Hn hahnium	109 Mt meitnerium										

58 Ce cerium 140	59 Pr praseodymium 141	60 Nd neodymium 144	61 Pm promethium 147	62 Sm samarium 150	63 Eu europium 152	64 Gd gadolinium 157	65 Tb terbium 159	66 Dy dysprosium 162.5	67 Ho holmium 165	68 Er erbium 167	69 Tm thulium 169	70 Yb ytterbium 173	71 Lu lutetium 175
90 Th thorium 232	91 Pa protactinium 231	92 U uranium 238	93 Np neptunium 237	94 Pu plutonium 242	95 Am americium 243	96 Cm curium 247	97 Bk berkelium 247	98 Cf californium 251	99 Es einsteinium 254	100 Fm fermium 253	101 Md mendelevium 256	102 No nobelium 254	103 Lr lawrencium 257

Key
- metal
- non-metal

atomic no.
symbol
name
relative atomic mass

The lines of elements going across are called **periods**
There are seven periods in the table

The columns of elements going down are called **groups**
Elements in the same group usually have similar properties

The reactivity series

	Element	Symbol	Reaction of metal with oxygen in the air	Reaction of metal with water	Reaction of metal with dilute hydrochloric acid	Reaction of oxide with hydrogen
Most reactive ↑	Potassium	K	burn easily with bright flame	burns violently in the cold	dangerous violent reaction	no reaction
	Sodium	Na		fast reaction in the cold		
	Calcium	Ca		slow reaction in the cold		
	Magnesium	Mg	react slowly with heating	reacts with steam	react quite well	
	Aluminium	Al		reaction stopped by oxide layer		
	Zinc	Zn		reacts with steam		
	Iron	Fe		reacts reversibly with steam		reduced reversibly
	Lead	Pb		no reaction with water or steam	slow reaction with concentrated acid	slow reduction
	Copper	Cu			no reaction	rapid reduction
	Mercury	Hg				oxides reduced to metal very easily
	Silver	Ag				
	Gold	Au	no reaction			
↓ **Least reactive**	Platinum	Pt				

The hazard symbols

- Harmful
- Corrosive
- Explosive
- Radioactive
- Flammable
- Toxic
- Oxidising

Glossary

Acid A compound that reacts with a base to form a salt. Solutions of acids in water have a pH of 1–6.

Alkali A water soluble base. Alkalis neutralise acids and have a pH of 8–14.

Alloy A solid mixture of two or more metals.

Allotropes Two or more physical forms of the same element.

Amphoteric A substance that will react with both an acid and a base.

Anhydrous Literally means 'without water' – a compound with no water of crystallisation.

Anion A negative ion – in electrolysis these are attracted to the anode.

Anode A positively charged electrode.

Aquifer A water-bearing rock.

Atom The smallest particle that can be obtained by chemical means.

Atomic number A number given to each element equal to the number of protons in the nucleus. Elements in the Periodic Table are arranged in atomic number order.

Avogadro's number The number of particles in one mole of a substance. It is 6.023×10^{23}.

Base A compound that neutralises an acid to make a salt.

Battery A series of cells connected together so as to provide an electric current.

Biodegradable Able to break down into simpler substances through the action of bacteria.

Brownian movement The random movement of tiny particles such as those in smoke caused by the bombardment of surrounding small molecules.

Carbohydrate A compound of carbon, hydrogen and oxygen in which the ratio of hydrogen to oxygen is 2:1.

Carbon 12 Scale A relative scale comparing the mass of all atoms to the mass of an atom of carbon 12.

Catalyst A substance that alters the rate of a chemical reaction. It remains unchanged chemically or in mass at the end of the reaction.

Cathode A negatively charged electrode.

Cation A positive ion – in electrolysis these are attracted to the cathode.

Cell A device for turning chemical energy into electrical energy.

Ceramic A clay-based material that has been fired in a kiln. This gives it unique heat-resistant properties.

Chemical reaction This happens when an element or compound reacts so as to form new substances.

Chemical properties The ways in which a substance reacts chemically.

Chromatography The separation of a mixture of substances. This is based on their relative solubility in a given solvent and the extent to which they are adsorbed onto the paper or other substance used.

Colloid A mixture in which small amounts of one substance are suspended in another.

Combustion The chemical name for burning. It involves a substance reacting rapidly with oxygen with the presence of a flame.

Composite A material that combines the useful properties of two or more substances.

Compound Two or more elements chemically joined together.

Concentration The amount of solute dissolved in a solvent.

Core The inner and outer core of the Earth, consisting of very hot solid and liquid materials.

Corrosion A chemical reaction of metals, either with water or solutions of other substances by which the metal is worn away.

Coulomb The amount of electricity flowing when 1 ampere (1A) is passed in 1 second. Coulombs = amps × seconds.

Covalent bond This is formed when atoms are joined by a shared electron pair.

Cracking Breaking down organic molecules by the action of heat and/or a catalyst to form smaller ones. One of the products formed is always unsaturated.

Crystallisation The formation of solid crystals when a solution is allowed to evaporate.

Density The mass of a given volume of a substance. For solids and liquids, density is usually given as the mass of 1 cm^3 (g/cm^3). For gases density is usually given as the mass of one litre (g/dm^3).

Diffusion The rapid random movement of particles in a liquid or gas.

Displacement reaction This is a chemical reaction in which a more reactive substance takes the place ('displaces') a less reactive one.

Dissolving When a solute is totally taken up into a solvent.

Dynamic equilibrium This occurs when two opposite reactions are happening at the same time and the same rate. It is shown in an equation by the symbol

Electrode The carbon or metal material that is given an electrical charge in electrolysis reactions.

Electrolysis This involves breaking down a compound containing ions by the passage of an electric current. The compound must either be melted or dissolved in water.

Electron Negatively charged particles with a negligible mass thatform the outer portion of all atoms. An electric current is a flow of electrons.

Electronic configuration This shows the arrangement of electrons round the nucleus of an atom.

Electroplating A process by which a thin layer of one metal is coated onto a substance during electrolysis.

Element A substance made from only one sort of atom.

Empirical formula The simplest ratio of atoms in a compound.

Endothermic A process that takes in heat energy and involves a fall in temperature. Denoted $\Delta H = + X$ kJ

Energy diagram A diagram showing the relative changes in energy involved in a physical or chemical process.

262

Glossary

Enzyme A biological catalyst.

Exothermic A process that gives out heat energy and involves a rise in temperature. Denoted ΔH = − X kJ.

Eutrophication A process by which water can become polluted, involving the presence of an excess of fertilisers.

Faraday The amount of electricity needed to discharge a singly charged ion. One Faraday is equal to a mole of electrons. 1 Faraday = 96 500 coulombs.

Fermentation A process by which the enzymes present in yeast assist the breakdown of carbohydrates into ethanol and carbon dioxide.

Fertiliser A substance that is taken in through the roots or leaves of a plant and assists healthy growth.

Filtrate The clear solution produced by filtering a mixture.

Formula The formula of a compound shows which elements are present and in what ratios.

Fractional distillation The separation of a mixture of liquids, using the difference in their boiling points.

Fuel A substance that burns well in air or oxygen, so that useful energy is produced.

Functional group An atom or group of atoms present in an organic molecule that gives it particular chemical properties.

Galvanising Coating iron or steel with a thin layer of zinc so as to prevent rusting.

Giant structure A regular arrangement of atoms or ions that is repeated throughout the structure of a substance.

Greenhouse effect The process by which various gases in the Earth's atmosphere trap heat.

Group A vertical column of elements in the Periodic Table.

Hardness The presence of dissolved compounds of calcium, magnesium and iron in a sample of water.

Homologous series A series of similar organic compounds having the same functional group.

Hydrated Literally means ''containing water' – hydrated salts contain water of crystallisation.

Hydrocarbon A compound of hydrogen and carbon.

Igneous rock Rocks that have formed when melted lava solidifies.

Immiscible Two liquids that do not mix with each other and form separate layers.

Indicator A chemical that changes colour at a particular pH.

Ion An atom or group of atoms with an electrical charge.

Ionic bond The bond which forms when ions of opposite charge attract each other in a compound.

Isomer A compound having the same molecular formula but different structures.

Isotope Atoms of the same element that contain different numbers of neutrons. Isotopes have the same atomic number but different mass numbers.

Kelvin Scale A temperature scale starting at absolute zero (0 K). A temperature of 0°C is equal to 273 K.

Le Chatelier's Principle When a constraint is applied to a system in equilibrium, the system responds so as to nullify the effect of the constraint.

Mantle A layer of rock between the inner core of the Earth and the outer crust.

Mass number The number of protons plus neutrons in an atom. It is denoted as a small number above the atom. E.g. an atom of $^{12}_{6}C$ has a mass number of 12.

Metallic bond The chemical bond that joins metal atoms together.

Metalloid An element with properties intermediate between those of metals and non-metals.

Metamorphic rock Rock formed by the action of heat and pressure.

Mineral A solid element or compound found in the ground.

Miscible Liquids that will mix with each other completely in all proportions.

Mixture Two or more substances that can be separated out using their different physical properties.

Molarity The concentration of a solution measured in moles per litre.

Mole The amount of substance that chemists often use in measuring, containing 6.023×10^{23} particles. One mole of an element contains its relative atomic mass in grams. E.g. C = 12 so 1 mole of carbon atoms has a mass of 12 g.

Molecular formula This shows the number of moles of each atom present in one mole of a substance.

Molecule A group of two or more atoms joined together by covalent bonds. Molecules may be elements (e.g. H_2) or compounds (e.g. H_2O). They may be small (e.g. NH_3) or large (e.g. poly(ethene)).

Monomer Small molecules capable of joining together to form polymers.

NPK An abbreviation of the symbols of the elements 'nitrogen, phosphorus and potassium' used to denote the relative amounts of each of these elements present in a sample of fertiliser.

Nanometre A very small unit of measurement used to define the size of atoms. One nanometre is equal to one meter, divided by ten, nine times over (1 nm = 1×10^{-9} m).

Neutralisation This happens when an acid and a base react together to form a salt.

Neutron Particle present in the nucleus of atoms that have mass but no charge.

Nucleon Any particle found in the nucleus of an atom (e.g. protons and neutrons).

Nucleus The small central core of an atom, containing protons and neutrons.

Ore A mineral from which a metal may be extracted.

Organic chemistry The study of the covalent compounds of carbon.

Oxidation This happens when a substance gains oxygen in a chemical reaction. Oxidation is also loss of electrons.

Period A horizontal row of elements in the Periodic Table.

Glossary

Physical change An easily reversed change brought about by altering physical properties such as temperature or pressure.

Physical properties Properties of a substance that can readily be measured or observed e.g. melting point, density, colour.

Polymer A compound formed when many monomer molecules join together.

Precipitation The formation of an insoluble solid when two solutions react together.

Proton Positively charged, massive particles found in the nucleus of an atom.

Radical An ion consisting of a group of atoms with an electrical charge, e.g. SO_4^{2-}; CO_3^{2-}; NH_4^+.

Rate A measure of how fast a process is happening, following the change in a particular property with time.

Reactivity series A list of elements showing their relative reactivity. More reactive elements will displace less reactive ones from their compounds.

Redox reaction A chemical reaction involving both reduction and oxidation.

Reducing agent A substance that brings about reduction. Reducing agents include reactive metals and hydrogen.

Reduction This happens when a substance loses oxygen in a chemical reaction. Reduction is also gain of electrons.

Relative Atomic Mass (A_r) A number comparing the mass of one mole of atoms of a particular element with the mass of one mole of atoms of other elements.

Relative Molar Mass (M_r) The sum of the relative atomic masses of each of the atoms in one mole of a substance.

Rock A mixture of minerals found in the Earth's crust.

STP An abbreviation applied to gases: 'standard temperature and pressure'. STP is one atmosphere pressure and 273 K.

Salt A substance formed when an acid is neutralised by a base. Salts always contain two ions – a cation from the parent base and an anion from the parent acid.

Saturated molecule Organic carbon compounds where each carbon atom is joined to four other atoms with single covalent bonds.

Saturated solution One that contains the maximum possible amount of solute dissolved in a solvent at a particular temperature.

Sedimentary rocks Rocks formed by layers of small particles laid down on top of each other over long time periods.

Simple distillation The separation of a solvent from a solute by boiling and condensing.

Solubility A measure of the extent to which a solute dissolves in a given solvent at a particular temperature. Measured in grams of solute per 100 g solvent.

Solute A substance that dissolves in a solvent.

Solution This is formed when a substance dissolves into a liquid. Aqueous solutions are formed when the solvent used is water.

Solvent The liquid in which solutes are dissolved.

State of matter Whether a substance is a solid, liquid or gas.

State symbol These denote whether a substance is a solid (s), liquid (l), gas (g) or is dissolved in aqueous solution (aq).

Strength When applied to an acid or alkali is a measure of the extent to which it is dissociated into ions.

Structural formula A diagram or model showing how the atoms in a molecule are arranged.

Sublimation The physical process by which a solid turns straight to a gas without forming a liquid in between.

Symbol One or two letters used to denote a particular element.

Tectonic plate Very large slabs of rock that form the Earth's crust and float on the slowly moving mantle.

Titration A chemical reaction used to find the concentration of a particular solution.

Unsaturated molecule Organic carbon compounds where carbon atoms are joined to two or three other atoms with double or triple covalent bonds.

Volatile Easily turning to a gas.

Water of crystallisation Water loosely held in the crystalline structure of a salt.

Weathering Process by which rocks and minerals are broken down into small particles such as those found in the soil.

Index

absolute zero 27, 33
acid rain 46–50, 72, 75
acid strength 134
acids 131–43, 186, 192, 237
activation energy 248
addition reaction 216
air 38–56, 197
air pressure 25
alcohols 218–20
alkali 135
alkali metals 93, 175
alkaline cells 190
alkaline strength 136
alkalis 237
alkanes 212–14
alkenes 215–17
allotropes 196, 202
alloys 169, 172
aluminium 48, 73, 137, 163, 173–4, 181
ammonia 198, 248–9
ammonium chloride 245–6
amphoteric oxides 137
anions 140
anodising 174
aqueous solutions 144–55, 157–8
aquifers 145
Arrhenius 50
atomic mass 85, 88–9
atomic number 83, 89, 92
atomic structure 81–7, 92–5
atoms 1–3, 117
Avogadro's law 122, 128
Avogadro's number 114

balanced equations 15
ballasting 79
bases 131–43, 169
batch processes 7
batteries 189–90
bauxite 73, 173
bedding planes 67
beds 67
biodegradable polymers 225
blast furnaces 172
boiling points 6, 32–6, 104, 167, 191, 229
bonding 96–112
bonds
    covalent 102–7
    double 104, 215, 216
    ionic 97–101
    metallic 108, 167
    reactions 240–1
    triple 104
Boyle's law 26
brine (see *sodium chloride*)
bromine 78, 205
Brownian motion 21, 22
buckminster fullerene 106

calcium carbonate 68, 73, 147–8
calcium sulphate 147
carbon 106, 195–6, 209–12
carbon cycle 195–6
carbon dioxide 50–1
carbonates, acid reaction 142
carboxylic acids 220–2
cars 46, 47, 49, 54
cassiterite 171
cast iron 172
catalysts 180, 198, 204, 247–9, 255
catalytic converters 49, 54
catalytic cracking 216
cations 140
cells 183–90
ceramics 231
CFCs (see *chlorofluorocarbons*)
chalk 68, 73
Charles' law 26, 27
chemical analysis 154
chemical change 10–16
chemical symbols 2
chlorine 205–7
chlorofluorocarbons (CFCs) 53
chromatography 8–9
classification, materials 230–4
closed systems 251–2
coal 210–12
colloids 231–2
combustion 43, 212, 214, 216, 239–40
composite materials 233
compound fertilisers 200
compounds 1–17
compressive strength 229
concentration
    acids 134
    equilibrium effects 253
    reaction rates 246
condensation point 34
conductivity 167, 192, 228
conservative margin 61
consolidation 66
constructive margin 61, 62
Contact process 203–4
continental crust 61
continuous processes 7
convection currents 58, 60, 61
copper 164
copper carbonate 127
copper (II) chloride 158
copper electrodes 159, 162
copper (II) sulphate 158–9, 162
coulombs 160
covalent bonding 102–7
covalent compounds 192
cracking 216
crude oil 6–7, 8, 79–80, 194, 210–12, 216
crust 57, 60, 61, 65–70, 73
cryolite 173
crystal shape 19
crystallising solutions 5
crystals 168

265

Index

Daniell cell 188
dehydrating agents 204
dehydration 219
density 29–30, 167, 229, 230
destructive margin 61, 62
detergents 80, 150, 222–6
diamond 106, 196
diaphragm cell 163
diatomic molecules 12
diffusion 22, 23–4
dislocations 168
displacement reactions 78, 187, 237
dissolving solutions 5, 152
distillation 6–7, 40, 211, 216
double bonds 104, 215, 216
dynamic equilibrium 252

Earth 57–60
earthquakes 61, 63–4
elasticity 229
electrical conductivity 167, 192, 228
electricity 188–90
electrode material 158–9
electrolysis 73, 76–7, 156–65, 185, 194, 206
electrolytic reduction 173
electronic configuration 86–7, 96
electrons 81–3, 86–7
electroplating 164
elements 1–17, 230
empirical formulae 120
emulsifiers 232
endothermic reactions 235, 238–9
energy 235–42
energy change 235–9
energy diagram 237, 238
enzymes 249
equations 13, 113–30
equilibrium 252–4
erosion 70
esters 222
ethanoates 221
ethanoic acid 221–2
ethanol 217, 218–20
eutrophication 149, 150, 202
evaporation 33
exothermic reactions 235, 237
extrusive igneous rocks 67

Faraday constant 161
Faraday, Michael 160
Faradays 161–2
fats 217, 222
fermentation 218–19
fertilisers 149, 200–2
fibreglass 231
fibres 232
filtrate 5
flexibility 229
flue gas desulphurisation plant 49
fluoride 146
fold mountains 61

forging 168
formulae 11–12, 15, 100–1, 119–21
fossil fuels 210–12
fossils 66
fractional distillation 6–7, 40, 211, 216
fractions 6
freeze-thaw effect 70
freezing point 34
fuel cells 190
fuels 209–12, 239–41
fullerene 106, 196
functional group 218
fungicides 150

galena 170
gas equation 28
gas laws 25–8
gas pressure 25
gases 18–37, 121–3, 128, 153
gasohol 220
giant structures 19, 98, 106–7, 156, 168
glasses 231
global warming 51
glycerol 222
grains 168
graphite 106, 196
greenhouse effect 50–2
Group 0 elements 92, 96–7
Group I elements 93, 175–6
Group II elements 177
Group IV elements 195–6
Group V elements 197–202
Group VI elements 202–4
Group VII elements 94, 205–7
groups 90
Gutenburg discontinuity 57

Haber process 180, 198, 248, 254–5
haematite 73, 172
half-life 59
halogens 94, 175, 205–7, 214, 216
hard water 147–9
hardness 229
hardness in water 147–9
heat of combustion 240
heat of neutralisation 237
heavy metals 179
herbicides 150
homologous series 213, 215, 218, 220
hydration 217, 237
hydrocarbons 210, 212
hydrochloric acid 158, 206
hydrogen 193–4
hydrogen chloride 207
hydroxonium ions 132

igneous rocks 67, 69
immiscible liquids 8
impurities 35
indicators 131–2
industrial waste 150

Index

inner core 57
insoluble salts 142
intrusive igneous rocks 67
iodine 9, 205
ion-electron equations 157
ion-exchange resin 148
ionic bonding 97–101
ionic compounds 156–7, 169, 192
ionic equations 138
ions 97–9, 117, 154, 169
iron 73, 172, 180
isomerism 213
isotopes 59–60, 84, 85

Kelvin scale 27
Kinetic Theory of Matter 19, 31–2

Lavoisier, Antoine 15
Law of Conservation of Mass 15
Le Chatelier's principle 253–4
lead 170
lead-acid accumulator 189
lead-acid battery 189
limestone 68, 72, 73–4, 147
liquids 6–8, 18–37
litmus 131

magma 65
magnesium 77–8, 163
magnetic field 58
magnetic north 58, 62
magnetite 73
malleability 167, 229
mantle 57
marble 68, 73
margarine 217
mass 30
mass number 83
materials science 228–34
melting points 32–6, 104, 167, 191, 229
membrane cell 76
Mendeleev, Dmitri 88
metallic bonds 108, 167
metalloids 195
metals 108, 142, 166–82, 183–90, 230–1
metamorphic rocks 68, 69
methane 50–1, 103, 193, 210, 213
methylated spirits 219
minerals 57–74
mines 170
miscible liquids 8
mixtures 1–17
Moho discontinuity 57
molar solutions 123
molarity 123, 128
molecular formulae 120, 212
molecules 12–13, 117
moles 113–30
monoclinic sulphur 202
monomers 223
mountain ranges 61

nanometres 1, 81
natural gas 210–12
natural materials 38
neutralisation 138–40, 237
neutrons 81–3
Newlands, John 88
nitrates 202
nitric acid 198–9
nitrogen 39, 41–2, 197, 198, 200
nitrogen cycle 197
nitrogen oxides 46–9
noble gases 44, 92, 96–7
non-metals 191–208, 230–1
NPK fertilisers 200
nucleons 81
nucleus 81–3

oceanic crust 61
oils 222
    (see also *crude oil*)
    slicks 79–80
open systems 251–2
optical properties 229
ores 73, 170
organic chemistry 195, 209–27
outer core 57
oxidation 43, 160, 183–8
oxides 43, 136–7, 169, 185, 192
oxidising agents 183, 204
oxygen 39–40, 42–4, 175, 177, 180, 185, 202
ozone depletion 52–3

paper chromatography 8–9
particles
    gases 22–3
    liquids 21
    solids 19–20
periodic table 88–95, 174–81
periods 90, 94
pesticides 150
pH 131–2
phases 231–2
phosphorus 197
photochromic glass 231
physical change 3–10
plasma 18
plastics 232
plate tectonics 58, 60–2
pollution 46–55, 79–80, 149–50
polymerisation 223
polymers 222–6
potassium 59
precipitation 142
pressure
    equilibrium effects 253–5
    gas effects 24–8
    liquids 21
    reaction rates 246
    solids effects 20
products 14
protons 81–3
purification 164
pyrex 231

Index

radicals 99–100, 101
radioactive decay 59
rates of reaction 243–50
raw materials 38–9
reactants 14
reactivity series 185
rechargeable cells 190
recycling 181, 231
redox reactions 183–90
reducing agents 170, 184, 194
reduction 160, 183–8
relative atomic mass 85, 88–9, 114–15
relative molar mass 115
reversible reactions 251–7
rhombic sulphur 202
rift valleys 62
rock cycle 69
rocks 57–74
rubidium 59
rust 180

salt (see *sodium chloride*)
salts 131–43, 169, 187
sandy soils 72
saponification 223
saturated solutions 5, 152
scum 148, 223
sea 75–80
sea water 75–9
sedimentary rocks 65–7, 69
seismographs 63
sewage 146, 150
silicon 195
silicon dioxide 106
silt soils 72
silver carbonate 127
silver oxide cells 189
simple distillation 6
smoke cell 22–3
soapless detergents 223
soaps 222–6
sodium 163
sodium chloride (salt/brine) 140, 159, 163, 185
    bonding 97
    distillation 6
    electrolysis 76–7, 157, 163, 185, 194, 206
sea 75–7
separation 4–5, 9
soft water 147
soil 70, 72, 200
solids 18–37
solubility 152, 229
solubility curve 152
solutes 5, 152
solutions 5, 123–6, 152
solvents 5, 152–5
spectator ions 138
standard temperature and pressure (STP) 121
state, changes of 31–7
state symbol 14
states of matter 18–19, 151
steel 172

STP (see *standard temperature and pressure*)
strength 167, 191, 229
structural formulae 212
sublimation 9
substitution reactions 214
sulphur 202
sulphur dioxide 46–50
sulphuric acid 158, 203–4
surface area, reaction rates 246–7
symbol equations 13
symbols 2, 12, 84

tectonic plates 58, 60–2
temperature
    equilibrium effects 253–4
    gas laws 26–8
    gas solubility 153
    reaction rates 245
    solids effects 20
    solubility curves 152
    weathering 70
tensile strength 229
thermal conductivity 167, 192, 228
tin 171
titrations 128, 138–9
toughness 229
transition metals 90, 99, 179–80
triple bonds 104

ultra-violet radiation 52–3
universal solvent 144, 152

vinegar 220
volcanoes 61, 62, 65
volume
    density relationship 30
    gas laws 25–8

washing soda 148
water 144–55
    of crystallisation 151
    cycle 144, 145
    density 230
    heating 236
    hydrogen production 194
    metals reaction 175, 177, 186
    state symbol 14
    states of matter 18
    treatment 145–6
weathering 70
weathering, rocks 70–2
word equations 13
working metals 168

zinc 171
zinc blende 171
zinc-carbon dry cells 189